Microsoft® Official Academic Course

Microsoft Excel 2010, EXAM 77-882

WILEY

EDITOR	Bryan Gambrel
DIRECTOR OF SALES	Mitchell Beaton
EXECUTIVE MARKETING MANAGER	Chris Ruel
ASSISTANT MARKETING MANAGER	Debbie Martin
MICROSOFT STRATEGIC RELATIONSHIPS MANAGER	Merrick Van Dongen of Microsoft Learning
EDITORIAL PROGRAM ASSISTANT	Jennifer Lartz
CONTENT MANAGERS	Micheline Frederick, Kevin Holm
SENIOR PRODUCTION EDITOR	Kerry Weinstein
CREATIVE DIRECTOR	Harry Nolan
COVER DESIGNER	Jim O'Shea
INTERIOR DESIGNER	Amy Rosen
PHOTO EDITORS	Sheena Goldstein, Jennifer MacMillan
EXECUTIVE MEDIA EDITOR	Tom Kulesa
MEDIA EDITOR	Wendy Ashenberg

This book was set in Garamond by Aptara, Inc. and printed and bound by Courier Kendallville. The covers were printed by Lehigh Phoenix.

Microsoft, ActiveX, Excel, InfoPath, Microsoft Press, MSDN, OneNote, Outlook, PivotChart, PivotTable, PowerPoint, SharePoint, SQL Server, Visio, Windows, Windows Mobile, and Windows Server are either registered trademarks or trademarks of Microsoft Corporation in the United States and/or other countries. Other product and company names mentioned herein may be the trademarks of their respective owners.

The example companies, organizations, products, domain names, e-mail addresses, logos, people, places, and events depicted herein are fictitious. No association with any real company, organization, product, domain name, e-mail address, logo, person, place, or event is intended or should be inferred.

The book expresses the author's views and opinions. The information contained in this book is provided without any express, statutory, or implied warranties. Neither the authors, John Wiley & Sons, Inc., Microsoft Corporation, nor their resellers or distributors will be held liable for any damages caused or alleged to be caused either directly or indirectly by this book.

Founded in 1807, John Wiley & Sons, Inc. has been a valued source of knowledge and understanding for more than 200 years, helping people around the world meet their needs and fulfill their aspirations. Our company is built on a foundation of principles that include responsibility to the communities we serve and where we live and work. In 2008, we launched a Corporate Citizenship Initiative, a global effort to address the environmental, social, economic, and ethical challenges we face in our business. Among the issues we are addressing are carbon impact, paper specifications and procurement, ethical conduct within our business and among our vendors, and community and charitable support. For more information, please visit our website: www.wiley.com/go/citizenship.

ISBN 978-0-470-90767-2

Printed in the United States of America

10 9 8 7 6 5 4 3 2

Foreword from the Publisher

Wiley's publishing vision for the Microsoft Official Academic Course series is to provide students and instructors with the skills and knowledge they need to use Microsoft technology effectively in all aspects of their personal and professional lives. Quality instruction is required to help both educators and students get the most from Microsoft's software tools and to become more productive. Thus our mission is to make our instructional programs trusted educational companions for life.

To accomplish this mission, Wiley and Microsoft have partnered to develop the highest quality educational programs for information workers, IT professionals, and developers. Materials created by this partnership carry the brand name "Microsoft Official Academic Course," assuring instructors and students alike that the content of these textbooks is fully endorsed by Microsoft, and that they provide the highest quality information and instruction on Microsoft products. The Microsoft Official Academic Course textbooks are "Official" in still one more way—they are the officially sanctioned courseware for Microsoft IT Academy members.

The Microsoft Official Academic Course series focuses on *workforce development*. These programs are aimed at those students seeking to enter the workforce, change jobs, or embark on new careers as information workers, IT professionals, and developers. Microsoft Official Academic Course programs address their needs by emphasizing authentic workplace scenarios with an abundance of projects, exercises, cases, and assessments.

The Microsoft Official Academic Courses are mapped to Microsoft's extensive research and job-task analysis, the same research and analysis used to create the Microsoft Office Specialist (MOS) exams. The textbooks focus on real skills for real jobs. As students work through the projects and exercises in the textbooks, they enhance their level of knowledge and their ability to apply the latest Microsoft technology to everyday tasks. These students also gain resume-building credentials that can assist them in finding a job, in keeping their current job, or in furthering their education.

The concept of lifelong learning is today an utmost necessity. Job roles, and even whole job categories, are changing so quickly that none of us can stay competitive and productive without continuously updating our skills and capabilities. The Microsoft Official Academic Course offerings, and their focus on Microsoft certification exam preparation, provide a means for people to acquire and effectively update their skills and knowledge. Wiley supports students in this endeavor through the development and distribution of these courses as Microsoft's official academic publisher.

Today educational publishing requires attention to providing quality print and robust electronic content. By integrating Microsoft Official Academic Course products, *WileyPLUS*, and Microsoft certifications, we are better able to deliver efficient learning solutions for students and teachers alike.

Joseph Heider
General Manager and Senior Vice President

Preface

Welcome to the Microsoft Official Academic Course (MOAC) program for Microsoft Office 2010. MOAC is the collaboration between Microsoft Learning and John Wiley & Sons, Inc. publishing company. Microsoft and Wiley teamed up to produce a series of textbooks that deliver compelling and innovative teaching solutions to instructors and superior learning experiences for students. Infused and informed by in-depth knowledge from the creators of Microsoft Office and Windows, and crafted by a publisher known worldwide for the pedagogical quality of its products, these textbooks maximize skills transfer in minimum time. Students are challenged to reach their potential by using their new technical skills as highly productive members of the workforce.

Because this knowledge base comes directly from Microsoft, architect of the Office 2010 offering and creator of the Microsoft Office Specialist (MOS) exams (www.microsoft.com/learning/mcp/msbc), you are sure to receive the topical coverage that is most relevant to your personal and professional success. Microsoft's direct participation not only assures you that MOAC textbook content is accurate and current; it also means that students will receive the best instruction possible to enable their success on certification exams and in the workplace.

THE MICROSOFT OFFICIAL ACADEMIC COURSE PROGRAM

The Microsoft Official Academic Course series is a complete program for instructors and institutions to prepare and deliver great courses on Microsoft software technologies. With MOAC, we recognize that, because of the rapid pace of change in the technology and curriculum developed by Microsoft, there is an ongoing set of needs beyond classroom instruction tools for an instructor to be ready to teach the course. The MOAC program endeavors to provide solutions for all these needs in a systematic manner in order to ensure a successful and rewarding course experience for both instructor and student—technical and curriculum training for instructor readiness with new software releases; the software itself for student use at home for building hands-on skills, assessment, and validation of skill development; and a great set of tools for delivering instruction in the classroom and lab. All are important to the smooth delivery of an interesting course on Microsoft software, and all are provided with the MOAC program. We think about the model below as a gauge for ensuring that we completely support you in your goal of teaching a great course. As you evaluate your instructional materials options, you may wish to use the model for comparison purposes with available products.

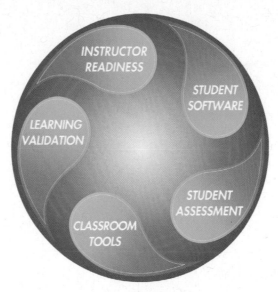

www.wiley.com/college/microsoft
or call the MOAC Toll-Free Number: 1+(888) 764-7001 (U.S. & Canada only)

PEDAGOGICAL FEATURES

The MOAC textbooks for Microsoft Office 2010 are designed to cover all the learning objectives for that MOS exam, which is referred to as its exam objective. The Microsoft Office Specialist (MOS) exam objectives are highlighted throughout the textbooks. Many pedagogical features have been developed specifically for Microsoft Official Academic Course programs. Unique features of our task-based approach include a Lesson Skill Matrix that correlates skills taught in each lesson to the MOS objectives; Certification, Workplace, and Internet Ready exercises; and three levels of increasingly rigorous lesson-ending activities, Competency, Proficiency, and Mastery Assessment.

Presenting the extensive procedural information and technical concepts woven throughout the textbook raises challenges for the student and instructor alike. The Illustrated Book Tour that follows provides a guide to the rich features contributing to Microsoft Official Academic Course program's pedagogical plan. Following is a list of key features in each lesson designed to prepare students for success on the certification exams and in the workplace:

- Each lesson begins with a **Lesson Skill Matrix**. More than a standard list of learning objectives, the skill matrix correlates each software skill covered in the lesson to the specific MOS exam objective domain.
- Each lesson features a real-world **Business scenario** that places the software skills and knowledge to be acquired in a real-world setting.
- **Software Orientations** provide an overview of the software features students will be working with in the lesson. The orientation will detail the general properties of the software or specific features, such as a ribbon or dialog box; and it includes a large, labeled screen image.
- Concise and frequent **Step-by-Step** instructions teach students new features and provide an opportunity for hands-on practice. Numbered steps give detailed instructions to help students learn software skills. The steps also show results and screen images to match what students should see on their computer screens.
- **Illustrations** provide visual feedback as students work through the exercises. The images reinforce key concepts, provide visual clues about the steps, and allow students to check their progress.
- When the text instructs a student to click a particular button, **button images** are shown in the margin or in the text.
- Important technical vocabulary is listed in the **Key Terms** section at the beginning of the lesson. When these terms are used later in the lesson, they appear in bold italic type with yellow highlighter and are defined. The Glossary contains all of the key terms and their definitions.
- Engaging point-of-use **Reader Aids**, located throughout the lessons, tell students why this topic is relevant (*The Bottom Line*), provide students with helpful hints (*Take Note*), or show alternate ways to accomplish tasks (*Another Way*), or point out things to watch out for or avoid (*Troubleshooting*). Reader aids also provide additional relevant or background information that adds value to the lesson.

- **Certification Ready** features throughout the text signal students where a specific certification objective is covered. They provide students with a chance to check their understanding of that particular MOS exam objective and, if necessary, review the section of the lesson where it is covered. MOAC provides complete preparation for MOS certification.

- The **New Feature** icon appears near any software feature that is new to Office 2010.

- Each lesson ends with a **Skill Summary** recapping the MOS exam skills covered in the lesson.

- The **Knowledge Assessment** section provides a total of 20 questions from a mix of True/ False, Fill in the blank, Matching, or Multiple Choice, testing students on concepts learned in the lesson.

- **Competency, Proficiency, and Mastery Assessment** sections provide progressively more challenging lesson-ending activities.

- **Internet Ready** projects combine the knowledge that students acquire in a lesson with web-based task research.

- Integrated **Circling Back** projects provide students with an opportunity to renew and practice skills learned in previous lessons.

- **Workplace Ready** features preview how Microsoft Office 2010 applications are used in real-world situations.

- The student companion website contains the **online files** needed for each lesson. These data files are indicated by the @ icon in the margin of the textbook.

Illustrated Book Tour

LESSON FEATURES

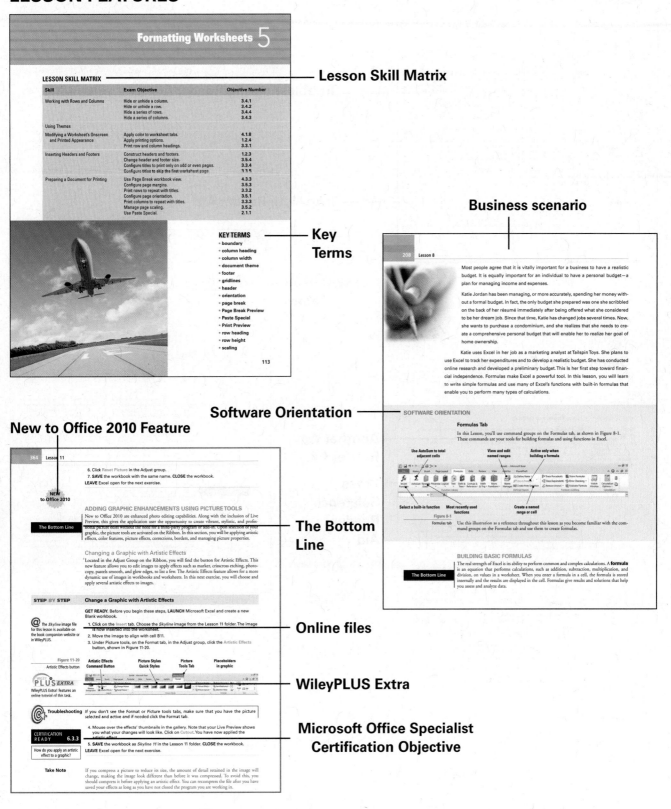

Lesson Skill Matrix

Key Terms

Business scenario

Software Orientation

New to Office 2010 Feature

The Bottom Line

Online files

WileyPLUS Extra

Microsoft Office Specialist Certification Objective

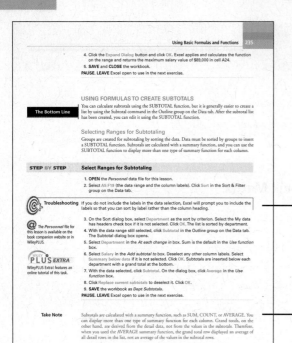

Troubleshooting Reader Aid

Take Note Reader Aid

Easy-to-read Tables

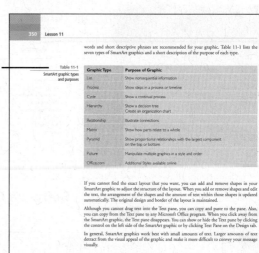

Step-by-Step Exercises

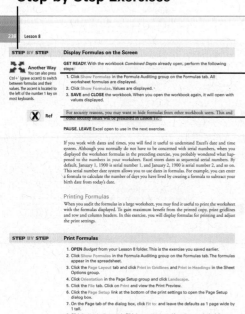

Another Way Reader Aid

Cross Reference Reader Aid

Skill Summary

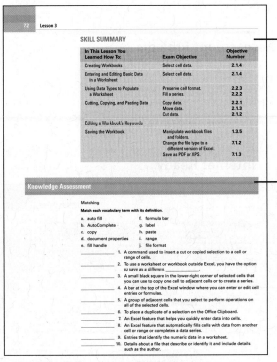

Knowledge Assessment Questions

Competency Assessment Projects

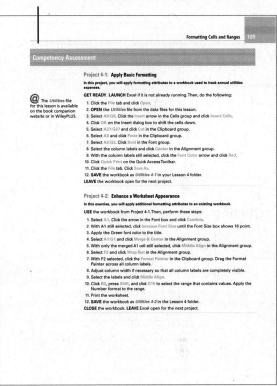

Proficiency Assessment Projects

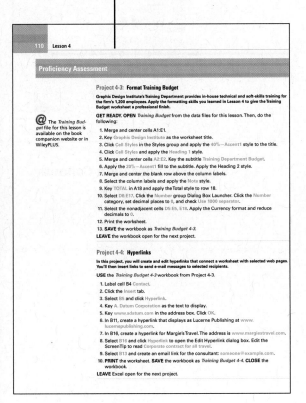

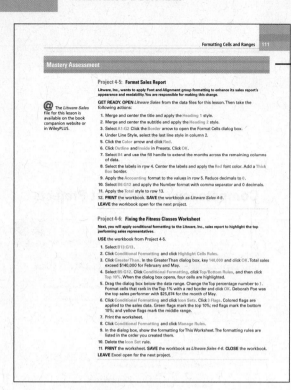

Mastery Assessment Projects

Internet Ready

Workplace Ready

Circling Back exercises

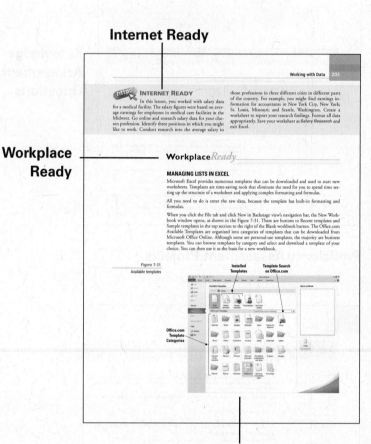

Screen Images with Callouts

Conventions and Features Used in This Book

This book uses particular fonts, symbols, and heading conventions to highlight important information or to call your attention to special steps. For more information about the features in each lesson, refer to the Illustrated Book Tour section.

NEW to Office 2010

This icon indicates a new or greatly improved Windows feature in this version of the software.

The Bottom Line

This feature provides a brief summary of the material to be covered in the section that follows.

CLOSE

Words in all capital letters indicate instructions for opening, saving, or closing files or programs. They also point out items you should check or actions you should take.

CERTIFICATION READY

This feature signals the point in the text where a specific certification objective is covered. It provides you with a chance to check your understanding of that particular MOS objective and, if necessary, review the section of the lesson where it is covered.

Take Note

Take Note reader aids, set in red text, provide helpful hints related to particular tasks or topics.

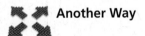 **Another Way**

Another Way provides an alternative procedure for accomplishing a particular task.

 Ref

These notes, set in gray shaded boxes, provide pointers to information discussed elsewhere in the textbook or describe interesting features that are not directly addressed in the current topic or exercise.

ALT+Tab

A plus sign (+) between two key names means that you must press both keys at the same time. Keys that you are instructed to press in an exercise will appear in the font shown here.

Key terms

Key terms appear in bold with highlighting.

Key My Name is

Any text you are asked to key appears in color.

Click OK

Any button on the screen you are supposed to click on or select will also appear in color.

Budget Worksheet 1

The names of data files will appear in bold, italic and red for easy identification.

Instructor Support Program

The *Microsoft Official Academic Course* programs are accompanied by a rich array of resources that incorporate the extensive textbook visuals to form a pedagogically cohesive package. These resources provide all the materials instructors need to deploy and deliver their courses. The following resources are available online for download.

- The **Instructor's Guide** contains solutions to all the textbook exercises as well as chapter summaries and lecture notes. The Instructor's Guide and Syllabi for various term lengths are available from the Instructor's Book Companion Site (www.wiley.com/college/microsoft).

- The **Solution Files** for all the projects in the book are available online from our Instructor's Book Companion Site (www.wiley.com/college/microsoft).

- The **Test Bank** contains hundreds of questions organized by lesson in multiple-choice, true/false, short answer, and essay formats and is available to download from the Instructor's Book Companion Site (www.wiley.com/college/microsoft). A complete answer key is provided.

  This title's test bank is available for use in Respondus' easy-to-use software. You can download the test bank for free using your Respondus, Respondus LE, or StudyMate Author software.

  Respondus is a powerful tool for creating and managing exams that can be printed to paper or published directly to Blackboard, WebCT, Desire2Learn, eCollege, ANGEL, and other eLearning systems.

- A complete set of **PowerPoint Presentations** is available on the Instructor's Book Companion site (www.wiley.com/college/microsoft) to enhance classroom presentations. Tailored to the text's topical coverage and Skills Matrix, these presentations are designed to convey key Microsoft Office 2010 concepts addressed in the text.

  All **images** from the text are on the Instructor's Book Companion Site (www.wiley.com/college/microsoft). You can incorporate them into your PowerPoint presentations, or create your own overhead transparencies and handouts.

  By using these visuals in class discussions, you can help focus students' attention on key elements of Office 2010 and help them understand how to use it effectively in the workplace.

- **DreamSpark Premium** is designed to provide the easiest and most inexpensive developer tools, products, and technologies available to faculty and students in labs, classrooms, and on student PCs. A free three-year membership is available to qualified MOAC adopters.

- **Office Grader** automated grading system allows you to easily grade student data files in Word, Excel, PowerPoint, or Access format, against solution files. Save tens or hundreds of hours each semester with automated grading. More information on Office Grader is available from the Instructor's Book Companion Site (www.wiley.com/college/microsoft).

- The **Student Data Files** are available online on both the Instructor's Book Companion Site and for students on the Student Book Companion Site.

- Microsoft Official Academic Course books can be bundled with MOS exam vouchers from Certiport and MOS practice tests from GMetrix LLC or Certiport, available as a single bundle from Wiley, to create a **complete certification solution**. Instructors who use MOAC courseware in conjunction with a practice MOS exam find their students best-prepared for the MOS certification exam. Providing your students with the MOS exam voucher is the ultimate workforce preparation.

- When it comes to improving the classroom experience, there is no better source of ideas and inspiration than your fellow colleagues. The **Wiley Faculty Network** connects teachers with technology, facilitates the exchange of best practices, and helps to enhance instructional efficiency and effectiveness. Faculty Network activities include technology training and tutorials, virtual seminars, peer-to-peer exchanges of experiences and ideas, personal consulting, and sharing of resources. For details, visit www. WhereFacultyConnect.com.

WILEYPLUS

Broad developments in education over the past decade have influenced the instructional approach taken in the Microsoft Official Academic Course programs. The way that students learn, especially about new technologies, has changed dramatically in the Internet era. Electronic learning materials and Internet-based instruction is now as much a part of classroom instruction as printed textbooks. WileyPLUS provides the technology to create an environment where students reach their full potential and experience academic success that will last a lifetime.

WileyPLUS is a powerful and highly integrated suite of teaching and learning resources designed to bridge the gap between what happens in the classroom and what happens at home and on the job. WileyPLUS provides instructors with the resources to teach their students new technologies and guide them to reach their goals of getting ahead in the job market by having the skills to become certified and advance in the workforce. For students, WileyPLUS provides the tools for study and practice that are available to them 24/7, wherever and whenever they want to study. WileyPLUS includes a complete online version of the student textbook; PowerPoint presentations; homework and practice assignments and quizzes; image galleries; test bank questions; grade book; and all the instructor resources in one easy-to-use website.

The following features are new to WileyPLUS for Office 2010:

- In addition to the hundreds of questions included in the WileyPLUS courses that are not included in the test bank or textbook, we've added over a dozen additional projects that can be assigned to students.
- Many more animated tutorials, videos, and audio clips to support students as they learn the latest Office 2010 features.

DREAMSPARK PREMIUM

Free Three-Year Membership Available to Qualified Adopters!

DreamSpark Premium is designed to provide the easiest and most inexpensive way for universities to make the latest Microsoft developer tools, products, and technologies available in labs, classrooms, and on student PCs. DreamSpark Premium is an annual membership program for departments teaching Science, Technology, Engineering, and Mathematics (STEM) courses. The membership provides a complete solution to keep academic labs, faculty, and students on the leading edge of technology.

Software available in the DreamSpark Premium program is provided at no charge to adopting departments through the Wiley and Microsoft publishing partnership.

As a bonus to this free offer, faculty will be introduced to Microsoft's Faculty Connection and Academic Resource Center. It takes time and preparation to keep students engaged while giving them a fundamental understanding of theory, and the Microsoft Faculty Connection is designed to help STEM professors with this preparation by providing articles, curriculum, and tools that professors can use to engage and inspire today's technology students.

Contact your Wiley rep for details.

For more information about the DreamSpark Premium program, go to **https://www.dreamspark.com.**

IMPORTANT WEB ADDRESSES AND PHONE NUMBERS

To locate the Wiley Higher Education Rep in your area, go to www.wiley.com/college, select Instructors under Resources, and click on the Who's My Rep link, or call the MOAC toll-free number: 1 + (888) 764-7001 (U.S. and Canada only).

To learn more about becoming a Microsoft Certified Professional and exam availability, visit www.microsoft.com/learning/mcp.

WHY MOS CERTIFICATION?

Microsoft Office Specialist (MOS) 2010 is a valuable credential that recognizes the desktop computing skills needed to use the full features and functionality of the Microsoft Office 2010 suite.

In the worldwide job market, Microsoft Office Specialist is the primary tool companies use to validate the proficiency of their employees in the latest productivity tools and technology, helping them select job candidates based on globally recognized standards for verifying skills. The results of an independent research study show that businesses with certified employees are more productive compared to non-certified employees and that certified employees bring immediate value to their jobs.

In academia, as in the business world, institutions upgrading to Office 2010 may seek ways to protect and maximize their technology investment. By offering certification, they validate that decision—because powerful Office 2010 applications, such as Word, Excel, and PowerPoint, can be effectively used to demonstrate increases in academic preparedness and workforce readiness.

Individuals seek certification to increase their own personal sense of accomplishment and to create advancement opportunities by establishing a leadership position in their school or department, thereby differentiating their skill sets in a competitive college admissions and job market.

BOOK COMPANION WEBSITE

The students' book companion site for the MOAC series, www.wiley.com/college/microsoft, includes any resources, exercise files, and web links that will be used in conjunction with this course.

WILEY DESKTOP EDITIONS

Wiley MOAC Desktop Editions are innovative, electronic versions of printed textbooks. Students buy the desktop version for 50% off the U.S. price of the printed text and get the added value of permanence and portability. Wiley Desktop Editions provide students with numerous additional benefits that are not available with other e-text solutions.

Wiley Desktop Editions are NOT subscriptions; students download the Wiley Desktop Edition to their computer desktops. Students own the content they buy and keep it for as long as they want. Once a Wiley Desktop Edition is downloaded to the computer desktop, students have instant access to all of the content without being online. Students can also print the sections they prefer to read in hard copy. Students also have access to fully integrated resources within their Wiley Desktop Edition. From highlighting their e-text to taking and sharing notes, students can easily personalize their Wiley Desktop Edition as they are reading or following along in class.

COURSESMART

CourseSmart goes beyond traditional expectations providing instant, online access to the textbooks and course materials you need at a lower cost option. You can save time and hassle with a digital eTextbook that allows you to search for the most relevant content at the very moment you need it. To learn more go to www.coursesmart.com.

PREPARING TO TAKE THE MICROSOFT OFFICE SPECIALIST (MOS) EXAM

The Microsoft Office Specialist credential has been upgraded to validate skills with the Microsoft Office 2010 system. The MOS certifications target information workers and cover the most popular business applications such as Word 2010, PowerPoint 2010, Excel 2010, Access 2010, and Outlook 2010.

By becoming certified, you demonstrate to employers that you have achieved a predictable level of skill in the use of a particular Office application. Employers often require certification either as a condition of employment or as a condition of advancement within the company or other organization. The certification examinations are sponsored by Microsoft but administered through exam delivery partners like Certiport.

To learn more about becoming a Microsoft Certified Application Specialist and exam availability, visit www.microsoft.com/learning/msbc.

Preparing to Take an Exam

Unless you are a very experienced user, you will need to use a test preparation course to prepare for the test to complete it correctly and within the time allowed. The Microsoft Official Academic Course series is designed to prepare you with a strong knowledge of all exam topics. With some additional review and practice on your own, you should feel confident in your ability to pass the appropriate exam.

After you decide which exam to take, review the list of objectives for the exam. This list can be found in Appendix A at the back of this book. You can also easily identify tasks that are included in the objective list by locating the Lesson Skill Matrix at the start of each lesson and the Certification Ready sidebars in the margin of the lessons in this book.

To take the MOS test, visit www.microsoft.com/learning/msbc to locate your nearest testing center. Then call the testing center directly to schedule your test. The amount of advance notice you should provide will vary for different testing centers, and it typically depends on the number of computers available at the testing center, the number of other testers who have already been scheduled for the day on which you want to take the test, and the number of times per week that the testing center offers MOS testing. In general, you should call to schedule your test at least two weeks prior to the date on which you want to take the test.

When you arrive at the testing center, you might be asked for proof of identity. A driver's license or passport is an acceptable form of identification. If you do not have either of these items of documentation, call your testing center and ask what alternative forms of identification will be accepted. If you are retaking a test, bring your MOS identification number, which will have been given to you when you previously took the test. If you have not prepaid or if your organization has not already arranged to make payment for you, you will need to pay the test-taking fee when you arrive.

Test Format

All MOS certification tests are live, performance-based tests. There are no multiple-choice, true/false, or short-answer questions. Instructions are general you are told the basic tasks to perform on the computer, but you aren't given any help in figuring out how to perform them. You are not permitted to use reference material other than the application's Help system.

As you complete the tasks stated in a particular test question, the testing software monitors your actions. Following is an example question.

Open the file named *Wiley Guests* and select the word *Welcome* in the first paragraph. Change the font to 12 point, and apply bold formatting. Select the words *at your convenience* in the second paragraph, move them to the end of the first paragraph using drag and drop, and then center the first paragraph.

When the test administrator seats you at a computer, you will see an online form that you use to enter information about yourself (name, address, and other information required to process your exam results). While you complete the form, the software will generate the test from a master test bank and then prompt you to continue. The first test question will appear in a window Read the question carefully, and then perform all the tasks stated in the test question. When you have finished completing all tasks for a question, click the Next Question button.

You have 45 to 60 minutes to complete all questions, depending on the test that you are taking. The testing software assesses your results as soon as you complete the test, and the test administrator can print the results of the test so that you will have a record of any tasks that you performed incorrectly. A passing grade is 75 percent or higher. If you pass, you will receive a certificate in the mail within two to four weeks. If you do not pass, you can study and practice the skills that you missed and then schedule to retake the test at a later date.

Tips for Successfully Completing the Test

The following tips and suggestions are the result of feedback received from many individuals who have taken one or more MOS tests.

- **Make sure that you are thoroughly prepared.** If you have extensively used the application for which you are being tested, you might feel confident that you are prepared for the test. However, the test might include questions that involve tasks that you rarely or never perform when you use the application at your place of business, at school, or at home. You must be knowledgeable in all the MOS objectives for the test that you will take.

- **Read each exam question carefully.** An exam question might include several tasks that you are to perform. A partially correct response to a test question is counted as an incorrect response. In the example question on the previous page, you might apply bold formatting and move the words *at your convenience* to the correct location, but forget to center the first paragraph. This would count as an incorrect response and would result in a lower test score.

- **Use the Help system only when necessary.** You are allowed to use the application's Help system, but relying on the Help system too much will slow you down and possibly prevent you from completing the test within the allotted time. Use the Help system only when necessary.

- **Keep track of your time.** The test does not display the amount of time that you have left, so you need to keep track of the time yourself by monitoring your start time and the required end time on your watch or a clock in the testing center (if there is one). The test program displays the number of items that you have completed along with the total number of test items (for example, "35 of 40 items have been completed"). Use this information to gauge your pace.

- **You cannot return to a question once you've skipped it.** If you skip a question, you cannot return to it later. You should skip a question only if you are certain that you cannot complete the tasks correctly.

- **Make sure you understand the instructions for each question.** As soon as you are finished reading a question and you click in the application window, a condensed version of the instruction is displayed in a corner of the screen. If you are unsure whether you have completed all tasks stated in the test question, click the Instructions button on the test information bar at the bottom of the screen and then reread the question. Close the instruction window when you are finished. Do this as often as necessary to ensure you have read the question correctly and that you have completed all the tasks stated in the question.

If You Do Not Pass the Test

If you do not pass, you can use the assessment printout as a guide to practice the items that you missed. There is no limit to the number of times that you can retake a test; however, you must pay the fee each time that you take the test. When you retake the test, expect to see some of the same test items on the subsequent test; the test software randomly generates the test items from a master test bank before you begin the test. Also expect to see several questions that did not appear on the previous test.

Office 2010 Professional Six-Month Trial Software

Some editions of the textbooks in the MOAC Office 2010 series come with six-month trial editions of Office 2010 Professional. If your book includes a trial, there is a CD adhered to the front or back cover of your book. This section pertains only to the editions that are packaged with an Office 2010 Professional trial.

STEP BY STEP **Installing the Microsoft Office System 2010 Six-Month Trial**

1. Insert the trial software CD-ROM into the CD drive on your computer. The CD will be detected, and the Setup.exe file should automatically begin to run on your computer.
2. When prompted for the Office Product Key, enter the Product Key provided with the software, and then click Next.
3. Enter [your name] and [organization user name], and then click Next.
4. Read the End-User License Agreement, select the *I Accept the Terms in the License Agreement* check box, and then click Next.
5. Select the install option, verify the installation location or click Browse to change the installation location, and then click Next.
6. Verify the program installation preferences, and then click Next.

Click Finish to complete the setup.

UPGRADING MICROSOFT OFFICE PROFESSIONAL 2010 SIX-MONTH TRIAL SOFTWARE TO THE FULL PRODUCT

You can convert the software into full use without removing or reinstalling software on your computer. When you complete your trial, you can purchase a product license from any Microsoft reseller and enter a valid Product Key when prompted during setup.

UNINSTALLING THE TRIAL SOFTWARE AND RETURNING TO YOUR PREVIOUS OFFICE VERSION

If you want to return to your previous version of Office, you need to uninstall the trial software. This should be done through the Add or Remove Programs icon in Control Panel (or Uninstall a program in the Control Panel of Windows Vista).

STEP BY STEP **Uninstall Trial Software**

1. Quit any programs that are running.
2. In Control Panel, click Programs and Features (Add or Remove Programs in Windows XP).
3. Click Microsoft Office Professional 2010, and then click Uninstall (Remove in Windows XP).

Take Note
If you selected the option to remove a previous version of Office during installation of the trial software, you need to reinstall your previous version of Office. If you did not remove your previous version of Office, you can start each of your Office programs either through the Start menu or by opening files for each program. In some cases, you may have to re-create some of your shortcuts and default settings.

STUDENT DATA FILES

All of the practice files that you will use as you perform the exercises in the book are available for download on our student companion site. By using the practice files, you will not waste time creating the samples used in the lessons, and you can concentrate on learning how to use Microsoft Office 2010. With the files and the step-by-step instructions in the lessons, you will learn by doing, which is an easy and effective way to acquire and remember new skills.

Copying the Practice Files

Your instructor might already have copied the practice files before you arrive in class. However, your instructor might ask you to copy the practice files on your own at the start of class. Also, if you want to work through any of the exercises in this book on your own at home or at your place of business after class, you may want to copy the practice files.

STEP BY STEP	Copy the Practice Files

OPEN Internet Explorer.

1. In Internet Explorer, go to the student companion site: www.wiley.com
2. Search for your book title in the upper-right corner.
3. On the Search Results page, locate your book and click on the Visit the Companion Sites link.
4. Select Student Companion Site from the pop-up box.
5. In the left-hand column, under "Browse by Resource" select Student Data Files.
6. Now select Student Data Files from the center of the screen.
7. On the File Download dialog box, select Save to save the data files to your external drive (often called a ZIP drive or a USB drive or a thumb drive) or a local drive.
8. In the Save As dialog box, select a local drive in the left-hand panel that you'd like to save your files to; again, this should be an external drive or a local drive. Remember the drive name that you saved it to.

Acknowledgments

We'd like to thank the many reviewers who pored over the manuscript and provided invaluable feedback in the service of quality instructional materials.

Access 2010

Tammie Bolling, *Tennessee Technology Center—Jacksboro*
Mary Corcoran, *Bellevue College*
Trish Culp, *triOS College—Business Technology Healthcare*
Jana Hambruch, *Lee County School District*
Aditi Mukherjee, *University of Florida—Gainesville*

Excel 2010

Tammie Bolling, *Tennessee Technology Center—Jacksboro*
Mary Corcoran, *Bellevue College*
Trish Culp, *triOS College—Business Technology Healthcare*
Dee Hobson, *Richland College*
Christie Hovey, *Lincoln Land Community College*
Ralph Phillips, *Central Oregon Community College*
Rajeev Sachdev, *triOS College—Business Technology Healthcare*

Outlook 2010

Mary Harnishfeger, *Ivy Tech State College—Bloomington*
Sandra Miller, *Wenatchee Valley College*
Bob Reeves, *Vincennes University*
Lourdes Sevilla, *Southwestern College—Chula Vista*
Phyllis E. Traylor, *St. Philips College*

PowerPoint 2010

Natasha Carter, *SUNY—ATTAIN*
Dr. Susan Evans Jennings, *Stephen F. Austin State University*
Sue Van Lanen, *Gwinnett Technical College*
Carol J. McPeek, *SUNY—ATTAIN*
Michelle Poertner, *Northwestern Michigan College*
Tim Sylvester, *Glendale Community College (AZ)*

Project 2010

Tatyana Pashnyak, *Bainbridge College*
Debi Griggs, *Bellevue College*

Word 2010

Portia Hatfield, *Tennessee Technology Center—Jacksboro*
Terri Holly, *Indian River State College*
Pat McMahon, *South Suburban College*
Barb Purvis, *Centura College*
Janet Sebesy, *Cuyahoga Community College*

We would also like to thank Lutz Ziob, Jason Bunge, Ben Watson, David Bramble, Merrick Van Dongen, Don Field, Pablo Bernal, and Wendy Johnson at Microsoft for their encouragement and support in making the Microsoft Official Academic Course program the finest instructional materials for mastering the newest Microsoft technologies for both students and instructors. Finally, we would like to thank Lorna Gentry of Content LLC for developmental editing and Jeff Riley and his team at Box Twelve Communications for technical editing.

About the Author

CATHERINE BINDER, ED.D.

Catherine Binder has over 15 years experience teaching computer technology courses—ranging from Microsoft Office and computer repair to networking and web development. She has developed curricula for Microsoft Office, operating systems, and networking courses at more than a dozen schools. Her specialty has been in revising existing curricula for use in entirely online and online/classroom hybrid course formats. She has her MOS, MCT, MCP, MCSE, A+, and ICW certifications. She was previously the department chair for Networking and Digital Lifestyle at the Katherine Gibbs School and currently resides in Fredericksburg, Pennsylvania.

Brief Contents

Contents

1 Overview 1

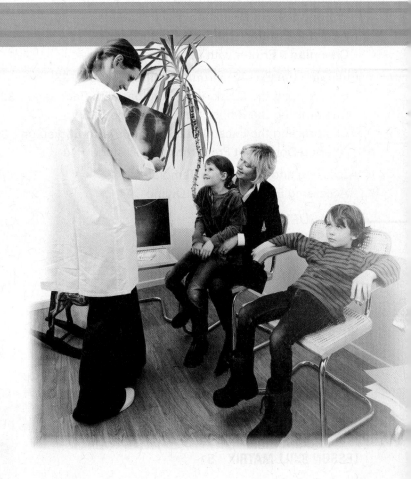

2 Using Backstage 22

3 Working with Microsoft Excel 2010   51

4   Formatting Cells and Ranges   76

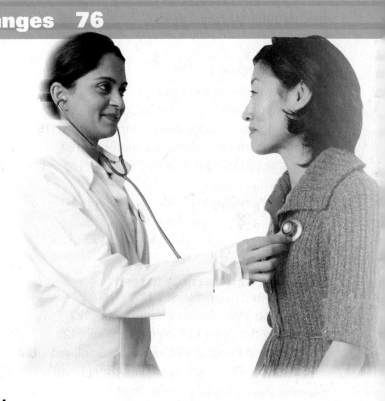

5　Formatting Worksheets　113

6 Managing Worksheets   149

7 Working with Data   174

8 Using Basic Formulas and Functions   207

9 Using Advanced Formulas and Securing Workbooks 248

11   Adding Pictures and Shapes to a Worksheet   342

LESSON SKILL MATRIX

Skill	Exam Objective	Objective Number
Starting Excel		
Working in the Excel Window	Manipulate the Quick Access Toolbar.	1.3.1
	Use Hotkeys.	1.1.1
Changing Excel's View	Use Page Layout workbook view.	4.3.2
	Use Normal workbook view.	4.3.1
	Split window views.	4.2.1
	Open a new window with contents from the current worksheet.	4.2.3
	Arrange window views.	4.2.2
Working with an Existing Workbook	Use the Name box.	1.1.2
Working with Excel's Help System		

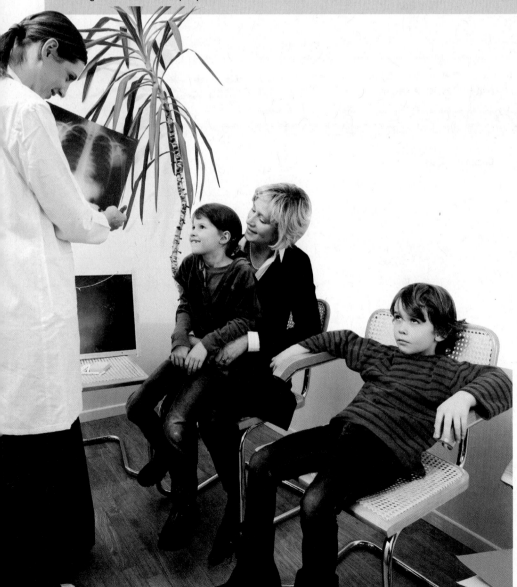

KEY TERMS

- active cell
- Backstage
- cell
- column
- command tab
- command group
- Dialog Box Launcher
- File tab
- Help system
- hotkey
- Keytip
- Name box
- Quick Access Toolbar
- Ribbon
- row
- ScreenTip
- workbook
- worksheet

Contoso, Ltd., provides specialty health care for the entire family—prenatal through geriatric care. The practice, owned by Dr. Stephanie Bourne, has an expanding patient list. It currently employs a staff of 36, which includes three additional family practice physicians. Each physician has unique patient contact hours; the office is open from 7 a.m. to 7 p.m. on Mondays and from 8 a.m. to 4 p.m. other weekdays. The office manager must track revenue and expenses for the practice and maintain a large volume of employee data. Microsoft Excel is an ideal tool for organizing and analyzing such data. In this lesson, you will learn how to enter text and numbers into an Excel worksheet to keep up-to-date employee records.

SOFTWARE ORIENTATION

Microsoft Excel's Opening Screen

NEW to Office 2010

Microsoft Office Excel 2010 provides powerful new and improved tools that enable users to organize, analyze, manage, and share information easily. When you open Excel, you immediately see some of its most important new features. A broad band, called the **Ribbon**, runs across the top of the window. The Ribbon is organized into task-oriented **command tabs**. Each

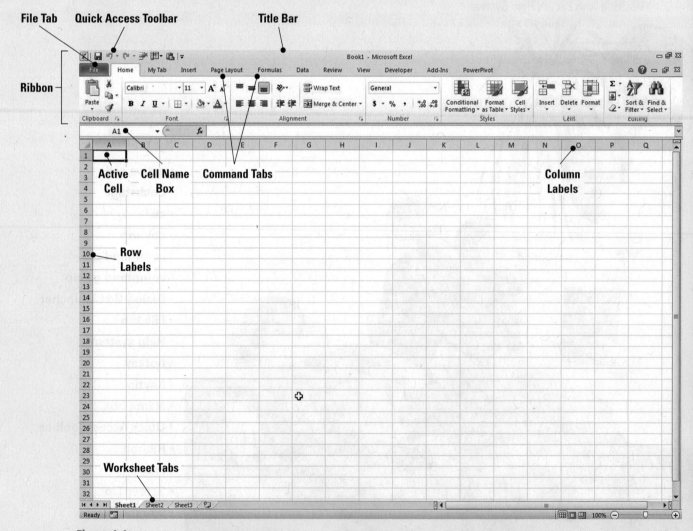

Figure 1-1

Excel's opening screen

tab is divided into task-specific **command groups** appropriate to the type of work the user is currently performing. The tabs and groups replace the menus and multiple toolbars that were present in Excel 2007. When you first launch Excel, you will see a screen similar to the one shown in Figure 1-1. (The Developer and Add-Ins tabs may not appear on your screen if the default settings have been changed or other preferences have been set.) Use Figure 1-1 as a reference throughout this lesson and the rest of this book.

STARTING EXCEL

The Bottom Line

To work efficiently in Microsoft Excel, you need to become familiar with its primary user interface. You can open Microsoft Office Excel 2010 by clicking the Start menu, All Programs, Microsoft Office, and then Office Excel 2010.

Excel opens with a blank **workbook**, or spreadsheet file, as shown in Figure 1-1. The filename (Book1) and the program name (Microsoft Excel) appear in the title bar at the top of the screen; the Book1 title remains until you save the workbook with a name of your choice. The new workbook contains three **worksheets**—similar to pages in a document or a book—where you can enter information. The sheet tabs are located just above the Status bar and are identified as Sheet1, Sheet2, and Sheet3. You can rename worksheets to identify their content and add additional worksheets as needed.

Starting Excel

In this exercise, you learn to use the Start menu to open Excel and view the new workbook's first blank worksheet.

STEP BY STEP	Start Excel

GET READY. To complete this exercise, make sure your computer is running and Microsoft Excel is installed. Then, follow these steps:

WileyPLUS Extra! features an online tutorial of this task.

1. Click the Start menu, and then click All Programs.
2. On the list of programs, click Microsoft Office 2010.
3. Click Microsoft Office Excel 2010. A blank workbook will open, and the worksheet named Sheet1 will be displayed.

PAUSE. LEAVE the worksheet open to use in the next exercise.

A worksheet is a grid composed of rows, columns, and cells. Worksheet **columns** go from top to bottom and are identified by letters; **rows** go from left to right and are identified by numbers. Each box on the grid is a **cell** and is identified by the intersection of a column and a row. Thus, the first cell in an open worksheet is A1. You enter information by keying it into the **active cell**, which is outlined by a bold black line; this is also called a highlighted cell.

WORKING IN THE EXCEL WINDOW

The Bottom Line

When you launched Excel in the previous exercise, the program opened a new workbook and displayed a blank worksheet. You just learned about some of the most important components of the Excel worksheet. In this lesson, you explore the Excel window and learn to identify and customize the Quick Access Toolbar, the Ribbon, and other important onscreen tools and components. You also learn to open and use Backstage view, Microsoft's replacement for the Office button and File tab commands found in previous versions of Office.

Using Onscreen Tools

The **Quick Access Toolbar** gives you fast and easy access to the tools you use most often in any given Excel session. It appears on the left side of the title bar, above the Ribbon (although you can move the toolbar below the Ribbon if you want it closer to your work area). You can add and remove commands to and from the toolbar so that it contains only those commands you use most frequently. In this lesson, you learn to move and customize the Quick Access Toolbar by adding and removing commands. You also learn how to use **ScreenTips**—small, onscreen windows that display descriptive text when you rest the pointer on a command or control.

STEP BY STEP   **Use Onscreen Tools**

GET READY. Use the workbook you opened in the previous exercise to perform these steps:

1. Place the cursor at the bottom of each command on the Quick Access Toolbar and read the description that appears as a ScreenTip.

Take Note   Use ScreenTips to remind you of a command's function. Enhanced ScreenTips display in a larger window that contains more descriptive text than a ScreenTip. Most Enhanced ScreenTips contain a link to a Help topic.

2. Click the drop-down arrow at the right side of the Quick Access Toolbar. From the drop-down list, select Open. The Open icon is added to the Quick Access Toolbar. Click the down arrow again and select Quick Print from the drop-down list (see Figure 1-2).

Figure 1-2

Customizing the Quick Access Toolbar

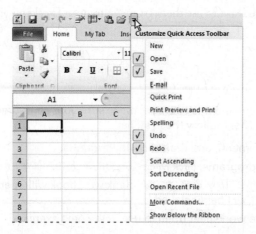

3. Next, right-click the toolbar, then select Show Quick Access Toolbar Below the Ribbon.
4. Right-click the Home tab and click Minimize the Ribbon; now, only the tabs remain on display, increasing your workspace.
5. Click the drop-down arrow on the right side of the Quick Access Toolbar to produce a menu of options, then select Minimize the Ribbon to turn off the option and make the Ribbon commands visible.
6. Right-click the Quick Access Toolbar again and choose Show Quick Access Toolbar Above the Ribbon from the pop-up menu.
7. Right-click the Open command, and select Remove from Quick Access Toolbar.

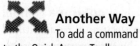

Another Way
To add a command to the Quick Access Toolbar, you can also right-click any icon on the Ribbon and then click Add to Quick Access Toolbar.

Take Note   If you want to add commands to the Quick Access Toolbar that do not appear in the drop-down list, click More Commands on the drop-down list. The Excel Options dialog box will open. You can also right-click the Quick Access Toolbar or any Ribbon tab and select Customize Quick Access Toolbar to open the Excel Options window.

PAUSE. LEAVE the workbook open to use in the next exercise.

CERTIFICATION READY **1.3.1**

How do you manipulate the Quick Access Toolbar?

By default, the Quick Access Toolbar contains the Save, Undo, and Redo commands. As you work in Excel, customize the Quick Access Toolbar so that it contains the commands you use most often. Do not, however, remove the Undo and Redo commands. These commands are not available on the command tabs.

Navigating the Ribbon

The Ribbon organizes tools from the Menu Toolbar into an easier, more useful user interface. Having commands visible on the work surface enables you to work more quickly and efficiently. As you've seen in earlier exercises, the Ribbon in Microsoft Office Excel 2010 is made up of a series of tabs, each related to specific kinds of tasks that users perform in Excel. By pressing and releasing the Alt key, you can reveal **Keytips**, or small "badges" displaying keyboard shortcuts for specific tabs and commands on the Ribbon and Quick Access Toolbar. In this exercise, you learn how to navigate between Excel tabs and use their commands and Keytips.

Take Note   Keytips are sometimes also referred to as **hotkeys** in Excel. Note, however, that when you use Microsoft Office 2010 Help, no reference is listed for hotkeys; only Keytips is referenced.

Within each tab on the Ribbon, commands are organized into related tasks called command groups, as shown in Figure 1-3. For example, consider the Home tab, which groups all the options that were part of the Standard and Formatting toolbars in previous Office versions. When the Home tab is displayed, you see the Clipboard group, which contains the command buttons to cut, copy, and paste data. These commands allow you to revise, move, and repeat data within a worksheet. Similarly, you can use commands in the Editing group to fill adjacent cells, sort and filter data, find specific data within a worksheet, and perform other tasks related to editing worksheet data.

Figure 1-3

Home tab command groups

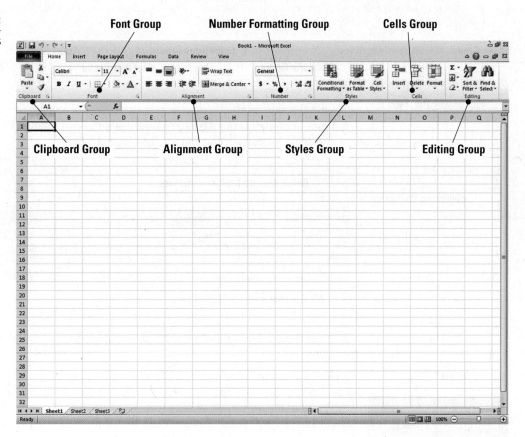

Font Group   Number Formatting Group   Cells Group

Clipboard Group   Alignment Group   Styles Group   Editing Group

Navigate the Ribbon

USE the previous worksheet for this exercise, making sure you complete the following steps:

1. With the Home tab active, click cell A1; your Ribbon should look similar to the one shown in Figure 1-4.

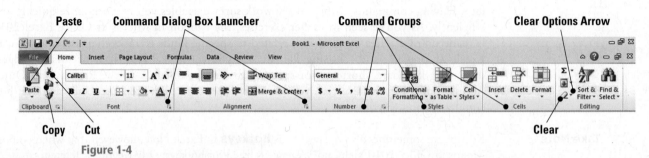

Figure 1-4

Ribbon with Home tab active

2. Click the Insert tab; your screen should now look similar to the one shown in Figure 1-5. Commands on the Insert tab enable you to add charts and illustrations and to perform other functions that enhance your Excel spreadsheets.

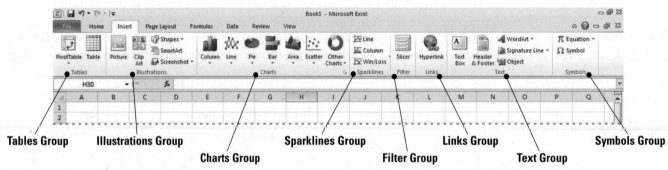

Figure 1-5

Ribbon with the Insert tab active

3. Click the Home tab.

4. Press and release the Alt key to produce onscreen Keytips that show keyboard shortcuts for certain commands (see Figure 1-6).

Figure 1-6

Keytips on the Ribbon

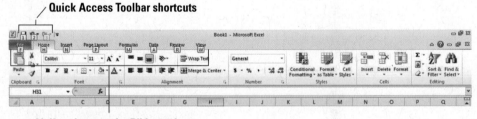

Quick Access Toolbar shortcuts

Alt Key shortcuts for Ribbon tabs

5. Press the Esc key or press the Alt key again to turn off the Keytips.

Take Note   Keyboard shortcuts enable you to issue commands in Excel without using the mouse (so you don't have to take your hands from the keyboard). You use keyboard shortcuts by pressing the key shown in the Keytip while also pressing and holding the Alt key. When you press and release the Alt key by itself, Excel displays the shortcuts for the Quick Access Toolbar.

**CERTIFICATION
READY   1.1.1**

How do you use hotkeys in Excel?

PAUSE. CLOSE the workbook.

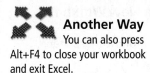

Another Way
You can also press Alt+F4 to close your workbook and exit Excel.

Introducing Backstage

The most noticeable new feature in Microsoft Office 2010 is Backstage. The Backstage view enables you to easily navigate and customize the different features you most frequently use in Excel. Backstage will be covered in more depth in Lesson 2—but first, you need to know how to access it.

STEP BY STEP   **Access Backstage**

OPEN a new workbook for this exercise. Then, follow these steps:

1. Click the File tab. This opens Backstage view (see Figure 1-7).

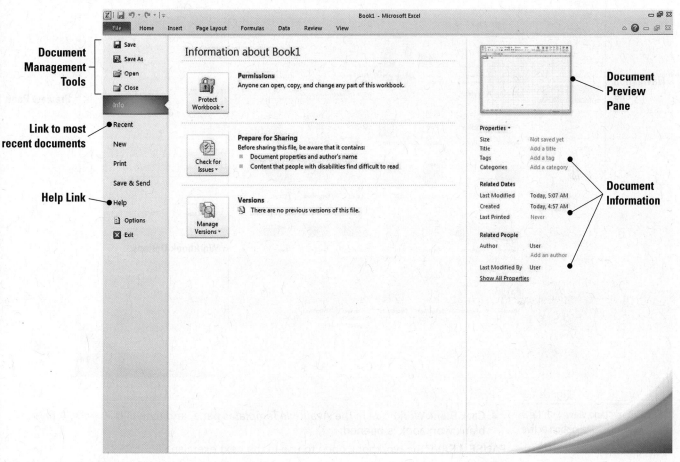

Document Management Tools

Link to most recent documents

Help Link

Document Preview Pane

Document Information

Figure 1-7

Backstage view

2. Notice that the Excel Backstage view is green. The Office suite has customized colors to designate which application you are using.

 Ref   The use and tools of Backstage are covered in depth in Lesson 2.

PAUSE. CLOSE the workbook and exit Excel.

Another Way
Pressing Alt+F also allows you to activate Backstage view.

NEW to Office 2010

Using the Microsoft Office File Tab and Backstage View

In Microsoft Office 2010, the Office button is replaced by the **File tab**. Clicking the File tab takes you to the Microsoft Office Backstage view, with its navigation bar of commands extending down the left side of the Excel window. **Backstage** view helps you access and use file management features, just as the Ribbon offers commands that control Excel's authoring features. In this exercise, you learn to use the File tab to open Backstage view. You also use Backstage commands to create a new, blank workbook.

STEP BY STEP   **Use the File Tab to Open Backstage View and Create a New Workbook**

GET READY. LAUNCH Excel to open a new, blank workbook. Then, follow these steps:

WileyPLUS Extra! features an online tutorial of this task.

1. Click the File tab to open Backstage view.
2. Click Close in the navigation bar; your workbook disappears, but Excel remains open.
3. Click the File tab again, then click New; the *Available Templates* pane opens (see Figure 1-8).

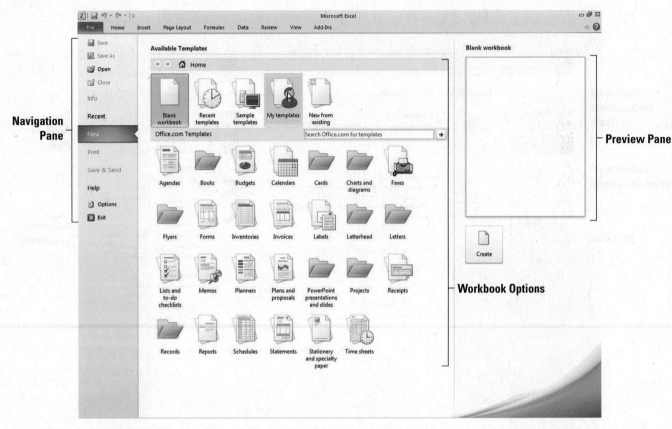

Figure 1-8

Backstage view with New option active

4. Click Blank Workbook in the *Available Templates* pane, and then click Create. A new blank workbook is opened.

PAUSE. LEAVE the workbook open to use in the next exercise.

As you have seen, a new blank workbook contains three worksheets. You can enter data in each of the worksheets, and Excel saves the worksheets as one workbook, rather than as separate documents.

CHANGING EXCEL'S VIEW

The Bottom Line

On the Ribbon, the View tab holds commands for controlling the appearance of the displayed document. You can also open and arrange new windows and split windows for side-by-side document views.

Changing Excel's View

Some command group headers in the Ribbon tabs have an arrow in their lower-right corner; this is called a **Dialog Box Launcher**. Clicking the arrow opens a dialog box, or a task pane containing more options for that particular group of commands. In this exercise, you learn how to use the View tab commands (including those you access through the Dialog Box Launcher) to change Excel's view within the open window.

STEP BY STEP   **Change Excel's View**

USE the open workbook from the previous exercise. Then, follow these steps:

1. The Home tab should be active. If it is not, click Home to activate it.
2. Select cell A1 to make it active. Then type 456 and press Tab.
3. Click the Dialog Box Launcher arrow in the lower-right corner of the Font group of commands. The *Format Cells* dialog box, shown in Figure 1-9, opens. In most cases, your default font in Excel will be Calibri, point size 11, with no bolding or italics.

Figure 1-9

Format Cells dialog box

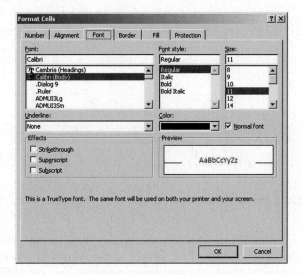

4. Notice that the Font tab of the dialog box is active. Change the font to Arial, then click OK.
5. Cell B1 should now be the active cell in your worksheet. Key 456 in this cell, then press Tab. Notice the difference in size and appearance between this number and the one you keyed in cell A1.
6. Click the View tab.
7. Click Page Layout view. Your workbook should look like Figure 1-10. In this view, you can see the margins, and you can add a header or footer.

Another Way
To change a font, you can type the first few letters of the name of the font you are searching for and Excel will locate it on the font list. You can also scroll through the list and choose your font type.

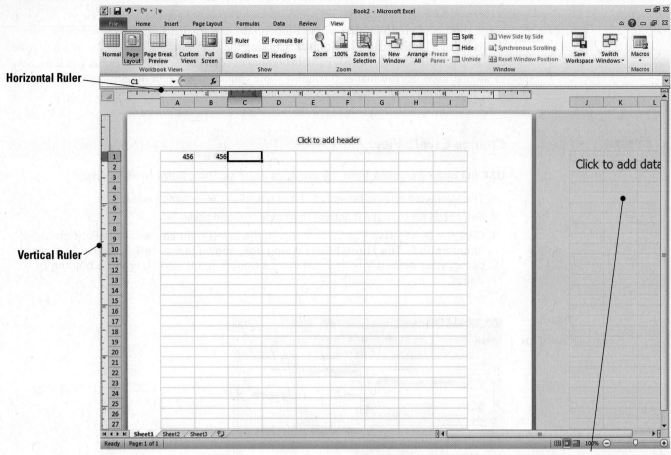

Horizontal Ruler

Vertical Ruler

Right Pane with additional cells

Figure 1-10

Page Layout view

PAUSE. LEAVE the workbook open to use in the next exercise.

CERTIFICATION READY   4.3.2

How do you change to Page Layout view?

As demonstrated in the exercise, you can preview your printed worksheet by clicking the Ribbon's View tab, then clicking Page Layout in the Workbook Views group (first section). This view enables you to fine-tune pages before printing. You can change your worksheet's layout and format in both this view and Normal view. You can also use the rulers to measure the width and height of your worksheet and determine whether you need to change its margins or print orientation.

 Ref   You will learn how to use additional commands in Lessons 2 and 3.

Splitting a Window

CERTIFICATION READY   4.3.1

How do you change back to Normal view?

When a worksheet contains a great deal of data, you can see only a small portion of the worksheet in Excel's Normal and Page Layout views. The Split command enables you to overcome this limitation by viewing the worksheet in four quadrants. After issuing this command, you can use the scroll bars on the right and at the bottom of the window to display different sections of the worksheet at the same time so that you can more easily compare or contrast data. In this exercise, you learn to split the Excel window and use the scroll bars to view different sections of a worksheet. You also practice keying data into cells within the split windows, and you learn how to remove the split to return to single-window view.

STEP BY STEP   ## Split a Window

USE the worksheet you left open in the previous exercise. Then, follow these steps:

1. Press Ctrl+Home to make cell A1 active.
2. With the View tab active, click the Split command in the Window group.
3. Choose the lower-right quadrant by clicking any cell in that area, then scroll down to Row 30.
4. Key 235 in cell H30 and press Enter. The data you entered in cells A1 and B1 should be visible along with what you just entered in cell H30, as shown in Figure 1-11.

Figure 1-11

Working in a split window

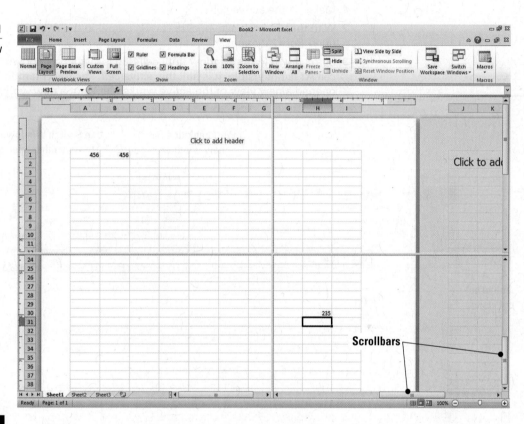

5. Click Split to remove the split. The data in cell H30 is no longer visible. However, if you click the Split command once more, you will again see all the data in this worksheet.

PAUSE. LEAVE the workbook open to use in the next exercise.

Take Note   The Split command is especially useful when you need to compare various portions of a long worksheet.

When you use a worksheet that contains a small amount of data, it is easy to scroll through the worksheet and focus on specific cells. As you become experienced in working with Excel, however, you may find yourself working on much larger worksheets. The ability to view more than one section of a worksheet at the same time by using split windows is especially useful when you need to compare different sections of data.

Opening a New Window

Splitting a window allows you to look at two sections of a worksheet side by side. You can also view two sections of a worksheet by using the New Window command. In this section, you learn to use the New Window command on the View tab to open a new window in Excel. You also learn to use the Switch Window command to change the active window, and you learn how to close multiple windows.

STEP BY STEP   **Open a New Window**

USE the open workbook from the previous exercise to complete these steps:

1. Make A1 the active cell.
2. With the View tab active, click New Window in the Window group. A new window titled *Book2:2* opens.
3. Scroll down in the window until cell H30 is visible, as shown in Figure 1-12. Although cell A1 is not visible, it is still the active cell. It is important to note that you have opened a new view of the active worksheet—not a new worksheet.

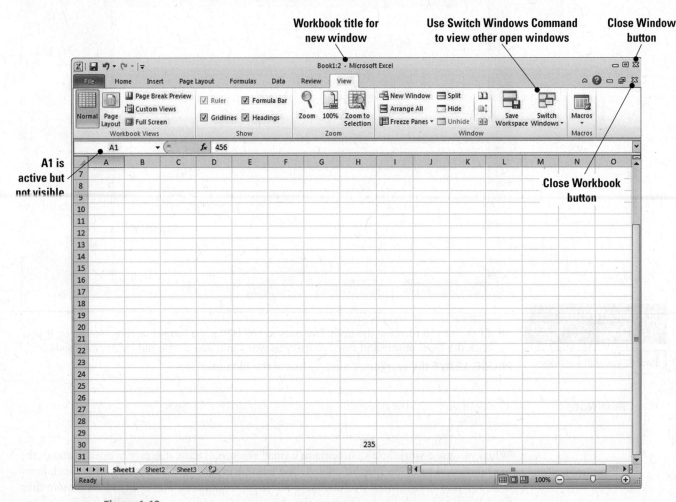

Workbook title for new window Use Switch Windows Command to view other open windows Close Window button

A1 is active but not visible

Close Workbook button

Figure 1-12

A new window

CERTIFICATION READY   **4.2.3**

How do you open and organize new windows?

4. Click Switch Windows; a drop-down list of all open windows appears. *Book2:2* is checked, which indicates that it is the active window.
5. Click Book2:1. You will now see the original view of the worksheet with cell A1 active.
6. Click Switch Windows and make Book2:2 active.

7. Click the Close Window button (in the upper-right corner of the workbook window) to close Book2:2. The window closes, and the title Book2 tells you that you are now looking at the only open view of this workbook.

Another Way
You also can use the Arrange All command on the View tab to display open windows side by side so that you can compare various parts of a worksheet. This function is especially useful when you work with workbooks that contain more than one worksheet.

The Bottom Line

**CERTIFICATION
READY   4.2.2**

How do you arrange multiple windows in Excel?

 The *Contoso Employee* Info file for this lesson is available on the book companion website or in WileyPLUS.

Clicking the Close Window button will close only the new window opened at the beginning of this exercise. If you use the Close command in the Microsoft File tab, you will close the entire workbook.

8. Click the File tab and then click Close.

9. When asked if you want to save the changes to Book2, click No.

PAUSE. LEAVE Excel open to use in the next exercise.

WORKING WITH AN EXISTING WORKBOOK

Many workbooks require frequent updating because existing data has changed or new data must be added. Workers frequently open an existing workbook, update information, and then save the workbook to be revised again at a later time. Often, files are created by one person, then used and/or updated by others. Filenames should reflect the type of data contained in the file. A descriptive filename enables workers to locate and retrieve files quickly. Filenames can be up to 255 characters long, including the filename extension. However, most workers use short, descriptive filenames that clearly identify the content of the workbook.

Opening an Existing Workbook

When you save an Excel 2010 file, the program automatically adds the .xlsx extension to the end of the file's name. This extension identifies the program in which the file can be opened. For example, .xlsx is the file extension used in Excel. To open a file, you must also identify the drive and folder that contain the file. In your local computer environment, generally by default, your local drive is designated as C:.

In this exercise, you will use commands from the File tab in Backstage view to find and open an existing workbook.

STEP BY STEP   **Open an Existing Workbook**

BEFORE you begin this exercise, log in to the WileyPLUS website for your course and download the appropriate data files for this lesson. Then, perform these steps:

Another Way
To display the Open dialog box without using the File tab, press Ctrl+O.

Take Note

1. Within Excel, click the File tab. Documents you recently created or edited will appear on the right side in the Recent Documents area.

2. Click Open. The Open dialog box will appear.

Throughout this chapter you will see information that appears in black text within brackets, such as [Press Enter], or [your email address]. The information contained in the brackets is intended to be directions for you rather than something you actually type word for word. It will instruct you to perform an action or substitute text. Do **not** type the actual text that appears within brackets.

3. In the Recent Workbooks area, click [the name of the data files for this lesson]. (Again, lesson files can be downloaded from the companion website or accessed for download from WileyPLUS.)

Take Note

By default, the Open dialog box lists only the files that were created in the program you are using—in this case, Excel. To see files created in other programs, you can select All Files in the Files of type box at the bottom of the Open dialog box.

4. Select *Contoso Employee Info* from the listed files, and then click Open. The file opens, as shown in Figure 1-13, with the workbook name displayed in the title bar.

Figure 1-13

Opening an existing worksheet

	A	B	C	D
1		Contoso, Ltd.		
2				
3	Last Name	First Name	Job Title	Hours
4	Bourne	Stephanie	Physician	36
5	Holliday	Nicole	Physician	36
6	Laszlo	Rebecca	Physician	36
7	Barnhill	Josh	Billing Clerk	36
8	Kane	John	Registered Nurse	30
9	Trenary	Jean	Registered Nurse	30
10	Da Silva	Sergio	Physician Assistant	36
11	Wang	Jian	Referral Specialist	36
12	Wilson	Dan	Physician	36
13	Valdez	Rachel	Receptionist	30
14	Giest	Jim	Office Manager	40
15	Gottfried	Jenny	Receptionist	30
16	Delaney	Aidan	Receptionist	20
17	Dellamore	Luca	Medical Assistant	36
18	Hamilton	David	Medical Assistant	36
19	Hoeing	Helge	Medical Assistant	36
20	Munson	Stuart	Referral Specialist	36
21	Murray	Billie Jo	Medical Assistant	36
22	Kenneth	Kevin	File Clerk	15
23	Hensien	Kari	File Clerk	20
24	Moore	Bobby	File Clerk	15
25	Moreland	Barbara	Billing Clerk	20
26	Metters	Susan	Billing Clerk	25
27	Poland	Carole	Nurse Practitioner	25
28				
29				
30				
31				
32				

PAUSE. LEAVE the workbook open to use in the next exercise.

If you are familiar with Microsoft Word, you know that when you open a file, the program places your cursor and screen display at the beginning of the document. When you open an Excel workbook, however, the active cell is the same one that was active when you last saved the file. For example, when you open the Contoso Employee Info workbook, A22 is the active cell in Normal view, because A22 was the active cell displayed in Normal view when the file was last saved. This feature enables you to continue working in the same location when you return to the workbook.

Navigating a Worksheet

An Excel worksheet can contain more than one million rows and more than sixteen thousand columns. There are several ways to move through worksheets that contain numerous rows and columns. You can use the arrow keys, the scrollbars, or the mouse to navigate through a worksheet. In the following exercises, you will explore the different methods for moving through a worksheet.

Navigate a Worksheet

USE the workbook you left open in the previous exercise to perform these steps:

1. Press **Ctrl+Home** to move to the beginning of the document (cell A1).
2. Press **Ctrl+End** to move to the end of the document (cell D27).
3. Click cell **A27** to make it the active cell, and press **Page Up**. The cursor moves to cell A1.
4. Click cell **A3** to make it active, then press **Ctrl+Page Down** to go to the last row of data (cell A27).
5. Press **Ctrl+Right Arrow**. The cursor moves to D27, the last column in the range of data. The unused cells below the data are considered a range.
6. Press **Ctrl+Down Arrow**. The cursor moves to the last possible row in the worksheet.

CERTIFICATION
R E A D Y   **1.1.2**

Where is the Name box located and what is it used for?

 Ref

Take Note

    Another Way
The cell **Name box** is located below the Ribbon at the left end of the formula bar. When you key a cell location in this box and press Enter, the cursor moves to that cell. This is another way to efficiently navigate your worksheet.

Take Note

You will learn about ranges in more depth in Lesson 3.

Ctrl+Arrow allows you to move to the start and end of ranges of data. The title, which spans all the columns, is not considered part of the worksheet's data range.

7. Press **Ctrl+Home**.
8. Press **Scroll Lock** while you press the **Right Arrow** key. This moves the active column one column to the right.
9. Use the vertical scrollbar (refer to Figure 1-11) to navigate from the beginning to the end of the data.
10. If your mouse has a wheel button, roll the wheel button forward and back to quickly scroll through the worksheet.

When Scroll Lock is on, *scroll lock* is displayed on the left side of the Status bar. If you want to use the arrow keys to move between cells, you must turn off Scroll Lock. Some keyboards come equipped with an onboard scroll lock key, while others do not. This is an option not a necessity.

PAUSE. CLOSE the workbook before moving to the next exercise.

WORKING WITH EXCEL'S HELP SYSTEM

The Bottom Line

The **Help system** in Excel 2010 is rich in information, illustrations, and tips that can help you complete any task as you create worksheets and workbooks. When you install Excel, you automatically install hundreds of help topics on your computer. Excel can also access thousands of additional help topics online.

Using the Help System

Finding the right information in Excel's Help system is easy: You can pick a topic from the Help system's table of contents, browse a directory of Help topics, or perform keyword searches by entering terms that best describe the task you want to complete. In this exercise, you learn to open the Help dialog box and move between its online and offline topics.

Take Note   If you aren't sure what an onscreen tool does, just point to it. Once the mouse pointer rests on a tool, a box called a ScreenTip appears. A basic ScreenTip displays the tool's name and shortcut key (if a shortcut exists for that tool). Some of the Ribbon's tools have enhanced ScreenTips, which also provide a brief description of the tool.

STEP BY STEP   Use the Help System

OPEN a new worksheet for this exercise. Then, follow these steps:

1. Position your mouse pointer over the Help button, as shown in Figure 1-14, in the upper-right corner of your Excel screen. A ScreenTip appears, telling you that this button enables you to access Excel's Help features.

Figure 1-14

Help button

Office Help Button

Microsoft Excel Help (F1)
Get help using Microsoft Office.

2. Click the Help button; the Help window opens, as shown in Figure 1-15.

Figure 1-15

Help window

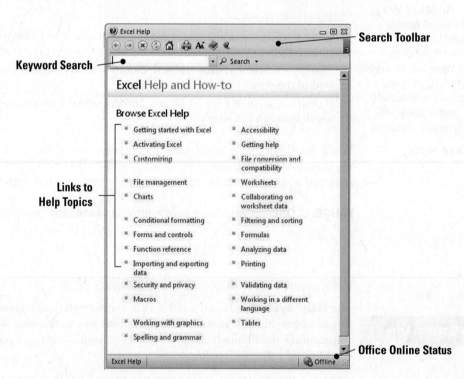

Search Toolbar

Keyword Search

Links to
Help Topics

Office Online Status

Another Way
Even if Excel is set to work offline, you can still search for help online. To do so, instead of clicking the Search button, click the drop-down arrow next to it. When the menu appears, click the Content from Office Online link. The choice will affect only the current search, not Excel's overall settings.

3. In the Help window, click on the Getting started with Excel hyperlink. The next screen gives you additional hyperlinked subcategories.
4. Navigate through three of the subtopics in the Help window.
5. Click the Office Help Connection Status button in the bottom-right corner of the Help window. This produces the Connection Status dialog box shown in Figure 1-16. This feature enables you to choose whether the Help window displays online or offline Help content.

Figure 1-16

Connection Status dialog box

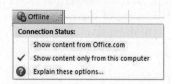

Another Way
You can access the Help Feature at any time by pressing the F1 key.

6. CLOSE the Help window.
CLOSE your workbook.

Excel's Help window gives you access to various help topics that offer information about specific Excel features or tools. Help topics can assist you with virtually any task, feature, or problem you encounter when working with Excel.

The Help window is set up like a browser, with links to specific categories and topics, and it features some of the same tools you will find in your web browser, including:

Back: Jumps to the previously opened Help topic

Forward: Jumps to the next opened Help topic

Stop: Stops any action in progress

Refresh: Reloads the current Help topic

Home: Returns to the initial Help Dialog Window

Print: Allows you to print the current Help topic

Take Note

Many Excel dialog boxes contain a Help button. When you click it, a Help window opens with information about that dialog box.

You can find help in several different ways. For example, you can open the table of contents and scan the list for help on a specific topic or feature. You can also enter a keyword or phrase in the Search box, then click the Search button. When you do this, related help topics appear in the Help window.

The Search button gives you additional options when looking for help. When you click the drop-down arrow next to the Search button, you have the option to search for help online or offline, look for Excel templates, find information about formulas and spreadsheet development, and more.

The Connection Status menu lets you use other help topics that are available online or just those topics installed on your computer (referred to as "offline help"). If your computer has an "always on" connection to the Internet, such as a cable modem or LAN connection, you may want to set the Connection Status to *Show content from Office Online*, which is Microsoft's online-based built-in help system. If your computer uses a dial-up modem, or if you simply choose not to use this feature, choose the *Show content only from this computer* option to work with the offline help feature and topics installed on your machine.

SKILL SUMMARY

In This Lesson You Learned How To:	Exam Objective	Objective Number
Starting Excel		
Working in the Excel Window	Manipulate the Quick Access Toolbar.	**1.3.1**
	Use Hotkeys.	**1.1.1**
Changing Excel's View	Use Page Layout workbook view.	**4.3.2**
	Use Normal workbook view.	**4.3.1**
	Split window views.	**4.2.1**
	Open a new window with contents from the current worksheet.	**4.2.3**
	Arrange window views.	**4.2.2**
Working with an Existing Workbook	Use the Name box.	**1.1.2**
Working with Excel's Help System		

Knowledge Assessment

Fill in the Blank

Complete the following sentences by writing the correct word or words in the blanks provided.

1. An arrow at the bottom of a group header on the Ribbon tells you that a(n) _____ is available that will offer additional options.
2. A selected cell is called the _____.
3. _____ view is a new feature in Office 2010 that enables you to easily navigate and customize different features in Excel.
4. After a file has been opened, the filename appears in the _____.
5. When you split a window, the window is divided into _____ panes.
6. When you click the Help button, the _____ opens.
7. A cell is formed by the intersection of _____.
8. The _____ can be customized and contains the commands you use most frequently.
9. A new Excel workbook opens with _____ worksheets.
10. An active cell is identified because it is the _____ cell.

True/False

Circle T if the statement is true or F if the statement is false.

T   F   1. Pressing the F1 key will activate Backstage.

T   F   2. Pressing the Alt key will activate ScreenTips that help you use the keyboard shortcuts.

T   F   3. Ctrl+O will open a new blank workbook.

T   F   4. The Quick Access Toolbar appears on the right side of the title bar, above the Ribbon.

T   F   5. Ctrl+F will activate Backstage.

T   F   6. Keytips can guide you to access the Backstage area.

T   F   7. Excel opens with a new blank workbook displayed.

T   F   8. The columns in a worksheet are identified by numbers.

T   F   9. The active cell in a worksheet is outlined by a bold black line.

T   F   10. Page Layout view is useful when preparing your data for printing.

Competency Assessment

Project 1-1: Utilizing Help

Use this lesson to better familiarize yourself with the Help System.

GET READY. LAUNCH Excel if it is not already running.

1. On the right side of the Ribbon, click the Help button.
2. When the Help window opens, key How to use Excel Help into the Search bar, and press Enter.
3. When the next screen appears, find the link to *What's New in Excel 2010* and click on it.
4. Choose three of the topics that interest you and examine them.
5. Click the Back button as needed to return to the previous topic searched. Click it again to go back to the Search results window.

6. Click on the article titled *Use Office Excel 2010 with earlier versions of Excel*. Examine and read the contents.

7. Close the Help window. The Close button is in the upper-right corner of the window.

CLOSE the workbook.

Project 1-2: Utilizing the Ribbon

GET READY. LAUNCH Excel if it is not already running.

1. Click the File tab. This is your instant access to Backstage. Click several of the commands in Backstage that are shown on the navigation bar on the left side of the Excel window. Get a feel for the environment.

2. Click the Home tab. Move your cursor over the Ribbon, reading the various ScreenTips that appear as your cursor rests over individual Ribbon elements.

3. In the Font command group area, click the arrow next to the font box. Note that the first font at the top of the font list is displayed. Click on the drop-down arrow again to hide the list.

4. In the font box, type a T. You will see the list change. Choose Times New Roman. Note the corresponding change in font.

5. Move your cursor up to the Quick Access Toolbar and click the Undo arrow. Note that your font returns to the default font face, either Times New Roman or Calibri.

6. Click the Insert tab. Move your cursor over the Ribbon and examine it while reading the ScreenTips.

7. Next click the View tab. Once again mouse over the Ribbon and examine its features.

8. Click the File tab again to display Backstage view.

Click the Exit command at the bottom of the navigation bar to close the application completely. If prompted to save the document, choose No.

Proficiency Assessment

Project 1-3: Organizing Data

You are consolidating your life and have items in storage you would like to sell. Because you are not yet sure about the value of these items, you need to gather research information (data) about them. Worksheets are excellent tools for organizing information so you can make easy comparisons between sets of data.

1. Identify a list of at least ten items that you have in storage that you would like to sell as quickly, efficiently, and inexpensively as possible. They can range from large items to small items.

2. **START** Excel and create a new workbook. Click the File tab and save this workbook as *Items for Sale_1*.

3. In cell A1, key Item. Press Enter.

4. In cell B1, type Cost.

5. In cell C1, key Sell For.

6. In cell D1, key Sold.

7. In cell E1, key Donated.

8. Beginning in cell A2, key the name of your first item. Repeat this step in cells A3–A11 until you have 10 items listed.

9. Minimize Excel.

10. Open a web browser on your computer and navigate to your favorite search engine.

11. In the keywords box for your search, key Price of [your item](Amount), then click Enter. View your results. Don't be discouraged—it might take a few tries to get some information.

12. When you have an estimated price for your first item, key it in cell B2.
13. Repeat steps 11 and 12 until you have keyed in the estimated values for all 10 items.
    SAVE the workbook. CLOSE Excel.

Project 1-4: Changing Data

In this exercise, you will use the previously created workbook to accommodate changes to your data.

LAUNCH Excel.

1. Click the File tab to engage Backstage.
2. Move your cursor to the Recent command; the command will highlight green.
3. Click the Recent command. The screen displays your most recent documents, including your workbook titled *Items for Sale_1*.
4. Click on this file to open it. SAVE the file as *Items for Sale_2*.
5. Make cell C2 active by clicking it, then key in the amount to sell that item at auction.
6. If you predict an item that you have might not sell, put an X in the appropriate box for donated in the cell created in column E.
7. Click the Close button in the upper-right corner of Excel. When prompted to save the worksheet, click OK.

PAUSE. CLOSE the workbook and LEAVE Excel open for the next exercise.

Project 1-5: Altering a Workbook

In this exercise, you will use the Home and File tabs to open and edit your worksheet titled *Items for Sale_1*.

OPEN Excel.

1. Click the File tab, and then click the Recent button in the navigation pane.
2. Open the worksheet *Items for Sale_1*. Save the file as *Items for Sale_3*.
3. Click Ctrl+Home to go to the beginning of the worksheet.
4. Now that cell A1 is active, click on the View tab.
5. Click the Full screen button. You are now in full screen view. Notice the split screen view and no Ribbon. To exit full screen view, press Esc.
6. Click Page Break Preview. The Welcome to Page Break Preview dialog box will appear to tell you how to drag break lines; click OK to close the box. Note that your active data cells are highlighted in blue. Click the Normal view button to return to your original state. Note that now a dotted line denotes your page breaks.

PAUSE. CLOSE Excel. If prompted to save the file, do so.

Project 1-6: Altering Excel's View

In this project, you will continue to explore the Ribbon and its features.

START Excel.

1. OPEN *Items for Sale_1* from Backstage. SAVE the file as *Items for Sale*.
2. Click the View tab on the Ribbon.
3. Click the Page Layout button. Examine your data in this view.
4. On the Ribbon, in the Zoom command group, click the Zoom to Selection button. Notice that you now see all your data in extreme close-up view.
5. On the Quick Access Toolbar, click the Undo arrow.

6. Click the New Window button in the Window command group.

7. Click the Arrange All button in the same command group.

8. When the Arrange Windows dialog box appears, choose Horizontal. Click OK. Take note of the arrangement of Book 1:1 and Book 1:2.

9. Click the Arrange All button again and choose Tiled. Click OK. Your windows are now side by side.

10. On the left side, in Book 1:2, click the Close button in the upper-right corner.

11. Now that only Book 1 is remaining, click the Maximize button to return the worksheet to full screen.

12. Return to Normal view by clicking the Normal button in the Workbook Views command group on the Ribbon.

CLOSE and **SAVE** this worksheet.

INTERNET READY

In this lesson, you learned how to navigate the Ribbon, use Onscreen Tools, and begin to manipulate a worksheet. Use Excel's Help system to gain further knowledge of these topics.

1. Click the Help button on the right side of the Ribbon.

2. Key Ribbon in the Search box at the top of the Help window.

3. Click Search. From the search result, open a topic that will provide information about selecting cells.

4. Repeat Steps 2 and 3 for Onscreen Tools, Backstage, and Excel views.

5. Share your findings with your instructor and classmates.

2 Using Backstage

LESSON SKILL MATRIX

Skill	Exam Objective	Objective Number
Accessing and Using Backstage View	Manipulate workbook files and folders.	**1.3.5**
Printing with Backstage	Apply printing options.	**1.2.4**
	Print only selected worksheets.	**1.2.1**
	Print an entire workbook.	**1.2.2**
Changing the Excel Environment in Backstage	Manipulate the Quick Access Toolbar.	**1.3.1**
	Customize the Ribbon.	**1.3.2**
	Manipulate Excel default settings.	**1.3.3**
	Manipulate workbook properties.	**1.3.4**
Accessing and Using Excel Templates		

KEY TERMS

- default settings
- Definitive Command
- Document properties
- Fast Command
- Print options
- tab
- template

Contoso, Ltd., employs hundreds of employees. The company likes to reward its employees by having monthly potluck dinners. They also like to share the homemade recipes within their company. These recipes are published for everyone on a quarterly basis. In particular, the recipes are housed and submitted for print in Excel worksheets. In this lesson, you will learn how to create the types of worksheets Contoso uses for this task. You will also learn how to share and send these worksheets to others.

SOFTWARE ORIENTATION

Microsoft 2010 Excel Backstage View

**NEW
to Office 2010**

As you learned in Lesson 1, Backstage view enables you to use and master Excel's file management features—functions that aren't related to creating workbooks. (The commands you use when creating and editing workbooks are contained in the Ribbon and the Quick Access Toolbar.) Backstage view replaces the system of layered menus, toolbars, and panes used in previous versions of Excel.

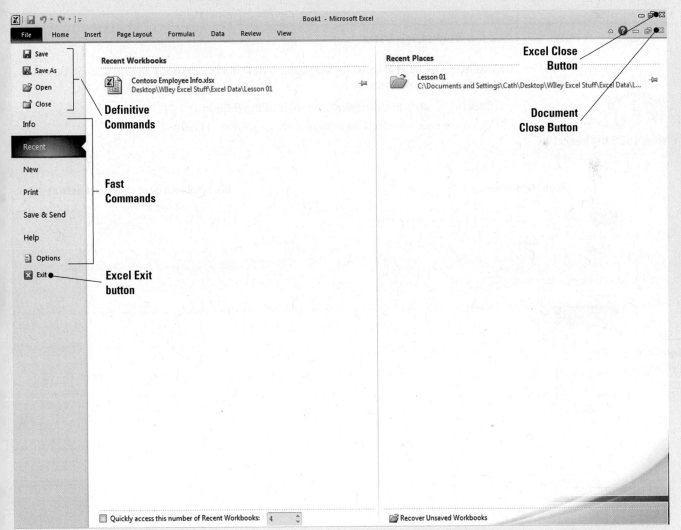

Figure 2-1

Backstage view

NEW to Office 2010

Backstage view's left-side navigation pane (Figure 2-1) gives you access to workbook and file-related commands, including Save, Save As, Open, and Close. The navigation pane also holds a series of **tabs**—Recent, Info, New, Print, Save & Send, Help, and Options—that you can click to access groups of related functions and commands. The Exit button on the navigation pane closes Excel.

ACCESSING AND USING BACKSTAGE VIEW

The Bottom Line

In the Excel 2010 window, you will see the green File tab in the upper-left corner. This is your access to Backstage view. When you click the File tab for Backstage, you will see a navigation pane containing many of the same commands that could be accessed through the Microsoft Office button in previous versions of Excel. In this section, you access Backstage view and use these commands to close a file.

By default, when you first enter Backstage view, the Info Fast Command is active. A **Fast Command** provides quick access to common functions and is located on the left navigation pane. Fast Commands include Print, Info, Recent, Save & Send, and New. Backstage view also contains Definitive Commands, such as Save, Save As, and Close. When you use **Definitive Commands**, these commands close Backstage view and return you to your workbook.

In this exercise, you revisit how to access Backstage view.

STEP BY STEP | **Access Backstage View**

GET READY. LAUNCH Microsoft Excel 2010. A new blank workbook should appear. Within the workbook, follow these steps:

1. Click the File tab in the upper-left corner of the Ribbon.
2. You have now accessed Backstage view, as shown in Figure 2-2

WileyPLUS Extra! features an online tutorial of this task.

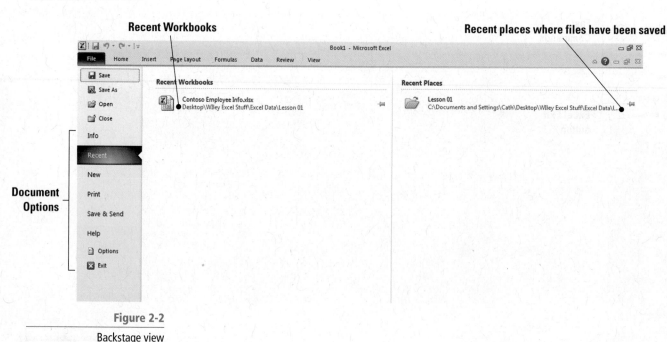

Figure 2-2

Backstage view

3. Take a few moments to familiarize yourself with this view and the tools in its navigation pane.

CLOSE Excel.

Another Way
If you use Print Preview quite often, you can save yourself time and steps by adding it to the Quick Access Toolbar in order to create a shortcut to Backstage view. This process will be explained in greater depth later in this lesson.

Saving a Document with Backstage

In Excel, you can use Backstage view to view, save, print, and organize workbooks or worksheets. In this exercise, you create a new workbook in Excel, edit its contents, and then save the workbook using Backstage view.

STEP BY STEP **Save a Document with Backstage**

Another Way
You can also click Ctrl+N to open a new workbook and activate the Backstage area.

GET READY. LAUNCH Microsoft Excel 2010; a new blank workbook will open. Using this workbook, complete the following steps:

1. In the new workbook, cell A1 should be the active cell. Key Recipe in this cell, and notice that the text appears in both the cell and the Formula Bar as you type.

2. Press Tab; the text is entered into cell A1, and B1 becomes the active cell.

3. Now key Recipe Description and press Tab. The text is entered into B1, and C1 becomes the active cell. Note that the text from B1 is flowing over into cell C1.

4. Key Cooking Directions into C1 and press Tab. Note that the text in cell B1 has now been hidden behind cell C1, and the contents of cell C1 are seen flowing into cell D1. In order to view the data in the column, you must double-click the column divider. Place your cursor on the divider between column B and C and double click. Note that the column resizes to accommodate the data. Refer to Figure 2-3.

Figure 2-3

Adjusting a column to fit data

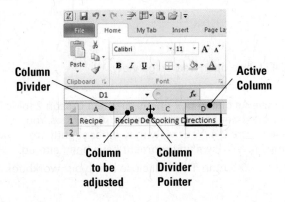

5. Key Main Ingredients into cell D1, then press Tab.

6. Key Alternate Ingredients into cell E1 and press Tab.

7. Key Serving Size into F1 and press Tab.

8. Repeat the process explained in step 4 to adjust all columns to fit the data. Refer to Figure 2-3 as needed.

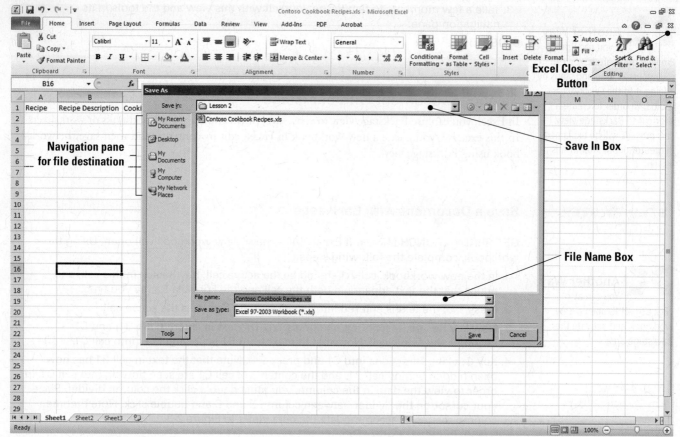

Figure 2-4

Save As dialog box

9. Click the File tab to open Backstage view.

10. Click the Save option.

11. When the **Save As** dialog box opens, create a Lesson 2 folder in My Documents and save your worksheet as *Contoso Cookbook Recipes*. Your window should appear as shown in Figure 2-4. Your view may differ slightly from the figure if the default settings in your Windows environment have been altered.

PAUSE. Click the Exit button. This will close both your workbook and Excel.

To use the Save As feature, you would follow the steps in the previous lesson, but choose Save As and complete your task. You should choose the Save As option to save to a different destination, change a file's name, and/or change a file's format.

Take Note

In Excel, the AutoRecover feature is installed by default. It will automatically save your workbook every 10 minutes. This can be customized to suit your needs. You can review and change these features in Excel Options.

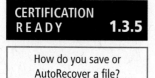

CERTIFICATION
READY **1.3.5**

How do you save or
AutoRecover a file?

PRINTING WITH BACKSTAGE

The Backstage area contains Excel's Print commands and options. You can use the Print dialog box to manipulate workbook elements such as margins, orientation, paper size, and so on.

Printing and Previewing with Backstage

Backstage view includes a Print Preview pane in the Print dialog box so you can preview your workbook as you choose Print options. In this exercise, you learn to use the Print and Print Preview features in Excel.

STEP BY STEP   **Print and Print Preview with Backstage**

GET READY. LAUNCH Microsoft Excel 2010. Then, follow these steps:

Another Way
You can also Click Ctrl+O to open a workbook on your computer. This keystroke activates the Open dialog box, which allows you to navigate to the file you want to open.

1. Click the File tab in the upper-left corner of the Ribbon to access Backstage.
2. Click the Recent command in the Backstage view navigation pane.
3. You should now see your recently created and used workbooks. Click on *Contoso Cookbook Recipes* to open the file. Your view should resemble Figure 2-5.

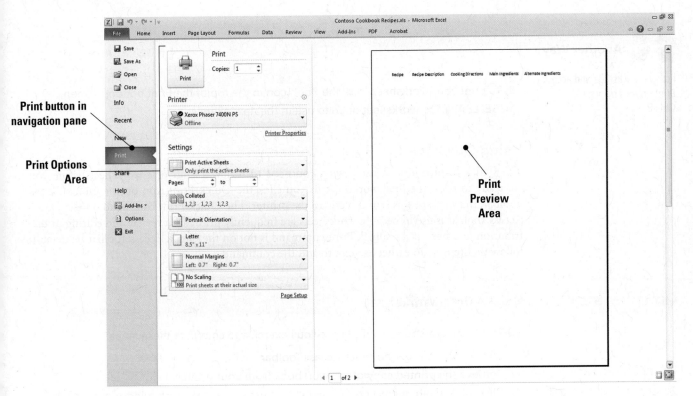

Figure 2-5

Document preview

4. Click the File tab to open Backstage. In the navigation pane, click Print. Note that this opens the Print options page of Backstage (See Figure 2-5). Take a moment to preview the workbook in the Print Preview section in the right pane and to read through the

Print options listed in the center section of the page. The printing options section of the window is shown in Figure 2-6.

Figure 2-6

Printing options

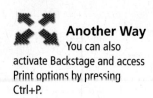

Another Way
You can also activate Backstage and access Print options by pressing Ctrl+P.

5. To print your worksheet, click the Print icon in the top of the Print options screen.

PAUSE. LEAVE the worksheet open to use in the next exercise.

Using Quick Print to Print a Worksheet

The Quick Print option is used when you need to review a draft of a worksheet before you are ready to print the final workbook. If you click the Quick Print icon on the Quick Access Toolbar, the worksheet is sent directly to the printer. The Quick Print command on the Quick Access Toolbar is useful because worksheets are frequently printed for review and editing or distribution to others. If the Quick Print command is not on the Quick Access Toolbar by default, follow the steps in an earlier exercise to add the command.

STEP BY STEP   **Quick Print a Worksheet**

USE the open workbook from the previous exercise to complete these steps:

1. Click Quick Print on the Quick Access Toolbar.
2. Retrieve the printed copy of the workbook from your printer.
3. Click the File tab, then click Print. From this pane, you can quick print or preview the printout before sending it to the printer.

PAUSE. LEAVE the workbook open to use in the next exercise.

Setting the Print Area

You can use the Print options in Backstage view to print only a selected portion, or print area, of an Excel workbook. **Print options** are options to customize and manipulate your workbook for printing; they include options for margins, orientation, scale, and collation. In this exercise, you learn to select an area of a workbook for printing and set it as the print area.

STEP BY STEP   ### Set a Print Area

GET READY. With *Contoso Cookbook Recipes* already open, follow these steps:

1. Click the Page Layout tab on the Ribbon.
2. Mouse over the Print Area button on the Ribbon in the *Page Setup* area. Note the tool tip that pops up defining the task to be completed.
3. On the worksheet, click cell A1, hold the mouse button, and drag the cursor to cell F6. Your cells should highlight in blue, as shown in Figure 2-7.

Figure 2-7

Setting print area

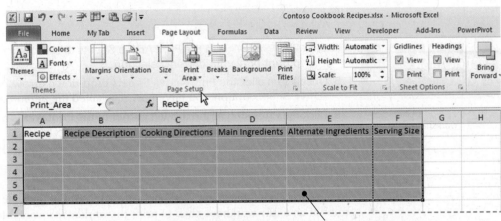

Highlighted Cells with dashed outline indicate Print Area has been set

4. With these cells highlighted, click the Print Area button drop-down arrow and choose Set Print Area from the menu that appears. You have now set the print area.
5. Click the File tab to access Backstage.
6. In the Print Preview pane on the right pane of the Print window, you should see the highlighted cells of your print area. You will not print at this time.
7. **PAUSE. SAVE** the workbook.

CLOSE Excel.

Printing Selected Worksheets with Backstage

In this exercise, you learn to access the options for printing individual worksheets within a workbook. You can use these options to print the current worksheet only or to print multiple worksheets that you have selected by page number.

STEP BY STEP   ### Print Selected Worksheets with Backstage

GET READY. LAUNCH Excel 2010. Then perform these steps:

1. Open Backstage view and click Recent in the navigation pane; in the list of Recent workbooks, click *Contoso Cookbook Recipes* to open the file.
2. Press Ctrl+P to activate Print options in the Backstage navigation pane.

3. In the *Settings* section of the center pane in Print options, click the Print Active Sheets drop-down arrow. In the drop-down menu that appears, as shown in Figure 2-8, you can choose several printing options for your workbook or worksheet.

Figure 2-8

Worksheet print options

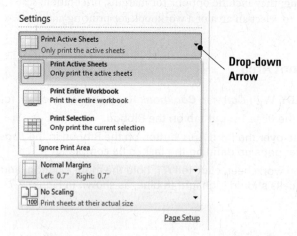

4. Click Print Selection in the Print Active Sheets drop-down menu; this option enables you to print *only* your current selection.

5. Once again click the Print Active Sheets drop-down arrow, then choose the Print Active Sheets option. You have now reselected the default option.

6. Click the Print icon at the top-left corner of the Print window.

CLOSE the workbook. **LEAVE** Excel open for the next exercise.

Printing Selected Workbooks with Backstage

In most scenarios in business, workbooks are composed of multiple worksheets. It is much easier to print an entire workbook than to print the workbook's worksheets individually. In this exercise, you will use Backstage commands to print an entire workbook.

STEP BY STEP   **Print Select Workbooks with Backstage**

GET READY. With Excel open from the previous exercise, perform these actions:

1. Click the File tab to produce Backstage view. Click the Recent command in the navigation pane.

2. In the Recent Workbooks section, open *Contoso Cookbook Recipes*.

3. Click the Print command in the navigation pane.

4. In the Print window Settings Options, click the Print Active Sheets drop-down arrow and choose Print Entire Workbook. Refer to Figure 2-9.

Figure 2-9

Printing an entire workbook

Print Entire Workbook

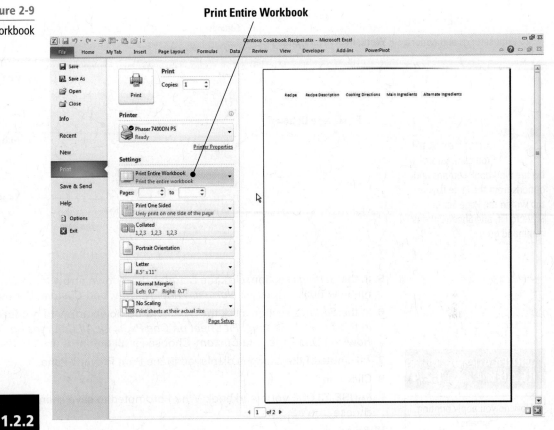

5. You will not print at this time.

PAUSE. LEAVE Excel open for the next exercise.

Applying Printing Options with Backstage

The Print command in Backstage view offers a number of options for customizing printed workbooks. This exercise prepares you to customize such options as page setup, scale, paper selection, and gridlines, all using the commands in Backstage view.

STEP BY STEP | **Apply Printing Options with Backstage**

GET READY. With Excel already open, carry out these steps:

1. **OPEN** *Contoso Cookbook Recipes*.
2. Click the File tab to access Backstage view.
3. Click the Print command on the left-hand navigation pane.

4. In the *Settings* section of the Print window, shown in Figure 2-10, click the Portrait Orientation drop-down arrow. Notice that there are two options: *Portrait* (default) and *Landscape*. Choose Landscape.

Figure 2-10

Print settings and options

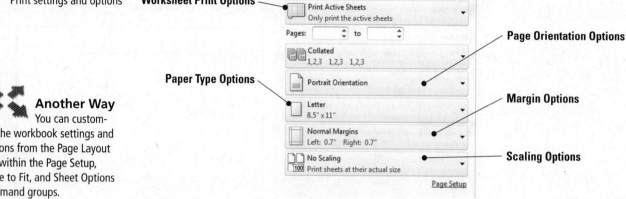

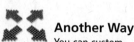

Another Way

You can customize the workbook settings and options from the Page Layout tab within the Page Setup, Scale to Fit, and Sheet Options command groups.

5. In the *Settings* section, click the Margins drop-down arrow to produce a drop-down menu with four options: *Normal, Wide, Narrow,* and *Custom*. Choose Wide.

6. In the *Settings* section, click the Scaling drop-down arrow to produce the five options in this area: *No Scaling, Fit Sheet on One Page, Fit All Columns on One Page, Fit All Rows on One Page,* and *Custom*. Choose Fit all Columns on One Page.

7. Take note of the changes displayed in the Print Preview Pane.

8. Click Print.

9. **PAUSE. CLOSE** your workbook. When prompted to save changes to your document, choose Don't Save.

CLOSE Excel.

CERTIFICATION READY   **1.2.4**

How do you apply printing options?

Changing a Printer with Backstage

In many business settings, you will print documents on multiple printers. In this exercise, you learn how to change the selected printer setting using Backstage.

STEP BY STEP   **Change a Printer with Backstage**

GET READY. LAUNCH Microsoft Excel 2010.

1. Click the File tab to access Backstage.

2. Click the Recent command in the navigation pane.

3. In the list of recently opened workbooks, click on *Contoso Cookbook Recipes*.

4. Click Ctrl+P to activate the Print options.

5. Your current default printer is displayed in the *Printer options* section of the Printer window. Click the drop-down arrow to produce a menu of installed printers, similar to the one shown in Figure 2-11. Note that the computer will let you know which printers are available (active or not active) for you to choose from.

Figure 2-11

Choosing a printer

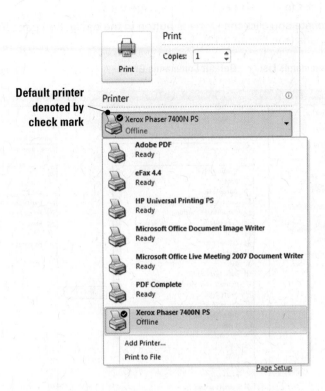

6. Click on a printer (other than your default printer) in the printer list. This printer should now be visible as your active printer. Should you attempt to print at this time with an inactive printer, you will likely get an error.

7. Once again, click the drop-down arrow next to the active printer and choose your default printer.

8. **PAUSE. CLOSE** your workbook. When prompted to save changes to your workbook, choose Don't Save.

CLOSE Excel.

CHANGING THE EXCEL ENVIRONMENT IN BACKSTAGE

The Bottom Line

Backstage view also offers a number of commands and options for changing the Excel work environment. In this section, you learn to manipulate various elements of the Excel environment, such as the Ribbon, Quick Access Toolbar, Excel Default Settings, and Workbook Properties.

Customizing the Quick Access Toolbar with Backstage

You can't change the size of the Quick Access Toolbar, but you can customize it by adding and subtracting command buttons. In this exercise, you customize the Quick Access Toolbar by adding commands for functions you use most frequently in Excel, and by organizing the command buttons on the toolbar to best suit your working needs and style.

STEP BY STEP   **Customize the Quick Access Toolbar with Backstage**

GET READY. LAUNCH Excel 2010. Then, take these actions:

1. Click the File tab to access Backstage view.
2. Locate and click the Options button in the navigation pane. The *Excel Options* window opens (see Figure 2-12).

Figure 2-12

Customizing the Quick Access Toolbar options

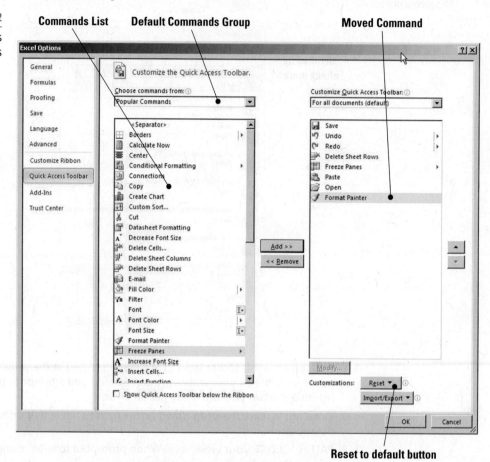

Reset to default button

3. In the left pane of the window, click Quick Access Toolbar item to open the *Quick Access Toolbar Options* dialog box. Refer to Figure 2-12. The left pane of this dialog box lists the commands that you could possibly add to the toolbar and the right pane shows the commands that are currently included on the toolbar.
4. In the left pane, click Format Painter, then Click the Add button in the center of the pane to move Format Painter to the Quick Access Toolbar.

5. Using the same process, move five more commands of your choice to the Quick Access Toolbar. When done, click OK to apply your changes (the changes don't take effect until you click OK).
6. Your Quick Access Toolbar should now include additional command buttons, much like the example shown in Figure 2-13. Similarly, you can remove any command that you add to the toolbar. Note that default commands cannot be removed. At any time you can reset the toolbar to its default settings. (See Figure 2-12.) Because your document was not affected by the toolbar changes, you will not be prompted to save any workbook changes.

Figure 2-13

Customized Quick Access Toolbar

New Quick Access Toolbar Icons

CLOSE Excel.

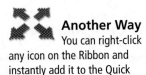 **Ref**

In Lesson 1, in Using Onscreen Tools, you were shown how to customize the Quick Access Toolbar by using the drop-down arrow to add commands.

Customizing the Ribbon with Backstage

 **Another Way**
You can right-click any icon on the Ribbon and instantly add it to the Quick Access Toolbar.

In the Backstage Options window, Excel Options also offers selections for customizing the Ribbon. You can add and remove commands, and you can change the location of Ribbon commands to make accessing those you use most frequently more convenient. In this exercise, you use the commands in the Options window to create a new tab and command group to contain your frequently used commands.

Take Note

Although you may add any command anywhere you choose, you do not have the option of removing any of the default commands from any of the default tabs.

STEP BY STEP | **Customize the Ribbon with Backstage**

GET READY. LAUNCH Excel 2010. Then, do the following:

1. Click the File tab to access Backstage view.
2. Click the Options button in the navigation pane.

WILEY PLUS EXTRA

WileyPLUS Extra! features an online tutorial of this task.

3. In the *Excel Options* window, click Customize Ribbon in the left-side menu. The *Customize the Ribbon* window opens, as shown in Figure 2-14. By default, Popular Commands is selected in the Choose Commands From drop-down box in the left pane; the list of Popular Commands appears in the list below the drop-down box. Also by default, the Main Tabs option appears in the Customize the Ribbon box in the right pane, with the Ribbon's main tabs listed below.

Figure 2-14

Customize the Ribbon window

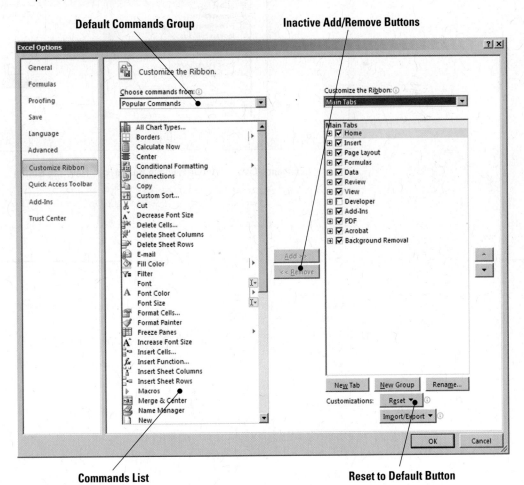

4. Click Format Painter in the list of Popular Commands to highlight; note the Add button in the center of the screen is now active.

5. In the *Customize the Ribbon* window on the right, click the + preceding *Home* to expand the list of command groups within the Home tab if it isn't already expanded.

6. Click the New Tab button below the Customize the Ribbon options, shown in Figure 2-15, to insert a new blank tab into the Customize the Ribbon list. When you create a New Tab, a New Group is automatically created inside that New Tab.

Figure 2-15

Customize the Ribbon

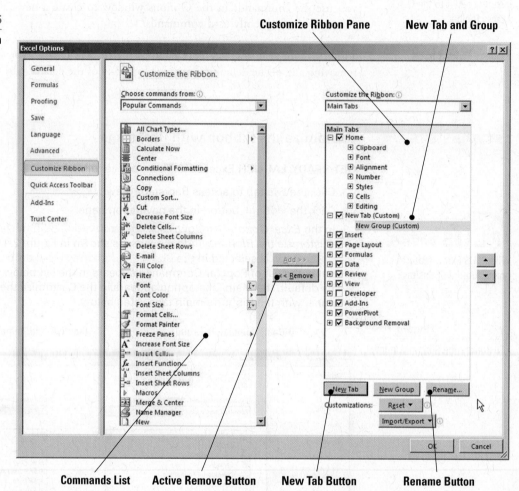

7. Click the New Tab list item on the right in the Customize Ribbon pane to highlight it, then click the Rename button on the bottom right. In the *Rename* dialog box that appears, Key My New Tab, as shown in Figure 2-16.

Figure 2-16

Rename dialog box and renamed tab

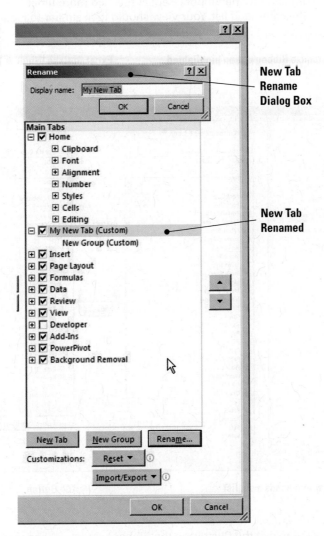

New Tab Rename Dialog Box

New Tab Renamed

8. Click New Group below your new tab to highlight it. Click the Rename button again, and Key My New Group in the *Rename* dialog box. You will see the New Group renamed.

9. In the *Customize the Ribbon* list on the right side of the pane, click the My New Group list item to highlight. In the command list on the left side of the pane, click on a command of your choice, then click the Add button. You have now successfully moved the command to the Ribbon. Repeat this two more times, choosing other commands from the command list. Your view should look similar to Figure 2-17.

Figure 2-17

Added commands

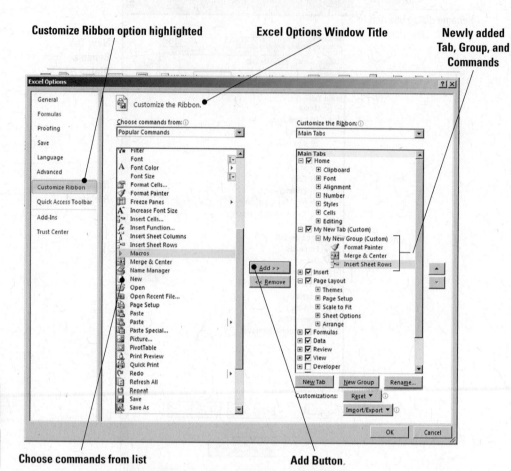

Customize Ribbon option highlighted Excel Options Window Title Newly added Tab, Group, and Commands

Choose commands from list Add Button

10. Click OK to exit the Customize the Ribbon window. When you exit, you will see your My New Tab tab appear on the Ribbon.

11. Click the My New Tab tab on the Ribbon. Note that your commands are now in the tab's My New Group command group, as shown in Figure 2-18.

Figure 2-18

New tab and group on Ribbon

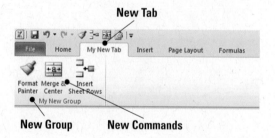

New Tab

New Group New Commands

12. Click New Tab and New Group within that tab to view your changes.

PAUSE. LEAVE Excel open for the next exercise.

Customizing the Excel Default Settings with Backstage

The Options window commands also enable you to modify the **default settings** in Excel. Default settings are standard settings installed by the application as presets so that the application has the same settings each and every time it is accessed. These defaults can include worksheet properties, printer settings, font style and size, and much more. By default, for example, Excel opens with three worksheets in a new workbook, specific settings, a particular font size, and so on. In this next lesson you will find, change and use new default settings in Excel. In this exercise, you learn to change Excel's default settings using Backstage view.

STEP BY STEP	**Customize the Excel Default Settings with Backstage**

GET READY. With Excel already open, perform the following steps:

1. Click the File tab to access Backstage.
2. Click Options in the navigation pane; by default, the *Options window* opens with the General options displayed.
3. In the *Creating New Workbooks* section of the *General options* window, click in the *Include This Many Sheets* option box and key 2 to change the number of worksheets that appear by default in new workbooks.
4. Click the User Name box in the *Personalize your copy of Microsoft Office* section and key [your first and last name] in the text box (see Figure 2-19). Click OK.

Figure 2-19

General options

General options highlighted   **Sheet Settings**

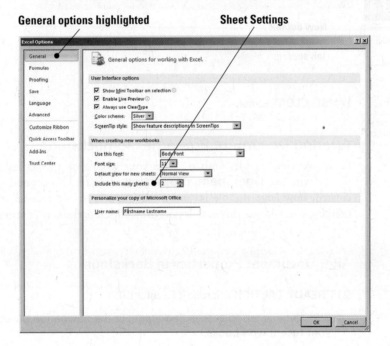

5. **EXIT** and **RESTART** Excel. Note that instead of three worksheet tabs, you now have two in your workbook, as shown in Figure 2-20.

Figure 2-20

Two worksheet tabs now appear by default

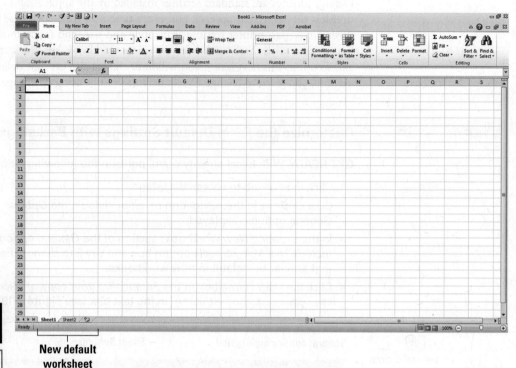

New default worksheet tab settings

CERTIFICATION READY 1.3.3

How do you customize Excel's default settings?

PAUSE. CLOSE Excel.

Altering Document Properties in Backstage

Backstage view enables you to access your workbook properties more easily and view them in one window. **Document properties** identify who created the document, when it was created, how large the file is, and other important information about the workbook. In this exercise, you will use this next lesson to manipulate those properties.

STEP BY STEP   **Alter Document Properties in Backstage**

GET READY. LAUNCH Microsoft Excel 2010.

1. Click the File tab to access Backstage; in the navigation pane, click Recent, to view your recent workbooks.

2. Open *Contoso Cookbook Recipes* from the list of recently opened workbooks.

3. Click Info in the navigation pane to open the Info window, as shown in Figure 2-21. The right pane of the window lists the workbook properties of the currently opened file.

Figure 2-21

Document properties

Info button in navigation pane   **Document Properties**

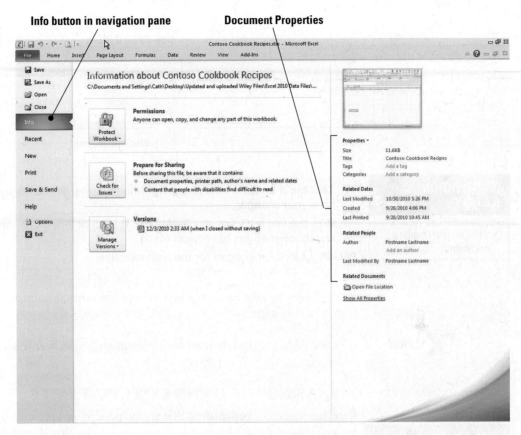

4. Click the Properties drop-down arrow to produce the drop-down menu shown in Figure 2-22. Click Show Document Panel to open the document panel.

Figure 2-22

Properties drop-down menu

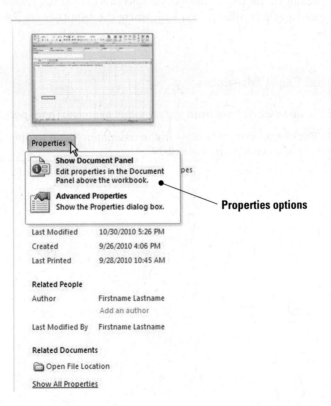

Properties options

5. In the document panel's Author text box, key [your name]. Key Contoso Cookbook Recipes in the *Title* text box, and Lesson 2 in the *Subject* text box. The document panel should resemble the one shown in Figure 2-23.

Figure 2-23

Changing document properties

Document Properties drop-down Options

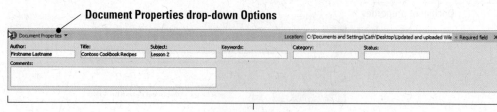

Document Panel

CERTIFICATION READY   1.3.4

How do you change a document's properties?

6. Click the X button in the upper right-hand corner of the document panel to close and save your changes.

7. Click the File tab to access Backstage, then click Info in the navigation pane. The workbook changes have been made.

PAUSE. LEAVE Excel open for the next exercise.

You will now be able to change and manipulate other document properties by accessing this feature in Backstage.

 Ref   We will address more advanced document properties in later lessons.

ACCESSING AND USING EXCEL TEMPLATES

The Bottom Line

Excel has numerous **templates** that are included in the application, and many more templates are available online at Office.com. Templates are files that already include formatting and formulas complete with designs, tools, and specific data types. Examples of these are budgets, loan models, invoices, calendars, and so on.

Many templates contain formulas and functions to help you customize them for your purposes. The exercise will familiarize you with where the templates are located and how to choose and use them.

STEP BY STEP   **Access Excel Templates**

USE the open worksheet from the previous exercise. Then, perform these steps:

1. In Backstage view, click New in the navigation pane to open the *Available Templates* window, as shown in Figure 2-24.

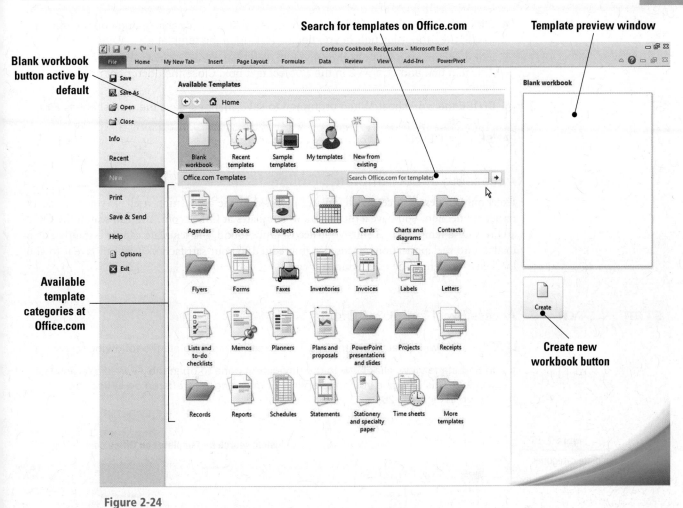

Figure 2-24

New File Options

2. Click the Sample Templates icon in the top-row gallery. The collection of sample templates included in Excel 2010 appears in the window.

3. Click the Personal Monthly Budget template listing; a preview of the template appears in the Preview pane. Your view should resemble Figure 2-25.

Figure 2-25

Templates

Template Preview

4. Click the Create button. The document properties panel opens, giving you the option to edit the properties before you begin working in the template.

5. In the document panel's Author text box, key [your name]. Key Using Templates in the *Title* text box and Lesson 2 in the *Subject* text box. Close the document properties pane.

6. **CLOSE** the worksheet. When prompted to save changes, save the worksheet as *First Template*.

PAUSE. LEAVE Excel open for the next exercise.

Accessing Excel Templates Online

Excel only comes with certain templates installed in the application itself. If you have an Internet connection, you have a direct link to templates at Office.com. You can search the Office archives for a template that suits your needs. Once found, the template can be instantly downloaded into the application and used. Once edited to your satisfaction, you can save it to your local environment to be used again and again.

STEP BY STEP   **Access Excel Templates Online**

USE the open worksheet from the previous exercise to complete the following steps:

1. In Backstage view, click New in the navigation pane to open the *Available Templates* window. This will give you an overview of the categories offered on Office.com as shown in Figure 2-26.

Figure 2-26

Template categories

Custom search for templates on Office.com

Available Office.com template categories

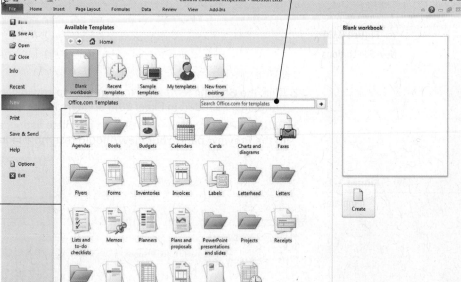

2. Click the Memos button to access the available templates in that category. You should see something similar to Figure 2-27. The templates are organized alphabetically and the first template should be *Credit memo (Blue Gradient design)*.

Figure 2-27

Sample templates online

Figure 2-27

Sample templates online

Highlighted template when memo group chosen

Template Preview

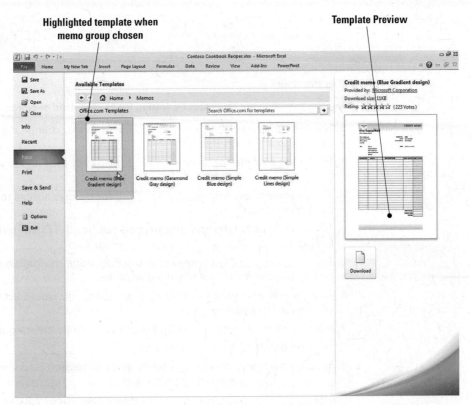

Before you implement a template, you have the option to preview the look and feel of it. You can actually see whether it fits your needs. In previous versions of Office, you had to go to the website to search for templates. This isn't the case with Office 2010. The preview is instantaneous. This means a much easier and simpler decision and download.

3. Click the Download button below the preview of the Credit Memo template. Note this instantly downloads the Memo and opens it as a new workbook.

4. **SAVE** the workbook as *First Online Template* in the Lesson 2 folder.

CLOSE Excel.

SKILL SUMMARY

In This Lesson You Learned How To:	Exam Objective	Objective Number
Accessing and Using Backstage View	Manipulate workbook files and folders.	1.3.5
Printing with Backstage	Apply printing options.	1.2.4
	Print only selected worksheets.	1.2.1
	Print an entire workbook.	1.2.2
Changing the Excel Environment in Backstage	Manipulate the Quick Access Toolbar.	1.3.1
	Customize the Ribbon.	1.3.2
	Manipulate Excel default settings.	1.3.3
	Manipulate workbook properties.	1.3.4
Accessing and Using Excel Templates		

Knowledge Assessment

Fill in the Blank

Complete the following sentences by writing the correct word or words in the blanks provided.

1. The area where you can save, choose a template, change document properties, and close or exit Excel is the _____.

2. To change a printer or margin settings, you click the File tab and use the _____ options.

3. You can customize the _____ for quicker access to the most commonly used commands.

4. To create custom tabs and groups, you can use the Customize the _____ feature.

5. The _____ command in the Backstage navigation pane enables you to view and open your most recently used workbooks.

6. To view and alter your workbook's properties, you would access the _____ window in Backstage.

7. When you are modifying the Ribbon, you begin by creating a custom _____.

8. To open Backstage, you click on the _____.

9. You can change Excel's default settings by accessing Backstage and clicking _____ in the navigation pane.

10. The _____ contain vital information about your workbook such as file size, author, and date created.

True/False

Circle T if the statement is true or F if the statement is false.

T   F   1. You do not have the ability to modify the number of default worksheets in a workbook.

T   F   2. Backstage view enables you to access the Microsoft website for custom templates.

T   F   3. Use Ctrl+N to create a new workbook.

T   F   4. When you want to access an Excel template, you click on the Template command in the Theme group on the Page Layout tab.

T   F   5. You cannot have more than one worksheet in an Excel workbook.

T   F   6. You can view templates in the Recent section of Backstage view.

T   F   7. You can access Backstage view by pressing Ctrl+N.

T   F   8. By default, Excel starts a new workbook with four worksheets.

T   F   9. In Excel, you can add your most commonly used commands to the Quick Access Toolbar.

T   F   10. Backstage view has replaced the Microsoft Office button.

Competency Assessment

Project 2-1: Setting Print Area

Create a worksheet listing several different movies and their genre, then set a specific print area within the worksheet.

GET READY. LAUNCH Excel if it is not already running.

1. From Backstage, Click New and then click the Create button in the right pane of the Available Templates window to create a new worksheet.

2. Select cell A1, key Movie, and press Tab.

3. With **B1** already active, key *Genre*.

4. Beginning in cell **A2**, key the data shown below. Ignore AutoComplete if prompted to use. You will learn more about this in future lessons.

Movie	Genre
Gone with the Wind	Drama
The Untouchables	Action
Frankenstein	Horror
Forrest Gump	Drama
Toy Story	Children's Animation

5. Double-click the column divider between columns A and B to adjust the column A width to display all of the text.

6. Double-click the label divider between columns B and C to adjust the column B width to display all of the text.

7. Click, hold, and drag the mouse from cell **A1** to **F3** to highlight. Click the *Page Layout* tab; in the *Page Setup* command group, click the *Print Area* drop-down arrow, and choose *Set Print Area*.

8. **SAVE** the worksheet as *Movies 2_1* and then close the file.

CLOSE Excel.

Project 2-2: Printing a Specific Area or Worksheet

You will print an active area and a specific worksheet.

GET READY. OPEN the file from the Lesson 2 folder titled *Movies 2_1*.

1. Open Backstage view.

2. Click *Print* in the Backstage navigation pane.

3. In the Settings section of the Print window, click the *Print Active Sheets* drop-down arrow, and click the *Print Selection* option in the drop-down menu.

4. Click the *Print* button in the upper section of the Print Settings to print the selected area of the worksheet.

5. Again in the *Settings* options, open the *Print Active Sheets* drop-down menu, and choose *Print Active Sheets*.

6. Click the *Print* button in the upper section of the Print Settings to print the active worksheet.

7. **PAUSE. SAVE** the workbook as *Movies 2_2*.

CLOSE Excel.

Proficiency Assessment

Project 2-3: Managing Document Properties

You are setting up a home office with new computer and communications equipment. Because you are not yet sure of your budget, you need several price options for each piece of equipment. Worksheets are excellent tools for organizing information so you can make easy comparisons between sets to data such as wholesale versus over the counter.

GET READY. LAUNCH Excel if it is not already running.

1. Identify a list of at least 12 pieces of equipment that a state-of-the-art home office needs. Some of these may include a desktop or laptop computer; a combination scanner, printer, and fax; a cordless phone; a cell phone; and so on.

2. **OPEN** Excel and **CREATE** a worksheet to store the list of equipment you have gathered. In Row 1, create column headings for your data. Beginning in cell A1, key *Item*, *Low End*, *Moderate*, and *High End* so that you can enter three prices (amounts) for each equipment item.

3. Using advertisements from office supply stores and other retailers (or Internet resources, if available), find low-end, moderate, and high-end options for each equipment item you have listed. These options can be sale prices from ads, or just everyday prices for the items you've found.

4. Key your amounts of the items into the worksheet.

5. Adjust column and cell width so that you can clearly see all of the data you have entered.

6. Access Backstage, and click on Info.

7. You will modify the following elements in document properties:

Author:	Your First and Last Name
Title:	Project 2-3
Subject:	Lesson 2 Project
Tags:	Equipment
Categories:	Excel Lesson 2

8. Close the Document Properties window. You have now saved your settings.

9. Access Backstage and click on Info in the navigation pane to view your changes to your workbook properties. You will be able to view some of your changes. In order to see more, click the Show All Properties link at the bottom of the workbook properties.

10. **SAVE** your document as *Equipment 2_3*.

PAUSE. LEAVE Excel open for the next project.

Project 2-4: Changing the Quick Access Toolbar

You will customize the Quick Access Toolbar to accommodate commands for users who are not familiar with Excel and the Ribbon.

GET READY. LAUNCH Excel if it is not already running.

1. With the Home tab active, on the Ribbon, in the Alignment group, right-click on Center and choose Add to the Quick Access Toolbar.

2. Repeating these steps as necessary, using the appropriate tabs and groups, add the following commands to the toolbar: Borders, Increase Indent, Copy, Cut, and Paste. Note the changes to the toolbar in the upper-left portion of the screen.

3. To remove the new icons from the Quick Access Toolbar, right-click an icon in the Quick Access Toolbar and select Remove From Quick Access Toolbar. Repeat the process to remove the other icons you added.

EXIT Excel.

Mastery Assessment

Project 2-5: Accessing a Template Online

You are in need of an invoice template for a client. You do not have an appropriate template available in Excel. You need to go to the website to search for one.

GET READY. LAUNCH Excel if it is not already running.

1. Access Backstage view.

2. Click on New.

3. Click in the Office.com Search box, and key Invoice. Press Enter. Note that if you have an Internet connection, you should be connected to Office.com. If you are without an Internet connection, this process will not work.

4. Browse the results for invoices on the website after it loads.

5. Click on a template to view it in the Preview pane. Click the Download button.

6. After choosing download, Excel automatically opens the template for you. Make note of what features the invoice you chose has to offer. Make changes to the template to see changes and actions.

7. **SAVE** the invoice as *Invoice 2_5*.

PAUSE. LEAVE Excel open for the next exercise.

Project 2-6: Managing a Custom Ribbon

In order for your client to use and maintain the invoice you downloaded in the previous exercise, he has requested that you customize several tabs on the Ribbon to make the worksheet easier to manage and edit.

GET READY. LAUNCH Excel if it is not already running.

1. **OPEN** *Invoice 2_5* from the Lesson 2 folder.

2. Open Backstage, and click Options in the navigation pane.

3. Click on the Customize Ribbon button in the Excel Options window.

4. Click the Reset button at the bottom right of the window and choose Remove All Customizations. When prompted to delete all customizations, click Yes.

5. Click Home in the Customize the Ribbon panel to highlight it and make it active.

6. Create a new tab named Invoice Edits.

7. Rename the new command group in Invoice Edits Invoice Tools.

8. Choose five commands to add to the Invoice Tools command group.

9. Create another new tab named My Edits.

10. Rename the new command group in My Edits My Tools.

11. Add five commands to the My Tools command group.

12. Click OK.

13. Examine your changes to the Ribbon.

14. Open Backstage and choose Options. Undo all the changes you just made to the Ribbon. When prompted, accept all changes.

CLOSE the workbook. **CLOSE** Excel.

INTERNET READY

As was mentioned at the beginning of this lesson, Contoso, Ltd., is dedicated to treating its employees well. Use web search tools to locate five additional recipes to add to the cookbook spreadsheet. Use family and friends for research in this venture if possible. I am sure there is a favorite, mouth-watering recipe that will come to mind that you would love to include and share with others. Include two main courses, two side dishes, and one dessert. Find out as much information about the recipe as you can and include this in the worksheet. If you are able, add a new column to your spreadsheet to include a history of the recipe and ethnic origin.

Workplace *Ready*

MANAGING THE ENVIRONMENT IN EXCEL

Many Excel users don't realize that they can arrange and manage the Excel environment to suit their individual needs.

With the ability in Excel to customize by adding and managing toolbars, changing default settings, managing the Quick Access Toolbar and Ribbon, you can give the end user a more manageable and workable environment.

Your accounting department in your firm needs both the Quick Access Toolbar and the Ribbon customized to accommodate frequently used commands for accounting. Take time to create three new Ribbon tabs that will organize commonly used commands from the following tab groups:

Home:	Number, Cells
Formulas:	Function Library, Formula Auditing
Insert:	Charts

You can also take time to add common commands not already on the Quick Access Toolbar that would be more convenient there than clicking through tabs to use them.

This will give you practice and offer you and the end user a way to organize and use Excel to its greatest potential.

LESSON SKILL MATRIX

Skill	Exam Objective	Objective Number
Creating Workbooks	Select cell data.	2.1.4
Entering and Editing Basic Data in a Worksheet	Select cell data.	2.1.4
Using Data Types to Populate a Worksheet	Preserve cell format. Fill a series.	2.2.3 2.2.2
Cutting, Copying, and Pasting Data	Copy data. Move data. Cut data.	2.2.1 2.1.3 2.1.2
Editing a Workbook's Keywords		
Saving the Workbook	Manipulate workbook files and folders. Change the file type to a different version of Excel. Save as PDF or XPS.	1.3.5 7.1.2 7.1.3

KEY TERMS

- auto fill
- AutoComplete
- copy
- copy pointer
- cut
- fill handle
- formula bar
- keywords
- label
- move pointer
- natural series
- Office Clipboard
- paste
- range
- selecting text

Purchasing a home is usually the biggest financial investment most people make in a life-time. Real estate agents advise and assist those who want to buy a new home or sell their present home. Agents must be licensed by their state. Many licensed agents also become Realtors®. This is a trademarked name that an agent can use only when he or she joins the local, state, and national associations of Realtors®. Fabrikam, Inc., located in Columbus, Ohio, is a real estate firm owned by Richard Carey and David Ortiz. Fabrikam has five full-time sales agents. Fabrikam uses an Excel workbook to track each agent's sales data by date of last sale. In this lesson, you will continue to view, add, and manipulate data in an Excel 2010 spreadsheet similar to that used by the Contoso, Ltd.

SOFTWARE ORIENTATION

Excel's Home Tab

The Ribbon in Microsoft Office Excel 2010 is made up of a series of tabs, each related to specific kinds of tasks that workers do in Excel. The Home tab, shown in Figure 3-1, contains the commands that people use the most when creating Excel documents. Having commands visible on the work surface enables you to work quickly and efficiently. Each tab contains groups of commands related to specific tasks or functions.

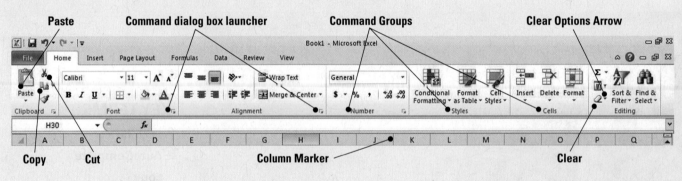

Figure 3-1

Worksheet/Workbook view

Below, in Figure 3-2, you see the Home tab, its command groups, and other Ribbon tools. Your screen may vary if default settings have been changed or if other preferences have been set. Use this figure as a reference throughout this lesson as well as the rest of this book.

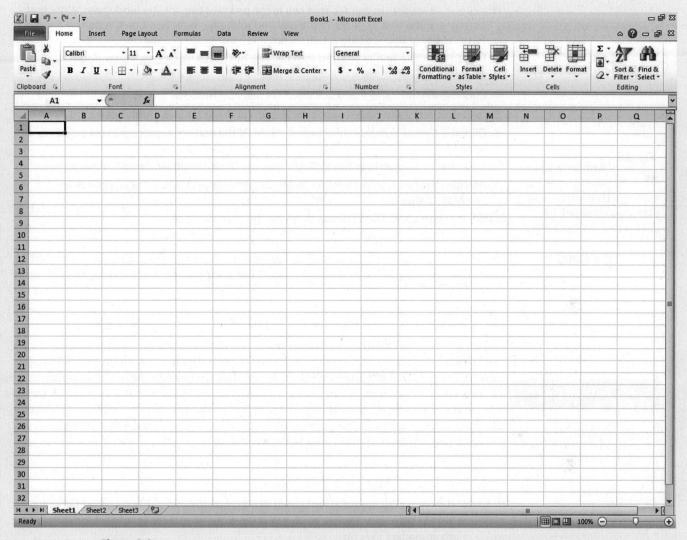

Figure 3-2

Home tab

CREATING WORKBOOKS

The Bottom Line

There are three ways to create a new Microsoft Excel workbook. You can open a new, blank workbook using the File tab to access Backstage. You can open an existing Excel workbook, enter new or additional data, and save the file with a new name, thus creating a new workbook. You can also use a template to create a new workbook. A template is a model that has already been set up to track certain kinds of data, such as sales reports, invoices, etc.

Starting a Workbook from Scratch

When you want to create a new workbook, launch Excel and a blank workbook is ready for you to begin working. If you have already been working in Excel and want to begin a new workbook, click the File tab, click New, and then click Create to create a blank workbook. Worksheets usually begin with a title that sets the stage for the reader's interpretation of the data contained in a worksheet. In this exercise, you will create a new Excel workbook to be used as a sales report.

| STEP BY STEP | **Start a Workbook from Scratch** |

GET READY. LAUNCH Excel. A blank workbook opens with A1 as the active cell.

1. Key Fabrikam, Inc. in cell A1. This cell is the primary title for the worksheet. Note that as you key, the text appears in the cell and in the formula bar. See the definition of formula bar in the "Editing a Cell's Contents" exercise on page 55.
2. Press Enter. The text is entered into cell A1, but looks like it flows over into B1.
3. In cell A2, key Monthly Sales Report. Press Enter.
4. Click the File tab, and then click the New fast command in the left pane.
5. In the center of the *Backstage* area, Blank Workbook will be highlighted.
6. Click the Create button on the bottom right of the screen. A second Excel workbook is opened.
7. Click the Close button in the top right corner. Book2 is closed. Book1 remains open.
8. **PAUSE.** Create a Lesson 3 folder in My Documents and **SAVE** the workbook as *Fabrikam Sales_3*.

CLOSE the workbook. **LEAVE** Excel open for the next exercise.

Another Way
When you are working in Excel, you can open a blank workbook with the shortcut combination Ctrl+N.

Take Note   Text is stored in only one cell even when it appears to extend into adjacent cells. If an entry is longer than the cell width and the next cell contains data, the entry appears in truncated form.

ENTERING AND EDITING BASIC DATA IN A WORKSHEET

The Bottom Line   You can key data directly into a worksheet cell or cells. You also can copy and paste information from another worksheet or from other programs. To enter data in a cell within a worksheet, you must make the desired cell active and then key the data. To move to the next column after text has been entered, press Tab. When you have finished keying the entries in a row, press Enter to move to the beginning of the next row. You also can use the arrow keys to move to an adjacent cell. Press Enter to accept the proposed entry or continue keying. In the following exercise, you will add a new employee's information to the worksheet.

Entering Basic Data in a Worksheet

In Excel, column width is established based on the existing data. When you add an entry in a column that is longer than other entries in the column, it is necessary to adjust the column width to accommodate the entry.

| STEP BY STEP | **Enter Basic Data in a Worksheet** |

GET READY. OPEN the workbook titled *Contoso Employee Info*.

@ The *Contoso Employee Info* file for this lesson is available on the book companion website or in WileyPLUS.

1. Move to cell A28.
2. Key Simon and press Tab.
3. Key Britta and press Tab.
4. Key Administrative Assistant and press Tab.
5. Key 36 and press Enter.
6. Double-click the column marker (line between two columns, refer to Figure 3-1) between columns C and D to so that the entire text is visible in column C.

PAUSE. LEAVE the workbook open to use in the next exercise.

Take Note   When you key text that is longer than the cell, the text extends into the next cell. However, when you press Tab and move to the next cell, the overflow text is not displayed. The text is still there. You will learn more about adjusting the column width later in this lesson.

Editing a Cell's Contents

One advantage of electronic records versus manual ones is that changes can be made quickly and easily. To edit information in a worksheet, you can make changes directly in the cell or edit the contents of a cell in the **formula bar**, located between the Ribbon and the worksheet. When you enter data in a cell, the text or numbers appear in the cell and in the formula bar. You can also enter or edit data directly in the formula bar. Before changes can be made, however, you must select the information that is to be changed. **Selecting text** means that you highlight the text that is to be changed. You can select a single cell, a row, a column, a range of cells, or an entire workbook. A range of cells is simply a group of more than one cell. They can be adjacent or nonadjacent.

STEP BY STEP	Select, Edit, and Delete Cell Contents

USE the workbook from the previous exercise.

1. Select cell A22 as shown in Figure 3-3.

Figure 3-3

Editing a selected cell

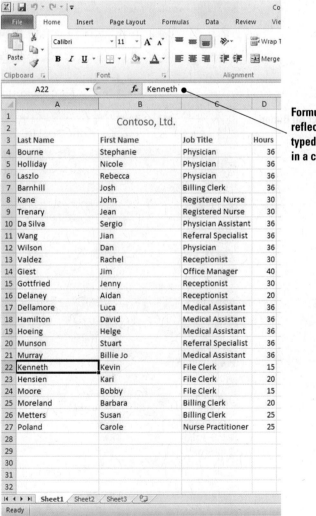

Formula bar reflects what is typed or present in a cell

2. Select the existing text in cell A22. Key Kennedy and press Enter.

3. **Click cell** A15 and, while holding down the left mouse button, drag the cursor to select all cells in that row through cell D15. You have selected the entire record for Jenny Gottfried.

4. **Press** Delete. The information is deleted and row 15 is now blank.

5. **With cells A15 to D15 still selected, right-click to display the shortcut menu.**

6. **Press** Delete. The *Delete* dialog box will be displayed.

7. Click the Shift cells up option as shown in Figure 3-4, and then click OK.

Figure 3-4

Delete a row

8. Click the Select All button, shown in Figure 3-5, to select all cells in the worksheet.

Figure 3-5

Select all cells

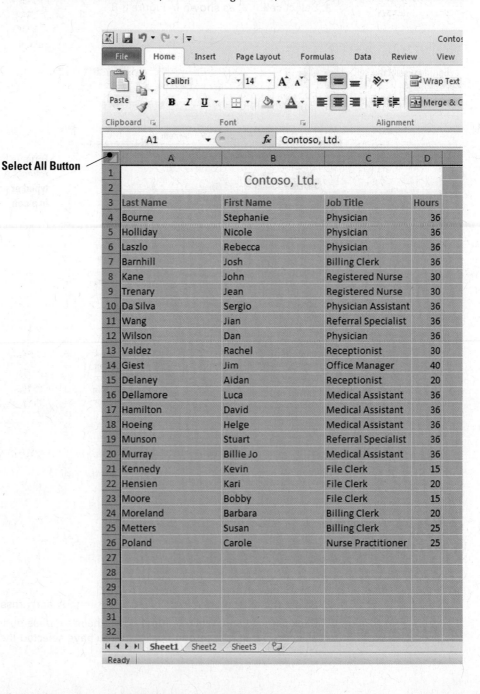

CERTIFICATION
R E A D Y   2.1.4

How do you select a cell's data?

9. Click **any worksheet cell** to deselect the worksheet.

10. **To select all cells containing data, select** A1 and press Ctrl+A. Click **any worksheet cell** to deselect the cells.

PAUSE. SAVE the workbook in the Lesson 3 folder and close the workbook. **LEAVE** Excel open to use in the next exercise.

Take Note

If you edit a cell's contents and change your mind before you press Enter, press Esc and the original text will be restored. If you change the content of a cell and then do not want the change, Click the undo button ↶ on the Quick Access Toolbar. The deleted text will be restored.

You can begin editing by double-clicking the cell to be edited and then keying the replacement text in the cell. Or you can click the cell and then click in the formula bar.

When you are in Edit mode:

- The insertion point appears as a vertical bar and other commands are inactive.
- You can move the insertion point by using the direction keys.

Use the Home key on your keyboard to move the insertion point to the beginning of the cell, and use End key to move the insertion point to the end. You can add new characters at the location of the insertion point.

To select multiple characters, press Shift while you press the arrow keys. You also can use the mouse to select characters while you are editing a cell. Just click and drag the mouse pointer over the characters that you want to select.

Another Way
You can right-click a cell or a selected range of cells and choose Delete from the menu that appears.

As you have seen in the preceding exercises, there are several ways to modify the values or text you have entered into a cell:

- Erase the cell's contents.
- Replace the cell's contents with something else.
- Edit the cell's contents.

Another Way
Place the cursor in the cell you want to edit, press F2, and edit directly in the cell.

To erase the contents of a cell, double-click the cell and press Delete. To erase more than one cell, select all the cells that you want to erase and then press Delete. Pressing Delete removes the cell's contents, but does not remove any formatting (such as bold, italic, or a different number format) that you may have applied to the cell.

USING DATA TYPES TO POPULATE A WORKSHEET

The Bottom Line

You can enter three types of data into Excel: text, numbers, and formulas. In the following exercises, you will enter text (labels) and numbers (values). You will learn to enter formulas in Lesson 7. Text entries contain alphabetic characters and any other character that does not have a purely numeric value. The real strength of Excel is its ability to calculate and to analyze numbers based on the numeric values you enter. For that reason, accurate data entry is crucial.

Entering Labels and Using AutoComplete

Labels are used to identify numeric data and are the most common type of text entered in a worksheet. Labels are also used to sort and group data. If the first few characters that you type in a column match an existing entry in that column, Excel automatically enters the remaining characters. This **AutoComplete** feature works only for entries that contain text or a combination of text and numbers.

| STEP BY STEP | **Enter Labels and Use AutoComplete** |

OPEN *Fabrikam Sales_3* from the Lesson 3 folder.

Troubleshooting To verify that AutoComplete is enabled, click the File tab accessing Backstage, click Options, and then click Advanced in the navigation pane. In the Editing options section, click the *Enable AutoComplete for cell values* check box if it is not already checked. Click OK.

WileyPLUS Extra! features an online tutorial of this task.

1. Click cell A4 to enter the first column label. Key Agent and press Tab.
2. Key Last Closing and press Tab.
3. In cell C4, key January and press Enter.

Take Note

When you press Tab to enter data in several cells in a row and then press Enter at the end of the row, the selection moves to the beginning of the next row.

4. Select A5 to enter the first-row label and key Richard Carey.
5. Select A6 and key David Ortiz.
6. Select A7 and key Kim Akers.
7. Select A8 and key Nicole Caron.
8. Select A9 and key R. As shown in Figure 3-6, AutoComplete is activated when you key the *R* because it matches the beginning of a previous entry in this column. AutoComplete displays the entry for Richard Carey.

Figure 3-6

AutoComplete

9. Key a Y. The AutoComplete entry disappears. Finish keying an entry for Ryan Calafato.
10. Double-click the marker between columns A and B. This resizes the columns to accommodate the data entered.
11. Double-click the marker between columns B and C. All worksheet data should be visible.

Take Note

Excel bases the list of potential AutoComplete entries on the active cell column. Entries that are repeated within a row are not automatically completed.

PAUSE. LEAVE the workbook open to use in the next exercise.

To accept an AutoComplete entry, press Enter or Tab. When you accept AutoComplete, the completed entry will exactly match the pattern of uppercase and lowercase letters of the existing entry. To delete the automatically entered characters, press backspace. Entries that contain only numbers, dates, or times are not automatically completed. If you do not want to use the AutoComplete option, the feature can be turned off.

Entering Dates

Dates are often used in worksheets to track data over a specified period of time. Like text, dates can be used as row and column headings. However, dates are considered serial numbers, which means that they are sequential and can be added, subtracted, and used in calculations. Dates can also be used in formulas and in developing graphs and charts. The way a date is initially displayed in a worksheet cell depends on the format in which you enter it. In Excel 2010, the default date format uses four digits for the year. Also by default, dates are right-justified in the cells.

Enter Dates

USE the workbook from the previous exercise.

1. Click cell **B5**, key **1/4/20XX** (with XX representing the current year), and press **Enter**. The number is entered in B5, and B6 becomes the active cell.
2. Key **1/25/XX** and press **Enter**. The number is entered in B6, and B7 becomes the active cell.
3. Key **1/17** and press **Enter**. *17-Jan* is entered in the cell, and if you were to go back and click on B7, then *1/17/20XX* appears in the formula bar.
4. Key **1/28** in B8 and press **Enter**.

Another Way
Ctrl+; (semicolon) will enter the current date into a worksheet cell; Ctrl+: (colon) will enter the current time.

5. Key **January 21, 2008** and press **Enter**. *21-Jan-08* will appear in the cell. (If you enter a date in a different format than specified, your worksheet may not reflect the results described.) The date formats in column B are not consistent. You will apply a consistent date format in the next lesson.

PAUSE. LEAVE the workbook open to use in the next exercise.

Excel interprets two-digit years from 00 to 29 as the years 2000 to 2029; two-digit years from 30 to 99 are interpreted as 1930 to 1999. If you enter 1/28/08, the date will be displayed as 1/28/2008 in the cell. If you enter 1/28/37, the cell will display 1/28/1937.

If you key January 28, 2008, the date will display as 28-Jan-08, as shown in Figure 3-7. If you key 1/28 without a year, Excel interprets the date to be the current year. 28-Jan will display in the cell, and the formula bar will display 1/28/ followed by the current year. In the next lesson, you will learn to apply a consistent format to series of dates.

Figure 3-7

Date formats

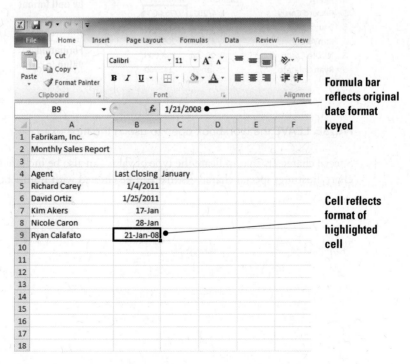

Formula bar reflects original date format keyed

Cell reflects format of highlighted cell

Take Note   When you enter a date into a cell in a particular format, the cell is automatically formatted. Subsequent numbers entered in that cell will be converted to the date format of the original entry.

Regardless of the date format displayed in the cell, the formula bar displays the date in month/day/four-digit-year format because that is the format required for calculations and analyses.

Entering Values

Numeric values are the foundation for Excel's calculations, analyses, charts, and graphs. Numbers can be formatted as currency, percentages, decimals, and fractions. By default, numeric entries are right-justified in a cell. Applying formatting to numbers changes their appearance but does not affect the cell value that Excel uses to perform calculations. The value is not affected by formatting or special characters (such as dollar signs) that are entered with a number. The true value is always displayed in the formula bar.

STEP BY STEP	Enter Values

USE the workbook from the previous exercise.

1. Click cell C5, key $275,000, and press Enter. Be sure to include the $ and the comma in your entry. The number is entered in C5, and C6 becomes the active cell. The number is displayed in the cell with a dollar sign and comma; however, the formula bar displays the true value and disregards the special characters.

2. Key 125000 and press Enter.

3. Key 209,000 and press Enter. The number is entered in the cell with a comma separating the digits; the comma does not appear in the formula bar.

4. Key 258,000 and press Enter.

5. Key 145700 and press Enter. Figure 3-8 illustrates how your spreadsheet should look with the values you have just keyed.

Figure 3-8

Value unaffected by formatting

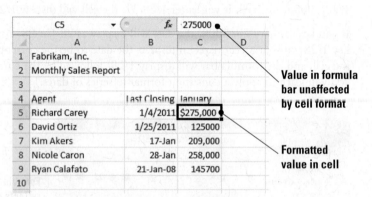

PAUSE. LEAVE the workbook open to use in the next exercise.

Special characters that indicate the type of value can also be included in the entry. The following chart illustrates special characters that can be entered with numbers.

Character	Used To
+	Indicate a positive value
– or ( )	Indicate a negative value
$	Indicate a currency value
%	Indicate a percentage
/	Indicate a fraction
.	Indicate a decimal
,	Separate the digits of an entry

Filling a Series with Auto Fill

Excel provides **auto fill** options that will automatically fill cells with data and/or formatting. To populate a new cell with data that exists in an adjacent cell, use the Fill command. The **fill handle** is a small black square in the lower-right corner of the selected cell. To display the fill handle, hover the cursor over the lower-right corner of the cell until it turns into a +. Click and drag the handle from cells that contain data to the cells you want to fill with that data, or have Excel automatically continue a series of numbers, numbers and text combinations, dates, or time periods, based on an established pattern. In this exercise, you use the auto fill option to populate cells with data.

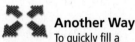**STEP BY STEP** | **Fill a Series with Auto Fill**

USE the workbook from the previous exercise.

1. Select D4 and click the Fill button in the Editing command group in the Home tab on the Ribbon; the Fill options menu appears, as shown in Figure 3-9.

Figure 3-9

Fill Command drop-down menu

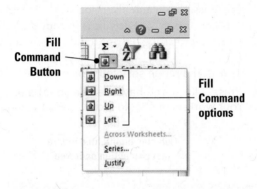

Another Way
To quickly fill a cell with the contents of the cell above, press Ctrl+D; press Ctrl+R to fill the cell to the right.

2. From the menu, click Right. The contents of C4 (January) is filled into cell D4.
3. Select C10 and click the Fill button. Choose Down. The content of C9 is copied into C10.
4. Click the Fill handle in cell C5, as shown in Figure 3-10, and drag to F5 and release. The *Auto Fill Options* button appears in G6.

Figure 3-10

Fill handle

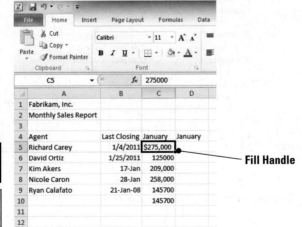

CERTIFICATION READY | **2.2.1**

How do you copy a cell's contents using Auto Fill?

Take Note   A **range** is a group of adjacent cells that you select to perform operations on all of the selected cells. When you refer to a range of cells, the first cell and last cell are separated by a colon (e.g., D5:F5).

5. Click the Auto Fill Options drop-down arrow, and choose *Fill Formatting Only* from the options list that appears.

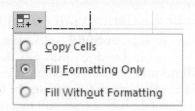

6. Click the **Fill handle** in **C4** and drag to **H4** and release. Excel recognizes January as the beginning of a natural series and completes the series as far as you take the fill handle. By definition, a **natural series** is a formatted series of text or numbers. For example, a natural series of numbers could be 1, 2, 3, or 100, 200, 300, or a natural series of text could be Monday, Tuesday, Wednesday, or January, February, March.

CERTIFICATION READY   **2.2.3**

How do you fill a series using Auto Fill without changing the formatting?

7. Select **C13**, key **2007**, and press **Enter**.

8. Click the **Fill handle** in **C13** and drag to **D13** and release. The contents of C13 are copied.

9. In D13, key **2008** and press **Enter**. You have created a natural series of years.

10. Select **C13** and **D13**. Click the **Fill handle** in **D13** and drag to **G13** and release. The cells are filled with consecutive years.

Take Note   When Excel recognizes a series, the default fill option is to complete the series. When you use the fill handle and a series is not present, the default is to copy the cell contents. The Fill Options button also allows you to fill formatting only or to fill without formatting.

11. Select cells **F4:H4**. With the range selected, press **Delete**.

12. Select **C10:G13**. Press **Delete**. You have cleared your Sales Report worksheet of unneeded data. Your worksheet should look like Figure 3-11.

Figure 3-11

Fabrikam worksheet

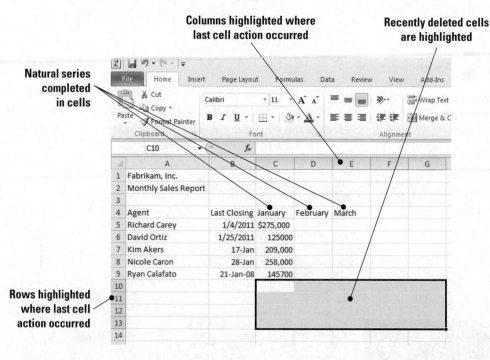

PAUSE. LEAVE the workbook open to use in the next exercise.

CERTIFICATION READY   **2.2.2**

How do you fill a series using Auto Fill?

After you fill cells using the fill handle, the Auto Fill Options button appears so that you can choose how the selection is filled. In Excel, the default option is to copy the original content and formatting. With auto fill you can select how the content of the original cell appears in each cell in the filled range.

If you choose to fill formatting only, the contents are not copied, but any number that you key into a cell in the selected range will be formatted like the original cell. If you click Fill Series, the copied cells will read $275,001, $275,002, and so on. The Auto Fill Options button remains until you perform another function.

Take Note   When you key sufficient data for Excel to recognize a series, the fill handle will do the rest. For example, to record daily sales, you might want to have consecutive columns labeled with the days of the week. If you key Monday in the first cell, you can fill in the rest of the days by dragging the fill handle from the Monday cell to complete the series.

CUTTING, COPYING, AND PASTING DATA

The Bottom Line

After you have entered data into a worksheet, you frequently need to rearrange or reorganize some of it to make the worksheet easier to understand and analyze. You can use Excel's cut, copy, and paste commands to copy or move entire cells with their contents, formats, and formulas. These processes will be defined and covered as the exercises in this section continue. You can also copy specific contents or attributes from the cells. For example, you can copy the format only without copying the cell value or copy the resulting value of a formula without copying the formula itself. You can also copy the value from the original cell but retain the formatting of the destination cell.

Cut, copy, and paste functions can be performed in a variety of ways by using:

- The mouse
- Ribbon commands
- Shortcut commands
- The Office Clipboard task pane

Copying a Data Series with the Mouse

By default, drag-and-drop editing is turned on so that you can use the mouse to **copy** (duplicate) or move cells. Just select the cells or range of cells you want to copy and hold down Ctrl while you point to the border of the selection. When the pointer becomes a **copy pointer**, you can drag the cell or range of cells to the new location. As you drag, a scrolling ScreenTip identifies where the selection will be copied if you released the mouse button. In this exercise, you practice copying data with the mouse.

STEP BY STEP   **Copy a Data Series with the Mouse**

USE the workbook from the previous exercise.

1. Select the range A4:A9.
2. Press Ctrl and hold the button down as you point the cursor at the bottom border of the selected range. The copy pointer is displayed.

Troubleshooting   Be sure to hold down the Ctrl key the entire time you are selecting a data series for copying with the mouse, or you will move the series instead of copying it.

3. With the copy pointer displayed, hold down the left mouse button and drag the selection down until A12:A17 is displayed in the scrolling ScreenTip below the copy box.
4. Release the mouse button. The data in A4:A9 appears in A12:A17.

PAUSE. LEAVE the workbook open to use in the next exercise.

CERTIFICATION READY   2.2.1

How do you copy a data series with the mouse?

Moving a Data Series with the Mouse

Data can be moved from one location to another within a workbook in much the same way as copying. To move a data series, select the cell or range of cells and point to the border of the selection. When the pointer becomes a **move pointer**, you can drag the cell or range of cells to a new location. When data is moved, it replaces any existing data in the destination cells. In this exercise, you practice moving a data series from one range of cells to another.

STEP BY STEP **Move a Data Series with the Mouse**

USE the workbook from the previous exercise.

1. Select B4:B9.
2. Point the cursor at the bottom border of the selected range. The move pointer is displayed.
3. With the move pointer displayed, hold down the left mouse button and drag the selection down until B12:B17 is displayed in the scrolling ScreenTip below the box.
4. Release the mouse button. In your worksheet, the destination cells are empty; therefore, you are not concerned with replacing existing data. The data previously in B4:B9 is now in B12:B17.
5. Select the range of cells from C4:E9.
6. Point the cursor at the left border of the selection to display the move arrows.
7. Drag left and drop the range of cells in the same rows in column B (B12:B17). Note that a dialog box will warn you about replacing the contents of the destination cells.
8. Click Cancel.
9. Move range C4:E9 to B4:D9.

PAUSE. LEAVE the workbook open to use in the next exercise.

<table>
<tr><td>

CERTIFICATION READY   **2.1.3**

How do you move a data series with the mouse?

</td></tr>
</table>

Take Note
When you attempt to move a selection to a location that contains data, a caution dialog box opens. "Do you want to replace the contents of the destination cells?" is a reminder that moving data to a new location replaces the existing data. You can click OK or cancel the event.

Copying and Pasting Data

The **Office Clipboard** collects and stores up to 24 copied or cut items that are then available to be used in the active workbook, in other workbooks, and in other Microsoft Office programs. You can **paste** (insert) selected items from the Clipboard to a new location in the worksheet. **Cut** (moved) data is removed from the worksheet but is still available for you to use in multiple locations. If you copy multiple items and then click Paste, only the last item copied will be pasted. To access multiple items, you must open the Clipboard task pane. In this exercise, you use commands in the Clipboard group and the Clipboard task pane to copy and paste cell data.

STEP BY STEP **Copy and Paste Data**

USE the workbook from the previous exercise.

Another Way
To copy, you can use Ctrl+C or right-click and then click Copy on the shortcut menu. You can use Ctrl+V to paste the last cut or copied data.

1. On the *Home* tab ribbon, click the Clipboard Dialog Box Launcher; the *Clipboard task pane* opens on the side of the worksheet. The most recently copied item is always added at the top of the list in this pane, and it is the item that will be copied when you click Paste or use a shortcut command.
2. Select C5 and key 305000. Press Enter.
3. Select C5 and click the Copy command button in the Clipboard group; the border around C5 becomes a flashing marquee.
4. Select C8; the flashing marquee (dotted flashing line around the highlighted cells) identifies the item that will be copied. Click the Paste button in the Clipboard group.
5. Select D5. Right-click and then click Paste on the shortcut menu (Figure 3-12). The flashing border remains active on cell C5. A copied cell will not deactivate until the data is pasted or another cell is double-clicked.

Take Note

With the new feature, Paste with Live Preview, if you mouse over the Paste options in either the right-click menu, or the paste menu in the Clipboard group, you will be able to view your changes before actually implementing them.

6. With D5 selected as the active cell, press Delete to remove the data from D5. When you perform any function other than Paste, the flashing border disappears from C5. You can no longer paste the item unless you use the Clipboard pane.

7. Select C6, key 185000, and press Enter.

8. You can copy data from one worksheet or workbook and paste it to another worksheet or workbook. Select A1:A9 and click Copy in the Clipboard command group.

9. Click the Sheet2 tab to open the worksheet.

10. Cell A1 will be highlighted as active. Click the Paste drop-down arrow in the Clipboard group. In the menu that appears, click Keep Source Column Widths. This will make sure that your column formatting does not change when you paste your copied selection.

Figure 3-12

Paste options

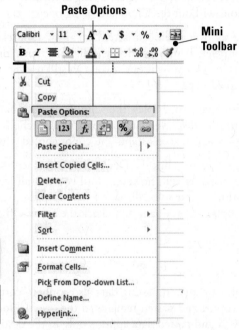

Paste Options

Mini Toolbar

**CERTIFICATION
READY   2.2.1**

How do you copy and paste a data series?

Take Note

If Collect Without Showing Office Clipboard is selected in Clipboard Options, cut or copied items will be stored on the Clipboard, but you must display the task pane to paste any item except the last one.

11. Click the Sheet1 tab to return to that worksheet. With cell C9 active, click the $305,000 item in the task pane to paste the item into cell C9. Click Undo to clear cell C9.

12. Close the Clipboard task pane.

PAUSE. LEAVE the workbook open to use in the next exercise.

Ⓧ Ref

In Lesson 5, you will use some of the Paste Special options.

Take Note

When you cut or copy data and then paste it into a new location, by default, Excel pastes the original cell contents and formatting. Additional options are available when you click the arrow below the Paste command. You can copy a range of data in a column and click Transpose to paste the data into columns. Other options allow you to copy formulas, to copy values instead of formulas, and to copy cells containing borders and paste the data without the border.

As illustrated in Figure 3-13, the Clipboard stores items copied from other programs as well as those from Excel. The program icon and the beginning of the copied text are displayed.

Figure 3-13

Office Clipboard task pane

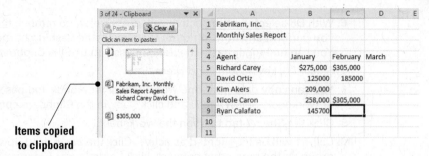

Items copied to clipboard

When you copy or cut data from a worksheet, a flashing border appears around the item and remains visible after you paste the data to one or more new locations. It will continue to flash until you perform another action or press Esc. As long as the marquee flashes, you can paste that item to multiple locations without the Clipboard being open.

When you move the cursor over a Clipboard item, an arrow appears on the right side that allows you to paste the item or delete it. You can delete individual items, or click Clear All to delete all Clipboard items. When the task pane is open, you can still use the command buttons or short-cuts to paste the last copied item.

Clipboard Options allow you to display the Clipboard automatically. If you do not have the Clipboard automatically displayed, it is a good idea to check Collect Without Showing Office Clipboard so that you can access items you cut or copied when you open the Clipboard.

To close the Clipboard task pane, click the Dialog Box Launcher or the Close button at the top of the pane. Clipboard items remain, however, until you exit all Microsoft Office programs. If you want the Clipboard task pane to be displayed when Excel opens, click the Options button at the bottom of the Clipboard task pane and check the Show Office Clipboard Automatically option.

Cutting and Pasting Data

Most of the options for copying and pasting data also apply to cutting and pasting. The major difference is that data copied and pasted remains in the original location as well as in the destination cell or range. Cut and pasted data appears only in the destination cell or range. In this exercise, you will cut and paste cell contents.

Another Way
Press Ctrl+C twice to display the Office Clipboard task pane. If this shortcut does not open the Clipboard, open the Clipboard with the Dialog Box Launcher, click Clipboard Options, and enable this shortcut. You can also press Alt+H then F and O to perform the same function. Repeat the last keystroke to close the Clipboard task pane.

STEP BY STEP   **Cut and Paste Data**

USE the workbook from the previous exercise.

Another Way
To cut, you can use Ctrl+X or right-click and then click Cut on the shortcut menu.

1. Click **Sheet2** to make it the active worksheet.
2. Select **A8** and click **Cut** in the Clipboard group; the contents of cell A8 are cut from that cell and moved to the clipboard.
3. Select **A9** and click **Paste** to add the former contents of cell A8 to A9.

Take Note   When you delete text, it is not stored on the Clipboard. If you want to remove data but think that you might use the text later, use Cut rather than Delete. By using the Cut feature, you will be able to access the data or information from the clipboard if needed. Deleted text can be restored only with Undo.

4. Click **Undo**. The data is restored to A8.

PAUSE. LEAVE the workbook open to use in the next exercise.

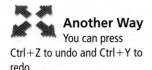

Another Way
You can press Ctrl+Z to undo and Ctrl+Y to redo.

CERTIFICATION
READY **2.1.2**

How do you cut and paste data and cell contents?

The Bottom Line

You can undo and repeat up to 100 actions in Excel. You can undo one or more actions by clicking Undo on the Quick Access Toolbar. To undo several actions at once, click the arrow next to Undo and select the actions that you want to reverse. Click the list and Excel will reverse the selected actions.

To redo an action that you undid, click Redo on the Quick Access Toolbar. When all actions have been undone, the Redo command becomes inactive.

In the preceding exercises, you learned that Excel provides a number of options for populating a worksheet with data. There are also several ways you can accomplish each of the tasks. To cut, copy, and paste, you can use Ribbon commands, shortcut key combinations, or right-click and use a shortcut menu. As you become more proficient in working with Excel, you will decide which method is most efficient for you.

EDITING A WORKBOOK'S KEYWORDS

Assigning **keywords** to the document properties makes it easier to organize and find documents. You can assign your own text values in the Keywords field of the Document Properties panel.

Assigning Keywords

For example, if you work for Fabrikam, Inc., you might assign the keyword *seller* to worksheets that contain data about clients whose homes the company has listed for sale. You could then search for and locate all files containing information about the owners of homes your company has listed. You can assign more than one keyword to a document.

STEP BY STEP | **Assign Keywords**

USE the workbook from the previous exercise.

1. Click the File tab to open the Backstage view, then click the drop-down arrow by Properties. Click the show Document Panel. In the Document Properties panel, click the Keywords field and key Agent, Closing.

2. Click the Document Properties drop-down arrow in the panel's title bar, and then click Advanced Properties in the drop-down menu (see Figure 3-14); the *Properties* dialog box opens.

Figure 3-14

Properties drop-down menu

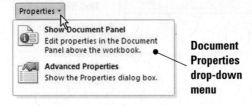

As covered in Lesson 2, altering the document properties by adding and modifying keywords makes changes to the document properties.

 Ref

3. Click the Summary tab in the dialog box to see the properties you entered.
4. Click the Statistics tab to see the date you created the file (today).
5. Click OK to close the Properties dialog box.
6. Click the Close button (X) at the top of the Document Information panel.

PAUSE. LEAVE the workbook open to use in the next exercise.

After a file has been saved, the Statistics tab will record when the file was accessed and when it was modified. It also identifies the person who last saved the file. After a workbook has been saved, the Properties dialog box title bar will display the workbook name. Because you have not yet saved the workbook you have been using, the dialog box title bar said *Book1 Properties*. You can view a document's properties from the Open dialog box or from the Save As dialog box when the workbook is closed. You can also view properties from the Print dialog box.

SAVING THE WORKBOOK

The Bottom Line

When you save a file, you can save it to a folder on your computer's hard drive, a network drive, a disk, CD, or any other storage location. You must first identify where the document is to be saved. The remainder of the Save process is the same, regardless of the location or storage device.

Naming and Saving a Workbook Location

When you save a file for the first time, you will be asked two important questions: Where do you want to save the file? What name will you give to the file? In this lesson, you practice answering these questions in the Save As dialog box. By default in all Office applications, documents are saved to the My Documents folder.

STEP BY STEP   **Name and Save a Workbook Location**

USE the workbook from the previous exercise.

1. Click Sheet1 to make it active. Click the **File** tab to open Backstage view. Click the **Save As** button in the navigation bar to open the Save As dialog box.

2. In the *Save As Type* text box at the bottom of the dialog box, choose **Excel Workbook** from the drop-down arrow (.xlsx extension if it is not already chosen as the default).

3. From the left-hand navigation pane in the *Save As* dialog box, click **Desktop**. This will make your new destination to save your file as the Desktop.

4. In the *Save As* dialog box, click the **Create New Folder** button 📁 to open the *New Folder* dialog box. The New Folder dialog box pops up to allow you to name the new folder you are about to create. Refer to Figure 3-15.

Figure 3-15

New Folder dialog box

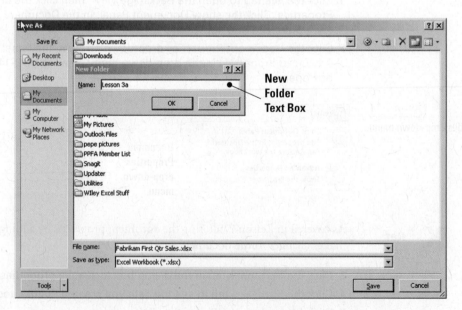

5. In the *New Folder* dialog box, key **Lesson 3a** and click **OK**. The New Folder dialog box closes and the Save As name box shows that the file will be saved in the Lesson 3a, folder.

6. Click in the **File Name** box and key *Fabrikam First Qtr Sales*.

7. Click the **Save** button.

PAUSE. LEAVE the workbook open to use in the next exercise.

CERTIFICATION READY   1.3.5

How do you name a workbook and save it to a specific location?

Saving a Workbook under a Different Name

You can resave an existing workbook to create a new workbook. For example, the sales report you created in the preceding exercises is for the first quarter. When all first-quarter data has been entered, you can save the file with a new name and use it to enter second-quarter data. You can also use an existing workbook as a template to create new workbooks. In this exercise, you learn how to use the Save As dialog box to implement either of these options.

STEP BY STEP   **Save a Workbook under a Different Name**

USE the workbook from the previous exercise.

1. Click the File tab and click Save As in the Backstage view navigation bar. The Save As dialog box opens with Excel Lesson 3a folder in the *Save In* text box, because it was the folder that was last used to save a workbook (See Figure 3-16).

Figure 3-16

Previously created folder as save destination

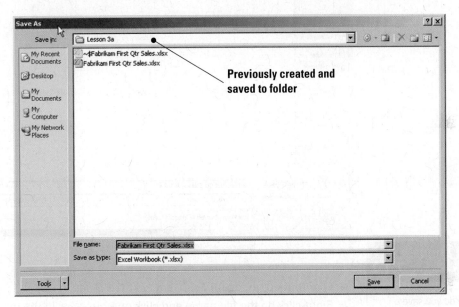

2. Click in the File Name box and key Fabrikam Second Qtr Sales.
3. **Click** Save. You have created a new workbook by saving an existing workbook with a new name.
4. Click File tab and click Save As in the Backstage view navigation bar to open the Save As dialog box.
5. **In the File Name box, key** Fabrikam Sales Template.
6. In the Save As Type box, click the drop-down arrow and choose Excel Template. By changing the file type to Excel Template, the location is automatically changed to save the workbook in the Templates folder. Change the destination to your Lesson 3 folder. Click the Save button.

PAUSE. LEAVE the workbook open to use in the next exercise.

CERTIFICATION READY 1.3.5

How do you rename and save an existing workbook?

Creating a template to use for each new report eliminates the possibility that you might lose data because you neglected to save with a new name before you replaced one quarter's data with another.

Saving a Workbook in a Previous Excel Format

Files created in earlier versions can be opened and revised in Excel 2010. You can save a copy of an Excel 2010 workbook (with the .xlsx file extension) that is fully compatible with Excel 97 through Excel 2010 (with the .xls file extension) versions. The program symbol displayed with the filenames will be different, but it is a good idea to give the earlier edition file a different name.

STEP BY STEP | **Save a Workbook for Use in a Previous Excel Version**

USE the workbook from the previous exercise.

1. Click the File tab and then click Save As.

2. In the *Save As* dialog box, in the *File Name* box, key Fabrikam First Qtr Sales 97-03. Click the Save as type dropdown box and select Excel 97-2003 Workbook (*.xls). (See Figure 3-17.) Click Save. Close the workbook.

3. Press Ctrl+O to display the Open dialog box. Select Fabrikam First Qtr Sales 97-03. Scroll to the right to view the file type and see that it is saved to be compatible with earlier Excel editions.

Figure 3-17

Dialog box with previous version options visible

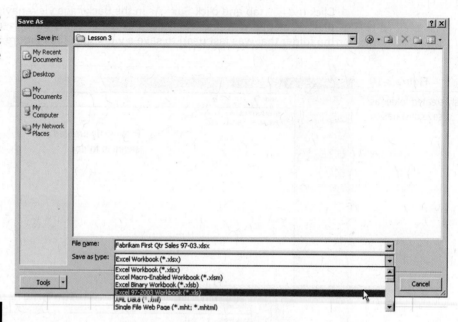

CERTIFICATION READY 7.1.2

How do you save a workbook for use in a previous version of Excel?

4. Click (but do not open) *Fabrikam First Qtr Sales*.

5. Right-click on the file name and click on Properties in the menu that opens. The properties you entered earlier are displayed. Click OK. Click Open.

PAUSE. LEAVE the workbook open to use in the next exercise.

Saving in Different File Formats

You can save an Excel 2010 file in a format other than .xlsx or .xls. The file formats that are listed as options in the Save As dialog box depend on what type of file format the application supports. When you save a file in another file format, some of the formatting, data, and/or features may be lost.

STEP BY STEP | **Choose and Save a Different File Format**

USE the workbook from the previous exercise.

1. Click the File tab and click Save As. When the *Save As* dialog box opens, click the Save as Type box.

2. Choose Single File Web Page from the drop-down menu, as shown in Figure 3-18.

Take Note   The screen shots in this book were taken using the Windows XP operating system. If your computer is running a different version of the Windows operating system (such as Windows 7 or Windows Vista), your screen may look slightly different than the images in this book.

Figure 3-18

Other file format options

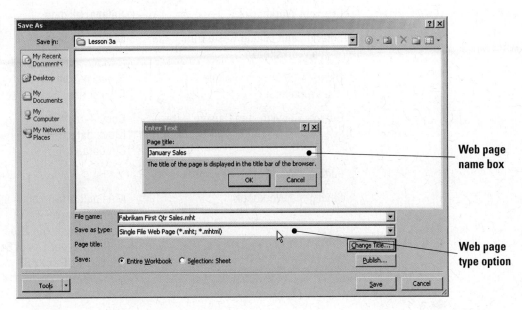

3. Click the **Change Title** button. In the Page title box, key **January Sales**. Click **OK**.

4. Click the **Selection: Sheet** radio button and click **Publish**. It is not necessary to publish the entire workbook at this time because it only contains one worksheet. The entire workbook option is appropriate when you have a workbook with two or more worksheets.

5. In the *Publish as Web Page* dialog box, select **Sheet**.

6. Click the check box in front of the *Open published web page in browser* option.

7. Click the **Publish** button. The default browser assigned to your Windows environment opens with the January Sales web page displayed.

8. Close the browser window.

9. Click the **File** tab and click **Close** in the Backstage view navigation bar.

10. If prompted to save changes, click **Yes**. The workbook is closed but Excel remains open.

CLOSE Excel.

CERTIFICATION READY   7.1.3

How do you save a workbook in PDF format?

CERTIFICATION READY   7.1.3

How do you save a workbook in XPS format?

Take Note   Excel 2010 also allows you to save your workbooks in PDF (Portable Documents Format) and XPS (XML Paper Specification) formats. Adobe PDF format ensures your printed or viewed file retains the formatting that you intended, and that data in the file cannot easily be changed. The Microsoft XPS format also ensures that when the file is viewed online or printed, it retains exactly the format that you intended, and that data in the file cannot be easily changed. Both of these options are available from the Save As Type drop-down menu.

SKILL SUMMARY

In This Lesson You Learned How To:	Exam Objective	Objective Number
Creating Workbooks	Select cell data.	2.1.4
Entering and Editing Basic Data in a Worksheet	Select cell data.	2.1.4
Using Data Types to Populate a Worksheet	Preserve cell format. Fill a series.	2.2.3 2.2.2
Cutting, Copying, and Pasting Data	Copy data. Move data. Cut data.	2.2.1 2.1.3 2.1.2
Editing a Workbook's Keywords		
Saving the Workbook	Manipulate workbook files and folders. Change the file type to a different version of Excel. Save as PDF or XPS.	1.3.5 7.1.2 7.1.3

Knowledge Assessment

Matching

Match each vocabulary term with its definition

a. auto fill
b. AutoComplete
c. copy
d. document properties
e. fill handle

f. formula bar
g. label
h. paste
i. range
j. file format

_____ 1. A command used to insert a cut or copied selection to a cell or range of cells.

_____ 2. To use a worksheet or workbook outside Excel, you have the option to save as a different _____.

_____ 3. A small black square in the lower-right corner of selected cells that you can use to copy one cell to adjacent cells or to create a series.

_____ 4. A bar at the top of the Excel window where you can enter or edit cell entries or formulas.

_____ 5. A group of adjacent cells that you select to perform operations on all of the selected cells.

_____ 6. To place a duplicate of a selection on the Office Clipboard.

_____ 7. An Excel feature that helps you quickly enter data into cells.

_____ 8. An Excel feature that automatically fills cells with data from another cell or range or completes a data series.

_____ 9. Entries that identify the numeric data in a worksheet.

_____ 10. Details about a file that describe or identify it and include details such as the author.

True/False

Circle T if the statement is true or F if the statement is false.

T   F   1. You can accept an AutoComplete entry by pressing Tab or Enter.

T   F   2. If you key June 5, 2010 in a cell, the formula bar will display June 5, 2010 as well.

T   F   3. Use Ctrl+: to enter the current date in a worksheet cell.

T   F   4. When you paste data into a cell or range of cells that contain data, the data that is replaced is copied to the Office Clipboard.

T   F   5. You can assign keywords so that others can search for your documents online.

T   F   6. Use the fill handle to create a natural series such as the months of the year.

T   F   7. When you open Excel, the application opens by default to the Backstage area.

T   F   8. The Office Clipboard collects items cut or copied from Excel worksheets only.

T   F   9. An existing workbook can be opened by pressing the Ctrl+N keys.

T   F   10. Workbooks can be saved as web pages, PDF files, and for use in previous versions of Excel.

Competency Assessment

Project 3-1: Advertising Budget

Create a new workbook for Fabrikam, Inc., that can be used to compare actual expenses with budgeted amounts.

GET READY. LAUNCH Excel if it is not already running.

1. Click the File tab and click New.

2. **Blank Workbook will be highlighted, then click the** Create button below the Preview pane.

3. Select A1 and key Fabrikam, Inc.

4. **Select** A2 and key Advertising Budget.

5. **Beginning in A4, key the following labels and values; press** Tab between each to move to a new cell:

Media	Vendor	Budgeted
Print	Lucerne Publishing	2000
Radio	Northwind Traders	$1,500
Door-to-Door	Consolidated Messenger	1200
Print	Graphic Design Institute	500
Television	Southridge Video	3000

6. If necessary, double-click the column marker between columns to adjust the column width to display all of the text in the column.

7. **SAVE** the workbook in the Lesson 3 folder you created in an exercise. Save the workbook as *Advertising Budget 3-1*.

8. **CLOSE** the file.

LEAVE Excel open for the next project.

Project 3-2: Set Document Properties and Assign Keywords

Use the Document Properties panel to assign document properties to an existing workbook.

OPEN the *Employees* file.

1. Click the File tab.

2. **Point to** Info in the left-hand panel and select Show Documents Panel from the Properties pull-down menu.

@ The *Employees* file for this lesson is available on the book companion website or in WileyPLUS.

3. **In the Author field, key** [your name]. Press Tab.

4. **In the Title field, key** Employees and press Tab.

5. **In the Subject field, key** Hours Worked and press Tab.

6. **In the Keywords field, key** Job Title, Hours.

7. Click the Close (X) button at the top of the Document Information Panel.

8. **SAVE** the workbook as *Employees 3-2* and **CLOSE** the file.

LEAVE Excel open for the next project.

Proficiency Assessment

Project 3-3: Monthly Advertising Expense

Use an existing workbook to create a new workbook that will track monthly advertising costs.

@ The *Advertising Expense* file for this lesson is available on the book companion website or in WileyPLUS.

OPEN the *Advertising Expense* file.

1. Select D4 and key January.

2. **Select** D4. Use the fill handle to enter the months of the year.

3. Select A10. Click Fill in the Editing group on the Home tab.

4. Choose Down and press Enter.

5. **Select** B10, key Trey Research, and press Enter.

6. Select C10, key 2500, and press Enter.

7. Open the Document Information Panel and key [your name] in the author, Advertising Expense in the title and Monthly Expenses in the subject text boxes.

8. Close the Document Information Panel.

9. **SAVE** the workbook in your Lesson 3 folder as *Advertising Expense 3-3*.

10. **CLOSE** the workbook.

LEAVE Excel open for the next project.

Project 3-4: Advertising Expenditures

Fourth Coffee specializes in unique coffee and tea blends. Create a workbook to track and classify expenditures for January.

GET READY. LAUNCH Excel if it is not already running.

1. Click the File tab. Open a new blank workbook.

2. In A1 key Fourth Coffee.

3. **In A2 key** January Expenditures.

4. Enter the following column headings in row 4. Date, Check No., Paid to, Category, and Amount.

5. Enter the following expenditures:
   - January 3, paid $3000 to Wide World Importers for coffee, Check No. 4076.
   - January 20, paid $600 to Northwind Traders for tea, Check 4077.
   - January 22, paid $300 to City Power and Light for utilities.
   - January 28, paid $200 to A. Datum Corporation for advertising.

6. Checks are written sequentially. Use the fill handle to enter the missing check numbers.

7. Adjust column headings as needed.

8. **SAVE** the workbook as *Expenses 3-4*. **CLOSE** the workbook.

LEAVE Excel open for the next project.

Mastery Assessment

@ The *Sales Research* file for this lesson is available on the book companion website or in WileyPLUS.

Project 3-5: Home Sales Data

Fabrikam receives sales research data from the local association of Realtors, which it uses as a benchmark for evaluating its sales performance.

OPEN the *Sales Research* file.

1. **OPEN** the Office Clipboard. If it contains items, click Clear All so that only data for this project will be on the Clipboard.
2. Use AutoFill to add the remaining months in column A.
3. **The data for March and April are reversed. Use the** Copy **command to place the data for March (B6:G6) on the Clipboard. Copy the data as one item.**
4. **Use the mouse to move B7:G7 to B6:G6. Paste the April data from the Clipboard to B7:G7.**
5. Beginning with A1, set the Print Area to include all data for January through June. Print the selected area.
6. Click the Select All button in the upper-left corner of the worksheet. Copy the entire worksheet to the Clipboard.
7. Paste the data to Sheet2. Adjust column widths if necessary.
8. **SAVE** the workbook as *Sales Research 3-5*. **CLOSE** the workbook.

LEAVE Excel open for the next project.

Project 3-6: Fourth Coffee

An employee has begun an inventory worksheet for Fourth Coffee. You want to use the company name and logo from the inventory sheet to create a banner for a website.

@ The *FC Inventory* file for this lesson is available on the book companion website or in WileyPLUS.

OPEN the *FC Inventory* file.

1. **SAVE** the workbook as a Single File Web Page.
2. **In** Print Area, in the publish web page dialog box, choose Selection A1:E1.
3. **Click** Publish. You have just created the banner for the company's new web page.
4. **CLOSE** the browser and all other open files.

LEAVE Excel open for the next project.

INTERNET READY

More than fifteen shortcut combinations were given in the first two lessons. Create a worksheet to list at least fifteen shortcut combinations. Decide how many columns you will need.

Each column must have a label that identifies its contents. Use the Excel Help on your computer and Microsoft Help online. Save your file as *Excel Shortcuts*.

When you have finished, close Excel.

4 Formatting Cells and Ranges

LESSON SKILL MATRIX

Skill	Exam Objective	Objective Number
Inserting and Deleting Cells	Move cell data.	2.1.3
	Cut cell data.	2.1.2
Manually Formatting Cell Contents	Select cell data.	2.1.4
	Align cell content.	3.1.1
	Apply a number format.	3.1.2
	Use Merge & Center.	3.2.1
	Merge across.	3.2.2
	Wrap text in a cell.	3.1.3
	Merge cells.	3.2.3
	Unmerge cells.	3.2.4
Copying Cell Formatting with the Format Painter	Use Format Painter.	3.1.4
Formatting Cells with Styles	Apply cell styles.	3.6.1
	Construct new cell styles.	3.6.2
Working with Hyperlinked Data	Create a hyperlink.	2.3.1
	Modify a hyperlink.	2.3.2
	Modify hyperlinked cell attributes.	2.3.3
	Remove a hyperlink.	2.3.4
Applying Conditional Formatting to Cells	Apply conditional formatting to cells.	8.3.1
	Use the Rule Manager to apply. conditional formats.	8.3.2
	Use icon sets.	8.3.5
	Use data bars.	8.3.6
Clearing a Cell's Formatting	Clear rules.	8.3.4

KEY TERMS

- attribute
- character
- conditional formatting
- default
- font
- Format Painter
- hyperlink
- merged cells
- Mini toolbar
- point
- select
- style

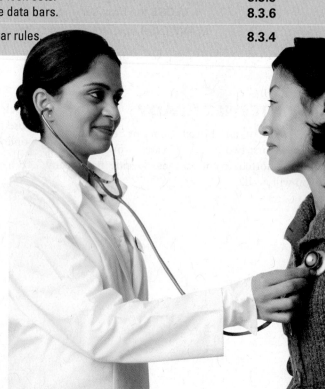

Contoso Ltd.'s income is generated by four physicians and the physician's assistant (PA). Ideally, physicians are scheduled to see no more than 35 patients per day, but every effort is made to accommodate patients who need immediate medical attention. Working in collaboration with the physicians, the PA sees patients who need an appointment when all the physicians' schedules are full. Many chronically ill patients whose conditions require frequent monitoring are scheduled with the PA. By law, a PA can treat no more than 25 patients a day. The firm is considering adding a nurse practitioner (NP) to balance the patient load. An NP is a registered nurse who provides some of the same care as a physician. For instance, in most states, an NP can prescribe medications. In this lesson, you will use Excel to manage and sort the relevant data associated with Contoso's physicians and their assistants.

SOFTWARE ORIENTATION

Formatting Excel Worksheets

The Home tab displayed in Figure 4-1 contains the formatting commands that you will use to enhance the appearance of the worksheets you create. You will use commands from every group on this tab as you learn to insert and delete cells, apply basic formatting to text, copy formatting, and apply styles and conditional formatting.

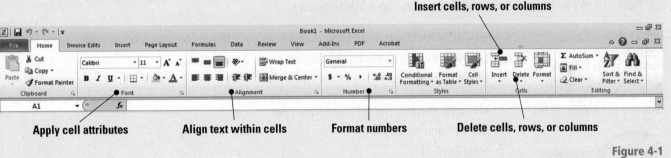

Figure 4-1

Home tab

The elements and features of the Home tab are those that are most often used to edit and develop workbooks and worksheets in Microsoft Excel. Your screen may vary if your default settings have been changed or if other preferences have been set. If so, use Figure 4-1 as a reference as needed throughout this lesson and the rest of the book.

INSERTING AND DELETING CELLS

The Bottom Line

As shown in Figure 4-2, when you click the arrow below the Insert command in the Cells group on the Ribbon, you can insert cells, worksheet rows, worksheet columns, or even a new worksheet into a workbook. Similar options apply to the Delete command—here, you can delete a cell, a worksheet row, a worksheet column, or an entire worksheet. Inserting and deleting items requires that you first select these items in your worksheet and workbook. To **select** means to click in an area to make it active. You can also select multiple areas by clicking, holding, and dragging to highlight a group of cells, rows, or columns. In the exercises that follow, you will explore the process of adding and deleting cells.

Figure 4-2

Insert options

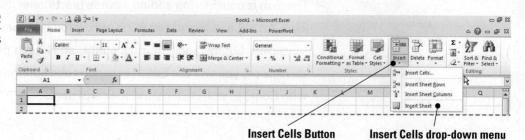

Insert Cells Button   Insert Cells drop-down menu

Inserting a New Cell in a Worksheet

After creating a worksheet, you may decide that you need to add additional data or delete unnecessary data. To enter additional text or values within the existing data, you need to insert cells in your worksheet. You can either insert a cell or cells and shift down the other cells in the same column, or you can shift other cells in the same row to the right.

STEP BY STEP

Insert a New Cell in a Worksheet

@ The *Contoso Patient Visits* Info file for this lesson is available on the book companion website or in WileyPLUS.

EXTRA

WileyPLUS Extra! features an online tutorial of this task.

Another Way
You can also select a cell or range, right-click on the selection, and then click Insert to open the Insert dialog box. In that dialog box, you can click the direction in which you want to shift the cells.

GET READY. Before you begin these steps, be sure to turn on or log on to your computer:

1. **LAUNCH** Excel. The Home tab will be active on the Ribbon.
2. **OPEN** the *Contoso Patient Visits* data file.
3. Select cell F5, then click Insert in the Cells group. F5 is now blank and the cells in the range F5:F8 have shifted down one row.
4. Key 604 and press Enter.
5. Select cell J4.
6. Click the Insert arrow, then click Insert Cells. The *Insert* dialog box opens.
7. Click Shift cells right, then click OK. A blank cell is inserted and the data is shifted to the right.
8. With cell J4 still active, key 580 and press Enter.
9. Select K7:L7 and click the Insert arrow.
10. Click Insert Cells.
11. Click Shift cells right and click OK. The data has shifted two cells to the right.
12. Select cell K7, key 475, and press Tab.
13. Key 611 and press Enter.
14. Select N3:N9. Click the Insert arrow and click Insert Cells.
15. The Shift cells right option is already selected; click OK. Cells are inserted so that November's data can be entered later. See Figure 4-3.
16. **PAUSE. SAVE** the workbook as *Contoso Patient 1*.

LEAVE the workbook open to use in the next exercise.

Figure 4-3

Group of cells moved and aligned

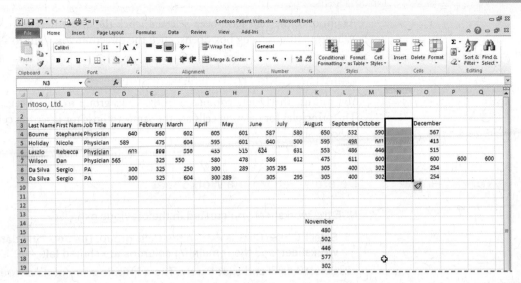

Additions and changes are common activities in Microsoft Office Excel 2010 workbooks. In the previous exercise, Contoso created an Excel workbook to track the number of patients treated during a month to determine whether to hire a nurse practitioner. After creating and saving the workbook, the administrative assistant discovered that corrections were needed and additional data must be added to the workbook.

CERTIFICATION READY   2.1.3

How do you move or insert a cell or a range of cells in a worksheet?

As demonstrated in the exercise, if you click Insert in the Cells group, a blank cell is inserted and, by default, the existing cells move down in the column. If, however, you click the arrow next to Insert and select Insert Cells, the Insert dialog box shown in Figure 4-4 opens, and you can choose to shift cells to the right. By default, the option box has the shift cells down option selected. The dialog box also allows you to insert a row or a column in a worksheet. Note that when working with active cells that have been inserted, when you continue to use these cells, the last action performed will be the selected option in the dialog box when you reuse the tool.

Figure 4-4

Insert dialog box

To insert blank cells in a worksheet, select the cell or the range of cells where you want to insert the new blank cells. The number of cells you select must match the number of cells that you want to insert. Thus, as Figure 4-5 illustrates, if you want to insert two cells, you must select two cells.

Figure 4-5

Your selection must match the number of cells to be inserted

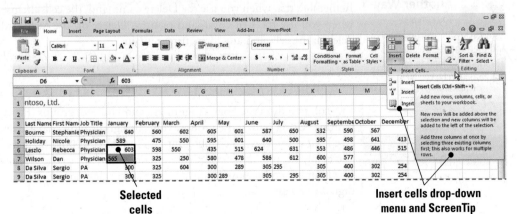

Selected cells

Insert cells drop-down menu and ScreenTip

Again, once the cells have been selected, click the arrow next to Insert, then click Insert Cells. When the Insert dialog box opens, click the direction you want to shift the cells.

Deleting Cells from a Worksheet

You can use the Delete command in the Cells group to delete cells, ranges, rows, or columns. The principles for deleting cells are the same as those for inserting cells except that the direction the cells shift is reversed.

STEP BY STEP   Delete a Cell from a Worksheet

USE the worksheet you created in the previous exercise.

1. Select C3:C9. Click Delete in the Cells group. The Job Title data is removed from the worksheet, and the remaining columns are shifted left.
2. Select A9:N9 and click Delete. The duplicate entry of data is removed.
3. Select K13:K18 and click Cut in the Clipboard group.
4. Select M3 and click Paste. The November data is now pasted into the space you made when you shifted cells in the previous exercise. Your worksheet should now resemble the one shown in Figure 4-6.

Figure 4-6

Completed paste of cell group

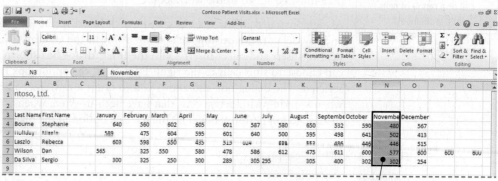

Moved Cells

5. **SAVE** your workbook.

PAUSE. LEAVE the workbook open to use in the next exercise.

CERTIFICATION
READY   **2.1.2**

How do you cut cells from a worksheet?

As shown, you can click Delete in the Cells group to eliminate cells from a worksheet. Any data to the right of the deleted cell or cells will automatically shift left. If you want to shift cells up rather than left, click the arrow next to Delete, then click Delete Cells to open the Delete dialog box.

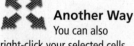

Another Way
You can also right-click your selected cells and then choose Delete on the shortcut menu to open the Delete dialog box.

Remember that when you use the Delete command, the cells themselves are deleted. In contrast, when you use the Cut command or press Delete on the keyboard, only the cell contents are deleted; the cells and any formatting remain.

MANUALLY FORMATTING CELL CONTENTS

The Bottom Line

The commands in the Font, Alignment, and Number groups (Figure 4-7) are used for basic formatting. Using only those groups, you can significantly change the appearance of a worksheet. Use Font commands to change font and font size; to bold, italicize, and underline data; and to add color, fill, and borders. Use Alignment commands to choose how data is aligned within cells. Use Number commands to apply a format to values and to increase or decrease the number of digits after a decimal.

Figure 4-7

Basic formatting command groups

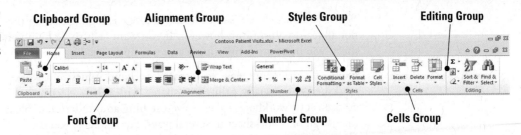

Selecting Cells and Ranges

To apply formatting to text and values in an existing worksheet, you must first select the data. When you select data, you identify the cell or range of cells in which you want to enter data or apply formatting. You can select cells, ranges, rows, columns, or the complete worksheet. The cells in a range can be adjacent or nonadjacent. You can also place a cell in editing mode and select all or part of its contents Table 4-1 offers information about making selections.

STEP BY STEP | **Select Cells and Ranges**

USE the workbook from the previous exercise to complete these steps:

1. Select cell A3. Hold down the left mouse button and drag to B8 to select the range, then release the mouse button.
2. Click the Row 3 heading to select the entire row.
3. Click the column C header, press and hold Ctrl, and click E, G, and I to select nonadjacent columns.
4. Click the File tab, then click Save As.
5. When the Save As dialog box opens, create a Lesson 4 folder.
6. SAVE your workbook in the folder and name it *Patient Visits*.

PAUSE. LEAVE the workbook open to use in the next exercise.

CERTIFICATION
READY   **2.1.4**

How do you select a
cell or cells?

Table 4-1

Making selections in Excel

To Select	Do This
A single cell	Click the cell or press the arrow keys to move the cell.
A range of cells	Click the first cell in the range and drag your cursor to the last cell, or hold down Shift while you press the arrow keys to extend the selection.
A large range of cells	Click the first cell in the range and hold down Shift while you click the last cell.
All cells in a worksheet	Click the Select All button (intersection of the column and row headings), or press Ctrl+A.
Nonadjacent cells or cell ranges	Select the first cell or range and hold down Ctrl while you select the other cells or ranges.
An entire row or column	Click the row or column heading.
Adjacent rows or columns	Drag your cursor across the row or column headings.
Nonadjacent rows or columns	Click the column or row heading of the first row or column of the selection. Hold down Ctrl while you click the column or row headings of other rows or columns you want to add to the selection.
The contents of a cell	Double-click the cell, then drag across the contents that you want to select.

When you make a selection, the cell or range is highlighted on the screen. These highlights do not appear in a printout, however. If you want cells to be highlighted when you print a worksheet, you must use formatting features to apply shading.

Excel provides many ways to format labels and values in a worksheet. In the business world, worksheets are usually printed or shared with others electronically. Therefore, you want your worksheet or workbook to be as eye-catching and understandable as possible. You can improve the design of a worksheet in several ways. For instance, you can:

- Change the alignment
- Change the font style and enlarge the text for titles
- Format titles and labels in bold and/or italics
- Apply special formatting attributes

Each of these formatting options is described in the following sections.

Aligning Cell Contents

Text and numbers in a worksheet can be aligned to the left, to the right, or at the center. By default, when you enter alphabetic characters or alphabetic characters combined with numbers or symbols, the cell content is left-aligned, but when you enter numbers, the content is right-aligned. You can use Alignment commands to change this default alignment or to override previous alignment formatting.

STEP BY STEP   **Align Cell Contents**

USE the worksheet you created in the previous exercise. Then, do the following:

1. Select **A3:N3**.
2. In the Alignment group, click **Center**. The column labels are now horizontally centered.
3. Click **C4**, press **Shift**, and click **N8**. The cell range containing the values is selected. Release the **Shift** key and click **Align Text Right**. All cells containing values are now right-aligned.

PAUSE. LEAVE the workbook open to use in the next exercise.

> **CERTIFICATION READY   3.1.1**
>
> How do you align cell content?

As illustrated in Figure 4-8, the alignment that has been applied to the active cell is shown by the highlighted commands in the Alignment group. Proper alignment and spacing greatly improve the readability of worksheet data.

Figure 4-8

Active cell alignment is highlighted

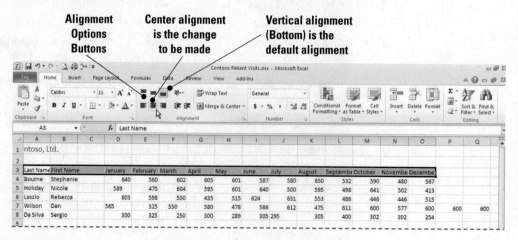

Choosing Fonts and Font Sizes

A **font** is a set of text characteristics designed to appear a certain way. The font determines the appearance of the cell contents. The **default**, or predefined, font for Excel 2010 is 11-point Calibri. This is an easy-to-read font that takes up less space than Arial, which was the default in earlier Excel versions.

STEP BY STEP   **Choose Fonts and Font Sizes**

USE the workbook from the previous exercise.

1. Select the column labels in row 3.

2. Click the Font arrow. Scroll up the list of font names and click Arial. Notice that the font size is unchanged (still 11 point), but Arial is larger than the default Calibri font. (See Figure 4-9.)

Figure 4-9

Changing fonts

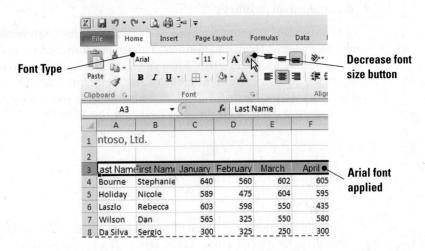

3. With row 3 still selected, click Decrease Font Size. The number 10 appears in the Font Size box, and the labels now fit within the column width.

4. SAVE the workbook.

PAUSE. LEAVE the workbook open to use in the next exercise.

On Excel's Options page, you can change the default font used in all new workbooks. If you chose a different default font and/or font size, that font is used only in workbooks that you create *after* you change the default and restart Excel. Existing workbooks are not affected.

Of course, you can also change the font for only a selected cell, a range of cells, or for characters within text. To change the font, select the font that you want in the Font box. You can then change the size in the Font Size box or click Increase Font Size or Decrease Font Size until the size you want is displayed in the Font Size box. To improve the overall design of a worksheet, the font size is usually enlarged for titles and labels.

Font size is measured in points. Each time you click Decrease Font Size or Increase Font Size, the size changes by a set amount that matches the size options on the Font Size list. **Points** refer to the measurement of the height of the characters in a cell. One point is equal to 1/72 inch.

Applying Special Character Attributes

In addition to changing font and font size, you can apply special **attributes** to a font that add visual appeal. An attribute is a formatting characteristic, such as bold, italic, or underlined text. Applying special characteristics to specific text or values adds interest to a worksheet and calls attention to specific data.

STEP BY STEP   **Apply Special Character Attributes**

USE the workbook from the previous exercise to carry out these steps:

1. Select A4. Hold down the left mouse button and drag to B8. Click Bold  in the Font group.
2. Click cell A3. Press Shift and click N3 to select the column labels. Click Italic in the Font group, then click Bold.
3. **SAVE** the workbook.

PAUSE. LEAVE the workbook open to use in the next exercise.

Although you are adding multiple instances of special formatting to the worksheets in these exercises to improve your skills, in real-life situations, it is wise to have a clear, logical design plan that presents data in an easy-to-understand format. To this end, it is best not to overuse special character attributes. Keep in mind that the focus of your worksheet should be on the data and the information it conveys.

When you select text for formatting, you can also use the **Mini toolbar**, shown in Figure 4-10, to apply selected formatting features. This unique formatting tool was new in Excel 2007 and has carried over to Excel 2010. When you right-click, the Mini toolbar displays above the short-cut menu. Just click any of the toolbar's available features to apply them to selected text. Unlike the Quick Access Toolbar, which can be customized, you cannot customize the Mini toolbar. However, you can turn off the Mini toolbar in Excel Options.

Figure 4-10

Mini toolbar

> Calibri ▾ 11 ▾ A˄ A˅ $ ▾ % , ▦
> B I ≡ ◇ ▾ A ▾ ⊞ ▾ ⁺₀₀ ⁰₀ ◈

Changing Font Color

Color enhances the visual appeal of a worksheet. To add color to the text in your worksheet, you must first select the cell, range of cells, text, or characters that you want to format with a different color. A **character** can be a letter, number, punctuation mark, or symbol.

STEP BY STEP   **Change Font Color**

USE the workbook from the previous exercise.

1. Select the column labels if they are not already selected. Click the Font Color arrow.
2. Click Blue in the list of standard colors. (See Figure 4-11.)

Figure 4-11

Font color options

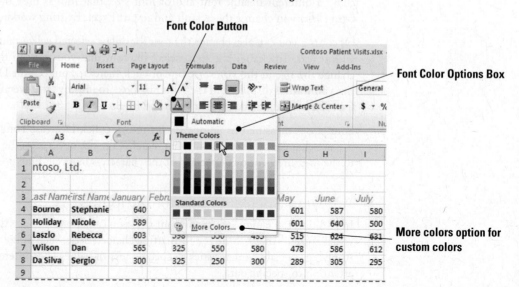

Font Color Button

Font Color Options Box

More colors option for custom colors

3. Select A4:B8. Click the Font Color arrow, then click Red in the standard colors.

4. **SAVE** the workbook.

PAUSE. LEAVE the workbook open to use in the next exercise.

Take Note   If you choose a color and change your mind, click Undo on the Quick Access Toolbar or press Ctrl+Z.

Black is the default, or automatic, font color in Excel, but you can easily change text color. The most recently applied color appears on the Font Color button. To apply that color, make a selection and click Font Color. To apply a different text color, click the arrow next to Font Color. You can choose a theme color or a standard color. You can also click More Colors to open the Colors dialog box, in which you can choose from additional standard colors or create colors to your own specifications.

 Ref

You will learn about Document Themes in Lesson 5. The default Office theme is the basis for the colors that appear under Theme Colors and Standard Colors on the Font Color menu.

Filling Cells with Color

You can also call attention to cells by adding a background color and/or pattern. You can use a solid color or apply special effects, such as gradients, textures, and pictures. Use the Fill Color command in the Font group to change the background color of a cell. The most recently used fill color appears on the Fill Color button.

STEP BY STEP   **Fill Cells with Color**

USE the workbook from the previous exercise and follow these steps:

1. Select A3:N3.

2. Click the Font Dialog Box Launcher.

3. Click the Fill tab.

4. In the Background Color section, click the light blue color (second box) in column 5, as shown in Figure 4-12.

Figure 4-12

New fill color

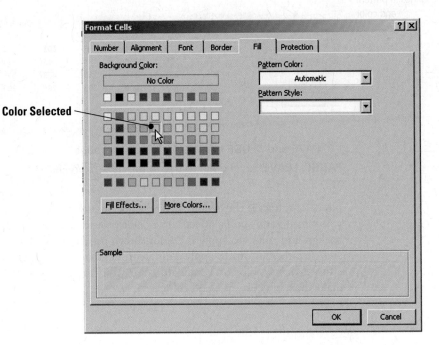

5. Add a second color in the Pattern Color box. Click the arrow and click the third box in column 5.

6. Click the Pattern Style arrow and click the pattern at the end of the first row. At the bottom of the dialog box, you can see a sample of how the pattern and color will look in the selected cells. Adjust any column widths to the appropriate size to accommodate the data. (See Figure 4-13.)

Figure 4-13

New pattern color and pattern style

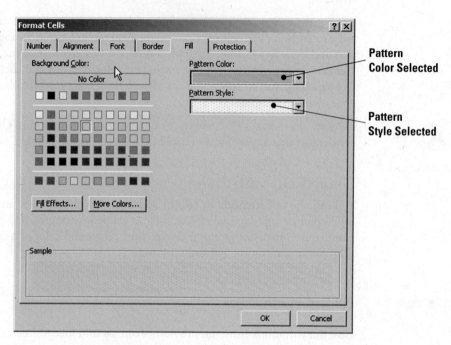

7. Click OK to apply the color and the fill pattern. Click in any empty cell to deselect your heading row. Your headings should resemble Figure 4-14.

Figure 4-14

Background changes in pattern and color

Pattern and color applied

	Last Name	First Name	January	February	March	April	May	June
4	Bourne	Stephanie	640	560	602	605	601	587
5	Holiday	Nicole	589	475	604	595	601	640
6	Laszlo	Rebecca	603	598	550	435	515	624
7	Wilson	Dan	565	325	550	580	478	586
8	Da Silva	Sergio	300	325	250	300	289	305
9								

8. SAVE and CLOSE the *Patient Visits* workbook.

PAUSE. LEAVE Excel open to use in the next exercise.

No color (clear) is the default background. To add color and shading, select the cells to which you want to add special effects. The color palette you used to apply font color is also used for background color. To apply the color shown on the Fill Color button, simply make a selection and click the button. To apply a different fill color, click the arrow next to Fill Color and apply either a theme color or a standard color. You can also click More Colors to open the Colors dialog box and custom blend colors.

As demonstrated, you can also apply a background color and add a pattern effect. To do so, first select the range of cells to which you want to apply a background color with fill effects, then click the Font group's Dialog Box Launcher. The Format Cells dialog box opens. Click the Fill tab. As shown in Figure 4-15, make a selection in the Pattern Style box to add a pattern to the background color.

Figure 4-15

Add a pattern to a cell's background color

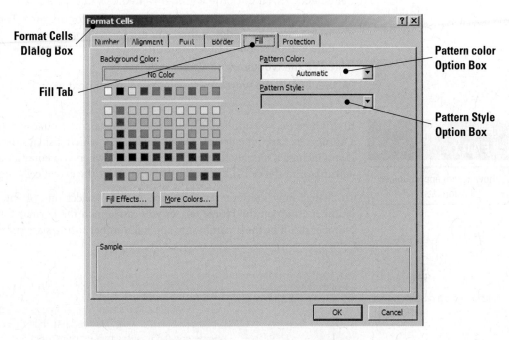

Applying Number Formats

Most of the data that you use in Excel is numeric. Applying accurate formatting to numeric data makes this information easier to interpret—and therefore more useful. Number formatting can be applied to cells before data is entered, or data can be selected and formatted after it has been entered. Formatting changes the appearance of numbers; it does not change their value. The actual value is always displayed in the formula bar.

STEP BY STEP   **Apply Number Formats**

GET READY. With Excel running, perform these actions:

 The *Contoso Revenue* file for this lesson is available on the book companion website or in WileyPLUS.

1. **OPEN** *Contoso Revenue*. Click the Sheet1 tab if necessary to make it the active worksheet.

2. Select B4:D10 and click the Accounting Number Format ($) button in the Number group. The selected data is reformatted to monetary values, the decimal points are aligned, and the column width is increased to accommodate the selected number format.

3. With the text still selected, click the Decrease Decimal button in the Number group twice. The data is rounded to whole dollars.

4. Select B10:D10. Click Comma Style (,) then click Decrease Decimal twice to show whole numbers. Row 10 data relates to the number of patients, not monetary values. Accounting style was inappropriately applied to this data.

WileyPLUS Extra! features an online tutorial of this task.

5. Click the Sheet2 tab.

6. Select B7:B11. Click the Number Dialog Box Launcher.

7. Click Number in the Category area. Key 0 in the *Decimal places* box and place a check mark in the *Use 1000 Separator* box. Click OK.

8. Format B6 with Accounting and zero decimals.

9. Select C7:C11. Click the Number Dialog Box Launcher.

10. The Number tab is active. Click Date in the Category area. Then click the 03/14/01 date style. Click OK. By doing this, you are formatting blank cells to accept data at a later date without having to reformat.

11. **SAVE** the workbook as *Revenue*.

PAUSE. LEAVE the workbook open to use in the next exercise.

CERTIFICATION READY   3.1.2

How do you apply number formats?

In this exercise, you applied formatting to Contoso's first-quarter revenue data. When you enter a number in Excel; the default format is General, which displays the data exactly as you enter it. If you include a special character such as $ or % when you enter a number, the special character will appear in the cell. The format does not affect the actual cell value.

To change how numeric data appears, you can select one of the formatting options in the Number group on the Home tab, or you can launch the Format Cells dialog box and click the Number tab. The most commonly applied number formats are summarized in Table 4-2.

Table 4-2

Number group buttons on the Home tab

Format Category	Description
General	This is the default number format that Excel applies when you key a number. Numbers are displayed just the way you key them. If a cell is not wide enough to show the entire number, a number with decimal places will be rounded.
Number	This format is used for the general display of numbers. You can specify the number of decimal places that you want to use, whether you want to use a thousands separator, and how you want to display negative numbers.
Currency	This format is used for general monetary values and displays the default currency symbol with numbers. You can specify the number of decimal places that you want to use, whether you want to use a thousands separator, and how you want to display negative numbers.
Accounting	This format is also used for monetary values. Currency symbols and decimal points are aligned in this format.
Date	This format displays days, months, and years in various styles, such as January 7, 2011, 7-Jan, and 1/7/2011.

If pound symbols (###) appear in a cell, it means that the numeric value entered is wider than the cell. If you plan to apply a number format to this data, it is not necessary to adjust column width first because the column width will be adjusted automatically when you apply a number format.

After you choose a number format, you will need to further specify how you want the numbers to appear. You can use the commands in the Number group to apply formats and to increase or decrease the number of decimal places displayed in worksheet data. When you decrease the number of decimal places, the data becomes less precise because the numbers following the decimal point are rounded. This lack of preciseness is insignificant, however, when you are dealing with large numbers.

Wrapping Text in a Cell

When a cell is formatted to wrap text, any data in the cell automatically breaks to fit the column width. If you later change the column width, the text wrapping adjusts automatically. When text is wrapped, row height is also adjusted to accommodate the wrap.

STEP BY STEP **Wrap Text in a Cell**

USE the workbook from the previous exercise to perform these steps:

1. Select **Sheet1**. Select cell **A7** and click **Wrap Text** in the Alignment group. The row height is adjusted and the cell's full text is displayed on two lines. (See Figure 4-16.)

Figure 4-16

Wrap Text button

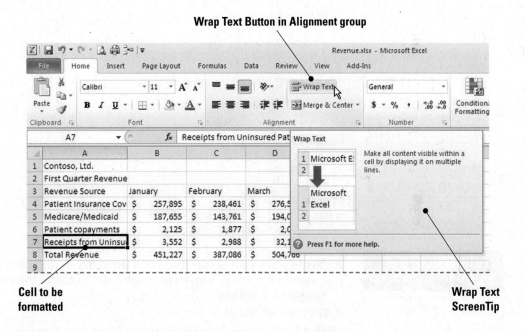

Wrap Text Button in Alignment group

Cell to be formatted

Wrap Text ScreenTip

Take Note   If you format a cell for text wrapping and all wrapped text is not visible, it may be because the row is set to a specific height. You will learn to modify row height in Lesson 5.

2. Double-click cell **A4**. The Status bar displays Edit, indicating that the cell is in edit mode. (See Figure 4-17.)

Figure 4-17

Cell in Edit mode

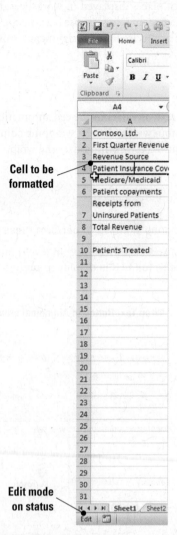

Cell to be formatted

Edit mode on status

CERTIFICATION READY   3.1.3

How do you wrap text in a cell?

3. Click to place your cursor just to the left of the word Coverage and press **Alt+Enter**. A manual line break is inserted. Press **Enter** to accept the change. You have manually wrapped the cell text.

4. **SAVE** the workbook.

PAUSE. LEAVE the workbook open to use in the next exercise.

Take Note   Remember that you can edit a cell in the formula bar as well as in the cell itself.

As demonstrated in this exercise, if you want the text in a cell to appear on multiple lines, you can format the cell so that the text wraps automatically, or you can enter a manual line break. To wrap text automatically, select the text you want to format and click Wrap Text in the Alignment group. To start a new line of text at a specific point in a cell, double-click the cell to place it in Edit mode, then click the location where you want to break the line and press Alt+Enter.

Merging and Splitting Merged Cells

You can use the Merge & Center command in the Alignment group to merge cells. A **merged cell** is created by combining two or more horizontally or vertically adjacent cells. When you merge cells, the selected cells become one large cell that spans multiple columns or rows. You can split cells that have been merged into separate cells again, but you cannot split a single worksheet cell that has not been merged. Merging is a useful tool when combining data from other sources.

STEP BY STEP   Merge and Split Merged Cells

USE the workbook from the previous exercise.

1. Select A1:D1. Click Merge & Center in the Alignment group. The content previously in cell A1 is now centered across columns A, B, C, and D. (See Figure 4-18.)

Figure 4-18

Merging and centering cells

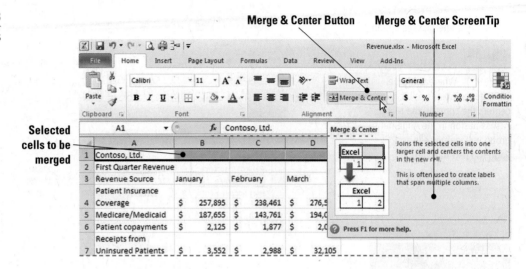

2. Select A2:D2. Click Merge & Center.
3. Select A4:A5 and click Merge & Center. A dialog box opens to remind you that the data in A5 will be deleted in the merge. (See Figure 4-19.)

Figure 4-19

Merge warning dialog box

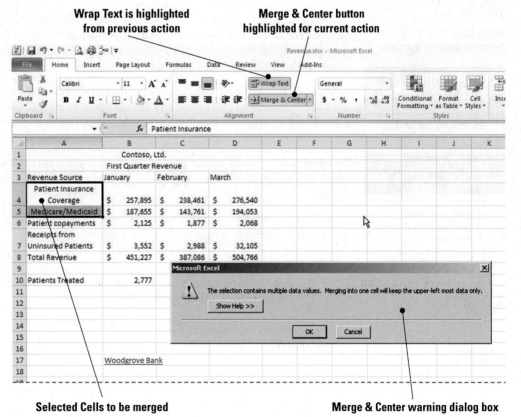

CERTIFICATION
READY   3.2.1

How do you merge and
center cells?

4. Click **OK**. Cells A4 and A5 are merged, and the data originally in A4 is centered in the merged cell.

5. Click the arrow next to **Merge & Center** and click **Unmerge Cells**. The cells are unmerged, but note that the data from cell A5 has been deleted.

6. Select **A5**, key **Medicare/Medicaid**, and press **Enter**. (See Figure 4-20.)

Figure 4-20

Unmerge cells option

Another Way
Whereas Merge
& Center combines cells and
centers the content, the Merge
Across button in the Alignment
group will merge cells and
align the text flush left.

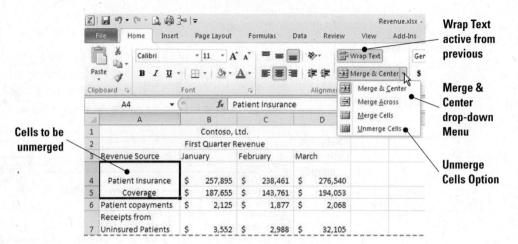

CERTIFICATION
READY   3.2.2

How do you merge
across cells?

Another Way
With a merged cell
active, you can click Merge &
Center to unmerge the cells.

7. Select **A4:A5** and click **Align Text Left** in the Alignment group.

8. **SAVE** the workbook.

PAUSE. LEAVE the workbook open to use in the next exercise.

As shown in the previous exercise, when you merge cells, the data that you want to appear in the merged cells will be the content from the upper-left cell of the selected range. Only the data in the upper-left cell will remain in the newly merged cell; data in the other cells included in the merge will be deleted.

CERTIFICATION
READY   3.2.3

How do you merge cells?

Cells can be merged in a row or a column—but in either situation, the content of the upper-left cell will be centered in the merged cell. If the cells to be merged contain information that will be deleted in the merge, the Excel dialog box shown in Figure 4-19 opens to caution you that only the content of the upper-left cell will remain after the merge.

CERTIFICATION
READY   3.2.4

How do you unmerge or
split merged cells?

To merge cells without centering the contents of the upper-left cell, click the arrow next to Merge & Center, then click Merge Cells. Any text you enter in such a merged cell will be left aligned.

With a merged cell active, click Merge & Center to split the merged cell. You can also click the arrow next to Merge & Center and choose Unmerge Cells.

Troubleshooting If the Merge & Center button is unavailable, the selected cells may be in editing mode. To cancel this mode, press Enter or Escape (Esc).

A merged cell takes the name of the original upper-left cell. As shown in Figure 4-21, when you merged cells A1:D1 in the previous exercise, the merged cell is named A1.

Figure 4-21

Merged cells have one name

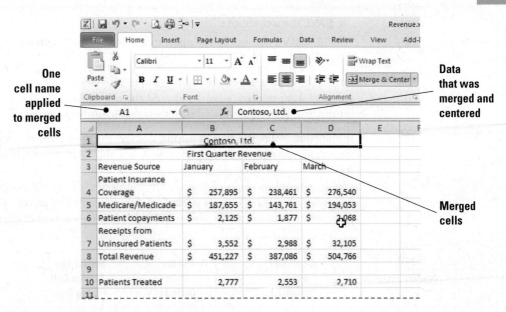

Placing Borders around Cells

You can use borders to enhance a worksheet's visual interest and to make it easier to read. You can either apply Excel's predefined border styles, or you can customize borders by specifying a line style and color of your choice. Borders are often used to set off headings, labels, or totals.

STEP BY STEP   **Place Borders around Cells**

USE the workbook from the previous exercise to complete these actions:

1. Select cell **A1** and click the arrow next to Bottom Border ⊞ ▾ in the Font group on the Ribbon.

2. Click **More Borders**. The *Format Cells* dialog box opens with the Border tab displayed.

3. Under Line, click the **Style** displayed in the **lower-right corner**.

4. Click the **Color arrow**, then click **Red**.

5. Under Presets, click **Outline**. The red border is previewed in the Border box.

6. Click **OK**. The dialog box closes and the border is applied to **A1**.

7. With **A1** selected, click **Increase Font Size** until the value in the Font Size box is 20 points. Click on cell A11. Your border should resemble Figure 4-22.

Figure 4-22

Formatted border

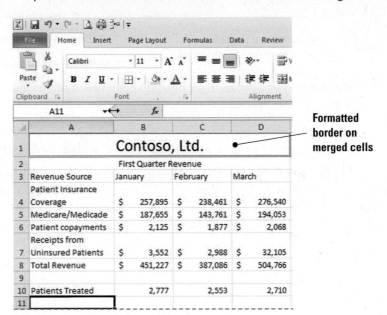

8. **SAVE** the workbook.

PAUSE. LEAVE the workbook open to use in the next exercise.

To add a border, select the cell or range of cells to which you want to call attention. For example, you may want to place a border around the titles, around the cells displaying the total revenue for the first quarter, or around the labels that identify the months.

In the Font group, the Border button displays the most recently used border style, and the button's name changes to that style name. Click the Border button (not the arrow) to apply that style, or you can click the arrow and choose a different border style. Click More Borders to apply a custom or diagonal border. On the Border tab of the Format Cells dialog box, click a line style and a color. You can select a border style from the presets or create a style with the line-placement options in the Border area. Notice that Figure 4-23 displays the two diagonal borders.

Figure 4-23

Borders options

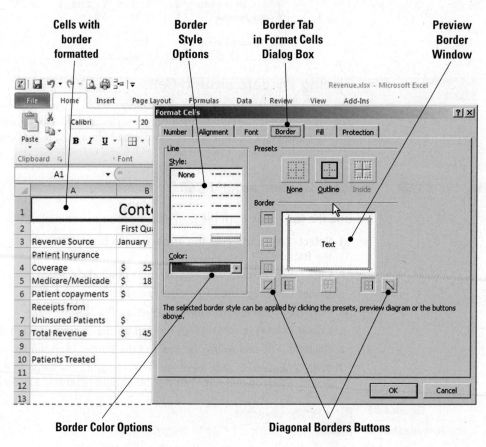

Cells with border formatted — **Border Style Options** — **Border Tab in Format Cells Dialog Box** — **Preview Border Window**

Border Color Options — **Diagonal Borders Buttons**

Take Note   If you apply two different types of borders to a shared cell boundary, the most recently applied border will be displayed.

COPYING CELL FORMATTING WITH THE FORMAT PAINTER

The Bottom Line

The **Format Painter** is an Excel feature that allows you to copy formatting from a cell or range of cells to another cell or range of cells. Located in the Clipboard group on the Home tab, it is one of Excel's most useful tools. It allows you to quickly copy attributes that you have already applied and "paint" those attributes onto other data.

CERTIFICATION READY   3.1.4

How do you use Format Painter?

Another Way
The Format Painter is available on the Mini toolbar as well as in the Clipboard group.

USE the workbook from the previous exercise.

1. With **A1** active, click **Format Painter**. A flashing border appears around A1, indicating this is the formatting to be copied.

2. Click cell **A2**.

3. With A2 selected, right-click to display the Mini toolbar. Click the Font Size arrow and choose 14. The font size of the subtitle is reduced.

4. Select **A1:A2** and click **Format Painter**.

5. Click the **Sheet2** tab and select **A1:A2**. The formatting from the Sheet1 titles have been applied to the Sheet2 titles.

6. Click the **Sheet1** tab.

7. **SAVE** the workbook.

PAUSE. LEAVE the workbook open to use in the next exercise.

You can use the Format Painter to copy formats, including font, font size, font style, font color, alignment, indentation, number formats, and borders and shading. To copy formatting from one location to another, select the cell or range that has the formatting you want to copy, then click Format Painter in the Clipboard group. The mouse pointer turns into a white plus sign with the paint brush beside it. Drag the mouse pointer across the cell or range of cells that you want to format.

To copy the formatting to several cells or ranges of cells, double-click Format Painter, and then drag the mouse pointer across each cell or range of cells that you want to format. When you're done, click Format Painter again or press Esc to turn off the Format Painter.

FORMATTING CELLS WITH STYLES

The Bottom Line

A **style** is a set of formatting attributes that you can apply to a cell or range of cells more easily than by setting each attribute individually. Style attributes include fonts and font sizes, number formats, and borders and shading. Excel has several predefined styles that you can apply; you can also modify or duplicate a cell style to create a custom cell style.

Applying a Cell Style

To apply a cell style to an active cell or range, click Cell Styles in the Styles group on the Home tab, then choose the cell style that you want to apply. You can apply more than one style to a cell or range.

STEP BY STEP   **Apply a Cell Style**

USE the workbook from the previous exercise.

1. With cells A1:A2 already selected, click **Cell Styles** in the Styles group. The Cell Styles gallery opens. (See Figure 4-24.)

Figure 4-24

Cell Styles gallery

Cell Styles Button

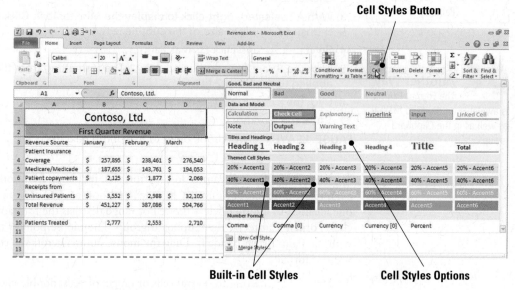

Built-in Cell Styles   **Cell Styles Options**

2. Click **20%—Accent4** under *Themed Cell Styles*. The themed shading is applied to A1 and A2. The style changes the font size as well as the cell shading.

3. Select **A1** and click **Cell Styles**.

4. Click **Heading 1** under *Titles and Headings*. This heading style is now applied to the cell.

5. Select **A2** and click **Cell Styles**. The cell style has just been applied to the cell.

6. Click **Heading 2** under *Titles and Headings*. This heading style is now applied to the cell.

7. Select **A8:D8** and click **Cell Styles**.

8. Click **Total** under *Titles and Headings*. This heading style is now applied to the range of cells. Then click cell A12. Your worksheet should resemble Figure 4-25.

Figure 4-25

Worksheet with styles applied

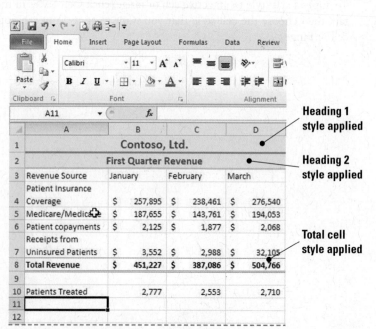

Heading 1 style applied

Heading 2 style applied

Total cell style applied

9. SAVE the workbook.

PAUSE. LEAVE the workbook open to use in the next exercise.

When you view defined styles in the Cell Styles gallery, you can see the formatting that will be used when you apply each style. This feature allows you to assess the formatting without actually applying it.

Experiment with combining styles to achieve your desired effect. For example, you can click a themed cell style, which will apply shading to the cell. Then, you can click Cell Styles again and click Heading 1, which applies font face, font size, and special formatting effects such as bold or italics.

If you are not pleased with a style you apply, you can Undo the style or apply another style to the cell or range. To remove a cell style from selected cells without deleting the cell style, select the cells that are formatted with that cell style. Click Cell Styles and click Normal. To delete the cell style and remove it from all cells formatted with that style, right-click the cell with the cell style, then click Delete.

Take Note   You cannot delete the Normal cell style.

Modifying a Cell Style

You can also modify or duplicate a cell style to create your own custom style. When doing so, you can either add or delete style attributes.

STEP BY STEP   **Modify a Cell Style**

USE the workbook from the previous exercise.

1. With A12 active, click **Cell Styles** in the *Styles* group. The *Cell Styles* gallery opens.
2. Right-click **20%—Accent6** under *Themed Cell Styles*. Click **Duplicate**. See Figure 4-26. The Style dialog box opens.

Figure 4-26

Right-click option on a style

Cell Styles Option Box   Cell Styles Button

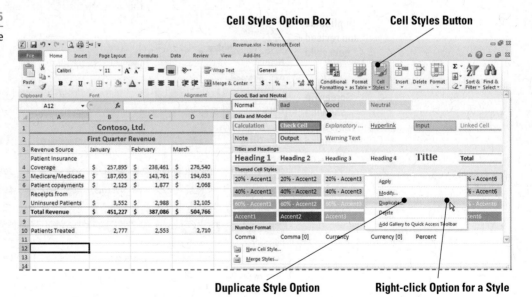

Duplicate Style Option   Right-click Option for a Style

3. Key **Accent Revised** in the Style name box.
4. Click **Format**. Click the Font tab.
5. Click **Italic** in the Font style box.

6. Click **12** in the Size box.

7. Click the **Border** tab and click your choice of a broken line in the Line Style box.

8. Click the two diagonal borders below the Border box. Click **OK**. Your formatting modifications will be shown in the Style dialog box. (See Figure 4-27.)

Figure 4-27

Formatting options changed in the Style dialog box

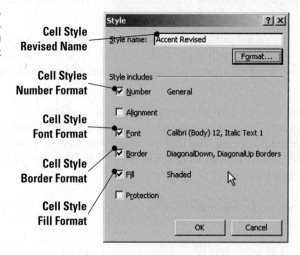

Cell Style Revised Name

Cell Styles Number Format

Cell Style Font Format

Cell Style Border Format

Cell Style Fill Format

9. Click **OK** to close the dialog box.

10. Click **Cell Styles** in the Styles group. Your Accent Revised cell style should be the first style in the *Custom* section. Click **Accent Revised** to apply the style to A12.

11. Use the **Format Painter** to apply your style to B12:D12. Double-click on cell **A15**. Your changes should resemble Figure 4-28.

Figure 4-28

New style in styles option box

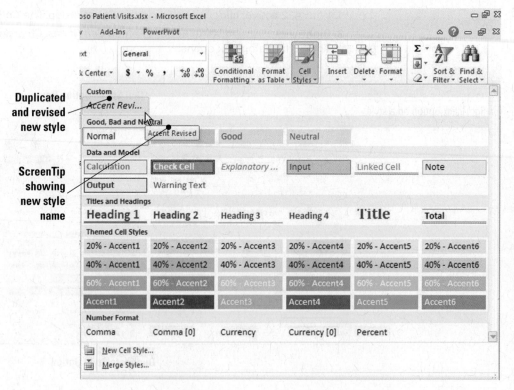

Duplicated and revised new style

ScreenTip showing new style name

12. **SAVE** the workbook.

PAUSE. LEAVE the workbook open to use in the next exercise.

CERTIFICATION READY 3.6.2

How do you create a new cell style?

In this exercise, you duplicated a cell style and then modified the style to create your own custom style. Your custom style was added to the styles gallery. If you had used the Modify command, the existing style would have reflected the formatting changes you made.

Duplicating an existing style and then modifying it is preferable. To modify an existing style, click Cell Styles in the Styles group. When the styles gallery is displayed, right-click the cell style that you want to change, then click Modify. The Style dialog box shown in Figure 4-29 will open with the current style name displayed but not accessible. This tells you that any changes you make to the style will be made to the existing style rather than a customized style.

Figure 4-29

Style dialog box

If you'd rather create a new customized style, right-click a style, then click Duplicate. Key an appropriate name for the new cell style you want to create. Then, to change the cell style, click Format. The Format Cells dialog box opens. On the various tabs in the dialog box, select the formatting that you want for the new style. Click OK when you have completed your changes. The changes will be reflected on the Style dialog box. When you are satisfied with the style attributes, click OK. The new cell style is added to the styles gallery and identified as a custom style.

WORKING WITH HYPERLINKED DATA

The Bottom Line

For quick access to related information in another file or on a web page, you can insert a hyperlink in a worksheet cell. Hyperlinks enable you to supplement worksheet data with additional information and resources.

A **hyperlink** is an image or a sequence of characters that opens another file or web page when you click it. The target file or web page can be on the World Wide Web, on an intranet, or on your personal computer. In a workbook containing your personal banking records, for example, you might insert a hyperlink to jump to your bank's online bill-paying service.

Placing a Hyperlink in a Cell

It is easy to embed a hyperlink in a workbook cell. Just click the cell where you want to create the hyperlink and identify the source to which you want to connect. The resulting hyperlink appears in the cell as blue underlined text. When you point to the hyperlink, a ScreenTip describing the link or giving the location of the file appears.

STEP BY STEP   **Place a Hyperlink in a Cell**

USE the workbook from the previous exercise. Verify that you can access the Internet, then perform these steps:

1. With cell A15 active, click the Ribbon's Insert tab.
2. Click Insert Hyperlink in the Links group. The Insert Hyperlink dialog box opens, as shown in Figure 4-30.

Figure 4-30

Insert Hyperlink dialog box

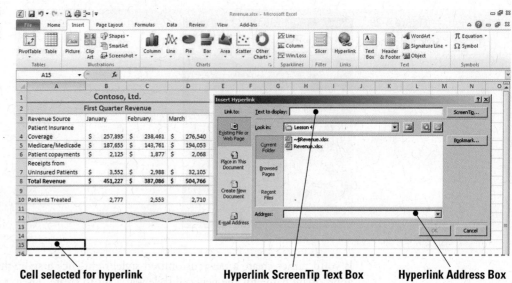

Another Way
Ctrl+K will open the Insert Hyperlink dialog box, or you can right-click and then select Hyperlink on the shortcut menu.

Cell selected for hyperlink   Hyperlink ScreenTip Text Box   Hyperlink Address Box

Take Note   When you key www, Excel recognizes it as the beginning of a web address and *http://* is supplied automatically.

3. In the *Text to display* box, key Microsoft. This is the blue, underlined text that will appear in A15.
4. Click ScreenTip. The *Set Hyperlink ScreenTip* dialog box opens.

CERTIFICATION
READY   2.3.3

How do you change the text that appears onscreen in a hyperlinked cell?

5. Key Go to Microsoft's Help and Support Center. Click OK. The text you keyed will replace the default ScreenTip.
6. In the Address box, key www.support.microsoft.com and click OK. The hyperlink text appears in A15. Click on cell B15.

7. Point to the cell containing the hyperlink. Notice the customized ScreenTip displays. The newly inserted hyperlink and ScreenTip are shown in Figure 4-31.

Figure 4-31

Hyperlink inserted in cell

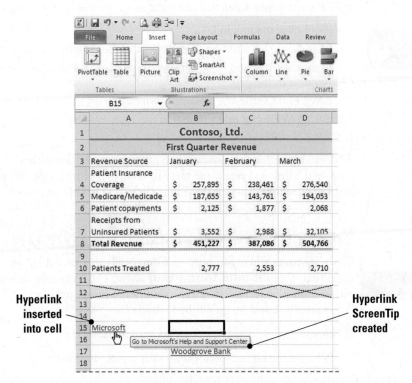

8. Click the left mouse button to open the hyperlink. The web browser opens and connects to Microsoft's Help and Support.

9. Click the **Excel** button on the taskbar to return to your workbook.

10. Key **[your email address]** in A17 and press **Enter**. If you do not have an email address, key *someone@example.com*.

11. **SAVE** the workbook.

PAUSE. LEAVE the workbook open to use in the next exercise.

In this exercise, you created a hyperlink using the Hyperlink command on the Insert tab. You can also create a hyperlink to an email address or an Internet address by typing the address directly in the cell. For example, if you key someone@example.com or www.microsoft.com in a worksheet cell, an automatic hyperlink is created.

The default ScreenTip identifies the full address of the hyperlink and provides instructions for following the link. You can specify the information you want in the tip when you create the link or you can edit it later, as shown in Figure 4-31.

To edit a hyperlink, click and hold to select the cell containing the hyperlink. Right-click and then click Edit Hyperlink to open the Edit Hyperlink dialog box. You can edit the text that displays in the link, the ScreenTip text, or the address where the link will take you. You also can cut or copy a hyperlink and paste it into another cell in the worksheet or another worksheet altogether.

Removing a Hyperlink from a Cell

Within Excel, you can delete a hyperlink and the text that represents it, turn off a single hyperlink, or turn off several hyperlinks at once.

Remove a Hyperlink from a Cell

CERTIFICATION
READY   **2.3.4**

How do you remove a
hyperlink from a cell?

USE the workbook from the previous exercise and do the following:

1. Right-click the link in D17.
2. Click Clear Contents on the shortcut menu. The hyperlink and text are removed.
3. Right-click B17 and click Remove Hyperlink. The hyperlink is removed and the text remains in the cell.
4. **SAVE** and **CLOSE** the *Revenue* workbook.

PAUSE. LEAVE Excel open to use in the next exercise.

As demonstrated in this exercise, you can remove a hyperlink and the associated text, or you can remove the link and retain the text. To remove multiple links, press Shift and select the hyperlinks to be removed or deleted. Right-click and click the appropriate action.

APPLY CONDITIONAL FORMATTING TO CELLS

The Bottom Line

There are times when you want to format cells in a particular way only if they meet a specific condition. **Conditional formatting** allows you to specify how cells that meet a given condition should be displayed. Thus, conditional formatting means that Excel applies formatting automatically, based on established criteria.

When you analyze data, you often ask questions, such as:

- Who are the highest performing sales representatives?
- In what months were revenues highest or lowest?
- What are the trends in profits over a specified time period?

Conditional formatting helps answer such questions by highlighting interesting cells or ranges of cells. With conditional formatting, fonts become visual guides that help the reader understand data distribution and variation.

Using the Rule Manager to Apply Conditional Formats

On what conditions or criteria do you want to analyze the data contained in a worksheet? The answer to this question provides the basis for establishing conditional formats. Once data is selected, you can choose one of five preset specific conditional formats that provide a visual analysis of a worksheet or selected range of data. For example, you can specify that when the value in a cell is greater than a given number, the value will be displayed with a particular font or background color. You can even establish multiple conditional formatting rules for a data range.

Use the Rule Manager to Apply Conditional Formats

@ The *Patient Visit Data* file for this lesson is available on the book companion website or in WileyPLUS.

WileyPLUS Extra! features an online tutorial of this task.

GET READY. OPEN the *Patient Visit Data* file. Then, do the following:

1. Click the Home tab if it is not active. Select A1:N1. Merge and center the range and apply the Heading 1 style. (Refer to the "Merge & Split Cells" and the "Apply a Cell Style" exercises as a reference if needed.)
2. Select A2:N2. Merge and center the range and apply the Heading 2 style.
3. Select C4:N8 and click Conditional Formatting in the Styles group.
4. Click Highlight Cells Rules and click Greater Than.
5. In the *Greater Than* dialog box, key 600 and click OK. The highlighted data represents the months in which the doctors were seeing more than the ideal number of patients.
6. With the range still selected, click Conditional Formatting.

7. Mouse over Highlight Cells Rules and click Less Than.

8. In the *Less Than* dialog box, key 560. In the *With* box, select Green Fill with Dark Green Text and click OK. The highlight now contrasts the months in which the patient load was less than expected. Refer to the *Conditional Formatting* dialog box in Figure 4-32.

Figure 4-32

Conditional formatting Less Than box

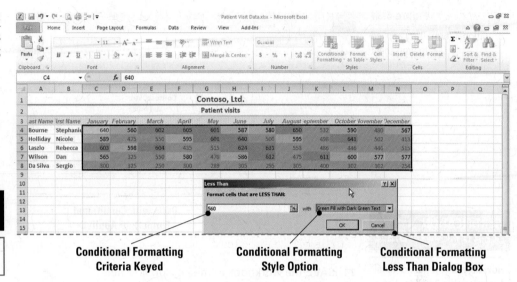

Conditional Formatting Criteria Keyed

Conditional Formatting Style Option

Conditional Formatting Less Than Dialog Box

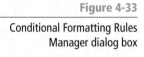

CERTIFICATION READY   8.3.1

How do you apply a conditional cell format?

9. Click Conditional Formatting and mouse over Top/Bottom Rules.

10. Click Top 10%. In the dialog box, accept 10% and click Yellow Fill with Dark Yellow Text. Click OK.

11. Click Conditional Formatting and click Manage Rules at the bottom of the list.

12. In the *Show formatting rules for* box, click This Worksheet. The three conditional formatting rules you have applied are displayed. Position the Conditional Formatting Rules Manager dialog box below the worksheet data so you can view the data and the conditional formatting rules. Notice that the first and third rules apply to overlapping data. Therefore, if a cell value exceeds 600 and that value also falls within the top 10%, the 10% formatting will be applied. See Figure 4-33.

Figure 4-33

Conditional Formatting Rules Manager dialog box

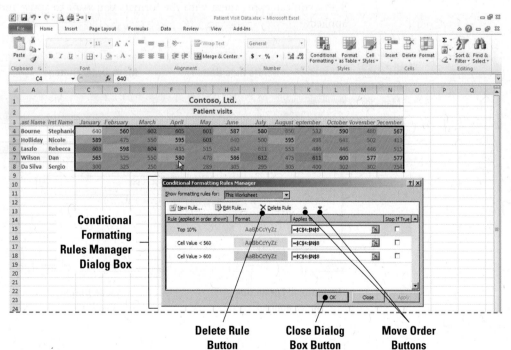

Conditional Formatting Rules Manager Dialog Box

Delete Rule Button

Close Dialog Box Button

Move Order Buttons

13. Click the Cell Value > 600 rule and click the up arrow twice to move the rule to the top of the list. Click Apply and then click OK. Click the Close button to close the *Conditional Formatting* dialog box. Click on any empty cell to deselect the range. All values greater than 600 are now formatted with the dark red font. Click in any empty cell. Your worksheet should resemble Figure 4-34.

Figure 4-34

Conditional formatting applied to worksheet

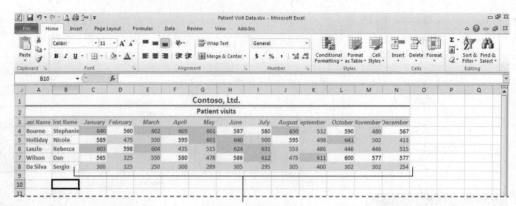

Cells with Conditional Formatting Applied

CERTIFICATION READY   8.3.2

How do you apply conditional formats using Rule Manager?

14. **SAVE** the workbook in the Lesson 4 folder.

PAUSE. LEAVE the workbook open to use in the next exercise.

In this lesson's exercises, you have worked with data related to the number of patients treated each month at Contoso, Ltd. You can use Excel's Rule Manager to apply conditional formatting to provide visual analyses of the data in the *Patient Visit Data* workbook.

In addition, you can display the Conditional Rules Manager to see what rules are in effect for the worksheet and apply those rules at an appropriate time. From the Conditional Formatting Rules Manager, you can add new rules, edit existing rules, or delete one or all of the rules. The rules are applied in the order in which they are listed in the Conditional Formatting Rules Manager. You can apply all the rules, or you can apply specific rules to analyze the data. As you can see in Figure 4-35, formatting is visible when the Conditional Formatting Rules Manager is open. Thus, you can experiment with the formats you want to apply and the order in which they are applied.

Figure 4-35

Conditional Formatting Rules Manager

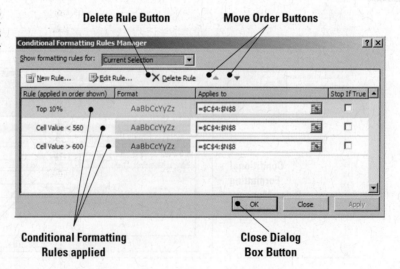

Delete Rule Button   Move Order Buttons

Conditional Formatting Rules applied

Close Dialog Box Button

Applying Multiple Conditional Formatting Rules

Multiple conditional formatting rules can be true. By default, new rules are always added to the top of the list and therefore have a higher precedence. Conditional formatting takes precedence over manual formatting that has been applied to the worksheet or any given cell or range, as shown in the following exercise.

STEP BY STEP | **Applying Multiple Conditional Formatting Rules**

USE the workbook from the previous exercise.

1. Click on the Column C header to highlight the entire column. Click on the arrow below the Insert Rows button then click Insert Sheet Columns. A new column is inserted. The Format Painter button emerges with your new column. Click on it and accept the first option (default) of *Format Same as Left*.

2. Click on C3 and key Job Title, then press Enter.

3. In cell C4, key Physician, then press Enter. Click C4 again to activate it, then click and hold and drag the contents to C7.

4. Click C8 and key PA. You have now reentered the data that was removed in a previous exercise.

5. Select D8:O8. Click Conditional Formatting and click Highlight Cells Rules.

6. Click Less Than. Key 300 in the value box and click Red Text. Click OK.

7. Click Conditional Formatting, then click Manage Rules. In the *Show formatting rules for* box, click This Worksheet. Although the last rule has the highest precedence, it applies only to the PA's schedule and therefore does not conflict with any of the rules that apply to the physicians' schedules.

8. Click the Close button to close the dialog box. You will not apply any changes in the *Conditional Formatting Manager* dialog box. Click on any empty cell to view your changes.

9. SAVE the workbook.

PAUSE. LEAVE the workbook open to use in the next exercise.

Applying Specific Conditional Formats

Excel has three preset conditional formats that use color and symbols to provide visual guides to help you understand data distribution and variation: color scales, icon sets, and data bars.

STEP BY STEP | **Apply Specific Conditional Formats**

USE the workbook from the previous exercise. Then, do the following:

1. Click Conditional Formatting.

2. Mouse over Clear Rules and then click Clear Rules from Entire Sheet. All conditional formatting is cleared from the data.

3. Select D4:O8. Click Conditional Formatting.

4. Mouse over Data Bars and click Blue Data Bar in the *Gradient Fill* section (first choice). Data bars show that the longer the dark blue portion of the bar is, the higher the value is in relation to other cells in the data range.

5. Repeat Steps 1 and 2 to clear the Data Bars. (See Figure 4-36.) The data range will still be selected.

Figure 4-36

Clear data bars or conditional formatting

Conditional Formatting Button

Conditional Formatting Drop-down Menu

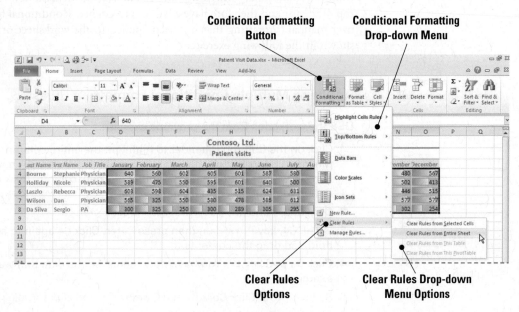

Clear Rules Options

Clear Rules Drop-down Menu Options

6. Click Conditional Formatting. Mouse over Color Scales and click the Red-Yellow-Green Color Scale (first option in the second column). The darker colors indicate the lower values.

7. Once again refer to Steps 1 and 2 to clear the Formatting Rules. Refer to Figure 4-36 if necessary. Click Conditional Formatting. Mouse over Icon Sets then click the 3 Flags set in the Indicators group.

8. **SAVE** the workbook as *Patient Visits with Icons*.

PAUSE. LEAVE the workbook open to use in the next exercise.

CERTIFICATION READY   8.3.5

How do you use icon sets?

CERTIFICATION READY   8.3.6

How do you use data bars?

A two-color scale helps you compare a range of cells by using a gradation of two colors. The shade of the color represents higher or lower values. The shade of the color in a three-color scale represents higher, middle, and lower values.

You can use an icon set to interpret and classify data into three to five categories. Each icon represents a range of values. For example, in the three-flag icon set, the green flag represents higher values, the yellow represents middle values, and the red represents lower values.

A data bar helps you see the value of a cell relative to other cells in the data range. The length of the data bar represents the value in the cell. A longer bar represents a higher value, and a shorter bar represents a lower value. Data bars are useful in spotting higher and lower numbers, especially with large amounts such as those in a retailer's after-Thanksgiving sales report.

CLEARING A CELL'S FORMATTING

The Bottom Line

The Clear command in the Editing group on the Home tab lets you clear contents and formatting or allows you to selectively remove contents or formatting. When you want to redesign the appearance of an existing worksheet, click Clear and then click Clear Formats. The content will remain, and you then can choose to apply manual formatting, styles, or conditional formatting. Clearing all formatting ensures that you are starting with a clean formatting slate.

STEP BY STEP   **Clear a Cell's Formatting**

USE the workbook from previous exercise.

1. Press **Ctrl+A** to select the entire worksheet.

2. Click the **Clear button** in the *Editing* group. (See Figure 4-37.)

3. Click **Clear Formats**. All formatting is cleared from the data. If you selected Clear All, the data would be removed as well as the formatting.

Figure 4-37

Clear button and options in the Editing group

Clear Button in Editing Group

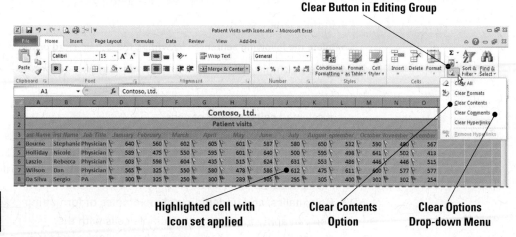

Highlighted cell with Icon set applied   **Clear Contents Option**   **Clear Options Drop-down Menu**

CERTIFICATION READY   8.3.4

How do you clear conditional formatting rules?

4. **CLOSE** the file without saving.

CLOSE Excel.

Take Note

If you select Clear All, contents and formatting are removed. Selecting Clear Contents will remove the data within the selected range, but the formatting will remain.

SKILL SUMMARY

In This Lesson You Learned How To:	Exam Objective	Objective Number
Inserting and Deleting Cells	Move cell data.	2.1.3
	Cut cell data.	2.1.2
Manually Formatting Cell Contents	Select cell data.	2.1.4
	Align cell content.	3.1.1
	Apply a number format.	3.1.2
	Use Merge & Center.	3.2.1
	Merge across.	3.2.2
	Wrap text in a cell.	3.1.3
	Merge cells.	3.2.3
	Unmerge cells.	3.2.4
Copying Cell Formatting with the Format Painter	Use Format Painter.	3.1.4
Formatting Cells with Styles	Apply cell styles.	3.6.1
	Construct new cell styles.	3.6.2
Working with Hyperlinked Data	Create a hyperlink.	2.3.1
	Modify hyperlinks.	2.3.2
	Modify hyperlinked cell attributes.	2.3.3
	Remove a hyperlink.	2.3.4
Applying Conditional Formatting to Cells	Apply conditional formatting to cells.	8.3.1
	Use the Rule Manager to apply conditional formats.	8.3.2
	Use icon sets.	8.3.5
	Use data bars.	8.3.6
Clearing a Cell's Formatting	Clear rules.	8.3.4

Knowledge Assessment

Fill in the Blank

Complete the following sentences by writing the correct word or words in the blanks provided.

1. When a single cell is created by combining two or more selected cells, the new cell is referred to as a(n) _____.

2. A(n) _____ is a set of formatting attributes that you can apply as a group to a selected cell or range of cells.

3. A shortcut or link that opens a stored document or connects with the Internet is called a(n) _____.

4. When formatting is applied to data based on established criteria, it is said to be _____ formatting.

5. Bold, italics, and underlining are examples of formatting _____.

6. You can apply formatting to multiple cells with the _____.

7. By default, a feature introduced in Excel 2007 called the _____ displays above the right-click shortcut menu.

8. Font sizes can be changed by clicking the _____ button on the Ribbon.

9. The _____ option allows you to change the font color, font type, and heading styles for a cell's content.

10. Right-clicking on a built-in Cell Style and selecting any option from the drop-down menu opens the _____ dialog box.

True/False

Circle T if the statement is true or F if the statement is false.

T F 1. When you insert a cell into a row, all data in that row is shifted down.

T F 2. When you shift cells down and data in another cell is replaced, that data is copied to the Office Clipboard.

T F 3. You can select a large range of cells by selecting the first cell in the range, pressing Shift, and selecting the last cell in the range.

T F 4. You can merge cells horizontally, but not vertically.

T F 5. If you want the dollar sign and decimals to align in a column, apply the Accounting format.

T F 6. When you wrap text in a cell, the row height is automatically adjusted to accommodate the multiple-line text.

T F 7. Any cell in a worksheet can be split.

T F 8. When you apply a style to text, any conflicting formatting in the cell or range is replaced by the style format.

T F 9. When you choose the Remove a hyperlink option, the link and the text are removed.

T F 10. If you select an entire worksheet and click Clear and Clear All, then the worksheet will be blank.

Competency Assessment

Project 4-1: Apply Basic Formatting

In this project, you will apply formatting attributes to a workbook used to track annual utilities expenses.

GET READY. LAUNCH Excel if it is not already running. Then, do the following:

@ The *Utilities* file for this lesson is available on the book companion website or in WileyPLUS.

1. Click the File tab and click Open.
2. **OPEN** the *Utilities* file from the data files for this lesson.
3. Select A8:G8. Click the Insert arrow in the Cells group and click Insert Cells.
4. Click OK on the Insert dialog box to shift the cells down.
5. Select A27:G27 and click Cut in the Clipboard group.
6. Select A8 and click Paste in the Clipboard group.
7. Select A2:G2. Click Bold in the Font group.
8. Select the column labels and click Center in the Alignment group.
9. With the column labels still selected, click the Font Color arrow and click Red.
10. Click Quick Print on the Quick Access Toolbar.
11. Click the File tab. Click Save As.
12. **SAVE** the workbook as *Utilities 4-1* in your Lesson 4 folder.

LEAVE the workbook open for the next project.

Project 4-2: Enhance a Worksheet Appearance

In this exercise, you will apply additional formatting attributes to an existing workbook.

USE the workbook from Project 4-1. Then, perform these steps:

1. Select A1. Click the arrow in the Font box and click Cambria.
2. With A1 still selected, click Increase Font Size until the Font Size box shows 16 point.
3. Apply the Green font color to the title.
4. Select A1:G1 and click Merge & Center in the Alignment group.
5. With only the merged A1 cell still selected, click Middle Align in the Alignment group.
6. Select F2 and click Wrap Text in the Alignment group.
7. With F2 selected, click the Format Painter in the Clipboard group. Drag the Format Painter across all column labels.
8. Adjust column width if necessary so that all column labels are completely visible.
9. Select the labels and click Middle Align.
10. Click B3, press Shift, and click G15 to select the range that contains values. Apply the Number format to the range.
11. Print the worksheet.
12. **SAVE** the workbook as *Utilities 4-2* in the Lesson 4 folder.

CLOSE the workbook. **LEAVE** Excel open for the next project.

Proficiency Assessment

Project 4-3: Format Training Budget

Graphic Design Institute's Training Department provides in-house technical and soft-skills training for the firm's 1,200 employees. Apply the formatting skills you learned in Lesson 4 to give the Training Budget worksheet a professional finish.

@ The *Training Budget* file for this lesson is available on the book companion website or in WileyPLUS.

GET READY. OPEN *Training Budget* from the data files for this lesson. Then, do the following:

1. Merge and center cells A1:E1.
2. Key Graphic Design Institute as the worksheet title.
3. Click Cell Styles in the Styles group and apply the 40%—Accent1 style to the title.
4. Click Cell Styles and apply the Heading 1 style.
5. Merge and center cells A2:E2. Key the subtitle Training Department Budget.
6. Apply the 20%—Accent1 fill to the subtitle. Apply the Heading 2 style.
7. Merge and center the blank row above the column labels.
8. Select the column labels and apply the Note style.
9. Key TOTAL in A18 and apply the Total style to row 18.
10. Select D6:E17. Click the Number group Dialog Box Launcher. Click the Number category, set decimal places to 0, and check Use 1000 separator.
11. Select the nonadjacent cells D5:E5, E18. Apply the Currency format and reduce decimals to 0.
12. Print the worksheet.
13. SAVE the workbook as *Training Budget 4-3*.

LEAVE the workbook open for the next project.

Project 4-4: Hyperlinks

In this project, you will create and edit hyperlinks that connect a worksheet with selected web pages. You'll then insert links to send email messages to selected recipients.

USE the *Training Budget 4-3* workbook from Project 4-3.

1. Label cell B4 Contact.
2. Click the Insert tab.
3. Select B5 and click Hyperlink.
4. Key A. Datum Corporation as the text to display.
5. Key www.adatum.com in the address box. Click OK.
6. In B11, create a hyperlink that displays as Lucerne Publishing at www.lucernepublishing.com.
7. In B16, create a hyperlink for Margie's Travel. The address is www.margiestravel.com.
8. Select B16 and click Hyperlink to open the Edit Hyperlink dialog box. Edit the ScreenTip to read Corporate contract for all travel.
9. Select B13 and create an email link for the consultant: someone@example.com.
10. PRINT the worksheet. SAVE the workbook as *Training Budget 4-4*. CLOSE the workbook.

LEAVE Excel open for the next project.

Mastery Assessment

Project 4-5: Format Sales Report

Litware, Inc., wants to apply Font and Alignment group formatting to enhance its sales report's appearance and readability. You are responsible for making this change.

GET READY. OPEN *Litware Sales* from the data files for this lesson. Then take the following actions:

@ The *Litware Sales* file for this lesson is available on the book companion website or in WileyPLUS.

1. Merge and center the title and apply the Heading 1 style.
2. Merge and center the subtitle and apply the Heading 2 style.
3. Select A1:G2 Click the Border arrow to open the Format Cells dialog box.
4. Under Line Style, select the last line style in column 2.
5. Click the Color arrow and click Red.
6. Click Outline and Inside in Presets. Click OK.
7. Select B4 and use the fill handle to extend the months across the remaining columns of data.
8. Select the labels in row 4. Center the labels and apply the Red font color. Add a Thick Box border.
9. Apply the Accounting format to the values in row 5. Reduce decimals to 0.
10. Select B6:G12 and apply the Number format with comma separator and 0 decimals.
11. Apply the Total style to row 13.
12. **PRINT** the workbook. **SAVE** the workbook as *Litware Sales 4-5*.

LEAVE the workbook open for the next project.

Project 4-6: Apply Conditional Formatting to the Sales Report

Next, you will apply conditional formatting to the Litware, Inc., sales report to highlight the top performing sales representatives.

USE the workbook from Project 4-5.

1. Select B13:G13.
2. Click Conditional Formatting and click Highlight Cells Rules.
3. Click Greater Than. In the Greater Than dialog box, key 140,000 and click OK. Total sales exceed $140,000 for February and May.
4. Select B5:G12. Click Conditional Formatting, click Top/Bottom Rules, and then click Top 10%. When the dialog box opens, four cells are highlighted.
5. Drag the dialog box below the data range. Change the Top percentage number to 1. Format cells that rank in the Top 1% with a red border and click OK. Deborah Poe was the top sales performer with $25,874 for the month of May.
6. Click Conditional Formatting and click Icon Sets. Click 3 Flags. Colored flags are applied to the sales data. Green flags mark the top 10%; red flags mark the bottom 10%; and yellow flags mark the middle range.
7. Print the worksheet.
8. Click Conditional Formatting and click Manage Rules.
9. In the dialog box, show the formatting for This Worksheet. The formatting rules are listed in the order you created them.
10. Delete the Icon Set rule.
11. **PRINT** the worksheet. **SAVE** the workbook as *Litware Sales 4-6*. **CLOSE** the workbook.

LEAVE Excel open for the next project.

INTERNET READY

In this lesson, you applied formatting styles that are preset in Excel. You also created a custom style. Open Excel Help and key create style in the Excel Help Search box. Open the Apply, create, or remove a cell style link. Click Create a custom cell style.

Merge four cells in an open worksheet and key your name in the cell. Follow the steps provided to create a custom style. Use your first name as the style name. Include the following formats in the style:

- **Alignment:** Horizontal Center Vertical Center
- **Font:** CG Omega, 16 point, Italic
- **Border:** Style: Broken line (your choice)
  Color: Green
  Presets: Outline
- **Fill:** Pattern Color: Yellow
  Pattern Style: Thin Vertical
  Stripe Pattern Style

Key your name in cell A1 of a new blank workbook. Apply the style to your name. Save the workbook as *My Style*.

Formatting Worksheets 5

LESSON SKILL MATRIX

Skill	Exam Objective	Objective Number
Working with Rows and Columns	Hide or unhide a column.	3.4.1
	Hide or unhide a row.	3.4.2
	Hide a series of rows.	3.4.4
	Hide a series of columns.	3.4.3
Using Themes		
Modifying a Worksheet's Onscreen and Printed Appearance	Apply color to worksheet tabs.	4.1.8
	Apply printing options.	1.2.4
	Print row and column headings.	3.3.1
Inserting Headers and Footers	Construct headers and footers.	1.2.3
	Change header and footer size.	3.5.4
	Configure titles to print only on odd or even pages.	3.3.4
	Configure titles to skip the first worksheet page.	3.3.5
Preparing a Document for Printing	Use Page Break workbook view.	4.3.3
	Configure page margins.	3.5.3
	Print rows to repeat with titles.	3.3.2
	Configure page orientation.	3.5.1
	Print columns to repeat with titles.	3.3.3
	Manage page scaling.	3.5.2
	Use Paste Special.	2.1.1

KEY TERMS
- boundary
- column heading
- column width
- document theme
- footer
- gridlines
- header
- orientation
- page break
- Page Break Preview
- Paste Special
- Print Preview
- row heading
- row height
- scaling

Margie's Travel is an agency that sells travel-related products and services to clients on behalf of third parties such as airlines, hotels, and cruise lines. The company also custom designs corporate and leisure travel packages for its clients. The agency's owner, Margie Shoop, specializes in creative, detailed, and personalized service to assure clients they will have an enjoyable and trouble-free travel experience. She employs experienced and knowledgeable travel consultants whose goal is to save clients time, effort, and money. The company maintains a 24/7 emergency service hotline and nationwide toll-free accessibility for business travelers and tourists. The company manages various aspects of its business, including travel itineraries, tour packages, vendor lists, frequent traveler lists, and customer requests, using the Excel workbook format.

SOFTWARE ORIENTATION

Page Layout Commands

One of the easiest ways to share information in a worksheet or workbook is to print copies for others to review. To prepare worksheets for printing and distribution, you will continue to use some of the Home tab command groups, but you will primarily use the Page Layout command groups shown in Figure 5-1. Applying formatting options from these command groups will ensure that your printed worksheets are more useful, more readable, and more attractive.

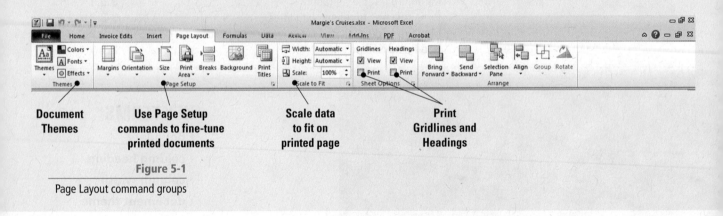

Figure 5-1

Page Layout command groups

WORKING WITH ROWS AND COLUMNS

The Bottom Line

When you open a new worksheet, the columns and rows in that worksheet are uniform. However, uniformity rarely fits the data you want to include in a worksheet or workbook. For some columns, you might need only two or three characters; for others, you will need to increase the **column width** to accommodate more data than will fit in the default column width of 8.43 characters.

Inserting or Deleting a Row or Column

Many times, after you've already entered data in a worksheet, you will need to insert additional rows or columns. To insert a row, select the row or a cell in the row *below* which you want the new row to appear. The new row will then be inserted *above* the selected cell or row. For example, to insert a row above row 10, click any cell in row 10. To insert multiple rows, select the same number of rows as you want to insert.

Inserting columns works the same way. If you want to insert a column to the left of column D, click any cell in column D. Columns are inserted to the left of the selected cell, and by default, the inserted column is formatted the same as the column to the left.

The same principles apply when you need to delete a row or column. In the following exercise, you will delete an entire row from a worksheet.

Take Note   It does not matter which column you use to select cells when you want to insert rows or which row you select when you want to insert columns.

STEP BY STEP   **Insert or Delete a Row or Column**

 The *Margie's Cruises* file for this lesson is available on the book companion website or in WileyPLUS.

GET READY. Locate the Lesson 5 folder to access the exercise files. Then, follow these steps:

1. **OPEN** the *Margie's Cruises* data file. The Home tab will be active.
2. Select any cell in row 12; then press Ctrl and select a cell in row 17. Click the arrow next to Insert in the Cells group and click Insert Sheet Rows.
3. Select any cell in column A. Click the arrow under the Insert cells button in the Cells group, then click Insert Sheet Columns.
4. In A5, key Destination.
5. Select A6:A11. Click Merge & Center in the Alignment group.
6. Select A13:17. Click Merge & Center.
7. Select A19:23. Click Merge & Center.
8. Label the merged cells Mexico (A6), Hawaii (A13), and Alaska (A19).
9. Select A6:A23. Click the Middle Align button in the Alignment group and Bold in the Font group.
10. Select any cell in row 2. Click the arrow under the Delete button in the Cells group and click Delete Sheet Rows.
11. Click the row header for the new row 2. Right-click the highlighted row and click Delete.

PAUSE. LEAVE the workbook open to use in the next exercise.

WileyPLUS Extra! features an online tutorial of this task.

 **Another Way**
After you insert a row or column, you can select the location where you want to insert another row or column and press Ctrl+Y.

Modifying Row Height and Column Width

By default, all columns in a new worksheet are the same width and all rows are the same height. In most worksheets, you will want to change some column or row defaults to accommodate more or less data. Changes can be made using the Format commands in the Cells group on the Home tab.

Modifying row height and column width can make a worksheet's contents easier to read and increase its visual appeal. You can set a row or column to a specific height or width, change the height or width to fit the contents, or change the height or width by dragging the **boundary**, or the line between rows or columns.

STEP BY STEP   **Modify Row Height and Column Width**

USE the workbook from the previous exercise to perform these steps:

1. Click the heading for column D. Press and hold the mouse button and drag to select column E. Release the mouse button.
2. Click Format in the Cells group.
3. Under *Cell Size*, click Column Width on the options list, as shown in Figure 5-2.

Figure 5-2

Cell Size options

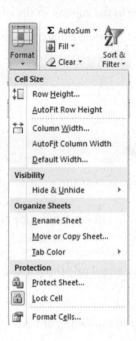

4. In the Column Width dialog box (shown in Figure 5-3), key 15. Click OK. You have adjusted the column width to the specific size of 15.

Figure 5-3

Column Width dialog box

5. Select column C. Click Format, then click AutoFit Column Width. This command adjusts the column width to fit the longest entry in the column.
6. Click the right boundary of column G and drag to the right until the ScreenTip says Width: 17.00.
7. Click any cell in column A. Click Format in the Cells group.
8. Under Cell Size, click Column Width.
9. In the *Column Width* dialog box, key 16. Click OK.
10. Set the width for column B to 30 characters.
11. Select row 3 and click Format. Click Row Height and key 25 in the Row Height dialog box. Click OK.

12. CREATE a Lesson 5 folder and **SAVE** the workbook.

Figure 5-4

Save the worksheet with changes applied

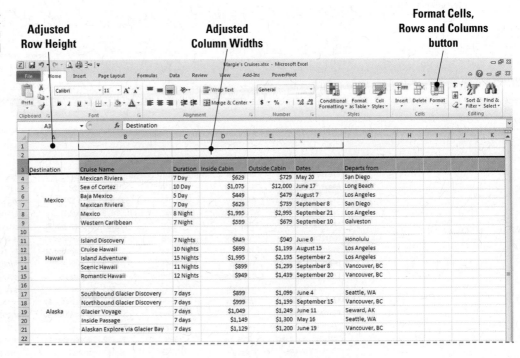

PAUSE. LEAVE the workbook open to use in the next exercise.

Another Way
When formatting rows and columns, you can press Enter instead of clicking the OK button in the dialog box.

Take Note
In previous lessons, when you double-clicked the right column boundary, you were utilizing the AutoFit Column Width option.

Row height, or the top-to-bottom height of a row, is measured in points; one point is equal to 1/72 inch. The default row height is 15 points, but you can specify a row height of 0 to 409 points. Although you can specify a column width of 0 to 255 characters, the default column width is 8.43 characters (based on the default font and font size). If a column width or row height is set to 0, then the corresponding column or row is hidden.

As you learned in Lesson 2, when the text you enter exceeds the column width, the text overflows to the next column, or it is truncated when the next cell contains data. Similarly, if the value entered in a column exceeds the column width, the #### symbols, shown in Figure 5-5, indicate the number is larger than the column width.

Figure 5-5

Symbols indicating a number is larger than the column width

Inside Cabin	Outsid	Dates
$629	$729	May 20
$1,075	#####	June 17

Indicates number is larger than column width

Another Way
To quickly autofit the entries in all rows on a worksheet, click Select All, then double-click one of the column boundaries.

Depending on the alignment of the data in your columns, worksheet data may appear crowded when you use the AutoFit Column Width option because this option adjusts column width to the exact width of the longest entry in the column. Therefore, after using this option, you may want to use the mouse to drag the right column boundary when a column with right-aligned data is adjacent to one with left-aligned data, as shown in Figure 5-6.

Figure 5-6

Separate right-aligned and
left-aligned columns

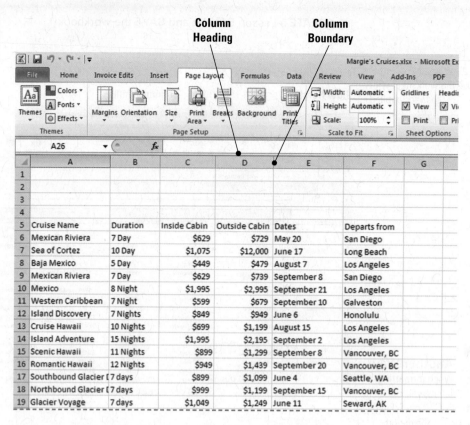

When you drag the boundary, the width of the column in characters and pixels appears in a
ScreenTip above the column headings. See Figure 5-7 for an example.

Figure 5-7

Column width is shown

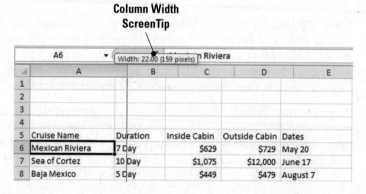

**Another Way**
You can also use
the Format Painter to copy the
width of one column to other
columns. To do so, select the
heading of the first column,
click the Format Painter, and
then click the heading of the
column or columns to which
you want to apply the column
width.

In Excel, you can change the default width for all columns on a worksheet or a workbook. To do
so, click Format; then, under Cell Size, click Default Width. In the Standard Width dialog box,
key a new default column measurement. Note that when changing the default column width
or row height, columns and rows that contain data or that have been previously formatted will
retain their formatting.

Take Note

When you are more familiar with the ways to modify rows and columns, you will likely use one
method consistently.

Formatting an Entire Row or Column

To save time, achieve a consistent appearance, and align cell contents in a consistent manner, you often want to apply the same format to an entire row or column. To apply formatting to a row or column, click the **row heading** or **column heading** (its identifying letter or number) to select it, then apply the appropriate format or style.

STEP BY STEP   **Format an Entire Row or Column**

USE the workbook from the previous exercise to carry out the following steps:

1. Select A1:G1, then click Merge & Center. With A1 selected, click Cell Styles in the Styles group and click Heading 1 under *Titles and Headings*.

2. Key Margie's Travel and press Enter.

3. With A1 selected, click Increase Font Size **A** until the font size is 20 points. Notice that the height of row 1 increased to accommodate the larger font size. (See Figure 5-8.)

Figure 5-8

Font size applied

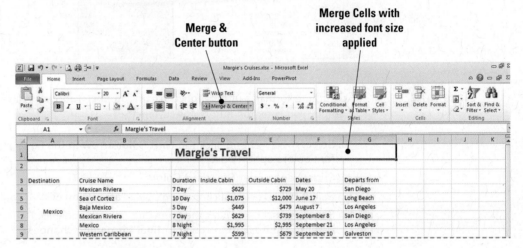

Troubleshooting If you select row 1 rather than the data range and apply the style, the bottom border style effect will extend to the end of the row (cell XFD1).

4. Merge and center A2:G2. Apply the Heading 2 style.

5. Key Cruise Options, Prepared for Fabrikam, Inc., and press Enter.

6. Click on the newly merged A2 and increase the font size to 16 points. Note that the period after Inc. is highlighted in light blue. Please include this when you key the heading.

7. Select A3:G3 and apply Heading 3 style to the column labels. Increase the font size to 12 points.

8. Select row 3. Click Middle Align and Center ☰ in the Alignment group.

9. Select columns D and E. Click the Number Format box and click Accounting. Refer to Figure 5-9 to view the formatting changes in your worksheet.

Figure 5-9

Heading, alignment, and font size applied

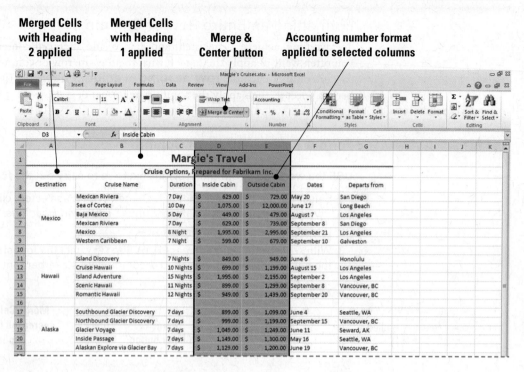

Merged Cells with Heading 2 applied | **Merged Cells with Heading 1 applied** | **Merge & Center button** | **Accounting number format applied to selected columns**

Take Note

Accounting format will be applied to any number you enter in column C or D, even if, for example, you enter the number as currency.

10. Select rows **4–9** and click the **Font Color** arrow in the Font group. This activates the font colors option box.

11. Click **Green** under Standard Colors.

12. Select rows **11–15**. Click the **Font Color** arrow and click **Purple** under Standard Colors.

13. Select rows **17–21**. Click the **Font Color** arrow and click **Red** under Standard Colors. Refer to Figure 5-10 to see your final formatting changes.

Figure 5-10

Formatting applied

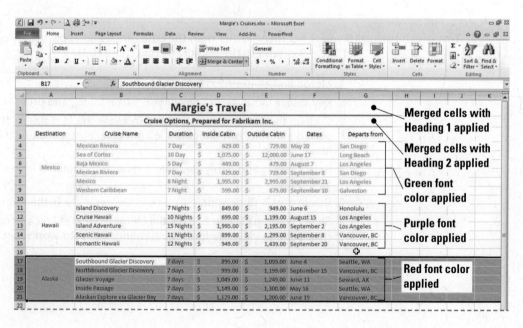

Merged cells with Heading 1 applied

Merged cells with Heading 2 applied

Green font color applied

Purple font color applied

Red font color applied

14. **SAVE** the workbook.
PAUSE. LEAVE the workbook open to use in the next exercise.

Formatting rows and columns rather than applying formatting to the range of cells that contain data has an advantage: Later, when you insert rows or columns or add additional data to a worksheet, it will be formatted correctly.

Hiding or Unhiding a Row or Column

You may not want or need all rows and columns in a worksheet to be visible all the time, particularly if the worksheet contains a large number of rows or columns. You can hide a row or a column by using the Hide command or by setting the row height or column width to zero. When rows are hidden, they do not appear onscreen or in printouts.

STEP BY STEP **Hide or Unhide a Row or Column**

CERTIFICATION READY   3.4.1

How do you hide and unhide columns in a worksheet?

Another Way
You can also hide a column by setting the column width to zero.

USE the workbook from the previous exercise. Then, do the following:

1. Click the column **D** header to select the entire column. Click **Format** in the Cells group.
2. Mouse over Hide & Unhide and click **Hide Columns** in the Visibility group. This process will hide column D from view. A thick line appears when you have hidden the column.
3. Click the row **11** header, press **Shift**, and click the row **15** heading. Click **Format** in the Cells group. This has selected all five rows.
4. Mouse over Hide & Unhide and click **Hide Rows** in the Visibility group. A thick line has once again appeared to show your action of hiding the rows.
5. Click **Quick Print** on the Quick Access Toolbar. As shown in Figure 5-11, you can recognize when rows or columns are hidden because numbers are skipped in the row headings or letters are skipped in the column headings. When you view your printed worksheet, note that it does not show the hidden rows or column.

Figure 5-11
Hidden column and rows

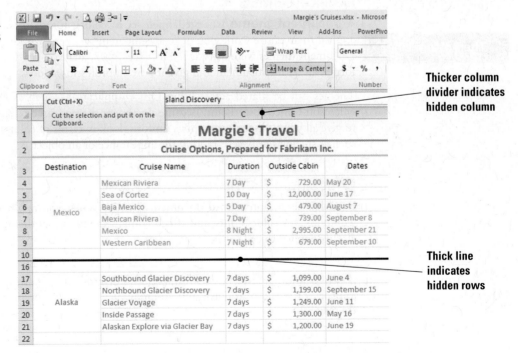

6. Select columns **C** and **E** (which are columns on each side of the hidden column).
7. Click **Format**, mouse over Hide & Unhide, and click **Unhide Columns** in the Visibility group. Column D is again visible.

Take Note

You must click the row or column heading to select the entire row or column when you want to display a hidden row or column. Selecting the data in the rows or columns will not release the hidden rows or columns.

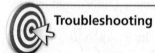

CERTIFICATION
READY **3.4.2**

How do you hide and unhide rows in a worksheet?

CERTIFICATION
READY **3.4.4**

How do you hide and unhide a series of rows in a worksheet?

CERTIFICATION
READY **3.4.3**

How do you hide and unhide a series of columns in a worksheet?

8. Select row **10**, press **Shift**, and select row **16**. Click **Format**. Point to Hide & Unhide and click **Unhide Rows** in the Visibility group. As a result of this action, your worksheet returns to its original state from before beginning the exercise.

9. **SAVE** the workbook.

PAUSE. LEAVE the workbook open to use in the next exercise.

A worksheet may contain rows or columns of sensitive data that you are not using or do not want to be visible while you are working in other areas of the worksheet. For example, if a person who is working with the Margie's Cruises worksheet wants to focus on or print the cruises to only one destination, the rows containing the data for the other destinations can be hidden.

To make hidden rows visible, select the row above and the row below the hidden row or rows and use the Format commands to Unhide Rows. If the first row is hidden, use the Go To feature to make the row visible. To display hidden columns, select the adjacent columns and follow the same steps used for displaying hidden rows.

You can also hide or unhide multiple rows or columns using this same method.

 Troubleshooting When you select rows 10 and 16 to unhide the hidden rows, you must select them in a way that includes the hidden rows. Press Shift when you select row 16 or select row 10 and drag to include row 16. If you select row 10, press Ctrl, and click row 16, the rows will not unhide.

(X) Ref You will learn more about the Go To feature in Lesson 6.

USING THEMES

The Bottom Line

A **document theme** is a predefined set of colors, fonts, lines, and fill effects that can be applied to an entire workbook or to specific items within a workbook, such as charts or tables. Document themes were introduced in Excel 2007, and you can use them to quickly and easily format an entire document and give it a fresh, professional look.

Themes can be shared across other Office applications, such as Microsoft Office Word and Microsoft Office PowerPoint. Because document themes can be shared, this feature enables you to give all your Office documents a uniform look in terms of colors, fonts, and effects. (Effects, such as shadows or bevels, modify the appearance of an object.)

Choosing a Theme for a Worksheet

Excel has several predefined document themes. When you apply a theme to a worksheet or workbook, the colors, fonts, and effects contained within that theme replace any styles that were already applied to cells or ranges.

 Troubleshooting If you or another user has customized one or more document themes, those themes will appear at the top of the list, and you may have to scroll down to see all of Excel's built-in themes.

Choose a Theme for a Worksheet

USE the workbook from the previous exercise.

1. Click the Page Layout tab to make it active.
2. Click Themes. The first 20 built-in themes are displayed in a preview window (see Figure 5-12). Mouse over each theme and observe the changes in the title lines of your worksheet.

Figure 5-12

Built-in document themes

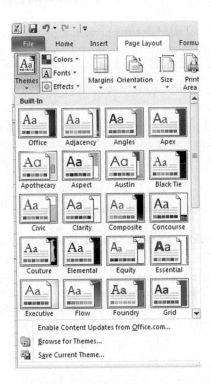

3. Scroll down and click Verve to apply that style to your worksheet.
4. Click the File tab to access Backstage. Click Save As and save the workbook in the Lesson 5 folder as *Verve Theme*. Here, you changed the default document theme by selecting another predefined document theme. As you can see, document themes that you apply immediately affect the styles that have already been applied in your document.

Take Note   Because you increased the font size after you applied Heading 1 to the title, the font size remains at 20 points. If you had changed the font size before applying the heading style, the title would be displayed in 14 points, because that is the default font size for themes.

5. Click Themes and click Opulent. The appearance of your document is significantly changed.
6. Click Save As and save the workbook in the Lesson 5 folder. Name your workbook *Opulent Theme*.

PAUSE. LEAVE the workbook open to use in the next exercise.

Figure 5-12 shows 20 built-in themes for Excel 2010, but when you scroll down, you can see all the built-in themes. The styles that you applied in the previous exercises were the styles associated with the default Office theme. When you opened the styles gallery, the colors, fonts, and effects that were displayed were those that make up the Office theme.

Remember that styles are used to format specific cells or ranges within a worksheet; document themes are used to apply sets of styles (colors, fonts, lines, and fill effects) to an entire document. All of the default Office theme styles you applied to the titles in a previous exercise were changed when you applied a different theme.

In this exercise, you applied two document themes so that the owner of Margie's Travel can select the one that will be used on all company documents. By saving both themes, the owner can compare the differences between the two and then choose which theme to use. Because themes are consistent in all Microsoft Office 2010 programs, all of the company documents for Margie's Travel can have a uniform appearance.

Many companies create a customized document theme and use it consistently. You can experiment by applying various predefined themes until you decide on the "look" that appeals to you, or you can design a customized theme, as you will do in the next exercise.

Customizing a Theme

You can create a customized theme by making changes to one or more of an existing theme's components—colors, fonts, or line and fill effects. The changes you make to one or more of a theme's components immediately affect the styles that you have applied in the active document.

STEP BY STEP   **Customize a Theme by Selecting Colors**

USE the *Opulent Theme* workbook, which should be open from the previous exercise, to complete the following steps:

1. On the Page Layout tab, in the Themes group, click Colors. Figure 5-13 illustrates the color array for some of the built-in themes. Remember, you have to scroll through the entire list to see them all. Each theme has an array of accent colors that are the same as the accents in the Styles group.

Figure 5-13

Theme colors

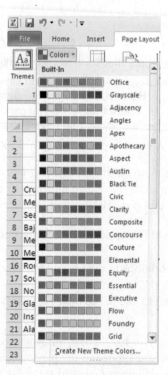

2. Click Create New Theme Colors. The *Create New Theme Colors* dialog box opens (see Figure 5-14), showing the colors used in the Opulent theme that is currently applied to the worksheet. Move the dialog box so that you can see the worksheet titles and column labels.

Figure 5-14

Create New Theme Colors dialog box

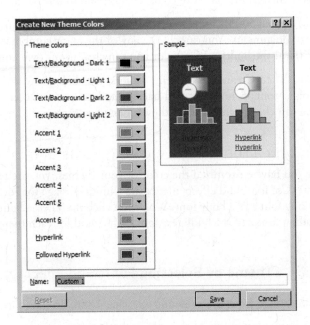

3. Click the Text/Background—Dark 2 arrow. The current color is highlighted under *Theme Colors*. Click Accent 6 to change the color to orange.

4. Click the arrow next to Accent 1 in the dialog box and click Accent 6 under *Theme Colors*. In the *Name* box, key My Colors. Click Save. The font and line color in the worksheet titles reflect the customized theme colors. Refer to Figure 5-15 to see the worksheet with custom theme colors.

Figure 5-15

Modified theme applied

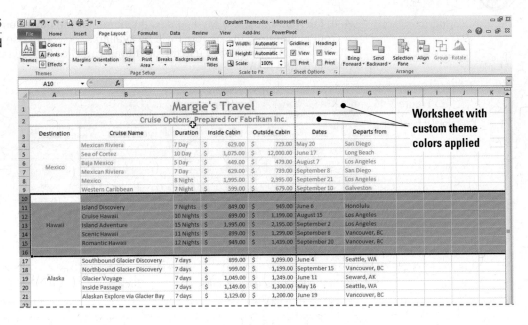

PAUSE. LEAVE the workbook open to use in the next exercise.

Take Note   To return all theme color elements to their original colors, click the Reset button in the Custom Colors dialog box before you click Save.

In the Create New Theme Colors dialog box, click the button next to the theme color element that you want to change. The theme colors are presented in every color gallery with a set of lines and shades based on those colors. By selecting colors from this expanded matched set, you can make formatting choices for individual pieces of content that will still follow the themes. When the theme colors change, the gallery of colors changes and so does all document content using them.

It is easy to create your own theme that can be applied to all of your Excel workbooks and other Office 2010 documents. You can choose any of the color combinations shown in Figure 5-13, which represent the built-in themes, or you can create your own combination of colors.

When you clicked Create New Theme Colors, the dialog box shown in Figure 5-14 opened. Theme colors contain four text and background colors, six accent colors, and two hyperlink colors. You can change any or all of these when you customize a theme.

Customizing a Theme by Selecting Fonts and Effects

Now that you have customized the color of your themes, you are ready to choose the font for your theme. Use fonts and effects that create a unique image for your documents. Themes contain a heading font and a body font. When you click the Theme Fonts button, you see the name of the heading font and the body text font that is used for each theme.

STEP BY STEP   **Customize a Theme by Selecting Fonts and Effects**

USE the workbook from the previous exercise. Then, do the following:

1. On the Page Layout tab, click Fonts in the Themes group.
2. Click Create New Theme Fonts. In the Heading font box, click Bookman Old Style.
3. In the Body font box, click Poor Richard. The sample is updated with the fonts that you selected.

 Troubleshooting If your customized theme font is not automatically applied, click Cell Styles and click the customized heading font to apply it.

4. In the Name box, key My Fonts as the name for the new theme fonts. Click Save. Your customized theme fonts will be available for you to use to customize any of the built-in themes or to use the next time you click Cell Styles on the Home tab. (See Figure 5-16.)

Figure 5-16

Customized font theme

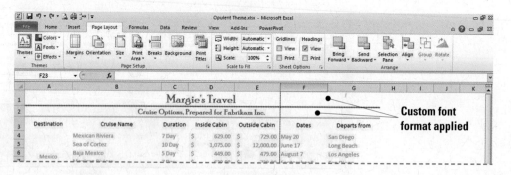

5. In the Themes group, click Themes. Click Save Current Theme.
6. In the *File name* box, key My Theme. Click Save. Your customized document theme is saved in the Document Themes folder, and it is automatically added to the list of custom themes that now appears at the top of the themes preview window.
7. Click on Themes. Your theme is now viewable in *Custom* themes.
8. On the Page Layout tab, in the Themes group, click Effects. Theme effects are sets of lines and fill effects. Mousing over the effects will show subtle changes in the cells. (See Figure 5-17).

Figure 5-17

Custom theme and effects

**Custom theme applied
to worksheet**

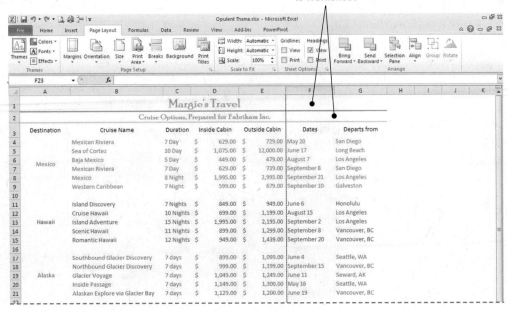

9. Click the Aspect effect to apply it to the workbook. Click Undo in the Quick Access Toolbar to undo the theme effect. Do not save the workbook.

PAUSE. LEAVE the workbook open to use in the next exercise.

You can customize any of the built-in themes by changing the attributes of the theme. For example, say you like the colors in the Verve theme but you want to use a different font. In this situation, first apply the Verve theme, then click Theme Fonts and apply the font of your choice.

You can then save the resulting theme and apply it to other documents. You cannot change the built-in theme effects, but you can apply a different built-in effect to modify the appearance of the theme you are editing, which can include changing the shading, beveling, or other effects.

MODIFYING A WORKSHEET'S ONSCREEN AND PRINTED APPEARANCE

The Bottom Line

You can draw attention to a worksheet's onscreen appearance by displaying a background picture. You can also add color to worksheet tabs. **Gridlines** (the lines that display around worksheet cells), row headings, and column headings also enhance a worksheet's appearance. Onscreen, these elements are displayed by default, but they are not printed automatically.

Formatting a Worksheet Background

You can use a picture as a sheet background for display purposes only. A sheet background is saved with your worksheet, but it is not printed and it is not retained in a worksheet or as an item that you save as a web page. Because a sheet background is not printed, it cannot be used as a watermark.

STEP BY STEP

Format a Worksheet Background

@ The *Sunset* image and the *Open Sea* image are available on the book companion website or in WileyPLUS.

USE the workbook from the previous exercise. Then, perform these steps:

1. On the Page Layout tab, in the Page Setup group, click Background.

2. Click the *Sunset* image from the student data files and then click Insert. The selected picture is displayed behind the text and fills the sheet. (See Figure 5-18.)

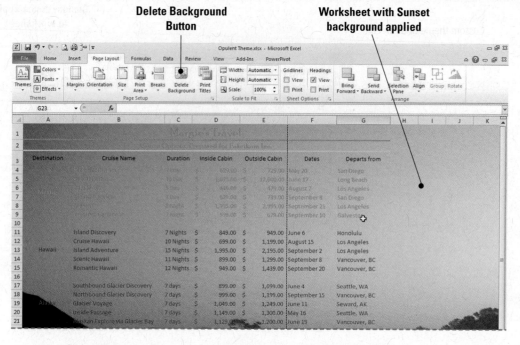

3. In the Sheet Options group, click **View** to remove the gridlines.

4. Select **A1:G21**, click the **Home** tab, and click the **Fill Color arrow**. To improve readability, click **Lavender Background 2, Darker 25%** to add solid color shading to cells that contain data. The higher the percentage of the fill color, the darker the fill that will be applied. Before you apply fill colors, you can mouse over them and their effect will preview in the worksheet.

5. Click anywhere in the worksheet. Click the **Page Layout** tab. In the Page Setup group, click **Delete Background**. The background is removed, but the shading applied to the data range remains.

6. On the Page Layout tab, in the Page Setup group, click **Background** and select the *Open Sea* image from the student data files. Click **Insert**. (See Figure 5-19.)

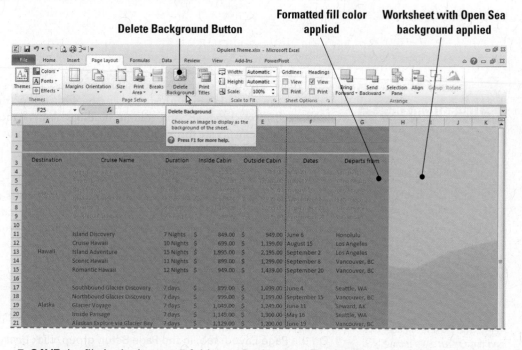

7. **SAVE** the file in the Lesson 5 folder as *Background*. The background will be saved with the worksheet.

8. Click **Delete Background** in preparation for the next exercise.

9. Select A1:G21. Right-click the selected cells, click the arrow on the fill button in the Mini-toolbar, and select No fill.

PAUSE. LEAVE the workbook open to use in the next exercise.

Say that the owner of Margie's Travel often uses worksheets in presentations to clients and also provides clients with printed copies. You can increase the effectiveness of these worksheet presentations by adding an appropriate background picture and adding color to worksheet tabs. It is best to remove gridlines when a sheet background is used, but printing gridlines makes printed worksheets easier to read. Printing column and row headings can also help identify the location of data during discussions.

Changing the Color of a Worksheet Tab

By default, a new workbook contains three blank worksheets identified as Sheet1, Sheet2, and Sheet3. You often use more than one worksheet to enter related data because it is easier to move between sheets than to scroll up and down through large amounts of data. Adding color to the worksheet tabs makes it easier to locate needed information.

STEP BY STEP **Change the Color of a Worksheet Tab**

USE the workbook from the previous exercise.

1. Right-click the Sheet1 tab and mouse over Tab Color. Under *Standard Colors*, click Green.
2. Right-click the Sheet2 tab and mouse over Tab Color. Click Purple.
3. Right-click the Sheet3 tab and mouse over Tab Color. Click Red.
4. Click the Sheet1 tab. Select A1:A3. Click Copy.
5. Click Sheet2. Select A1 and click Paste.
6. Click the Paste Options button and click Keep Source Column Widths. (See Figure 5-20.)

Figure 5-20

Keep Source Column Widths

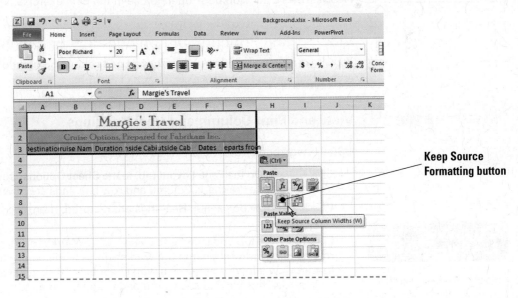

Keep Source Formatting button

7. Click Sheet3. Select A1 and click Paste.
8. Click the Paste Options button and click Keep Source Column Widths.
9. On the Sheet1 worksheet, select A11:G15 and click Cut.
10. On the Sheet2 worksheet, select A4 and click Paste.
11. Cut the Alaska data from Sheet1 and paste it to A4 on Sheet3. Note that each worksheet tab is color coded to match the font format in that worksheet.

PAUSE. LEAVE the workbook open to use in the next exercise.

CERTIFICATION READY **4.1.8**

How do you change the tab color in a worksheet?

The original workbook contained data about cruises to three destinations all in a single work-sheet. In this exercise, you separated the data so that data related to each destination is now on a separate worksheet in the workbook.

Viewing and Printing a Worksheet's Gridlines

You can have gridlines visible on your work surface or work without them. By default, gridlines are present when you open a worksheet. You can also choose whether gridlines are printed. A printed worksheet is easier to read when gridlines are included.

Take Note   Worksheets print faster if you print without gridlines.

STEP BY STEP   **View and Print a Worksheet's Gridlines**

USE the workbook from the previous exercise.

1. Click the Sheet1 tab. On the Page Layout tab, in the Sheet Options group, remove the check mark from the View option in the Gridlines section.
2. In the Page Setup group, click Orientation, then click Landscape. In the Scale to Fit group, click 1 page in the Width box.
3. Click Quick Print on the Quick Access Toolbar. Gridlines should not be present on the work surface or in the printout.
4. Click the Sheet2 tab to make it the active worksheet. Click the Print check box under Gridlines. Click Orientation, then click Landscape. Each worksheet has its own properties. When you access orientation for Sheet2, you will notice that Portrait is the default.
5. In the Scale to Fit group, click 1 page in the Width box. Click Quick Print. Although gridlines are not present on the work surface, they are included on the printout.
6. With Sheet3 as the active worksheet, check View and Print under Gridlines. Click Orientation and Landscape.
7. Click Quick Print. Gridlines are present on both the work surface and the printout.

PAUSE. LEAVE the workbook open to use in the next exercise.

CERTIFICATION
READY   **1.2.4**

How do you show and print gridlines?

Viewing and Printing Column and Row Headings

You also can choose whether to have the row and column headings of your worksheet print. This exercise shows you how.

STEP BY STEP   **View and Print Column and Row Headings**

USE the workbook from the previous exercise.

1. Click Sheet1. On the Page Layout tab, in the Sheet Options group under Headings, click View to remove the check. Column and row headings are now removed from the display.
2. Check the View box again. Headings are restored. Then, click the Print check box under Headings.
3. Click the View tab and click Page Layout in the Workbook Views group. Column and row headings now appear in the worksheet as it will be printed. Remember, Page Layout view allows you to see a worksheet exactly as it will appear on a printed page. You can use this view to see where pages begin and end.

PAUSE. LEAVE the workbook open to use in the next exercise.

CERTIFICATION
READY   **3.3.1**

How do you show and print column and row headings?

INSERTING HEADERS AND FOOTERS

The Bottom Line

You can add headers or footers to your worksheets to provide useful information about the worksheet, such as who prepared it, the date it was created or last modified, the page number, and so on. Headers and footers are visible in Page Layout view and appear on printouts.

A **header** is a line of text that appears at the top of each page of a printed worksheet. **Footers** are lines of text that appear at the bottom of each page. You can add predefined header or footer information to a worksheet; insert elements such as page numbers, date and time, and filename; or add your own content to a header or footer.

Adding Page Numbers to a Worksheet

To add or change a header or footer, click the Insert tab, then click Header & Footer in the Text group. The worksheet displays in Page Layout view, a Design tab (as shown in Figure 5-21) is added to the Ribbon, and the Header & Footer Tools command groups are displayed.

Figure 5-21

Design tab for Headers and Footers

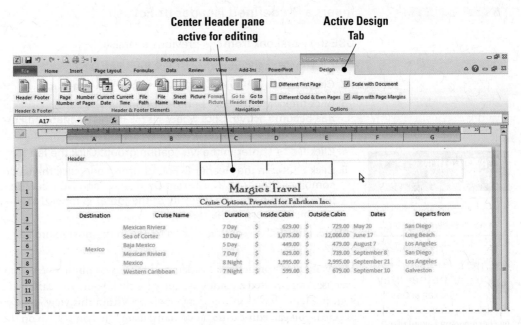

Take Note   The addition of the Design tab illustrates one advantage of Excel's Ribbon interface. With the Ribbon, instead of every command being available all the time, some commands appear only in response to specific user actions.

STEP BY STEP   **Add Page Numbers to a Worksheet**

USE the workbook from the previous exercise to perform these steps:

1. With Sheet1 active, click the Insert tab, then click the Header & Footer button in the Text group. The worksheet is now displayed in Page Layout view. Note that the center Header text box is active and the Design tab is added to the Ribbon. The Header & Footer Design tab command groups are thus available for you to use in the worksheet.

2. By default, your cursor will appear in the center Header section. Press Tab to move to the right pane in the Header section of the worksheet.

3. Click Page Number in the Header & Footer Elements group. The code **&[Page]** appears in the text box. This symbol (&) indicates that the appropriate page number will be added to each page of the printed worksheet.

4. Click the Go to Footer button in the Navigation group.

5. Click the left text box in the footer and click Sheet Name in the Header & Footer Elements group. Press Tab twice to go to the right footer pane.

CERTIFICATION READY   1.2.3

How do you add headers and footers to worksheets?

6. Click Current Date in the Header & Footer Elements group. Then click anywhere in the worksheet outside the header and footer to close the Design tab.

7. **SAVE** the workbook in the Lesson 5 folder as *Cruises*.

PAUSE. LEAVE the workbook open to use in the next exercise.

You can create headers and footers by keying the text that you want to appear, or, as you practiced in this exercise, you can click one of the predefined elements to insert codes for headers or footers that Excel provides. When your workbook is printed, Excel replaces these codes with the current date, current time, and so on.

Inserting a Predefined Header or Footer

On the Design tab, the Header & Footer group contains predefined headers and footers that allow you to automatically add text to the header or footer, such as the date, page number, number of pages, name of the sheet, and so on.

STEP BY STEP   **Insert a Predefined Header or Footer**

USE the workbook from the previous exercise.

1. Click the Sheet3 worksheet. Click the View tab.
2. Click Page Layout view in the Workbook Views group.
3. Click the center Header pane. Click on the Header & Footer Tools Design tab now that it has become active. Click Sheet Name in the Header and Footer Elements group. &Tab appears in the pane.
4. Click Go to Footer in the Navigation group. Click the left footer pane.
5. Click Footer in the Header & Footer group and click the last option in the list, which combines Prepared by, Current Date, and Page Number. Because the footer is wider than the left pane, the majority of the footer is moved to the center pane, and the page number appears in the right pane.

PAUSE. LEAVE the workbook open to use in the next exercise.

> **CERTIFICATION READY** **3.5.4**
>
> How do you change the size of your headers or footers?

Many of Excel's predefined headers and footers combine one or more elements. In the previous exercise, you inserted a combined entry by clicking it. You can then customize the appearance of your header or footer in Page Layout view. Within this view, once you have the header or footer selected, you can edit the text It contains using the Font group on the Home tab. In this way, you can change font type or size, add special effects, or add other options to your text.

 **Another Way** You can access the Header and Footer text boxes by clicking Page Layout view on the right side of the status bar.

Adding Content to a Header or Footer

Excel's predefined headers and footers will not always meet your needs. When this happens, you can simply key text into any of the header or footer text boxes.

Text isn't the only type of content you can add to a header or footer, though. For instance, you may be familiar with the watermark functionality that is available in Microsoft Word. You cannot insert a watermark in Excel, but you can mimic one by displaying a graphic in a header or footer. This graphic will appear behind the text, and it will display and print in the style of a watermark.

STEP BY STEP   **Insert Text and Graphics into a Header or Footer**

USE the workbook from the previous exercise.

1. With Sheet3 still active, click the center Header pane and delete the existing header.
2. Key For Presentation to Client in the center pane. Then press Tab to move to the right Header pane.
3. Click the Design tab if it is not already active. Click Picture in the Header and Footer Elements group. Select the *Sailing* image from student data files for Lesson 5 and click Insert.
4. Click Format Picture on the ribbon.
5. In the *Format Picture* dialog box, under *Size and rotate*, set the height to 8.5" and press Tab. Notice the width changes automatically. This happens because *Lock aspect ratio* is checked. Press OK.
6. Click anywhere on the worksheet to deselect Headers & Footers editing. The image now appears behind the header and footer text.

> @ The *Sailing* image is available on the book companion website or in WileyPLUS.

7. **SAVE** the workbook.

LEAVE the workbook open for the next exercise.

Using Headers to Print Titles

Using the headers in Excel will allow you to customize the title printing options and how they appear on the printed page. You can use these options to skip printing first page titles and print to odd pages only. In this next section you will apply these printing options to your worksheet.

STEP BY STEP   **Use a Header to Print Titles on Specific Pages**

CERTIFICATION READY   **3.3.4**

How do you use headers to print custom titles on odd pages?

CERTIFICATION READY   **3.3.5**

How do you use headers to skip printing first page titles?

USE the workbook from the previous exercise.

1. Click the **Insert** tab on the Ribbon. In the Text group, click **Header & Footer**. By default Excel will open the Header in the Center pane for editing.

2. Key **Margie's Client List for Printing**.

3. On the Headers & Footers Design tab, in the Options group, select the **Different Odd & Even Pages** check box. This will allow you to specify that the headers and footers on odd-numbered pages should be different from those on even-numbered pages.

4. Again on the Design tab, in the Options group, select the **Different First Page** check box. This option allows you to ignore the header title on the first page. You will not have a title because you will be leaving the center Header text box blank.

5. Click on the **File** tab to enter Backstage. Click on **Print**. You will now be able to view the title printing options that you selected for both the first page and odd and even pages.

6. Do not save the worksheet.

CLOSE Excel.

PREPARING A DOCUMENT FOR PRINTING

The Bottom Line

When worksheet data prints on more than one page, you can use the Page Break Preview command on the View tab to control where page breaks occur. This allows you to break data where it is most logical, so that printed documents are well-organized and easy to read.

In the next set of exercises, you will use Page Layout view on the View tab to view headers and footers, change page breaks, and change page margins at the top, sides, and bottom of a worksheet (see Figure 5-22).

Figure 5-22

Page Layout view

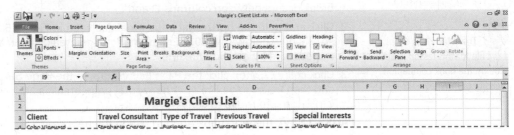

Adding and Moving a Page Break

The **Print Preview** window displays a full-page view of a worksheet just as it will be printed. With Print Preview, you can check the format and overall layout of a worksheet before actually printing it. You cannot make changes to the document in Print Preview, however.

A **page break** is a divider that breaks a worksheet into separate pages for printing. Excel inserts automatic vertical page breaks (shown as a broken line) based on paper size, margin settings, scaling options, and the positions of any manual page breaks (shown as a solid line) that you insert. In the **Page Break Preview** window, shown in Figure 5-23, you can quickly adjust automatic page breaks to achieve a more desirable printed document.

As you learned in Lesson 2, all printing options in Excel 2010 are now organized in Backstage view.

Figure 5-23

Page Break Preview window

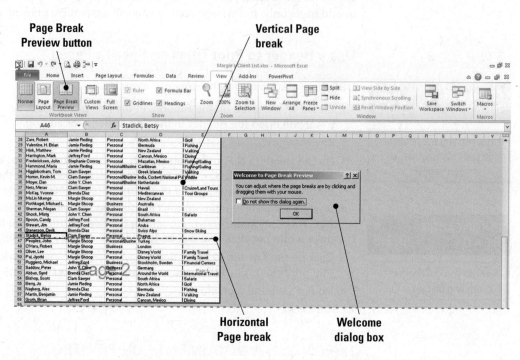

Page Break Preview button

Vertical Page break

Horizontal Page break

Welcome dialog box

STEP BY STEP   **Add and Move a Page Break**

OPEN the *Margie's Client List* workbook from the student data files in the Lesson 5 folder. Then, follow these steps:

1. On the View tab, click Page Break Preview if necessary. If a dialog box welcoming you to the view is displayed, read its contents and click OK to continue. (See Figure 5-23.) Note that an automatic page break occurs after row 46, and another automatic page break occurs between columns D and E.

2. Click and hold the horizontal page break (as seen in Figure 5-23) and drag it upward so it is now below row 40. The automatic page break is now a manual page break represented by a solid blue line.

3. Click cell A22, then click the Page Layout tab. In the Page Setup group, click Breaks and then Insert Page Break. A horizontal page break is added above row 22. Press Ctrl+Home to move to cell A1.

PAUSE. LEAVE the workbook open to use in the next exercise.

@ The *Margie's Client List* file for this lesson is available on the book companion website or in WileyPLUS.

Take Note   When you move an automatic page break, it becomes a manual page break.

Use manual page breaks to control page break locations. You can drag an automatic page break to a new location to convert it to a manual page break.

CERTIFICATION READY   4.3.3

How do you insert or move a page break?

Setting Margins

Margins are an effective way to manage and optimize the white space on a printed worksheet. Achieving balance between data and white space adds significantly to the readability and appearance of a worksheet. In Excel. you can choose one of three built-in margin sets (shown in Figure 5-24), or you can create customized margins using the Page Setup dialog box.

Figure 5-24

Built-in margin options

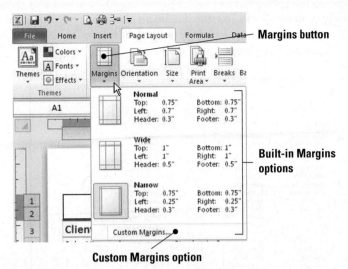

Margins button

Built-in Margins options

Custom Margins option

Set Margins

USE the workbook from the previous exercise.

1. Click the View tab on the Ribbon. In the Workbook Views group, click the Page Layout button.

2. Click the Page Layout tab. In the Page Setup group, click the arrow on the Margins button, then click Narrow.

3. Mouse over the Zoom slider on the right corner of the status bar and increase the zoom to 100% if necessary. Depending on whether this feature has been previously used, the zoom might be set to a different value. The Zoom slider allows you to zoom out or in, depending on how you need to view a worksheet's contents.

4. Click Page Break Preview on the Status bar. The margin adjustment has moved the vertical page break to between columns E and F. Again the Page Break welcome dialog box appears. Click OK to continue.

5. Click Margins, then click Custom Margins. In the Page Setup dialog box, change the left and right margins to 0.5. Click OK.

6. Click cell A22, click Breaks in the Page Setup group, then click Remove Page Break.

7. Click the vertical page break line and drag it to the right of column E.

8. Click the File tab. Click Print and Print Preview. The worksheet will now print on two pages, with all columns fitting to one page wide.

9. Print the worksheet or click on the Home tab to leave Backstage and Print Preview without printing.

PAUSE. CLOSE the workbook without saving any changes.

CERTIFICATION
READY   3.5.3

How do you set margins?

Another Way
You can also alter the margins in Page Layout view by clicking the top or bottom border on the margin area in the ruler. When a vertical two-headed arrow appears, drag the margin to the size you want.

The Normal margin setting is the default for a new workbook. You can also set custom margins in Excel. Narrower margins, for example, allow more area for data when you print a workbook. When you click Custom Margins at the bottom of the Margins list, the Page Setup dialog box will open with the settings that have been applied to the open worksheet. You can change any of the settings to create a custom margin setting. Header and footer margins automatically adjust when you change the page margins.

Worksheets that do not fill an entire page can be centered vertically and horizontally, thereby evenly distributing the page's white space. Use the Margins tab of the Page Setup dialog box for this function.

Setting a Worksheet's Orientation

Printed worksheets are easiest to read and analyze when all of the data appears on one piece of paper. Excel's orientation and scaling features give you control over the number of printed pages of worksheet data. You can change the **orientation** of a worksheet so that it prints either vertically or horizontally on a page. A worksheet that is printed vertically uses the Portrait orientation and looks like the document shown on top in Figure 5-25. Portrait orientation is the default setting. A worksheet printed horizontally uses the Landscape orientation, shown in Figure 5-25 at the bottom of the page.

Figure 5-25

Portrait and landscape orientation

Margie's Client List

Client	Travel Consultant	Type of Travel	Previous Travel
Coho Vineyard	Stephanie Conroy	Business	Tuscany Valley
Coho Winery	Stephanie Conroy	Business	France
Contoso Pharmaceuticals	Margie Shoop	Business	Vienna, Austria
Trey Research	John Y. Chen	Business	Copenhagen, Denmark
Fabrikam, Inc.	Brenda Diaz	Business	Lisbon, Portugal
Ashton, Chris	Jeffrey Ford	Personal	Brussels, Belgium
Bolender, Corinna	Jamie Reding	Personal	Oslo, Norway
Caro, Fernando	Clam Sawyer	Personal	Stockholm, Sweden
Ihrig, Ryan	Margie Shoop	Personal	Barcelona, Spain
Ingle, Marc J.	Margie Shoop	Personal	Naples, Italy
Keil, Kendall	Stephanie Conroy	Personal	Athens, Greece
Kim, Jim	Brenda Diaz	Personal	Athens, Greece
Li, Yale	John Y. Chen	Personal	Naples, Italy
McAskill-White, Katie	Jeffrey Ford	Personal	Rome, Italy
McGuel, Alejandro	Jeffrey Ford	Personal	Israel
Myer, Ken	Clam Sawyer	Personal	Latin America
Nash, Mike	Margie Shoop	Personal	Mexico
Seidl, Birgit	Margie Shoop	Personal	Bahamas
Sutton, Brad	John Y. Chen	Personal	Australia
Teal, Andy	Clam Sawyer	Personal	Hawaii
Tiano, Mike	Jeffrey Ford	Personal	Mediterranean
Vargas, Garrett R.	Stephanie Conroy	Personal	Alaska
Waldal, Deb	Brenda Diaz	Personal	Around the World
Walton, Bryan	Brenda Diaz	Personal	South Africa
Zare, Robert	Jamie Reding	Personal	North Africa
Valentine, H. Brian	Jamie Reding	Personal	Bermuda
Hink, Matthew	Jamie Reding	Personal	New Zealand
Harrington, Mark	Jeffrey Ford	Personal	Cancun, Mexico
Fredericksen, John	Stephanie Conroy	Personal	Mazatlan, Mexico
Hammond, Maria	Jamie Reding	Personal/Business	Caribbean
Higginbotham, Tom	Clam Sawyer	Personal	Greek Islands
Horner, Kevin M.	Clam Sawyer	Personal/Business	India, Corbett National Park
Moyer, Dan	John Y. Chen	Personal/Business	Netherlands
Netz, Merav	Clam Sawyer	Personal	Hawaii
McKay, Yvonne	Brenda Diaz	Personal	Mediterranean
McLin Nkenge	Margie Shoop	Personal	New Zealand
Rothkugel, Michael L.	Margie Shoop	Business	Australia

Portrait Orientation

Margie's Client List

Client	Travel Consultant	Type of Travel	Previous Travel	Special Interests
Coho Vineyard	Stephanie Conroy	Business	Tuscany Valley	Vineyard/Winery
Coho Winery	Stephanie Conroy	Business	France	Vineyard/Winery
Contoso Pharmaceuticals	Margie Shoop	Business	Vienna, Austria	Medical Research
Trey Research	John Y. Chen	Business	Copenhagen, Denmark	Medical Research
Fabrikam, Inc.	Brenda Diaz	Business	Lisbon, Portugal	
Ashton, Chris	Jeffrey Ford	Personal	Brussels, Belgium	History
Bolender, Corinna	Jamie Reding	Personal	Oslo, Norway	
Caro, Fernando	Clam Sawyer	Personal	Stockholm, Sweden	
Ihrig, Ryan	Margie Shoop	Personal	Barcelona, Spain	
Ingle, Marc J.	Margie Shoop	Personal	Naples, Italy	
Keil, Kendall	Stephanie Conroy	Personal	Athens, Greece	Cruise/Land Tours
Kim, Jim	Brenda Diaz	Personal	Athens, Greece	Cruise/Land Tours
Li, Yale	John Y. Chen	Personal	Naples, Italy	Museums, Art History
McAskill-White, Katie	Jeffrey Ford	Personal	Rome, Italy	Religion
McGuel, Alejandro	Jeffrey Ford	Personal	Israel	Religion
Myer, Ken	Clam Sawyer	Personal	Latin America	
Nash, Mike	Margie Shoop	Personal	Mexico	Diving
Seidl, Birgit	Margie Shoop	Personal	Bahamas	
Sutton, Brad	John Y. Chen	Personal	Australia	
Teal, Andy	Clam Sawyer	Personal	Hawaii	Sailing
Tiano, Mike	Jeffrey Ford	Personal	Mediterranean	
Vargas, Garrett R.	Stephanie Conroy	Personal	Alaska	Cruise/Land Tours
Waldal, Deb	Brenda Diaz	Personal	Around the World	International Travel
Walton, Bryan	Brenda Diaz	Personal	South Africa	Safaris
Zare, Robert	Jamie Reding	Personal	North Africa	Golf
Valentine, H. Brian	Jamie Reding	Personal	Bermuda	Fishing
Hink, Matthew	Jamie Reding	Personal	New Zealand	Walking
Harrington, Mark	Jeffrey Ford	Personal	Cancun, Mexico	Diving
Fredericksen, John	Stephanie Conroy	Personal	Mazatlan, Mexico	Fishing/Sailing
Hammond, Maria	Jamie Reding	Personal/Business	Caribbean	Fishing/Sailing

Landscape Orientation

STEP BY STEP   Set a Worksheet's Orientation

@ The *Margie's Client List* document file for this lesson is available on the book companion website or in WileyPLUS.

OPEN *Margie's Client List* again from the student data files. Then, do the following:

1. Click the Page Layout tab.
2. Click Orientation in the Page Setup group and click Landscape. Scroll through the document to see that it will now print on two pages with each page containing all columns.
3. In the Page Setup group, click Print Titles. The *Page Setup* dialog box opens. Click the Collapse dialog box icon next to *Rows to repeat at top*.
4. Click row 3 (the column labels). Row 3 data is identified in the dialog box. Press Enter. Click OK to accept the changes and close the dialog box.
5. Click the File tab, click Print, and view the Print Preview. Click the Next Page arrow at the bottom of the Print Options window to advance to page 2 in the Print Preview. Notice that the column labels appear on page 2 of the document.
6. Click on the Home tab.

PAUSE. LEAVE the workbook open to use in the next exercise.

WILEY PLUS EXTRA

WileyPLUS Extra! features an online tutorial of this task.

CERTIFICATION READY   3.3.2

How do you select a row of data to repeat at the top of each printed page?

CERTIFICATION READY   3.5.1

How do you change the orientation of a worksheet?

CERTIFICATION READY   3.3.3

How do you select a column of data to repeat at the top of each printed page?

Orientation is the way your workbook or worksheet appears on the printed page. There are two settings: Portrait and Landscape. Portrait is a vertical printing of the workbook, and Landscape is the horizontal aspect. By default, all workbooks and worksheets are printed in Portrait. Use the Landscape orientation when the width of the area you want to print is greater than the height. Data is easier to read when all the columns fit on one page. This can often be accomplished by changing a worksheet's orientation to Landscape. When you can't fit all of the data on one printed page by changing the orientation, you can shrink or reduce it using Excel's scaling options, as described in the next exercise.

Scaling a Worksheet to Fit on a Printed Page

Scaling refers to shrinking or stretching printed output to a percentage of its actual size. One use for scaling is to resize a document so that it fits on a single page. Before attempting to change the scaling for a worksheet's output, the maximum width and height must be set to "Automatic" (see Figure 5-26).

Figure 5-26

Scaling a worksheet to fit on one page

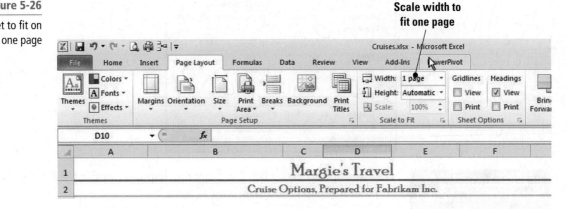

STEP BY STEP   Scale a Worksheet to Fit on a Printed Page

USE the workbook from the previous exercise.

1. On the Page Layout tab, click Orientation, then click Portrait. Notice that column E no longer fits on the same page with columns A–D.
2. In the Scale to Fit group, click the Width arrow and click 1 page. Then click the Height arrow and select 1 page. The scale of the worksheet is reduced so that all columns and rows fit on the same page.

CERTIFICATION READY   **3.5.2**

How do you scale a worksheet to fit on a printed page?

3. Click the File tab, then click Print. View the Print Preview pane to the right. Notice that all columns appear on the page, and the height is one page as well. When output is reduced, it shrinks the height and width proportionally.

4. **SAVE** the workbook as *Client List* and **CLOSE** the workbook.

CLOSE Excel.

The most common reason for scaling a worksheet is to shrink it so that you can print it on one page. You can also enlarge the sheet so that data appears bigger and fills up more of the printed page. When the Width and Height boxes are set to automatic, you can click the arrows in the Scale box to increase or decrease scaling of the printout. Each time you click the arrow, the scaling changes by 5%.

Take Note   Remember that width and height must be set to automatic if you want to specify a scale, such as 75%.

Using Paste Special to Copy Special Data

You may not always want to copy everything from source cells to your destination cells. For example, you may want to copy only the current values of formulas rather than the formulas themselves. In such cases, you can use **Paste Special** to perform irregular cell copying.

When you paste data, Excel normally copies all the information in the range of cells you selected. However, there are times when you only need to paste formula results or the formatting of a cell rather than all of the cell's content. This is where Excel's Paste Special command comes into play. You can use this command to specify a number of options, such as pasting only cell contents without formatting or only formatting without cell contents.

To paste particular parts of a cell selection, on the Home tab, click the arrow below the Paste button. Then, click Paste Special on the drop-down menu to open the Paste Special dialog box, which is shown in Figure 5-27.

Figure 5-27

Paste Special dialog box

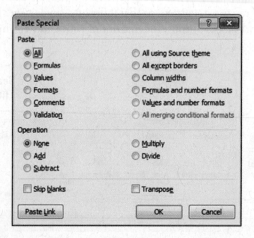

The Paste Special dialog box has many different paste options. Table 5-1 describes each option in the Paste group of the Paste Special dialog box.

CERTIFICATION READY   **2.1.1**

How do you paste only the formatting from a selection of cells?

Table 5-1

Paste group options

CERTIFICATION READY **2.1.1**

How do you paste only the formulas from a selection of cells?

CERTIFICATION READY **2.1.1**

How do you paste only the values from a selection of cells?

CERTIFICATION READY **2.1.1**

How do you paste a cell's comments?

CERTIFICATION READY **2.1.1**

How do you paste a cell's data validation rules?

CERTIFICATION READY **2.1.1**

How do you perform addition between cells you copy and paste?

Option	Resulting Action
All	Pastes your cell selection, including all formatting, formulas, content, etc. This is also the default Paste.
Formulas	Pastes the formulas, text, and numbers in your cell selection without the formatting.
Values	Pastes the calculated value of formulas in the current cell selection.
Formats	Pastes only the formatting from the cell selection—and none of the content.
Comments	Pastes only the Comments or notes attached to the current cell selection.
Validation	Pastes only the data validation rules that you set up with the Data Validation command.
All using Source theme	Pastes all the content and information in the cell selection plus the cell styles.
All except borders	Pastes all the content and information in the cell selection without copying any borders.
Column widths	Applies the column widths of the cells copied to the Clipboard to the columns where the cells are pasted.
Formulas and number formats	Pastes all the cell content, including formulas, and retains any formatting applied to the numbers and formulas.
Values and number formats	Pastes all cell content, converting formulas to their calculated values, and applies any number or formula formatting from the original cells.
All merging conditional formats	Pastes any conditional formatting that was applied to the original cell content.

You can also perform an arithmetic operation on values in the destination range. Table 5-2 explains the options in the Operation group of the Paste Special dialog box.

Table 5-2

Operation group options in the Paste Special dialog box

CERTIFICATION READY **2.1.1**

How do you perform division between cells you copy and paste?

Option	Resulting Action
None	Performs no mathematical operation between the original data in the Clipboard and your selected destination cell range.
Add	Adds the values you cut or copy to the Clipboard to the values in the cell range where you paste.
Subtract	Subtracts the values you cut or copy to the Clipboard from the values in the cell range where you paste.
Multiply	Multiplies the values you cut or copy to the Clipboard with the values in the cell range where you paste.
Divide	Divides the values you cut or copy to the Clipboard by the values in the cell range where you paste.

Take Note

The new Paste with Live Preview feature is also available with Paste Special. If you mouse over the Paste options in either the right-click menu, or the paste menu in the Clipboard group, you will be able to view your changes before actually implementing them.

Finally, there are a few more options available at the bottom of the Paste Special dialog box, shown in Table 5-3.

CERTIFICATION READY   2.1.1

How do you use the Paste Special Preview Icons when doing a copy and paste?

Table 5-3

Additional Paste Special options

CERTIFICATION READY   2.1.1

How do you transpose rows or columns of data when copying and pasting?

Option	Resulting Action
Skip blanks	Selecting this check box will paste only from the cells in your copied selection that aren't empty.
Transpose	Selecting this check box will cause your cell data to change orientation. Row data will become column data, and column data will become row data.
Paste Link	Click this button when you want to establish a link between the copies you're pasting and the original entries. This ensures that any changes to the original cells will be automatically updated in the pasted copies.

CERTIFICATION READY   2.1.1

How do you paste as a link?

SKILL SUMMARY

In This Lesson You Learned How To:	Exam Objective	Objective Number
Working with Rows and Columns	Hide or unhide a column.	3.4.1
	Hide or unhide a row.	3.4.2
	Hide a series of rows.	3.4.4
	Hide a series of columns.	3.4.3
Using Themes		
Modifying a Worksheet's Onscreen and Printed Appearance	Apply color to worksheet tabs.	4.1.8
	Apply printing options.	1.2.4
	Print row and column headings.	3.3.1
Inserting Headers and Footers	Construct headers and footers.	1.2.3
	Change header and footer size.	3.5.4
	Configure titles to print only on odd or even pages.	3.3.4
	Configure titles to skip the first worksheet page.	3.3.5
Preparing a Document for Printing	Use Page Break workbook view.	4.3.3
	Configure page margins.	3.5.3
	Print rows to repeat with titles.	3.3.2
	Configure page orientation.	3.5.1
	Print columns to repeat with titles.	3.3.3
	Manage page scaling.	3.5.2
	Use Paste Special.	2.1.1

Knowledge Assessment

Fill in the Blank

Complete the following sentences by writing the correct word or words in the blanks provided.

1. The _____ option allows you to enlarge or shrink worksheet data to achieve a more logical fit on the printed page.
2. There are _____ header and footer text boxes on a workbook page where you can enter information.
3. You can manually adjust page breaks in the _____ view.
4. You can mimic a watermark on printouts by adding a(n) _____ to a header or footer.
5. Applying a(n) _____ will override any formatting styles that have been applied to a data range.
6. To format an entire row or column, you must select its _____.
7. A(n) _____ is a block of text that appears at the top of each printed page.
8. Row _____ will automatically expand to accommodate increased font size.
9. Document themes are used to apply sets of styles, including colors, fonts, and _____.
10. _____ is a setting that specifies the direction a worksheet appears on the printed page.

True/False

Circle T if the statement is true or F if the statement is false.

T F 1. You can insert a graphic in the header or footer of a worksheet.

T F 2. Column width and row height can be changed.

T F 3. After you enter a manual page break, you cannot remove it.

T F 4. You can center a worksheet's data horizontally, but not vertically.

T F 5. You can hide a column by setting its width to zero.

T F 6. Hidden rows are not displayed onscreen, but they will appear when the page is printed.

T F 7. You can change page endings in Page Break Preview view.

T F 8. You can use one of Excel's predefined Header & Footer elements to enter the name of a worksheet's author.

T F 9. You cannot make changes to a worksheet in the Print Preview window.

T F 10. By default, gridlines will print in an Excel worksheet.

Competency Assessment

Project 5-1: Working with Rows and Columns

The School of Fine Arts has developed a workbook to track enrollment for the academic year. Enrollments for courses in two departments have been entered. In the following exercise, you will apply the formatting techniques you learned in this lesson to enhance the appearance of the two worksheets in the workbook.

@ The *SFA Enrollment* file for this lesson is available on the book companion website or in WileyPLUS.

GET READY. LAUNCH Excel if it is not already running. Then, do the following:

1. **OPEN** the *SFA Enrollment* data file. Sheet1 should be active and the Home tab should be displayed.
2. Click A1, click the Insert arrow in the Cells group, then click Insert Sheet Rows.
3. Select A1:C1 and click Merge & Center in the Alignment group.
4. With A1 selected, key School of Fine Arts.
5. Select A2:C2 and click Merge & Center. To overwrite the exiting text, key Fine Arts Department.
6. Merge and center A3:C3 and key Enrollment, replacing the existing text.
7. Select row 4, click the Insert arrow, then click Insert Sheet Rows.
8. In A5, key Call No.. Please include the period to abbreviate "number."
9. In B5, key Course.
10. In C5, key Fall, replacing the existing text.
11. Select row 5. Click Bold and Italic in the Font group. Click the Center button in the Alignment group.
12. Select row 1. Click Format in the Cells group and click Row Height under Cell Size.
13. Key 20 in the Row Height dialog box and click OK.
14. Click the bottom boundary for row 2 and drag down until the ScreenTip says the height is 18.00 points (24 pixels).
15. Click the Sheet2 tab and repeat steps 2–14. If necessary, double-click the boundary between columns to adjust the column width to display all of the text.
16. In A2, key Media Studies Department.
17. **SAVE** the workbook in your Lesson 5 folder. Name the workbook *SFA Enrollment 5-1*.

CLOSE the workbook. **LEAVE** Excel open for the next project.

Project 5-2: Working with Rows and Columns

In this exercise, you will insert columns and rows to add additional data to the client list for Margie's Travel. You'll also apply styles and a document theme to add visual appeal.

@ The *Client Update* file for this lesson is available on the book companion website or in WileyPLUS.

OPEN the *Client Update* file for this lesson, then perform these steps:

1. With column E selected, click the Insert arrow in the Cells group and click Insert Sheet Columns.
2. In E3, key Anticipated Travel.
3. Insert a row above row 3.
4. Select columns C and D. Click Format in the Cells group. Under Visibility, point to Hide & Unhide and click Hide Columns.
5. Click the Page Layout tab, then click Themes in the Themes group. Click Metro.
6. Select cell A1. Open the Home tab and click Middle Align in the Alignment group.
7. Select A4:F4. Click Cell Styles. Apply Heading 3 to the column labels.

8. Enter the following anticipated travel for the listed clients:

Keil, Kendall   Romantic Hawaii Cruise
Nash, Mike   Aruba
Li, Yale   Paris

9. **SAVE** the workbook as *Client Update 5-2*.

LEAVE the workbook open for the next project.

Proficiency Assessment

Project 5-3: Modifying a Worksheet's Onscreen Appearance

In this project, you will create a customized theme for Margie's Travel and prepare the document for printing on two pages.

USE the workbook from Project 5-2.

1. With the Home tab active, select A1. Increase the font size to 20.
2. Select row 4. Increase the font size to 14.
3. Click the Page Layout tab.
4. In the Themes group, click the Colors button, then click Create New Theme Colors.
5. Change the third Text/Background to Purple.
6. Key your name in the Name box. Click Save.
7. Set gridlines to print.
8. Insert a footer that prints the file name in the left Footer pane.
9. Insert a footer that prints the page number in the right Footer pane.
10. On the Page Layout tab, click the Print check box under Headings. Set the column headings to print on the second page. Click Page Break Preview. Move the horizontal automatic page break to the bottom of row 40 and move the vertical page break to the right of column F.
11. Print the worksheet.
12. **SAVE** the workbook in your Lesson 5 folder as *Client Update 5-3*.

CLOSE the workbook. **LEAVE** Excel open for the next project.

Project 5-4: Preparing a Worksheet for Printing

In this project, you will apply styles and a theme to a School of Fine Arts worksheet. You will also create and apply a custom margin setting and print the worksheet with gridlines and headings.

OPEN the *SFA Enrollment Update* data file for this lesson.

@ The *SFA Enrollment Update* file for this lesson is available on the book companion website or in WileyPLUS.

1. The workbook should open to Sheet1. Apply Heading 1 to cell A1.
2. Apply Heading 2 to A2.
3. Apply Heading 3 to A3.
4. Apply the Oriel theme to the worksheets.
5. Click Margins and Custom Margins to open the Page Setup dialog box.
6. For Sheet1, set the top, bottom, left, and right margins to 1.5.
7. Center the data horizontally and vertically.
8. Print Sheet2 with gridlines.
9. Print Sheet1 with headings.
10. Add blue color to the Sheet1 tab and green to the Sheet2 tab.
11. **SAVE** the workbook as *SFA Enrollment 5-4*.

LEAVE the workbook open for the next project.

Project 5-5: Updating and Printing a Workbook

In this project, you will add additional data to an existing workbook and prepare the workbook for printing.

USE the workbook from Project 5-4.

1. On Sheet1, select A1:C5. Copy the heading to Sheet3.
2. Click the Paste Options button. Click Keep Source Column Widths.
3. On Sheet3, enter the following data for the Biomedical Art Department enrollments:

MED114	Principles of Biology	463
MED115	Human Forms	236
MED116	Biomedical Art Methods	365
MED351	Traditional and Digital Color	446
MED352	3D Modeling	234
MED353	Advanced Problem in Biomedical Art	778
MED354	3D Texture	567
ILL302	Digital Imaging and Illustration	643
ILL303	Storyboarding	234
ILL304	Drawing Beyond Observation	123
DRG333	Visual Editor	434

4. Color the Sheet3 tab orange.
5. Insert a footer in the center text box that reads Academic Year 20XX (with XX being the current year).
6. In the left Footer text box, key Current as of and click Current Date.
7. Center Sheet3 vertically and horizontally.
8. Access Backstage. Print the sheet with gridlines.
9. **SAVE** the workbook as *SFA Enrollment 5-5*.

CLOSE the workbook; **LEAVE** Excel open for the next project.

Project 5-6: Fixing the Fitness Classes Worksheet

The owner of Margie's Travel plans to meet with each travel consultant to discuss his or her client list. For this project, you will insert manual page breaks in a worksheet so that each consultant's data prints on a separate page.

OPEN the *Anticipated Travel* file from the student data files for this lesson.

@ The *Anticipated Travel* worksheet and *Lighthouse* image file for this lesson are available on the book companion website or in WileyPLUS.

1. Check the worksheet for existing headers and footers.
2. In the right Header box, insert the *Lighthouse* image from the student data files for this lesson. Click Format Picture. Set the scale to 10% of its original size, so that the image appears only in the header.
3. In the center Footer box, click Footer and click the last option in the predefined footers.
4. Unhide columns C and D.
5. Set the orientation to Landscape.
6. Open the Page Break Preview and move and add page breaks so that each consultant's client list appears on a different page.
7. Titles and column labels should print on each page.
8. Scale the data so that it is only one page wide.

9. Print the complete worksheet with gridlines. You should have a page for each consultant.

10. **SAVE** the workbook as *Anticipated Travel 5-6*. **CLOSE** the workbook.

LEAVE Excel open for the next project.

INTERNET READY

Use the *Anticipated Travel 5-6* workbook from the previous project.

You and two friends from class have an appointment with Stephanie Conroy, a travel consultant with Margie's Travel, to plan your next vacation.

Add your name and your friends' names to the client list. Identify Stephanie as your consultant.

List at least one special interest for each of you.

Go online and find an ideal vacation spot that will fulfill the special interests for all of you. For example, if the three interests were golfing, theater, and swimming, where could you vacation that would satisfy the three interests?

Save the revised workbook as *My Vacation*. When you have finished, close Excel.

Circling Back 1

Cross-Cultural Solutions is a nonprofit organization that is recognized by the United Nations as an expert in the field of international volunteering. Whereas well-known programs such as the Peace Corps and Volunteer Service Overseas (VSO) require a two-year commitment, Cross-Cultural Solutions provides volunteer opportunities ranging from one to twelve weeks. The organization offers a choice of three programs with year-round start dates. The goal is to provide a balance of volunteer work, cultural activities, and learning activities with time to explore the host country.

As an employee in the organization's home office, part of your job is to create, edit, and format workbooks related to the programs and the individuals who volunteer.

Project 1: Creating and Formatting a Workbook

The two- to twelve-week Volunteer Abroad program is Cross-Cultural Solutions' most popular program because it offers the greatest flexibility in terms of locations and start dates. Volunteer work is personalized to the volunteer's skills and interests. In this exercise, you will create a worksheet that contains details about this program.

GET READY. LAUNCH Excel if it is not already running.

1. Click the File tab. Click New in the navigation area. Click the Create button. The Home tab should now be active.
2. Select cell A2 and key Volunteer Abroad. You have now created your worksheet header.
3. In row 4, key the following column labels:

   Country
   Location
   Language

4. **CREATE** a folder named Circling Back 1, and save the document as *Volunteer Abroad*.
5. Select columns A and C. Click Format, then click Column width, and then change the column width to 20 characters.
6. Change the width of column B to 25 characters.
7. Enter the following data for the countries and locations where the Volunteer Abroad program is available:

   Ghana, Volta Region
   Tanzania, Arusha
   Tanzania, Kilimanjaro
   China, Xi'an
   Thailand, Bangkok
   Thailand, Trang
   India, New Delhi
   India, Dharamsala
   Brazil, Salvador
   Costa Rica, San Carlos
   Costa Rica, Cartage
   Guatemala, Guatemala City
   Peru, Lima
   Peru, Ayacucho
   Russia, Yaroslavl

8. Click any cell in column A. In the Cells group, click the Insert arrow, then select Insert Sheet Columns. A new column is inserted to the left of the original column A.
9. Select cell A4 and key Continent.

10. Select the cell range A5:A7. Click Merge & Center in the Alignment group, then key Africa.

11. Select the cell range A8:A12. Click Merge & Center in the Alignment group, then key Asia.

12. Select the cell range A13:A18. Click Merge & Center in the Alignment group. Key Latin America. Next, click Wrap Text.

13. Select A19, and key Europe. Click Center in the Alignment group.

14. Using the Home tab and its groups, format column A as follows.

    Click Middle Align.

    Increase the font size to 14.

    Set the font color to blue.

    Double-click the column A boundary to AutoFit the contents.

15. Select a continent and the three columns associated with that continent. Click Format, then click Format Cells. Click the Border tab. Place an outline around each continent's data.

16. Using the Alignment group, merge and center A2:D2. Click Cell Styles, then apply Heading 2 style.

17. With A1 active, click Insert, then select Insert Sheet Rows.

18. In A1, key Cross-Cultural Solutions. Merge and center the title above the columns and apply Heading style 1.

19. Merge and center A2:D2, then merge and center A4:D4.

20. Apply Heading 3 style to the column labels and add a light blue fill color.

21. Click the File tab, click Print, and view the Print Preview.

22. In the Page Setup area, make the following selections:

    Portrait Orientation

    Center Vertically and Horizontally

23. PRINT the worksheet.

24. SAVE the changes. CLOSE the workbook.

LEAVE Excel open for the next project.

Project 2: Formatting Cells and Ranges

In addition to its Volunteer Abroad program, Cross-Cultural Solutions offers a two- to twelve-week Intern Abroad program for students interested in an international internship or academic credit and a one-week Insight Abroad program. You have prepared a workbook with data related to the volunteers who will depart for their assignments within the next two months. After preparing the workbook, you learned the volunteers' assignments from the organization's on-site coordinators. Therefore, you need to edit and format your worksheet.

The *Cross Cultural Volunteers* file for this lesson is available on the book companion website or in WileyPLUS.

OPEN *Cross Cultural Volunteers* from the student data files.

1. With Sheet1 active and the Home tab displayed, delete column E.

2. Click the row 18 heading to select the entire row. Press Ctrl and select row 23. Continue to scroll through the worksheet, selecting the blank rows.

3. Click Delete, then click Delete Sheet Rows.

4. On the Insert tab, click Header & Footer. Key July and August Departures in the center Header pane.

5. Click Go To Footer, and key Prepared by (your name) in the left Footer pane.

6. Tab to the center Footer pane, then click the Current Date option.

7. Tab to the right Footer pane, then click the Page Number button.

8. Right-click the Sheet1 tab, and change the tab color to purple.

9. Right-click the Sheet2 tab and change the tab color to green.

10. With Sheet1 active, select column E, click the Home tab, and display the Number dialog box. Format the dates to display as day-month (i.e., 20-Jul).

11. Click the Sheet2 tab to make it the active worksheet. Format columns B and C as Currency and decrease the decimals to zero.

12. **SAVE** the workbook as *Volunteers, Project 2*.

LEAVE the workbook open for the next project.

Project 3: Preparing a Workbook for Printing and Display

Now that you have completed the data entries for the Cross-Cultural Volunteers workbook, you will format and prepare the worksheet for printing.

USE the *Volunteers, Project 2* workbook from the previous project.

1. With Sheet1 active, set a Wide margin.

2. Click Page Break Preview, then move the page breaks so that page 1 ends with row 30 and page 2 ends with row 60.

3. Prepare the workbook for printing as follows:

   Use Landscape Orientation.

   Print the Guidelines.

   Print the titles (row4) at the top of all pages.

4. Examine the Print Preview in Backstage to verify that the printout will be in landscape orientation, that the column labels print on pages 2 and 3, and that only the cells that contain data are included in the printout.

5. Print the entire workbook.

6. Prepare Sheet1 for display at a meeting. On the Page Layout tab, click Background. Select the *Blue Hills* image from the student data files, and click Insert.

7. **SAVE** the workbook as *Volunteers, Project 3*.

CLOSE Excel.

@ The *Blue Hills* image file for this lesson is available on the book companion website or in WileyPLUS.

LESSON SKILL MATRIX

Skill	Exam Objective	Objective Number
Organizing Worksheets	Move worksheets.	**4.1.5**
	Copy worksheets.	**4.1.4**
	Rename worksheets.	**4.1.6**
	Reposition worksheets within a workbook.	**4.1.3**
	Hide worksheet tabs.	**4.1.9**
	Unhide worksheet tabs.	**4.1.10**
	Insert worksheets.	**4.1.1**
	Delete worksheets.	**4.1.2**
Working with Multiple Worksheets	Group worksheets.	**4.1.7**
	Open a new window with contents from the current worksheet.	**4.2.3**
	Arrange window views.	**4.2.2**
Using Zoom and Freeze to Change the Onscreen View		
Finding and Replacing Data		

KEY TERMS

- **freeze**
- **group worksheets**
- **hide**
- **string**
- **unhide**
- **zoom**

The School of Fine Arts (SFA) is a private college that is recognized as a leader in art education. More than 2,500 students are enrolled in its four-year programs of study. Admission requires an audition and/or portfolio presentation. Students pursue a BA degree in one of six majors: Fine Arts, Media Studies, Biomedical Arts, Dramatic Arts, Interior Design, Advertising, and Graphic Arts. The school also offers a degree program for students who wish to combine major areas of concentration. In addition to its degree programs, SFA offers continuing education courses and Saturday and summer courses for children, teens, and adults who hope to pursue a career in the creative arts or who have exceptional artistic talent.

SOFTWARE ORIENTATION

Worksheet Management

An Excel workbook should contain information about a unique subject. For example, SFA might have one workbook for enrollment data, one for faculty course assignments, and one for summer workshop course offerings. Each worksheet within a workbook should contain a subset of information about that workbook. The number of worksheets that a workbook can contain is limited only by the available memory of your computer.

Figure 6-1

Commands to organize worksheets

In this lesson, you will learn to copy worksheets between workbooks, manage and reorganize sheets by hiding and unhiding worksheets, and use Excel's search tools to find and replace information in a worksheet or workbook. To accomplish these tasks, you will use commands in the Home tab's Cells and Editing groups. (See Figure 6-1.)

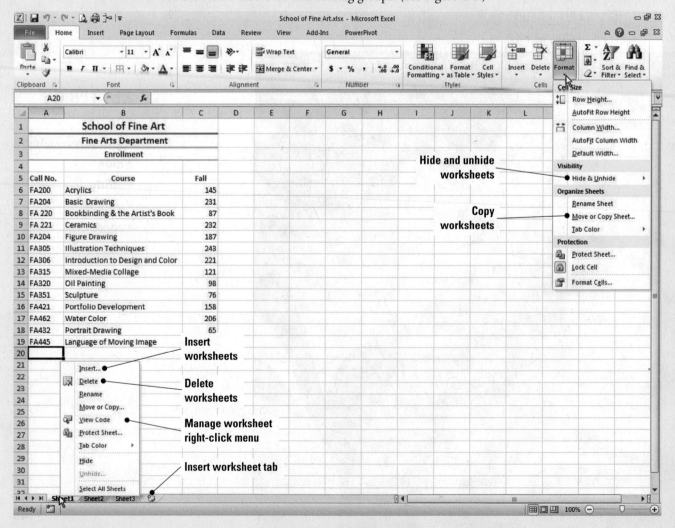

ORGANIZING WORKSHEETS

A new, blank Excel workbook has three worksheets. You can add to, delete from, and move and copy these worksheets as desired. You can also rename worksheets and hide and unhide worksheets when you need to do so. The flexibility to organize worksheets with similar subject matter together in one file enables you to effectively and efficiently manage related data.

Copying a Worksheet

Just as you can copy data from one cell or range in a worksheet to another cell or range, you can copy data from one worksheet to another within a workbook. For example, when a new worksheet will contain information similar to that contained in an existing worksheet, you can copy the worksheet and delete cell contents or overwrite existing data with new data. When you copy a worksheet, you retain the structure and formatting of the original worksheet so that you don't need to rebuild it from scratch. You can copy a worksheet using the Home tab's Format commands, the mouse, or the shortcut menu.

STEP BY STEP   **Copy a Worksheet**

The *School of Fine Arts* file for this lesson is available on the book companion website or the WileyPLUS website.

GET READY. Before you begin these steps, **LAUNCH** Microsoft Excel 2010.

1. **OPEN** the *School of Fine Arts* data file for this lesson.
2. With the Sheet1 tab active, click Format in the Cells group on the Home tab.
3. Click Move or Copy Sheet. The dialog box shown in Figure 6-2 opens.

Figure 6-2

Move or Copy dialog box

WILEY
PLUS *EXTRA*

WileyPLUS Extra! features an online tutorial of this task.

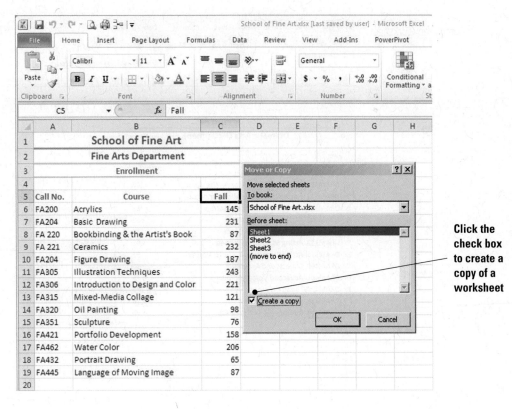

Click the check box to create a copy of a worksheet

4. Sheet1 is selected by default. Select the Create a copy box as shown in Figure 6-2 and click OK. A copy of Sheet1 is inserted to the left of Sheet1 and is named Sheet1 (2).
5. Click the Sheet3 tab and hold down the left mouse button. A down arrow appears at the boundary between Sheet2 and Sheet3, and the cursor becomes an arrow pointing to the left of a blank document symbol.
6. Press and hold Ctrl. A plus sign appears in the cursor document. Move the cursor to the right until the down arrow appears on the right side of Sheet3. Release the mouse button and Ctrl key. The new sheet is named Sheet3 (2).

Another Way
You can also right-click a sheet tab to display the shortcut menu, then click Move or Copy to display the corresponding dialog box.

CERTIFICATION READY   4.1.5

How do you move a worksheet?

7. With Sheet3 (2) active, select cell A2 and key **Dramatic Arts Department**.

   When you use the Format command or the shortcut menu to copy a worksheet, the Move or Copy dialog box shown in Figure 6-2 lets you identify the worksheet you want to copy. By default, the copied worksheet is inserted before the sheet you select in the dialog box. You can, however, place the worksheet in other locations by choosing the destination in the Move or Copy dialog box.

8. Select **A6:C18** and press **Delete**.

9. Enter the following data for the Dramatic Arts Department, beginning in cell A6:

Another Way
Rather than delete the existing data, you can over-write it. Select A6 and begin keying new data. Press Tab and key the data for B6. Press Tab and key the data for C6 and press Enter, etc. As you move to the next cell, the existing text is selected and it will be deleted when you enter new text.

DRAM321	Acting Studio I: Discover the Actor	106
DRAM322	Naturalism and Realism Techniques	95
DRAM326	Acting Studio: Improvisation	87
DRAM302	Acting Studio: Comedy	69
DRAM301	Fundamentals of Dance	110
DRAM312	Acting Studio: Shakespeare	95
DRAM315	Acting Studio: Iconoclastic Voices	95
DRAM400	Dialects and Accents	95
DRAM401	Advanced Voice and Diction	75
DRAM420	Theatre History	125
DRAM435	Acting for Film and TV	76
DRAM460	Auditioning Techniques	95

10. Adjust all column widths to display all data. (See Figure 6-3.)

Figure 6-3

Completed worksheet

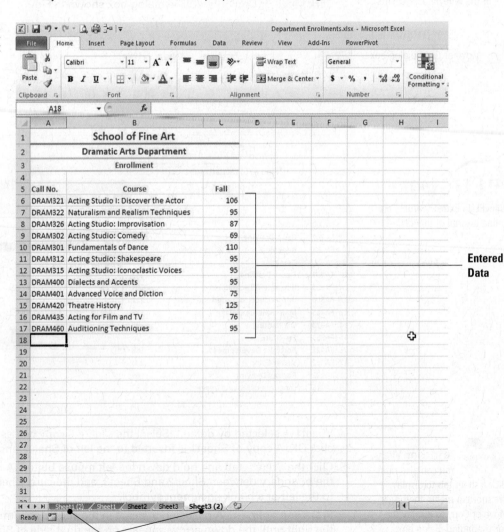

CERTIFICATION
READY   4.1.4

How do you copy a worksheet within a workbook?

11. Click the File tab and select Save As. Create a Lesson 6 folder. **SAVE** the workbook in the folder as *Department Enrollments*.

PAUSE. LEAVE the workbook open to use in the next exercise.

When an existing worksheet contains formatting that you want to use in a new worksheet, it is more efficient to copy the existing worksheet than to start the new worksheet from scratch. You can then delete or overwrite the existing data with new data. You will not need to format the new worksheet—the formatting is copied with the data. By copying worksheets, you can be assured that formatting is consistent among all the worksheets in a workbook.

In the preceding exercise, you used two methods to copy a worksheet, resulting in a workbook that has five worksheets. Notice that when you copy a worksheet, the new sheet is identified as a copy by a number in parentheses following the worksheet name. When you click and hold the left mouse button on the worksheet tab, the cursor becomes a new worksheet icon and an arrow appears next to the active worksheet tab, as shown in Figure 6-4.

Figure 6-4

Copying a worksheet using the mouse

Move or Copy mouse pointer

Take Note   Notice that when a worksheet is copied, the tab color is copied as well as the worksheet, contents, and formatting.

Renaming a Worksheet

When a workbook contains multiple worksheets with data, it is helpful to replace the generic names Sheet1, Sheet2, and so on with names that identify the data contained in each sheet. In our example, each of the worksheets contains information about one department in the School of Fine Arts. Renaming the tabs with department names will allow you to quickly locate enrollment data.

STEP BY STEP　　　　**Rename a Worksheet**

Another Way
You can also right-click the sheet tab to activate the sheet tab drop-down menu.

USE the workbook you saved in the previous exercise to carry out these steps:

1. Double-click the Sheet1 (2) tab to select the tab name.
2. Key Interior Design and press Enter. The new name appears on the worksheet tab.
3. Key Interior Design Department in A2 of the sheet. Select A6:C19 and press Delete. You will enter data for this department in a later exercise.
4. Click the Sheet1 tab. Click Format and click Rename Sheet. Key Fine Arts and press Enter.
5. Click the Sheet2 tab. Rename the sheet Media Studies and press Enter.
6. Click the Sheet3 tab. Rename the sheet Biomedical Arts and press Enter.
7. Click Sheet3 (2). Rename the sheet Dramatic Arts and press Enter.
8. Check each worksheet to ensure that the shortened name on the sheet tab matches the department name in A2.

PAUSE. LEAVE the workbook open to use in the next exercise.

CERTIFICATION READY 4.1.6

How do you rename a worksheet?

By naming the worksheets, you make it much easier to locate enrollment data for any course in a department. Each worksheet name indicates the type of data contained in the sheet.

Repositioning the Worksheets in a Workbook

Now that the worksheets in the Department Enrollments workbook are appropriately named, you can rearrange them in any way you wish. An alphabetical arrangement is a logical way to organize the worksheets in this workbook.

STEP BY STEP　　　　**Reposition the Worksheets in a Workbook**

USE the workbook from the previous exercise.

1. Click the Biomedical Arts tab. Click Format in the Cells group.
2. Click Move or Copy Sheet. The *Move or Copy* dialog box opens. You want this sheet to be the first sheet listed in the *Before sheet* box, so click OK to move Biomedical Arts before Interior Design.
3. Click the Dramatic Arts tab. Hold down the mouse button and move the worksheet to the left. Release the mouse when the down arrow is on the right side of the Biomedical Arts tab.
4. Click the Fine Arts tab. Click Format, then click Move or Copy Sheet.
5. Click Interior Design in the dialog box. Click OK to move Fine Arts before Interior Design. The Fine Arts sheet is moved to the third position and the sheets are now in alphabetic order.
6. Click the Dramatic Arts tab. Click Format and then Tab Color. Click Red under Standard Colors. As noted previously, when you copied worksheets, the tab color was copied as well as the contents and formatting. Changing the tab color for the copied worksheets ensures that each tab has a different color.
7. Right-click the Interior Design tab, click Tab Color, and click Purple under Standard Colors.
8. **SAVE** the workbook with the same name.

PAUSE. LEAVE the workbook open to use in the next exercise.

CERTIFICATION READY 4.1.3

How do you reposition a worksheet in a workbook?

Hiding and Unhiding a Worksheet

You may hide columns and rows when you want to exclude particular columns or rows from a printout or when you want to hide sensitive or confidential information while you are working with other data in a worksheet. You can apply the same procedure to **hide** (make a worksheet invisible) and **unhide** (make visible again) worksheets. For example, because the Interior Design worksheet does not contain data at this time, you would hide that sheet if you wanted to print the entire workbook. In the exercise that follows, you will learn how to hide and unhide worksheets.

STEP BY STEP   Hide and Unhide a Worksheet

USE the workbook from the previous exercise.

1. Select the Interior Design worksheet. Click Format in the Cells group.
2. Click Hide & Unhide and click Hide Sheet. The Interior Design worksheet is no longer visible. Click the Fine Arts tab.

Take Note   Right-click any worksheet tab. If worksheets are hidden, the Unhide option will be active on the shortcut menu.

3. Click Format, click Hide & Unhide, and then click Unhide Sheet. The Unhide dialog box shown in Figure 6-5 opens.

Figure 6-5

Unhide dialog box

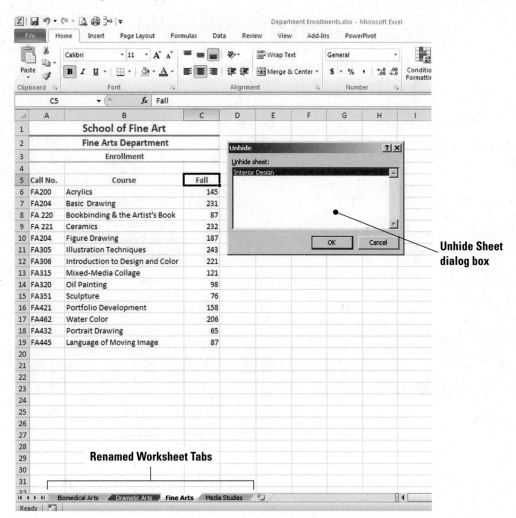

Unhide Sheet dialog box

Renamed Worksheet Tabs

4. Click OK to unhide the Interior Design worksheet. Enter the following enrollment information:

ID201	Elements of Design I	103
ID205	Interior Design I	106
ID207	History of Interiors	110
ID232	Drawing and Composition	121
ID320	Interior Design II	86

CERTIFICATION
READY   4.1.9

How do you hide a worksheet
in a workbook?

CERTIFICATION
READY   4.1.10

How do you unhide a
worksheet in a workbook?

ID322	Architectural Drafting	98
ID325	Elements of Design II	95
ID330	Color Theory	89
ID335	Textiles	121
ID405	CAD I	82
ID432	CAD II	75
ID430	Perspectives in Design	63
ID461	Furniture Design	59
ID465	Lighting Design	49

5. **SAVE** your workbook.

PAUSE. LEAVE the workbook open to use in the next exercise.

You can hide several worksheets at the same time. To do so, hold down Ctrl and click the tab(s) of the sheet(s) you want to hide. You cannot, however, select multiple worksheets in the Unhide dialog box; you must unhide worksheets individually.

Inserting a New Worksheet into a Workbook

You can insert one or multiple worksheets into an existing workbook. The Insert Worksheet tab (Figure 6-6) at the bottom of a worksheet was introduced in Excel 2007 as a new feature that

Figure 6-6

Insert Worksheet tab

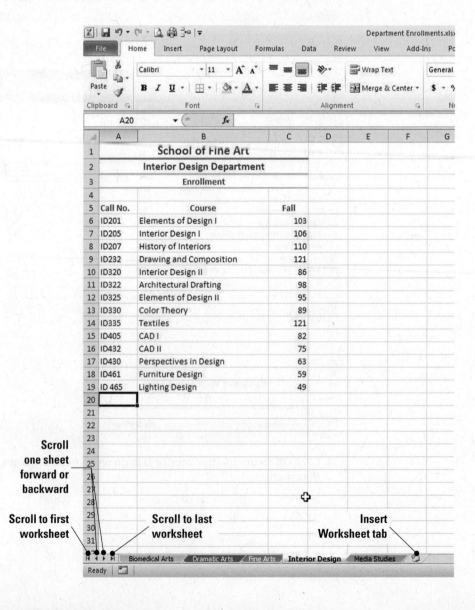

Scroll one sheet forward or backward

Scroll to first worksheet

Scroll to last worksheet

Insert Worksheet tab

allows you to quickly insert a new worksheet at the end of the existing worksheets. To insert a new worksheet before an existing worksheet, select the worksheet tab before the place where you want to insert the new sheet and use the Insert command in the Cells group.

STEP BY STEP   **Insert a New Worksheet into a Workbook**

USE the workbook from the previous exercise.

1. Click the Insert Worksheet tab next to the Media Studies tab. A new worksheet (Sheet6) is inserted. When you insert a new worksheet, it is blank and has the generic Sheet1 title. When you inserted a worksheet before the existing sheets were named, the new sheet was given the next consecutive number, such as Sheet6.

2. Click the Biomedical Arts tab and click the Insert arrow in the Cells group to display the options shown in Figure 6-7. Click Insert Sheet. A blank sheet (Sheet7) is inserted before the Biomedical Arts worksheet. As more worksheets are added to a workbook, you may not be able to see all worksheet tabs. When this happens, use the scroll arrows, shown in Figure 6-6, to move through all worksheets.

Figure 6-7

Insert options menu

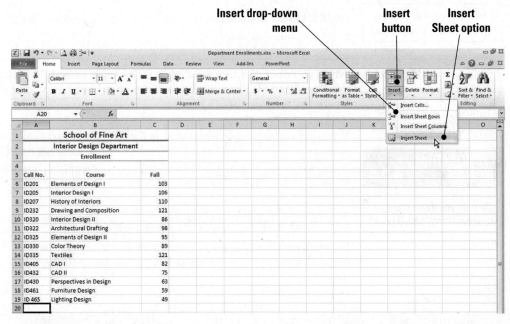

6. Click Insert and Insert Sheet. Based on the previous step's selection, two worksheets, Sheet9 and Sheet10, are inserted before the Biomedical Arts worksheet.

 Troubleshooting If the Biomedical Arts tab is not visible, use the scroll arrow to move to the first worksheet.

3. Double-click the Sheet7 tab, key Advertising, and press Enter.

4. Click the Dramatic Arts tab and click the Insert arrow in the Cells group. Click Insert Sheet. A new Sheet8 is inserted.

5. Click Advertising, press and hold Shift, and click Biomedical Arts. You have now selected two sheets.

6. Click Insert and Insert Sheet. Based on the previous step's selection, two worksheets, Sheet9 and Sheet10, are inserted before the Biomedical Arts worksheet.

Figure 6-8

Insert dialog box

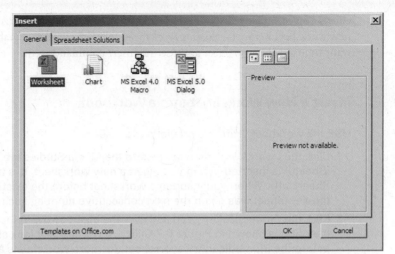

 Another Way
You can right-click a worksheet tab and click Insert on the shortcut menu to insert a worksheet. The Insert dialog box shown in Figure 6-8 will open, and you can insert a blank worksheet from the General tab, insert a worksheet based on a template from the Spreadsheet Solutions tab, or insert an online template if you are connected to the Internet.

CERTIFICATION READY **4.1.1**

How do you insert a new worksheet into a workbook?

PAUSE. LEAVE the workbook open to use in the next exercise.

 **Troubleshooting** When you open the Insert dialog box, multiple Excel files may be shown on the General tab. The listed files represent templates that have been downloaded, created by you, or created by another user.

Take Note When inserting multiple worksheets at the same time, press and hold Shift, then select the same number of worksheet tabs that you want to insert in the open workbook. Recall that in the exercise, when you selected the tabs of two existing worksheets, clicked Insert, and clicked Insert Sheet, two new worksheets were inserted.

CERTIFICATION READY **4.1.1**

How do you insert multiple worksheets into a workbook?

Deleting a Worksheet from a Workbook

If a workbook contains blank worksheets or worksheets that hold data that is no longer needed, you can delete the unnecessary sheets. In the next exercise, you will learn how to delete worksheets.

STEP BY STEP **Delete a Worksheet from a Workbook**

CERTIFICATION READY **4.1.2**

How do you delete one worksheet in a workbook?

USE the workbook from the previous exercise.

1. Use the scroll sheets arrow to locate and click Sheet6, then click the Delete arrow in the Cells group.
2. Click Delete Sheet.
3. Use the scroll sheets arrow to go back to the beginning of the worksheets. Click the Sheet8 tab, press and hold Ctrl, and click the Sheet9 tab. The selection should include Sheet10 as well as Sheet8 and Sheet9.

Take Note You can delete more than one worksheet at a time. To select adjacent sheets, click the first sheet tab, press and hold the Shift key, and then click the second sheet tab. To select nonadjacent sheets, click the first sheet tab, click and hold the Ctrl key, and then click all the sheet tabs you want to include.

CERTIFICATION READY **4.1.2**

How do you delete multiple worksheets in a workbook?

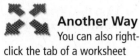

Another Way
You can also right-click the tab of a worksheet you do not need and click Delete. The worksheet will be deleted.

Bottom Line

4. Click the Delete arrow, then select Delete Sheet.
5. SAVE the workbook.

PAUSE. LEAVE the workbook open to use in the next exercise.

WORKING WITH MULTIPLE WORKSHEETS

In Excel, you can **group worksheets**, a feature that allows you to enter and edit data on several worksheets at the same time or apply formatting to multiple worksheets. When sheets are grouped, you can enter data in one worksheet and have it appear in multiple worksheets in a workbook. When multiple worksheets are selected, [*Group*] appears in the title bar at the top of the worksheet. Be cautious. When you change data in grouped sheets, you may accidentally replace data on other sheets.

Working with Multiple Worksheets in a Workbook

Working with a group of worksheets is a time-saving technique. You can view several worksheets within a workbook at the same time. This feature allows you to make quick visual comparisons and ensures that changes made to grouped sheets will not overwrite existing data. You can group worksheets and enter data on all worksheets within the group at the same time. In the next exercise, you will learn to work with multiple worksheets by grouping and ungrouping and arranging them.

STEP BY STEP **Work with Multiple Worksheets in a Workbook**

USE the workbook from the previous exercise.

1. Right-click any worksheet tab and click Select All Sheets. The title bar now reads Department Enrollments.xlsx [Group].
2. In cell B20, key Total Enrollment and press Enter. You have just added the contents of cell B20 in all the selected sheets.

Take Note

If you copy a data range from a worksheet to grouped worksheets, the Paste Options button does not appear. Some formatting, such as column width, is not copied.

Another Way
If you want to group some but not all worksheets within a workbook, press Ctrl and click the tab of each worksheet you want to include in the group.

3. Right-click any worksheet tab and click Ungroup Sheets.
4. Click the View tab and then the Biomedical Arts tab. Next, click New Window in the Windows group.
5. Click the Dramatic Arts tab and click New Window.

CERTIFICATION READY 4.1.7

How do you group worksheets?

6. Click the Fine Arts tab to make the sheet active and click Arrange All in the Windows group. The *Arrange Windows* dialog box opens. Click Vertical, as shown in Figure 6-9. Click on Windows of active workbook.

Figure 6-9

Arrange Windows dialog box

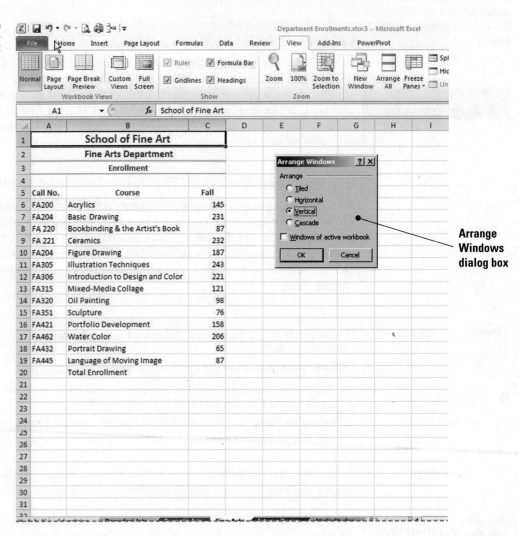

Arrange Windows dialog box

Take Note   Data that you copy or cut in grouped sheets cannot be pasted on another sheet because the size of the copy area includes all layers of the selected sheets and is different from the paste area in a single sheet. Therefore, make sure that only one sheet is selected before you attempt to copy or move data from a grouped sheet to another worksheet.

7. Click OK. Your screen should look like Figure 6-10, with the three worksheets displayed side by side.

Figure 6-10

Vertically tiled worksheets

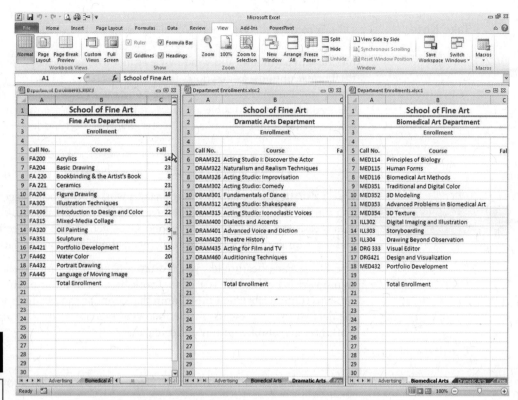

CERTIFICATION
READY 4.2.3

How do you open worksheet windows from the current worksheet?

PAUSE. LEAVE the workbook open to use in the next exercise.

Take Note   The New Window and Arrange All options enable you to display worksheets side by side for a quick visual comparison. You can enter and edit data, scroll, and move around in the individual windows just as you would in a "normal" view window. You can also click a cell in any of the displayed worksheets to make changes or to select cells or ranges.

Hiding and Unhiding Worksheet Windows in a Workbook

Any worksheet can be used and viewed in a separate window in the workbook view by applying it to a new window. These new windows can be arranged so that you can work in them without having to click back and forth on the worksheet tabs. This is an important feature to use when comparing like sheets and data. In the next exercise, you will use this tool.

STEP BY STEP   **Hide and Unhide Worksheet Windows in a Workbook**

USE the workbook from the previous exercise.

1. Click any cell in the Fine Arts window.

2. Click Hide in the Window group of the View tab. The Fine Arts window is closed; the Dramatic Arts and Biomedical Arts windows remain visible.

3. Click Unhide. Select the worksheet you want to unhide from the dialog box and click OK.

CERTIFICATION
READY 4.2.2

4. Click the Close button in the upper-right corner of the Fine Arts and Dramatic Arts windows. Restore the Biomedical Arts window to full-screen view.

5. SAVE and CLOSE the workbook.

PAUSE. LEAVE Excel open to use in the next exercise.

How do you arrange worksheet windows from the current worksheet?

If you click Hide in the Window group with one worksheet window open, the entire workbook is hidden. Excel remains open, but the taskbar no long displays the worksheet name. This feature allows you to quickly mask confidential data from view.

Take Note

Do not confuse the Hide and Unhide commands you used in this lesson with those you may have learned in an earlier lesson. The View tab commands in this exercise are used to hide and unhide active windows and window views in a workbook. The Hide and Unhide commands in the Format options, as described in previous exercises, are used to hide and unhide rows, columns, and worksheets. When you hide a sheet with the Format command, other worksheets in the workbook remain visible and accessible. When you use the Hide Window command, you must use the Unhide command to access any worksheet hidden in the workbook.

USING ZOOM AND FREEZE TO CHANGE THE ONSCREEN VIEW

The Bottom Line

Excel's **Zoom** feature allows you to make a worksheet appear bigger or smaller on your screen. You can use this feature to zoom in on a portion of a worksheet so that it appears larger and the data is easier to read. Or, you can zoom out to get a better perspective of the entire worksheet, making it easier to identify formatting inconsistencies or problematic spacing or alignment.

The Freeze Panes feature lets you **freeze** a pane, which means that you keep certain rows or columns visible while the rest of the worksheet scrolls. You often want to freeze the row that contains column labels and the column that contains row headings so that it is always clear what the data you see represents. In the following exercise, you will learn to zoom in and out of a worksheet and also freeze and unfreeze panes.

STEP BY STEP   **Using Zoom and Freeze to Change the Onscreen View**

GET READY. OPEN *SFA Staff Directory* from the data files for this lesson.

The *SFA Staff Directory* file for this lesson is available on the book companion website or in WileyPLUS.

1. Select any cell in the *SFA Staff Directory* worksheet. Click Zoom to Selection on the View tab. Zoom is increased to 400%.

2. Click Undo on the Quick Access Toolbar to return to 100% zoom.

3. Click Zoom on the View tab. In the *Zoom* dialog box, under *Magnification*, click 200%. Click OK.

4. Click Zoom and under *Magnification*, click Custom. Key 150 in the percentage box and click OK.

5. Click 100% in the Zoom group.

6. Select A5. Click Freeze Panes in the Window group on the View tab. Click Freeze Panes in the drop-down list.

Figure 6-11

Freeze Panes options

Another Way

The Freeze First Column and Freeze Top Row commands shown in Figure 6-11 are quick and easy to use if your worksheet begins with column and row headings, but when the data is preceded by a title and subtitle, you must tell Excel where you want the "freeze" to be located. That is why you need to select the cell below the line that you want to be visible as you move through the worksheet.

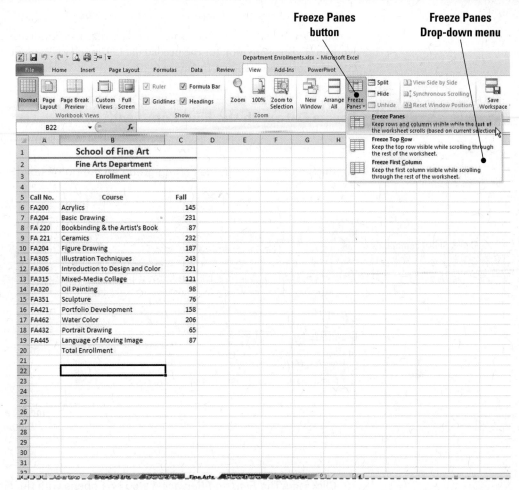

7. Press **Ctrl+End**. Row 4 with the column labels appears at the top of the screen to let you know what each column represents, even when the active cell is the last cell in the data range.

8. Press **Ctrl+Home** to return to the top of the data. Click **Freeze Panes** and select **Unfreeze panes**.

PAUSE. LEAVE the workbook open to use in the next exercise.

You can also use the Zoom scale on the Status bar to customize magnification. To zoom in (magnify), select a size greater than 100%; to zoom out (shrink), select a size less than 100%.

Some mouse devices have built-in zooming capabilities. If your mouse has a wheel, hold down Ctrl while you rotate the wheel forward or backward to increase and decrease zoom.

Take Note   The Freeze Top Row and Freeze First Column commands do not work together. When you want to freeze the first row and first column at the same time, locate the "freeze point" and use the Freeze Panes command.

FINDING AND REPLACING DATA

The Bottom Line   The Find and Replace options let you locate specific data quickly and, if necessary, replace it with new data. These features are most effective in large worksheets in which all of the data is not visible on the screen, thus saving you the time of scanning through vast amounts of data to find the information you need.

Locating Data with the Find Command

If you want to locate a particular item of data that isn't immediately visible, you can scan the worksheet visually to look for the needed data. A much easier and quicker way is to use the Find & Select commands shown in Figure 6-12.

STEP BY STEP   **Locate Data with the Find Command**

USE the workbook from the previous exercise.

1. Click **Find & Select** in the Editing group on the Home tab. (See Figure 6-12.)

Figure 6-12

Find & Select commands

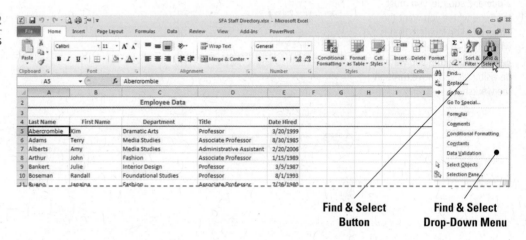

Find & Select
Button

Find & Select
Drop-Down Menu

2. Click **Find**. The *Find and Replace* dialog box opens with the Find tab displayed.
3. Key **tutor** in the *Find what* box. It does not matter whether you key the text in uppercase or lowercase; Excel will find each instance of the word.

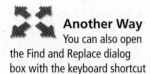
Troubleshooting If you had selected the Match case check box when you searched for *tutor,* the search would not have found any data because the word *tutor* is capitalized each time it occurs in the worksheet. Therefore, a data match would not be found if you searched for a lowercase word. When the search was completed, a dialog box would have informed you that Excel could not find the data you requested.

Take Note It does not matter which cell is currently the active cell when you enter a search string. If you do not select a range of cells, Excel will search the entire worksheet.

Another Way
You can also open the Find and Replace dialog box with the keyboard shortcut **Ctrl+F.**

4. Click **Find All**. The box is expanded to list all occurrences of "tutor" in the worksheet. You see that the search results lists both academic and writing tutors, so you need to refine the search criteria. If you click **Find Next** after you key the search string, Excel selects the cell in which the first occurrence of the string is found. You can edit the cell or click Find Next and continue to browse through the worksheet. The cursor will stop at each cell where the search string is located.
5. Key **writing tutor** in the *Find what* box and click **Find All**. The worksheet contains data for two individuals whose title is Writing Tutor.
6. Click **Options** on the dialog box to view the default settings for the Find feature.
7. **CLOSE** the dialog box.

PAUSE. LEAVE the workbook open to use in the next exercise.

When you enter the text or number that you want to find and click Find All, Excel locates all occurrences of the search string and lists them at the bottom of the dialog box, as shown in Figure 6-13. A **string** is any sequence of letters or numbers in a field.

Figure 6-13

Find All search results

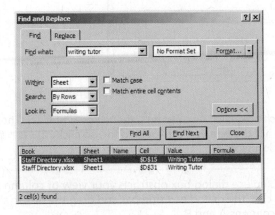

The Options button on the Find tab allows you to set additional parameters for the search. As shown in Figure 6-14, the default is to search the active worksheet, but you can also search an entire workbook. You can locate instances in which only the case (capitals or lowercase) matches the search string you key or the entire cell contents match the search string—more precise search strings create more concise search results.

Figure 6-14

Set search parameters

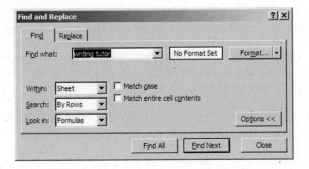

Replacing Data with the Replace Command

To look for specific data and replace it with other data, you can use the Replace tab on the Find and Replace dialog box. You can quickly find and replace all or some occurrences of a character string in a worksheet. Replacing data with the click of a button can save you the time of finding occurrences of the data and repeatedly keying replacement data.

STEP BY STEP   **Replace Data with the Replace Command**

Another Way
To display the Replace dialog box without using the Find & Replace feature, press Ctrl+H.

USE the workbook from the previous exercise.

1. Click **Find & Select** in the Editing group.
2. Click **Replace**. The Find and Replace dialog box opens with the Replace tab displayed.
3. In the *Find what* box, key **Johnson**.

4. In the *Replace with* box, key Johnston, as shown in Figure 6-15.

Figure 6-15

Replace tab of the Find and
Replace dialog box

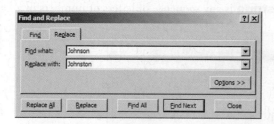

5. In the *Search* box, click By Columns, then click Find Next. The first occurrence of Johnson is not the one you are looking for, so click Find Next until you locate the entry for Tamara Johnson.

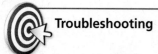 **Troubleshooting** If the Find and Replace dialog box obstructs your view of column A where the search data will be located, click the dialog box title bar and drag the box to the right so that you have a clear view of columns A and B.

6. Click Replace and click Close.

7. Click Find & Select and then click Replace. Key Advertising in the *Find what* field and key Advertising and Graphic Arts in the *Replace with* field.

8. Click Replace All. A dialog box tells you that Excel made nine replacements. Click OK, then click Close to close the dialog box.

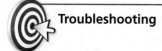 **Troubleshooting** Use discretion when deciding whether to use Replace All or Find Next when looking for specific data. For instance, when you needed to correct the spelling of the last name of a specific individual, you did not know whether there were other entries with the last name Johnson. Therefore, as a precaution, you needed to find each entry and decide whether to replace it with the corrected spelling. If you had chosen Replace All, you would have incorrectly changed two other last names in the directory.

9. **SAVE** your workbook in the Lesson 6 folder. Name the file *Staff Directory*.

PAUSE. LEAVE the workbook open to use in the next exercise.

As you have seen in this exercise, the Replace All command allows you to quickly change the contents of multiple cells. When the staff directory was created, it was easier to key *Advertising* rather than the complete name, *Advertising and Graphic Arts*. You corrected all nine occurrences of the department name, however, by clicking Replace All.

Navigating Data with the Go To Command

As you learned in an earlier lesson, you can key a cell location in the Name box, press Enter, and Excel makes the designated cell active. Another method of moving to a specific cell is to use the Go To feature. In the following exercise, you will use the Go To feature to navigate the worksheet and enter new data and to unhide the first worksheet row.

STEP BY STEP | **Navigate Data with the Go To Command**

USE the workbook you saved in the previous exercise.

1. If necessary, on the View tab, click Freeze Panes and select Unfreeze Panes. This removes the freeze so you can display all rows.

2. Click Find & Select, then click Go To. The Go To dialog box is displayed.

3. Key **A1** in the *Reference* box and click **OK**. Column headers A through E become highlighted. A1 is still hidden.

Take Note The Reference box is not case sensitive. Entering A1 or a1 will have the same effect.

4. In the Cells group, click **Format**, click **Hide & Unhide**, and click **Unhide Rows**. Row 1 is displayed.
5. Click **Find & Select**, then click **Go To**. Key **E67** in the Reference box and click **OK**.
6. Key **5/15/06** in E67 as the date on which Professor Young was hired. Press **Enter**.
7. Click **Find & Select** and click **Go To Special**.
8. In the *Go To Special* dialog box, click **Blanks** and select **OK**, as shown in Figure 6-16. The blank cells within the data range are highlighted.

Figure 6-16

Go To Special dialog box

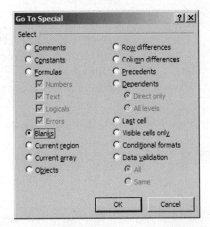

9. Press **Tab** three times until E13, the first blank cell in the Date Hired column, is the active cell. Enter **6/8/87** and press **Tab** to move to the next blank cell. Enter the following dates. Press **Tab** after each entry:

Gronchi	12/8/05
Hasselberg	10/20/00
Kahn	11/2/03
Liu	6/5/07
Male	7/10/00
Vande Velde	3/1/01
Wadia	6/1/02
Yang	6/1/02

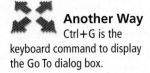
Another Way
Ctrl+G is the keyboard command to display the Go To dialog box.

10. **SAVE** the *Staff Directory* workbook and **CLOSE** the workbook.
CLOSE Excel.

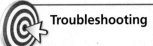
Troubleshooting The reason you needed to tab three times to reach E13 is the blank cells in the heading rows. Remember that when cells are merged, entries in the merged cells are considered to be in the upper-left cell. Therefore, Excel considers the remaining cells in the merge to be blank.

Take Note As you experienced in the preceding exercises, the Find & Select features allow you to find and, if necessary, quickly replace existing data. The Go To feature is a fast way to move to specific cell references, especially in a large worksheet.

In the exercises you completed in this lesson, you worked with relatively small amounts of data. In the business world, however, people often work with worksheets that contain massive amounts of data. The Find & Select and Go To features are most effective in large worksheets where it can take a significant amount of time to scan numerous rows and/or columns to find the data you need.

SKILL SUMMARY

In This Lesson You Learned How To:	Exam Objective	Objective Number
Organizing Worksheets	Move worksheets.	4.1.5
	Copy worksheets.	4.1.4
	Rename worksheets.	4.1.6
	Reposition worksheets within a workbook.	4.1.3
	Hide worksheet tabs.	4.1.9
	Unhide worksheet tabs.	4.1.10
	Insert worksheets.	4.1.1
	Delete worksheets.	4.1.2
Working with Multiple Worksheets	Group worksheets.	4.1.7
	Open a new window with contents from the current worksheet.	4.2.3
	Arrange window views.	4.2.2
Using Zoom and Freeze to Change the Onscreen View		
Finding and Replacing Data		

Knowledge Assessment

Matching

Match each vocabulary term with its definition.

a. Hide command

b. freeze

c. group worksheets

d. string

e. search and replace

f. Unhide command

g. zoom in

h. zoom out

i. Go To Special

j. Arrange All command

_____ 1. To make a hidden workbook or worksheet visible.

_____ 2. To make certain rows or columns remain visible on your screen even when you scroll your worksheet.

_____ 3. To make a worksheet appear larger on the screen.

_____ 4. To make a workbook or worksheet invisible.

_____ 5. Any sequence of letters or numbers that you type.

_____ 6. To make a worksheet appear smaller on the screen.

_____ 7. Selecting multiple worksheets in which you enter and edit data.

_____ 8. A command you can use to locate blank cells in a worksheet.

_____ 9. A feature you can use to locate and replace specific data in a worksheet.

_____ 10. A feature that allows you to visually compare worksheets.

Multiple Choice

Circle the choice that best completes or responds to the following statements.

1. To find data using the Find and Replace dialog box, you must enter a sequence of characters called a:
   a. range.
   b. string.
   c. cell address.
   d. menu.

2. You can tell that worksheets are grouped by:
   a. a bracket around the grouped sheets.
   b. the word *group* on the sheet tabs.
   c. the word *group* in the title bar.
   d. the words *grouped sheets* on the Status bar.

3. When Sheet1 has been copied, the new worksheet tab is named:
   a. copy of Sheet1.
   b. Sheet1 (2).
   c. Sheet1 Copy.
   d. Sheet2.

4. Which of the following is **not** a way to insert a new worksheet into a workbook?
   a. On the Home tab, click Insert and click Insert Sheet.
   b. Right-click a sheet tab, click Insert, and then click Insert Worksheet.
   c. On the Insert tab, click New Sheet.
   d. On the Home tab, click Format, click Move or Copy Sheet, and click Create a Copy.

5. To insert multiple worksheets at one time, what action is needed in addition to selecting the same number of tabs as the number of sheets to insert?
   a. Press and hold Shift as you select the tabs.
   b. Press and hold Ctrl as you select the tabs.
   c. Press Shift after you select the tabs.
   d. Press Ctrl after you select the tabs.

6. To enter data in multiple worksheets at one time, you must:
   a. use the Arrange command in the Window group on the View tab.
   b. use the Freeze command in the Window group on the View tab.
   c. use the Format command in the Cells group on the Home tab.
   d. group all worksheets and enter data in the open worksheet.

7. If you want to magnify the data on the screen:
   a. decrease zoom to less than 100%.
   b. increase zoom to 100%.
   c. increase zoom to more than 100%.
   d. increase the font size in the data range.
   e. both b & c.
   f. both b & d.

8. When a worksheet is hidden:
   a. Unhide is active on the shortcut menu.
   b. a bold line appears where the sheet is hidden.
   c. the word Hidden appears on the Status bar.
   d. the word Hidden appears in the title bar.

9. To hide a workbook that has multiple worksheets:
   a. click Format and click Hide in the Cells group on the Home tab.
   b. click Hide in the Window group on the View tab.

   c. right-click a sheet tab and click Hide.

   d. group all worksheets and click Format, click Hide & Unhide, and click Hide Sheet.

10. When you use the Freeze command,

   a. data cannot be entered in the worksheet.

   b. you cannot scroll through the worksheet.

   c. you cannot change the worksheet view.

   d. the column and/or row headings remain visible as you scroll through the worksheet card.

Competency Assessment

Project 6-1: School of Fine Arts Enrollments

In this exercise, you will move and copy worksheets, rename worksheets, change the tab color, and rearrange worksheets within a workbook.

GET READY. LAUNCH Excel if it is not already running.

The *SFA Enrollments* file for this lesson is available on the book companion website or in WileyPLUS.

1. **OPEN** the *SFA Enrollments* data file for this lesson.

2. With the Advertising tab active, click Ctrl+A. This selects the entire worksheet.

3. Click Format in the Cells group on the Home tab. Click Move or Copy Sheet.

4. In the Move or Copy dialog box, click the Create a copy box and click OK.

5. On the Advertising (2) worksheet, select A2 and key Foundational Studies. Press Enter.

6. Select A6:C20 and press Delete.

7. Click Format, click Rename Sheet, and key Foundations. Press Enter.

8. Click Format, click Tab Color, and click Dark Red.

9. Click Format and click Move or Copy Sheet. In the Before sheet box, click (move to end) and click OK.

10. **SAVE** the workbook as *SFA Enrollments 6-1* and then **CLOSE** the file.

LEAVE Excel open for the next project.

Project 6-2: Graphic Design Institute, Part 1

For this project, you will rename worksheets, hide and unhide worksheets, and insert and delete worksheets from a workbook.

GET READY. LAUNCH Excel if it is not already running.

The *Training Expenditures* file for this lesson is available on the book companion website or in WileyPLUS.

1. **OPEN** the *Training Expenditures* data file for this lesson.

2. Right-click Sheet1. Click Rename and key Budget. Press Enter.

3. Double-click the Sheet2 tab. Key January. Press Enter.

4. Rename Sheet3 March and press Enter.

5. Rename Sheet4 Previous Qtr. and press Enter.

6. Click the Insert Worksheet tab. Rename the new sheet Summary.

7. Click the March tab and click the Insert arrow in the Cells group on the Home tab. Click Insert Sheet.

8. Name the new worksheet February.

9. Click the Previous Qtr. tab. Click Format, click Hide & Unhide, and click Hide Sheet.

10. Click Format, click Hide & Unhide, and click Unhide Sheet. In the Unhide dialog box, click OK.

11. With the Previous Qtr. tab selected, click the arrow next to Delete and click Delete Sheet. Click Delete on the dialog box to confirm that you want to delete the Previous Qtr. sheet.

12. SAVE the workbook as *Training Expenditures 6-2*.

LEAVE the workbook open for the next project.

Proficiency Assessment

Project 6-3: Graphic Design Institute, Part 2

In this project, you will move between worksheets, change the workbook view, and group worksheets to enter data on multiple sheets.

USE the workbook from the previous project.

1. Click the View tab to make it active.

2. On the Budget worksheet, select E18 and click Zoom to Selection in the Zoom group.

3. Click 100% in the Zoom group.

4. Click Zoom In on the Status bar and increase magnification to 150%.

5. Click the January tab and click Select All. Click Copy.

6. Click the Summary sheet tab, select A1, and click Paste.

7. On the February worksheet, select A1, right-click, and click Paste. Click the Paste Options button and select Keep Source Formatting.

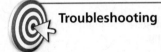 **Troubleshooting** If the formatting is not copied, make the January worksheet active and select the text containing the formatting. Double-click the Format Painter and apply the formatting to the necessary cells.

8. Double-click A2 to put it in Edit mode (noted on Status bar). Select January, key February, and press Enter.

9. Select C4 and key February.

10. Delete the January expenditures from C5:C17. Then enter the February expenditures for the items listed next. (Not all items have February expenditures; leave those cells blank.)

Courseware development	$2,500
Courseware purchase	400
Certification	250
Train-the-trainer	1,200
Hardware purchases	10,500
Consulting fees	150
Instructor fees	4,000
Travel	600
Per diem	400

11. Select A2 on the Summary worksheet and key Quarterly Expenditures.

12. Copy C4:C18 from the February worksheet to the Summary sheet. Paste the data next to the January data.

13. Copy C4:C18 from the March worksheet to the Summary sheet. Paste the data next to the February data.

14. Select A1:E1 and click Merge & Center two times.

15. Click Merge & Center two times for cells A2:E2.

16. SAVE the workbook as *Training Expenditures 6-3*. CLOSE the workbook.

LEAVE Excel open for the next project.

Project 6-4: School of Fine Arts Directory

For this project, you will update the school's staff directory.

GET READY. LAUNCH Excel if it is not already running.

@ The *Updated Directory* file for this lesson is available on the book companion website or in WileyPLUS.

1. **OPEN** the *Updated Directory* data file for this lesson.
2. At the bottom of the worksheet, add information for three new staff members:

DeGrasse, Kirk	Media Studies	Associate Professor	2/15/07
Sheperdidian, Janet	Student Services	Academic Advisor	3/1/07
Playstead, Craig	Administration	Associate Dean	4/1/07

3. Gail Erickson has been promoted to Professor. Click Find & Select. Change her title.
4. Use the Find & Select feature to replace BioMedical with Biomedical Art.
5. Use Find & Select to go to A33. Sidney Higa's title should be Vice President.
6. Click Format and change the name of Sheet1 to Directory.
7. Click Sheet2. Press Ctrl and click Sheet3. Click Format and hide the blank worksheets.
8. Name the workbook *Staff Directory 6-4*.
9. **SAVE** and **CLOSE** the workbook.

LEAVE Excel open for the next project.

Mastery Assessment

Project 6-5: School of Fine Arts Course Recommendations

Debra Core, an academic advisor, has asked you to search the enrollment data and highlight courses for some of the continuing education students with whom she is working.

GET READY. LAUNCH Excel if it is not already running

@ The *Advisor Recommendations* file for this lesson is available on the book companion website or in WileyPLUS.

1. **OPEN** the *Advisor Recommendations* data file for this lesson.
2. Identify the courses that investigate various aspects of color.
    a. Use the Find & Select options to search the entire workbook.
    b. Use *color* as the search string.
    c. In the Within field, click Workbook.
    d. Find all courses that have color as part of the course name.
3. Your search should return a list of six courses. Add yellow fill color to highlight each course.
    a. Click the first course (Biomedical Arts). Click Fill Color.
    b. Click the second course and click Fill Color in the Fonts group.
    c. Continue until the six courses have been highlighted.
4. Identify the available painting courses.
    a. Use *painting* as the search string.
    b. Search the workbook and mark painting courses with a light blue fill.
5. Mark photography courses with a light green fill.
6. **SAVE** the workbook as *Advisor Recommendations 6-5*. **CLOSE** the file.

LEAVE Excel open for the next project.

Project 6-6: Contoso, Ltd.

This exercise has you use the Find & Select command to locate specific information and fill blank spaces in a worksheet. Be sure to freeze the column headings so they remain visible as you scroll through the list of Contoso employees.

GET READY. LAUNCH Excel if it is not already running.

@ The *Contoso Employees* file for this lesson is available on the book companion website or in WileyPLUS.

1. **OPEN** the *Contoso Employees* data file for this lesson.

2. Use the Freeze Panes command so that the column headings in row 4 remain visible as you scroll to the end the data range.

3. Find and Replace all occurrences of Billing Clerk with Accounts Receivable Clerk.

4. Use Find and Replace options to find all blank cells on the worksheet. Key Records Management in each blank in column C.

5. **SAVE** the workbook as *Contoso Employees 6-6*.

LEAVE Excel open for the next project

INTERNET READY

In this lesson, you worked with data files for the School of Fine Arts. Open *College Comparisons* in the data files for this lesson. Go online and investigate colleges that offer degrees in your career interest area. Use the College Comparisons worksheet to record information about three colleges that offer a degree program in your area of interest. Fill in as much information as you can locate about each college. Based on your limited research, indicate which college would be your choice to pursue the degree you investigated. Save the file and exit Excel.

7 Working with Data

LESSON SKILL MATRIX

Skill	Exam Objective	Objective Number
Ensuring Your Data's Integrity		
Sorting Data	Use Sort options.	8.2.1
	Apply conditional formatting to cells.	8.3.1
Filtering Data	Filter lists using AutoFilter.	8.1.4
	Remove a filter.	8.1.3
	Define a filter.	8.1.1
	Apply a filter.	8.1.2
Subtotaling Data		
Setting Up Data in a Table Format		

KEY TERMS

- ascending order
- AutoFilter
- comparison operator
- criteria
- descending order
- duplicate value
- filter
- grouping
- outline symbols
- placeholders

An employee's name is added to the list of Contoso, Ltd.'s employees whenever a person joins the company. However, viewing the employee list according to the employees' positions would be more useful to the office manager when he develops the work schedule. Reorganizing the data enables the office manager to ensure that the office is fully staffed when it is open. The office manager also needs to update employee data files with additional data. Because other employees often need to access the files, he plans to restrict the data that can be entered in some files to ensure that valid results are obtained when data entry is complete and the data is analyzed for decision making. Excel is primarily a tool for organizing, analyzing, and presenting numerical information. Sorting data from highest to lowest or smallest to largest, for example, lets you quickly and easily identify trends and generate forecasts or probabilities. In this lesson, you will learn to use commands on Excel's Data tab to sort, filter, and display data needed for specific purposes.

SOFTWARE ORIENTATION

Excel's Data Tab

The command groups on Excel's Data tab, shown in Figure 7-1, enable you to sort and filter data, convert text to columns, ensure valid data entry, conduct what-if analyses, and outline data. You can also get external data into Excel by using Data commands.

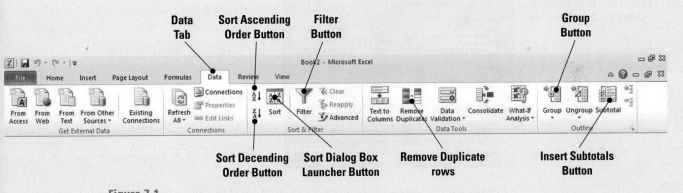

Figure 7-1

Data tab

In this lesson, you will learn many ways to use the command groups on Excel's Data tab to manage spreadsheet data. Use Figure 7-1 throughout this lesson as a guide to these powerful commands.

ENSURING YOUR DATA'S INTEGRITY

The Bottom Line

Ensuring valid data entry is an important task for Excel users. In many worksheets that you create, other users may enter data to get desired calculations and results. Restricting the type of data that can be entered in a cell is one way to ensure data integrity. You may want to restrict data entry to a certain range of dates, limit choices by using a drop-down list, or make sure that only positive whole numbers are entered. And, because it's not uncommon for users to inadvertently enter duplicate rows of information in lengthy spreadsheets, you need to have a mechanism for finding and eliminating duplicate information.

Restricting Cell Entries to Certain Data Types

When you decide what data type you want to use in a cell or range of cells and how you want it used, formatted, or displayed, you are ready to set up the validation **criteria** for that data. Data Validation is the feature in Excel that will manage data that is to be entered or displayed based on your specified criteria. When you restrict (validate) data entry, it is necessary to provide immediate feedback to instruct users about the data that is permitted in a cell. This feedback is on the form of alerts and error messages that you create. You can provide an input message when a restricted cell is selected or provide an instructive message when an invalid entry is made. In this exercise, you learn how to validate data and restrict data entry while supplying clear feedback to users to assure a smooth, trouble-free data entry experience. This is vital to worksheet performance because it restricts errors in data entry.

STEP BY STEP   **Restrict Cell Entries to Certain Data Types**

The *Employee Data* data file for this lesson is available on the book companion website or in WileyPLUS.

WileyPLUS Extra! features an online tutorial of this task.

GET READY. Before you begin these steps, be sure to **LAUNCH** Microsoft Excel.

1. **OPEN** the *Employee Data* data file for this lesson.
2. Select the cell range D3:D50.
3. On the Data tab, in the Data Tools group, click Data Validation. You will now begin to set your validation criteria.
4. On the Settings tab of the Data Validation dialog box, select Whole number in the Allow box. This sets the number format for your validation.
5. Key 15 in the Minimum box and 40 in the Maximum box. You have now set your whole number range. The *Data Validation* dialog box should look like Figure 7-2.

Figure 7-2

Restrict data entry using the Data Validation dialog box

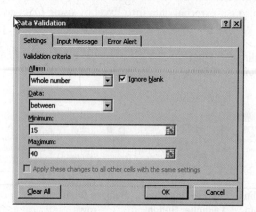

6. Click the Error Alert tab in the dialog box. Be sure the Show error alert after invalid data is entered check box is selected. Key Invalid Entry in the Title box. This will display an alert when an invalid entry has been made to the cell.
7. Key Only whole numbers can be entered in the error message box as shown in Figure 7-3. This will display the error message that you want the user to see.

Figure 7-3

Error alert message

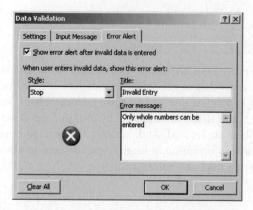

8. Click the Input Message tab and in the Input Message box, key Enter a whole number between 15 and 40. Click OK. This will create the message for the user to follow to correct their error.

9. Select cell D6, key 35.5, and press Enter. The Invalid Entry dialog box (Figure 7-4) opens, displaying the error message you created.

Figure 7-4

Invalid entry message

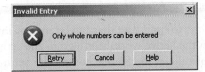

10. Click Retry to close the error message; key 36, and press Enter.

11. Use the following employee information to key values in row 29. Patricia Doyle was hired today as a receptionist. She will work 20 hours each week.

12. Create a Lesson 7 folder and **SAVE** the file as *Contoso Data*.

PAUSE. LEAVE the workbook open to use in the next exercise.

You have just taken the first step toward ensuring the integrity of data entered in the *Contoso Data* workbook. An employee cannot inadvertently enter text or values that are outside the parameters you set in the validation criteria. By extending the range beyond the current data, when new employee data is entered, the validation criteria will be applied.

You can specify how you want Excel to respond when invalid data is entered. In the preceding exercise, you accepted the default value, Stop, in the Style box on the Error Alert tab (Figure 7-3). If you select Warning in the Style box, you will be warned that you have made an entry that is not in the defined range, but you can choose to ignore the warning and enter the invalid data.

Take Note   If you do not enter an Error Alert title or text, the Excel default message will be displayed: *The value you entered is not valid. A user has restricted values that can be entered in this cell.*

Allowing Only Specific Values to Be Entered in Cells

To make data entry easier, or to limit entries to predefined items, you can create a drop-down list of valid entries. The entries on the list can be forced-choice (i.e., yes, no) or can be compiled from cells elsewhere in the workbook. A drop-down list displays as an arrow in the cell. To enter information in the restricted cell, click the arrow and then click the entry you want.

STEP BY STEP   **Allow Only Specific Values to Be Entered in Cells**

USE the workbook from the previous exercise.

1. Select E3:E29. Click Data Validation in the Data Tools group on the Data tab.

2. Click the Settings tab, in the Allow box, select List. The In-cell drop-down check box is selected by default.

3. In the Source box, key Yes, No. Click OK to accept the settings. An arrow now appears to the right of the cell range.

4. Click E3. Click the arrow to the right of the cell. You now see the list options you created in the previous step.

5. If the value in column D is 30 or more hours, from the newly created drop-down list, choose Yes. If it is less than 30 hours, select No.

6. Continue to apply the appropriate response from the list for each cell in E4:E29.

7. **SAVE** the workbook.

PAUSE. LEAVE the workbook open to use in the next exercise.

In the previous exercise, Contoso, Ltd. provided health insurance benefits to those employees who work 30 or more hours each week. By applying a Yes, No list validation, the office manager can quickly identify employees who are entitled to insurance benefits. You restricted the input for column E to two choices, but a list can include multiple choices. As you did in the exercise, the choices can be defined in the Source box on the Settings tab.

Use a comma to separate choices. For example, if you wanted to rate a vendor's performance, you might have three choices: Low, Average, and High.

There are a variety of other ways to limit data that can be entered into a cell range. You can base a list on criteria contained in the active worksheet, within the active workbook, or in another workbook. Enter the range of cells in the Source box on the Settings tab or key the cell range for the criteria. You can calculate what will be allowed based on the content of another cell. For example, you can create a data validation formula that enters yes or no in column E based on the value in column D. You will learn to create formulas in the next lesson.

Data validation can be based on a decimal with limits, a date within a timeframe, or a time within a timeframe. You can also specify the length of the text that can be entered within a cell.

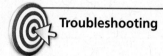

Troubleshooting Always test the data validation to make sure that it works correctly. Try entering both valid and invalid data in the cells to make sure that your settings work as you intend and that the expected message appears when invalid data is entered.

Removing Duplicate Cells, Rows, or Columns from a Worksheet

A **duplicate value** occurs when all values in the row are an exact match of all the values in another row. In a very large worksheet, data may be inadvertently entered more than once. This is even more likely to happen when more than one individual enters data in a worksheet. Duplicate rows or duplicate columns need to be removed before data is analyzed. When you remove duplicate values, only the values in the selection are affected. Values outside the range of cells are not altered or removed. In the next exercise, you will learn how to remove duplicate cells, rows, or columns from a worksheet.

STEP BY STEP   **Remove Duplicate Cells, Rows, or Columns from a Worksheet**

USE the workbook from the previous exercise.

1. Select A3:E29. In the Data Tools group, click Remove Duplicates. The Remove Duplicates dialog box shown in Figure 7-5 opens.

Figure 7-5

Identify duplicate values to be removed

Data selections to search for duplicate values

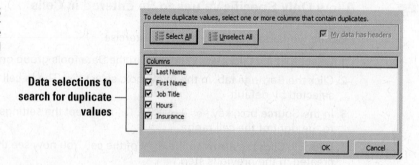

2. Remove the check from Hours and Insurance. You will identify duplicate employee data based on last name, first name, and job title.

3. My data has headers is selected by default. Click **OK**. Duplicate rows are removed and the confirmation box shown in Figure 7-6 appears informing you that two duplicate values were found and removed.

Figure 7-6

Duplicate values removed

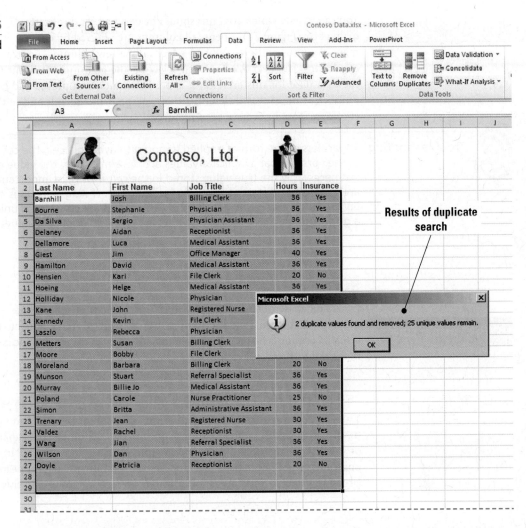

Results of duplicate search

4. Click **OK**. **SAVE** the workbook.

Take Note

Because you are permanently deleting data, it is a good idea to copy the original range of cells to another worksheet or workbook before removing duplicate values. You saved the file at the end of the previous exercise; therefore, you have a backup if you inadvertently remove data that you do not intend to remove.

Later in this lesson you will to learn to filter data. You can filter for unique values first to confirm that the results of removing duplicate values will return the result you want.

PAUSE. LEAVE the workbook open to use in the next exercise.

Take Note   You are working with a relatively small amount of data in the practice exercises, and it would not take a great deal of time to review the data and identify duplicate entries. However, if a company has hundreds of employees, you can see the benefit of this Excel feature.

You can specify which columns should be checked for duplicates. When the Remove Duplicates dialog box (Figure 7-5) opens, all columns are selected by default. If the range of cells contains many columns and you want to select only a few columns, you can quickly clear all columns by clicking Unselect All and then selecting the columns you want to check for duplicates. In the data used for this exercise, it is possible that an employee had been entered twice, but the number of hours was different. If you accepted the default and left all columns selected, that employee would not have been removed.

Troubleshooting   Regardless of the format applied to and displayed in a cell, the cell's true value is displayed in the Formula bar. Duplicate values are determined by the value displayed in the cell and not necessarily the true value stored in the cell. This is an important distinction when dates are entered in different formats. For example, if Aug 5, 2008 is entered in one row and 08/05/2008 is entered in another row, the values are considered unique—not duplicate. It is a good idea to check formatting before removing duplicate values.

SORTING DATA

The Bottom Line   Excel's database functions allow you to sort by text, numbers, dates, and times in one or more columns, that is, on a single criterion or on multiple criteria. Sorting data enables you to quickly visualize and understand the data better. You can rearrange and locate the data that you need to make more effective decisions.

Sorting Data on a Single Criterion

Data can be sorted on a single criterion (one column) in ascending or descending order. In **ascending order**, alphabetic data appears A to Z, numeric data appears from lowest to highest or smallest to largest, and dates appear from oldest to most recent. In **descending order**, the opposite is true—alphabetic data appears Z to A, numeric data appears from highest to lowest or largest to smallest, and dates appear from most recent to oldest. In this exercise you will sort data.

STEP BY STEP   **Sort Data on a Single Criterion**

USE the workbook from the previous exercise.

1. Before you begin, Delete the contents of row 1 from your worksheet.
2. Select D2:D27 (column heading and data in column D).
3. On the Data tab, click the Sort button. 🔳

4. A Sort Warning message appears and by default prompts you to expand the data selection. Click Expand the selection option and click the Sort button. The *Sort* dialog box opens. Excel will automatically organize your column information. It recognizes the header, understands the numeric values, and gives you the sort options. You will accept what Excel has selected. See Figure 7-7. Click OK to accept the first single sort criteria.

Figure 7-7

Sort dialog box

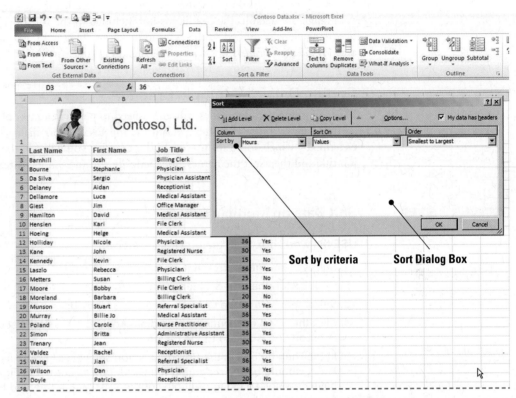

Sort by criteria   Sort Dialog Box

5. Select any cell in column A and click the Sort A to Z button. Data is sorted by last name. You have chosen your second single criteria of sorting alphabetically from A–Z.

6. Select A2:E27 and click the Sort button to launch the Sort dialog box shown in Figure 7-8.

Figure 7-8

Single sort criterion

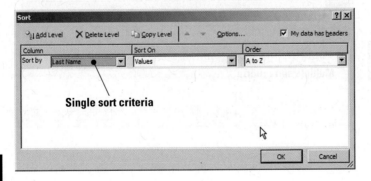

Single sort criteria

7. In the Column section's Sort by box, click the arrow to activate the drop-down list and select Job Title. Click OK. You have selected the third single sort criteria. Note that your worksheet is now sorted by Job Title.

8. Click the Sort button in the Sort & Filter group; the data range is automatically selected and the Sort dialog box opens. Select Hours in the Column section's Sort by box. Change the order options to smallest to largest. Click OK. You have now selected you last single sort criteria. Note that your worksheet is once again sorted by the data in the Hours column.

PAUSE. LEAVE the workbook open to use in the next exercise.

Take Note   Sort and Filter commands are in the Editing group on the Home tab as well as the Sort & Filter group on the Data tab.

In this exercise, you sorted data on one criterion. Unless the worksheet contains multiple merged cells, you do not need to select data to use the Sort commands. The Sort A to Z and Sort Z to A commands automatically sort the data range on the column that contains the active cell.

It is best to have column headings that have a different format than the data when you sort a data range. By default, the heading is not included in the sort operation. In your worksheet, a heading style was applied to the column headings. Therefore, Excel recognized the header row and *My data has headers* was selected by default on the Sort dialog box.

Sorting Data on Multiple Criteria

When working with large files, you often need to perform a multiple-criteria sort, for example, sorting data by more than one column. Using Excel's Sort dialog box, you can identify each criterion by which you want to sort. In this exercise, you will sort the Contoso employee data by job title and then sort the names alphabetically within each job category.

STEP BY STEP   **Sort Data on Multiple Criteria**

USE the workbook from the previous exercise.

1. Select the range A2:E27, if it isn't already selected.
2. Click Sort in the Sort & Filter group on the Data tab to open the dialog box.
3. Select Job Title in the Column section's Sort by box and A to Z in the Order box.
4. Click the Add Level button in the dialog box to identify the second sort criteria. A new criterion line is added to the dialog box.
5. In the Then by box in the Column section select Last Name as the second criterion. A to Z should be the default in the Order box as shown in Figure 7-9. Click OK. You have now sorted using multiple criteria; first by job title and then alphabetically by last name.

Figure 7-9

Multiple-criteria sort

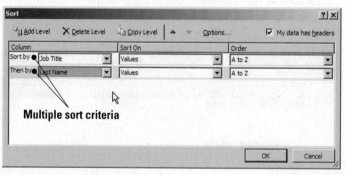

Multiple sort criteria

CERTIFICATION READY   8.2.1

How do you sort data using multiple criteria?

6. **SAVE** the workbook.

Take Note   In Excel, you can sort by up to 64 columns. For best results, the range of cells that you sort should have column headings.

PAUSE. LEAVE the workbook open to use in the next exercise.

You can continue to add levels in the Sort dialog box to expand your sort criteria, and you can delete or copy a criterion level. To change the sort order, select the criterion and click the up or down arrow. Entries higher in the list are sorted before entries lower in the list. To sort by case sensitivity, so that Excel sorts lowercase entries before uppercase entries, click the Options button in the Sort dialog box to open the Sort Options dialog box shown in Figure 7-10.

Figure 7-10

Case sensitive sort criteria

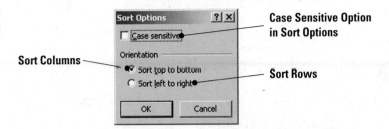

Case Sensitive Option
in Sort Options

Sort Columns

Sort Rows

Sorting Data Using Conditional Formatting

If you have conditionally formatted a range of cells with an icon set, you can sort by the icon. Recall that an icon set can be used to annotate and classify data into categories. Each icon represents a range of values. For example, in a three-color arrow set, the green up arrow represents the highest values, the yellow sideways arrow represents the middle values, and the red down arrow represents the lower values.

STEP BY STEP   **Sort Data Using Conditional Formatting**

USE the workbook from the previous exercise.

1. On the Home tab, click **Find & Select** in the Editing command group, and click **Conditional Formatting** in the drop-down menu. A message is returned that no cells in the worksheet contain conditional formatting. Click **OK** to close the message box. This step is to make sure there are no conditional formatting rules in place.

 Ref   You learned about applying conditional formatting in Lesson 4, Formatting Cells and Ranges.

2. Select **D3:D27**. Click **Conditional Formatting** in the Styles group, and then open the **Icon Set** gallery. See Figure 7-11.

Figure 7-11

Icon Set styles gallery

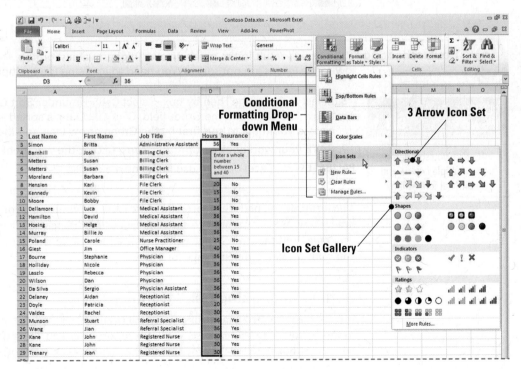

Conditional Formatting Drop-down Menu

3 Arrow Icon Set

Icon Set Gallery

3. Click the 3 Arrows icon set. Each value in the selected column now has an arrow that represents whether the value falls within the high, middle, or low range of your data.

4. Select A3:E27. On the Home tab, click Sort & Filter and then click Custom Sort (see Figure 7-12); the Sort dialog box opens.

Figure 7-12

Sort and Filter drop-down menu

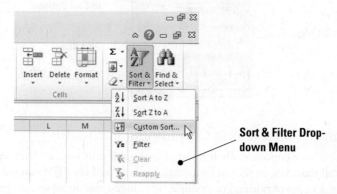

Sort & Filter Drop-down Menu

5. Select Hours in the Sort by box. Select Cell Icon in the Sort On section's drop-down list. Click the green arrow under *Order* (see Figure 7-13).

Figure 7-13

Sort dialog box

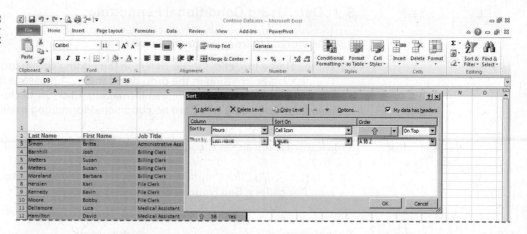

 **Troubleshooting** This sort will result in the green arrows (highest values) on top. However, the medium and low range values are not sorted. You need to implement a multiple-criteria sort.

CERTIFICATION READY   8.3.1

How do you sort data using multiple criteria and conditional formatting?

6. Select Hours in the Then by box. Select Cell Icon under Sort On and accept the yellow arrow and On top in the Order field. Click OK. Data is sorted by icon set. Your criteria caused your data to sort first by the Green arrow Icon and then by the Yellow.

7. SAVE your workbook as *Contoso Icons*. CLOSE the workbook.

PAUSE. LEAVE Excel open to use in the next exercise.

The first time you perform a sort, you must select the entire range of cells, including the column header row. When you want to sort the data using different criteria, select any cell within the data range and the entire range will be selected for the sort. You need to select the data only if you want to use a different range for a sort.

Sorting Data Using Cell Attributes

If you have formatted a range of cells by cell color or by font color, you can create a custom sort to sort by colors. In this exercise, you learn to sort by cell attribute (in this case, color) using the Sort dialog box to select the order in which you want the colors sorted.

At Contoso, Ltd., each medical assistant is assigned to work with a specific physician. To assist with scheduling, the office manager created the *MA Assignments* worksheet with color-coded assignments for the physician/medical assistant. The color coding serves as a reminder that the two must be scheduled for the same days and hours when the weekly schedule is created. Color coding enables you to sort the data so that the work assignments are grouped for the physician and his or her medical assistant.

STEP BY STEP	Sort Data Using Cell Attributes

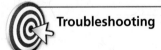

The *MA Assignment* file for this lesson is available on the book companion website or in WileyPLUS.

GET READY. OPEN the *MA Assignments* data file for this lesson.

1. Select the entire data range (including the column headings). On the Data tab, click Sort.
2. In the Sort dialog box, accept Last Name in the Sort by box. Under Sort On, select Cell Color.
3. Under Order, select Pink and On Top.
4. Click the Add Level button in the dialog box and select Last Name in the Sort By box. In the Sort On section, select Cell Color. Select Yellow and On Top in the Order section.

Take Note   Excel also allows you to sort by font color. To do this, in the Sort On section, you would select Font Color instead of Cell Color.

5. Using the same method you used in step 4, add a level for Green and then add a level for Blue. You should have a criterion for each color as illustrated in Figure 7-14. Click OK.

Figure 7-14

Multiple cell attribute sort

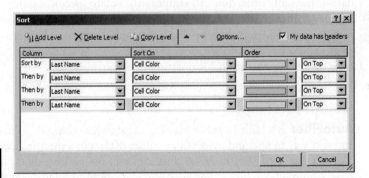

6. **SAVE** the workbook in your Lesson 7 folder as *MA Assignments*.

PAUSE. LEAVE the workbook open to use in the next exercise.

Troubleshooting When a worksheet contains unevenly sized merged cells, if you do not select data before you open the Sort dialog box, you will receive an error message that tells you a sort requires merged cells to be identically sized. The *MA Assignments* worksheet contained two rows with merged cells. Therefore, you had to select the data range (including column labels) the first time you sorted the worksheet. If you performed additional sorts, Excel would remember the data range and you would not need to select it again.

Most sort operations are by columns, but you can custom sort by rows. Create a custom sort by clicking Options on the Sort dialog box. You can then choose *Sort left to right* under Orientation (refer to Figure 7-10).

Sort criteria are saved with the workbook so that you can reapply the sort each time the workbook is opened. Table 7-1 summarizes Excel's default ascending sort orders. The order is reversed for a descending sort.

Table 7-1

Default ascending sort order

Value	Ascending Sort Order
Numbers	Smallest negative number to largest positive number.
Dates	Earliest date to most recent date.
Text	Alphanumeric data is sorted left to right, character by character. For example, A5, A501, A51 are correctly sorted. Numbers and symbols are sorted before text. If the Case sensitive option is active, lowercase text is sorted before uppercase text.
Logical values	False is placed before true.
Blank cells	In both ascending and descending sorts, blank cells are placed last.

FILTERING DATA

Worksheets can hold as much data as you need, but you may not want to work with all of the data at the same time. You can temporarily isolate specific data in a worksheet by placing a restriction, called a **filter**, on the worksheet. Filtering data enables you to focus on the data pertinent to a particular analysis by displaying only the rows that meet specified criteria and hiding rows you do not want to see. You can use Excel's AutoFilter feature to filter data, and you can filter data using conditional formatting or cell attributes.

Using AutoFilter

AutoFilter is a built-in set of filtering capabilities. Using AutoFilter to isolate data is a quick and easy way to find and work with a subset of data in a specified range of cells or table columns. You can use AutoFilter to create three types of filters: list value, format, or criteria. Each filter type is mutually exclusive. For example, you can filter by list value or format, but not both. In the next exercise, you will use AutoFilter to organize your data.

STEP BY STEP **Use AutoFilter**

USE the workbook from the previous exercise.

1. Select A3:E28. Click Filter on the Data tab in the Sort & Filter group; a filter arrow is added to each column heading.
2. Click the filter arrow in the Job Title column. The AutoFilter menu shown in Figure 7-15 is displayed.

Figure 7-15

Text values to filter

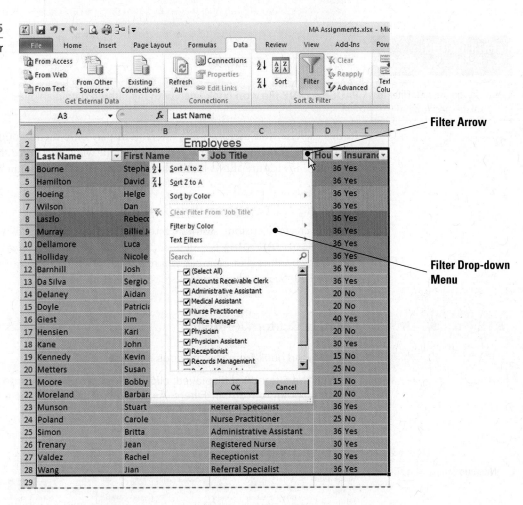

Filter Arrow

Filter Drop-down Menu

Troubleshooting To make the AutoFilter menu wider or longer, click and drag the grip handle at the bottom

3. Currently the data is not filtered, so all job titles are selected. Click Select All to deselect all titles.
4. Click Accounts Receivable Clerk and Receptionist. Click OK. Data for six employees who hold these titles is displayed. All other employees are filtered out. See Figure 7-16.

Figure 7-16

Filtered data

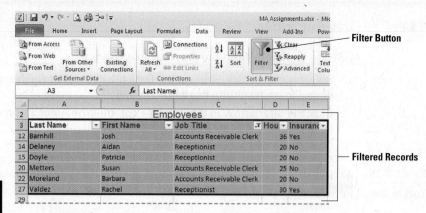

Filter Button

Filtered Records

CERTIFICATION
R E A D Y **8.1.4**

How do you use AutoFilter to
isolate specific data?

PAUSE. LEAVE the workbook open with the filtered data displayed to use in the next exercise.

In this exercise, you used two text filters to display only the receptionists and accounts receivables clerks. This information is especially useful when the office manager is creating a work schedule. This feature allows him or her to isolate relevant data quickly.

Creating a Custom AutoFilter

You can create a custom AutoFilter to further filter data by two comparison operators. A **comparison operator** is a sign, such as *greater than* or *less than*, that is used in criteria to compare two values. For example, you might create a filter to identify values *greater than* 50 but *less than* 100. Such a filter would display values from 51 to 99.

STEP BY STEP **Create a Custom AutoFilter**

USE the workbook from the previous exercise.

1. With the filtered list displayed, click the filter arrow in column D. In the AutoFilter menu, point to Number Filters. As shown in Figure 7-17, the menu expands to allow you to customize the filter.

Figure 7-17

Numeric comparison criteria

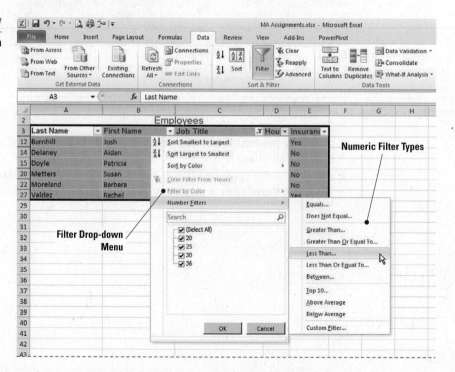

Numeric Filter Types

**Filter Drop-down
Menu**

2. Select Less Than on the expanded menu and key 30 in the amount box. Click OK. The AutoFilter menu closes and the filtered list is reduced to four employees who work fewer than 30 hours per week.

3. Click the Filter button in the Sort & Filter group on the Data tab to display all data. With the data range still selected, click Filter again.

4. Click the filter arrow in column D to open the AutoFilter menu. Point to Number Filters and select Greater Than. Key 15 and press Tab twice to move to the second comparison operator criteria box.

5. Click the arrow for the comparison operator drop-down list and select is less than as the second comparison operator and press Tab. Key 30 and click OK. The list should be filtered to six employees.

6. Click the Filter button to once again display all data.

CERTIFICATION READY   8.1.4

How do you create a custom AutoFilter?

Take Note   To remove a filter from a set of data (and see all the data in the worksheet again), you click on the Filter button again. This will make all the data visible again.

7. **SAVE** and **CLOSE** the workbook.

PAUSE. LEAVE Excel open to use in the next exercise.

CERTIFICATION READY   8.1.3

How do you remove a filter?

Comparison operators are used to create a formula that Excel uses to filter numeric data. The operators are identified in Table 7-2.

Table 7-2

Comparison operators

Button Name	Formatting Applied
=	Equal to
>	Greater than
<	Less than
>=	Greater than or equal to
<=	Less than or equal to
<>	Not equal to

Equal to and *Less than* are options for creating custom text filters. Text Filter options also allow you to filter text that begins with a specific letter (Begins With option) or text that has a specific letter anywhere in the text (Contains option).

As illustrated in Figure 7-18, you can design a two-criterion custom filter that selects data that contains both criteria (*And* option) or selects data that contains one or the other of the criteria (*Or* option). If you select *Or*, less data will be filtered out, giving a much wider filter. When choosing the *And* option, it narrows your filtered data.

Figure 7-18

Two-criterion custom AutoFilter

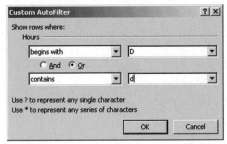

CERTIFICATION READY   8.1.1

How do you define a filter?

Creating a filter is also known as "defining" a filter.

Filtering Data Using Conditional Formatting

If you have conditionally formatted a range of cells, you can filter the data by that format. A conditional format is a visual guide that helps you quickly understand variation in a worksheet's data. By using conditional formatting as a filter, you can easily organize and highlight cells or ranges in order to emphasize the values based on one or more criteria. In the following exercise, you learn to use icon sets to identify the number of hours employees work each week.

STEP BY STEP **Filter Data Using Conditional Formatting**

OPEN *Conditional Format* from the data files for this lesson.

1. Select A3:E32. On the *Data* tab, click Filter.
2. Click the filter arrow in column D. Point to Filter by Color in the *AutoFilter* menu that appears. Click the green flag under the *Filter by Cell* icon. Data formatted with a green flag (highest number of work hours) is displayed.
3. Click the filter arrow in column D. Point to Filter by Color. Click the red flag under the *Filter by Cell* icon. The data formatted by a green flag is replaced in the worksheet by data formatted with a red flag (lowest number of work hours).
4. Click Filter to remove the filter arrows.

PAUSE. LEAVE the workbook open to use in the next exercise.

> **CERTIFICATION READY**   **8.3.1**
>
> How do you filter data using conditional formatting?

Filtering Data Using Cell Attributes

If you have formatted a range of cells with fill color or font color, you can filter on those attributes. It is not necessary to select the data range to filter using cell attributes. Excel will search for any cell that contains either background or font color. In the following exercise, icon sets are used to identify the number of hours employees work each week, and font color has been used to identify the medical assistant assigned to each physician. In the next exercise, you will use font attributes as your filter criteria.

STEP BY STEP **Filter Data Using Cell Attributes**

USE the workbook from the previous exercise.

1. Select any cell in the data range and click the Filter button in the Sort & Filter group on the Data tab.
2. Click the arrow next to the Title header (Contoso, Ltd.) and point to Filter by Color. Click More Font Colors. A dialog box opens that displays the font colors used in the worksheet.
3. As in Figure 7-19, the first color appears in the Selected field. Click OK. The heading rows are displayed. These are the colors in the Office theme that was applied to this worksheet.

Figure 7-19

Available font colors

First font color
available in
selection box

Recognized worksheet
font colors are available
as filter criteria

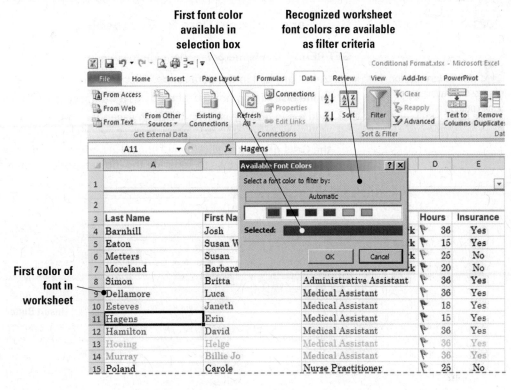

First color of
font in
worksheet

4. Click the filter arrow next to the Title header again and click Clear Filter From "Contoso, Ltd."

5. Click the Title header filter arrow again and point to Filter by Color. Select Purple in the *Filter by Font Color* drop-down menu (3rd selection). Data for Dr. Blythe (new physician) and his two medical assistants is displayed because you chose the Purple font in your sort criteria.

CERTIFICATION READY   8.1.2

How do you filter data using cell attributes?

6. Click the Filter button to clear the filter arrows.

7. **CLOSE** the file. You have not made changes to the data, so it is not necessary to save the file.

PAUSE. LEAVE Excel open to use in the next exercise.

In the preceding exercises, you used Excel's Sort and Filter features to organize data using a variety of criteria. Both Sort and Filter allow you to select and analyze specific data. The two functions have a great deal in common. In both instances, you can focus on data that meets specific criteria. Unrelated data is displayed when you sort; it is hidden when you use the filter command.

SUBTOTALING DATA

The Bottom Line

Excel provides a number of features that enable you to organize large groups of data into more manageable groups. Data in a list can be summarized by inserting a subtotal. Before you can subtotal, however, you must first sort the list by the field on which you want the list subtotaled.

Grouping and Ungrouping Data for Subtotaling

If you have a list of data that you want to group and summarize, you can create an outline. **Grouping** refers to organizing data so that it can be viewed as a collapsible and expandable outline. To group data, each column must have a label in the first row and the column must contain similar facts. The data must be sorted by the column or columns for that group.

| STEP BY STEP | **Group and Ungroup Data for Subtotaling** |

GET READY. OPEN the *Salary* data file for this lesson.

@ The *Salary* file for this lesson is available on the book companion website or in WileyPLUS.

1. Select any cell in the data range. Click Sort on the Data tab.
2. In the Sort dialog box, sort first by Job Category in ascending order.
3. Add a sort level, sort by Job Title in ascending order, and click OK.
4. Select row 14, press Ctrl, and select row 27. On the Home tab, click the Insert arrow in the Cells group and click Insert Sheet Rows from the drop-down menu that appears. This step inserts rows to separate the job categories. Refer to Figure 7-20.

Figure 7-20

Insert options

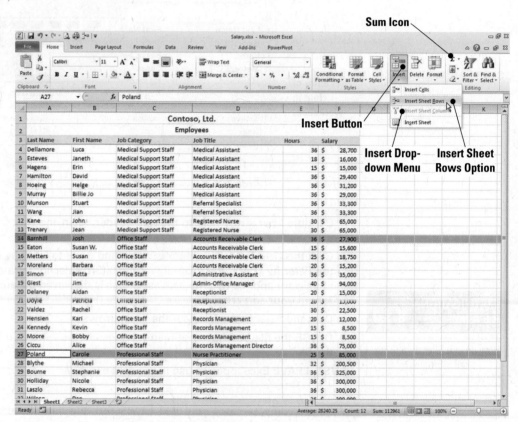

5. In C14, key Subtotal. Select F14 and click the Sum icon (also shown in Figure 7-20). The values above F14 are selected. Press Enter and Excel subtotals the category.
6. In C28, key Subtotal. Select F28 and click Sum. Press Enter.
7. In C36, key Subtotal. Select F36 and click Sum. Press Enter.
8. In C37, key Grand Total. Select F37 and click Sum. The three subtotals are selected. Press Enter.

9. Select a cell in the data range. On the Data tab, click the Group arrow in the Outline group, and then click Auto Outline from the drop-down menu. A three-level outline is created. Figure 7-21 shows your worksheet complete with subtotals and grand total. To view your worksheet as in the figure, adjust your zoom to 75%.

Figure 7-21

Three-level outline

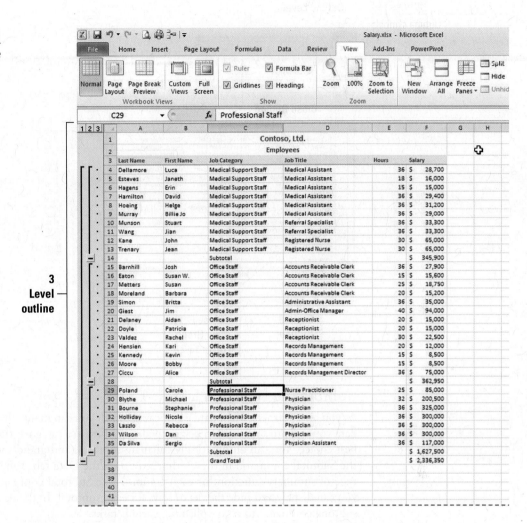

PAUSE. LEAVE the workbook open to use in the next exercise.

In the preceding exercises, you manually grouped and subtotaled salary data for Contoso, Ltd. You will use Excel's automatic subtotal feature in the next exercise.

To outline data by rows, you must have summary rows that contain formulas that reference cells in each of the detail rows for that group. In the preceding exercise, your outline contained three levels: the grand total level, the subtotals level, and the detail rows level. You can create an outline of up to eight levels.

Each inner level displays detail data for the preceding outer level. Inner levels are represented by a higher number in the **outline symbols**, which are symbols that you use to change the view of an outlined worksheet. You can show or hide detailed data by pressing the plus sign, minus sign, or the numbers 1, 2, or 3 that indicate the outline level to hide, unhide, and view your data. Refer to the example in Figure 7-22.

Figure 7-22

Outline symbols

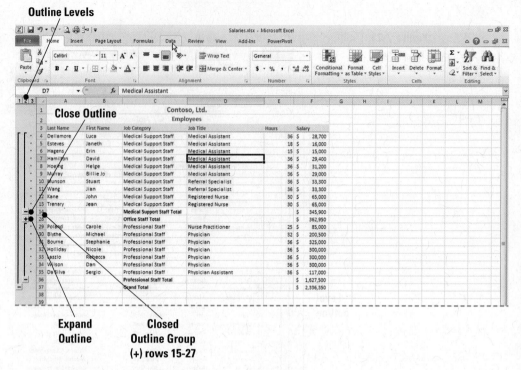

Subtotaling Data in a List

As you have learned, when data is not categorized, you can manually insert subtotals. When the data you want to subtotal can be grouped according to a category, the Subtotal command is the best choice. You can automatically calculate subtotals and grand totals for a column by using the Subtotal command in the Outline group on the Data tab. You can display more than one type of summary function for each column. The Subtotal command outlines the list so that you can display and hide the detail rows for each subtotal. In the next exercise, you will use the subtotal command to accomplish the various tasks.

STEP BY STEP   **Subtotal Data in a List**

USE the worksheet from the previous exercise.

1. In the Outline group on the Data tab, click the Ungroup arrow and then click Clear Outline.

2. Select rows 14, 28, 36, and 37, right-click and Delete all selected rows. Remember, to select nonadjacent rows, click the first row then press and hold the Ctrl key and proceed to click the additional rows you wish to select.

3. Select the data range (A3:F33), including the column labels in the selection.

4. Click Subtotal in the Outline group on the Data tab. The Subtotal dialog box is displayed.

5. Select Job Category in the *At Each Change in* box.

6. Under *Add Subtotal To*, Salary should already be checkmarked. Click **OK** to accept the remaining defaults. Subtotals are inserted for each of the three job categories, and a grand total is calculated at the bottom of the list. Figure 7-23 illustrates the outline groups with subtotals and grand total.

Figure 7-23

Subtotals and grand total

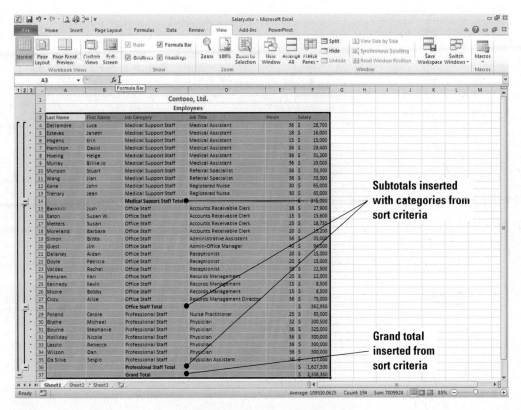

7. **SAVE** the workbook as *Salaries*.

CLOSE the workbook, but **LEAVE** Excel open for the next exercise.

Take Note

If the workbook is set to automatically calculate formulas, the Subtotal command recalculates subtotal values automatically as you edit the detail data.

You can subtotal groups within categories, as well. For example, you could subtotal the salaries for the accounts receivable clerks or the records management employees as well as find a total for the entire office staff.

SETTING UP DATA IN A TABLE FORMAT

The Bottom Line

When you create a table in Excel, you can manage and analyze data in the table independently of data outside the table. For example, you can filter table columns, add a row for totals, apply table formatting, and publish a table to a server.

Formatting a Table with a Quick Style

You can turn a range of cells into an Excel table and manage and analyze a group of related data independently. When you create a table, a Design tab appears on the Ribbon offering Excel's Table Tools. You can use the tools on the Design tab to customize or edit the table. Four table styles are displayed in the Table Styles group. Click the arrows to the right of the styles to display additional styles. You can view the styles samples in Figure 7-24. In the next exercise, you will learn how to use a quick style.

Figure 7-24

Formatting tables with styles

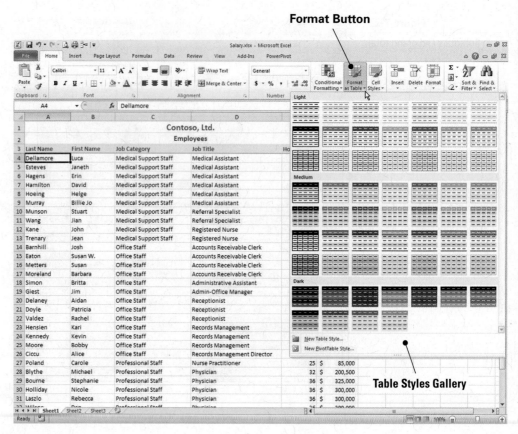

Format Button

Table Styles Gallery

STEP BY STEP   **Format a Table with a Quick Style**

@ The *Salary* file for this lesson is available on the book companion website or in WileyPLUS.

GET READY. OPEN *Salary* from the data files for this lesson.

1. Select any cell in the data. Click **Sort** on the Data tab.

2. In the Sort dialog box, sort first by **Job Category** in ascending order.

3. Add a sort level and sort by Job Title in ascending order. Click **OK**. Your data has been sorted first by Job Category and then by Job Title.

4. On the Home tab, click **Format as Table** in the Styles Group. The Table styles gallery opens.

5. Mouse over the Table styles to Table Style Medium 5 from the gallery. The *Format as Table* dialog box opens.

6. Click the **hide dialog box** icon ![icon] in the *Where Is the Data for Your Table?* box to collapse the *Format as Table* dialog box so you can select the data to be included in the table.

7. Select **A27:F32** as shown in Figure 7-25 and press **Enter**. The Create Table dialog box appears. Your table does not have headers, so click **OK**. The Table Style Medium 5 format is applied and filtering column headers are inserted as illustrated in Figure 7-26.

Figure 7-25

Identify data to include in table

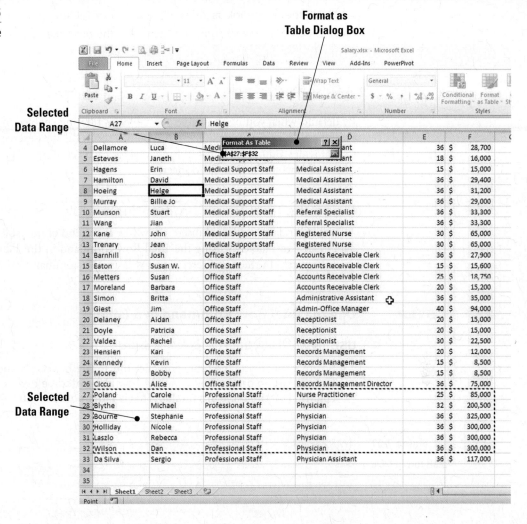

Figure 7-26

Formatted table with style

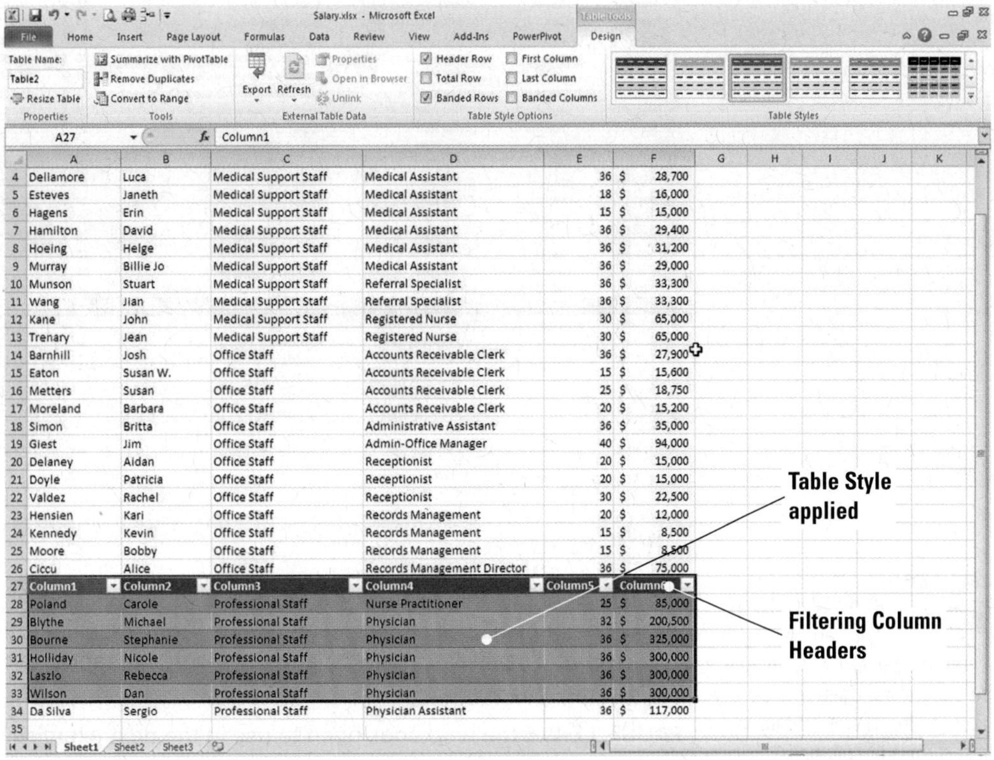

8. SAVE the workbook as *Table* in the Lesson 7 folder.

PAUSE. LEAVE the workbook open to use in the next exercise.

Take Note
Because the data selected for the table did not have headers, default names (i.e., Column1) are displayed above the table.

By default, when you insert a table, the table has filtering enabled in the header row so that you can filter or sort your table quickly. As you will see in the next exercise, you can add a Totals row that provides a drop-down list of functions for each cell in the Totals row. You can insert more than one table in the same worksheet.

Using the Total Row Command in a Table

To total your data, you could insert a new row at the end of the table. But it is faster to total the data in an Excel table by using the Total Row command in the Table Styles Options group on the Design tab. In the next exercise, you will use this command.

STEP BY STEP   **Use the Total Row Command in a Table**

USE the workbook from the previous exercise.

1. Select a cell inside the table and click the Total Row command box in the Table Style Options group on the Design tab. A row is inserted below the table and the salaries in column F of the table are totaled. This is illustrated in Figure 7-27.

Figure 7-27

Totals row in table

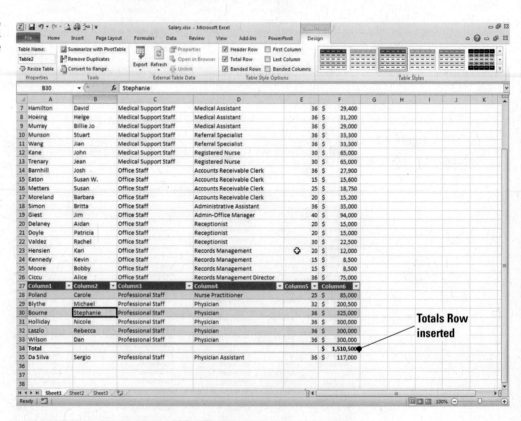

2. Click any blank cell to deselect the table. Adjust the column width to display the total amount if necessary. Click on any cell inside the table.

3. **SAVE** the workbook.

PAUSE. LEAVE the workbook open to use in the next exercise.

Another Way
You can also right-click on a table row or column to open the shortcut menu. Point to Insert and options to insert rows or columns.

If you press Tab in the last cell of the last row of the table, a blank row will be added at the end of the table, which would allow you to add new data to the table. Once a Totals row has been added to the table, however, pressing Tab will not add a new row.

Adding and Removing Rows or Columns in a Table

After you create a table in your worksheet, you can easily add rows or columns. You can add adjacent rows to the table by using the mouse to drag the resize handle down to select rows or drag to the right to select columns. You can enter text or values in an adjacent row or column that you want to include in the table. You can add a blank row at the end of the table, or insert table rows or columns anywhere in the table. In the next exercise, you will learn to add and remove rows and columns.

STEP BY STEP   **Add and Remove Rows or Columns in a Table**

USE the workbook from the previous exercise.

1. On the Design tab, in the Properties group, click Resize Table. The Resize Table dialog box opens.

2. Collapse the Resize Table dialog box by clicking the collapse dialog box button, and select A27:F35. Press Enter to accept the new range of cells. Click OK to accept the change to the table and apply the new settings. The physician assistant data is moved above the total line, and the total is recalculated. Refer to Figure 7-28.

Figure 7-28

New row moved into table

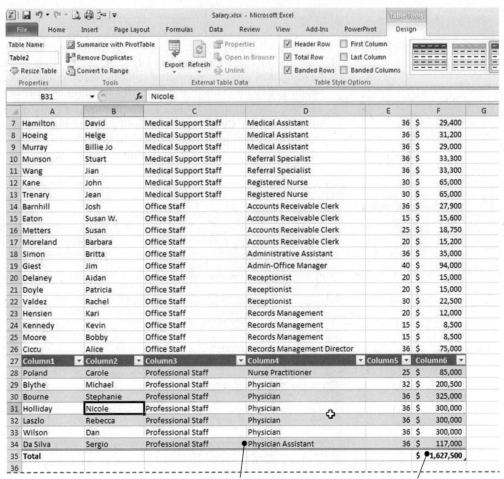

Moved Record   **New Total and Total Row**

3. Select C28. On the Home tab, click the Delete arrow in the Cells group, and click Delete Table Columns from the drop-down menu that appears. Column C is deleted. Refer to Figure 7-29 for the drop-down menu for this step.

Figure 7-29

Delete cells drop-down menu

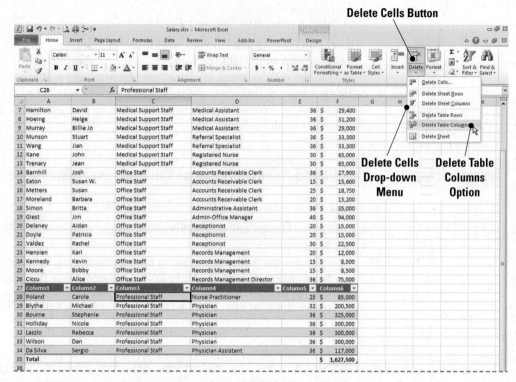

4. Click the Column1 heading and key Last Name. Press Tab to move to the Column 2 heading. Key First Name in that column heading and press Tab to advance to the next heading. Key Job Title in the column 4 heading and press Tab.

5. Key Hours in column 5. Press Tab. In the Invalid Entry dialog box that displays, click Yes to continue. Clicking Yes here will override the data restrictions and dismiss the Invalid Entry dialog box. Key Salary in the column 6 heading and press Enter. Your table headings should appear as illustrated in Figure 7-30.

Figure 7-30

Table headers complete

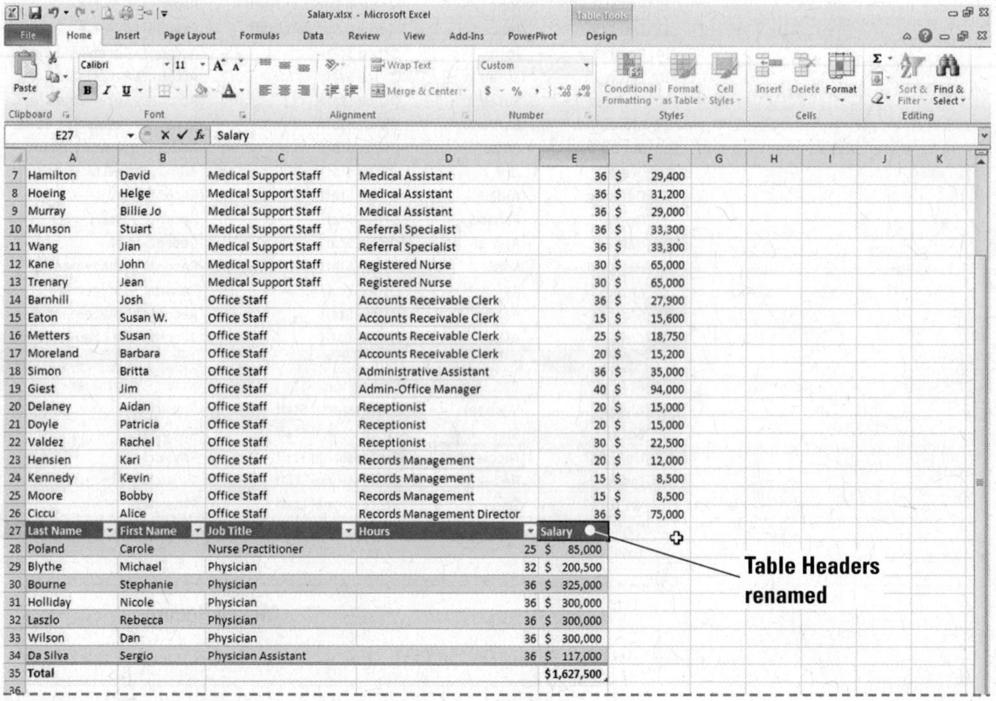

6. If necessary, adjust the column E width to display the total salary amount.

7. In the Properties group on the Design tab, select the text in the Table Name box and key **Schedule** and press **Enter**. This table represents the individuals with whom patients schedule appointments.

8. **SAVE** the file and then **CLOSE** the file.

CLOSE Excel.

When you resize a table, the table headers must remain in the same row, and the revised table range must overlap the original table range. In the exercise, you added a row from below to the table, but you would not be able to add a row from above the table. You can click the resizing handle in the lower-right corner of the table and drag it to the right to add a column.

When you finish working with a table, you can click Convert to Range in the Tools group and convert the table to a data range. The formatting, column headers, and table total remain.

SKILL SUMMARY

In This Lesson You Learned How To:	Exam Objective	Objective Number
Ensuring Your Data's Integrity		
Sorting Data	Use Sort options.	8.2.1
	Apply conditional formatting to cells.	8.3.1
Filtering Data	Filter lists using AutoFilter.	8.1.4
	Remove a filter.	8.1.3
	Define a filter.	8.1.1
	Apply a filter.	8.1.2
Subtotaling Data		
Setting Up Data in a Table Format		

Knowledge Assessment

Fill in the Blank

Complete the following sentences by writing the correct word or words in the blanks provided.

1. The process of organizing data so that it can be viewed as a collapsible and expandable outline is _____.

2. Values in the row that are an exact match of all the values in another row are referred to as _____.

3. Excel uses _____ rules to determine which worksheet rows to display.

4. In _____, sorted values appear Z to A or highest to lowest.

5. The _____ are conditions specified to limit which records to include in the result of a sort or filter.

6. A sign used in criteria to compare two values is a(n) _____.

7. Using a(n) _____ allows you to apply a built-in set of filtering capabilities.

8. In _____ sort order, values appear A to Z or smallest to largest.

9. You can use outline _____ to change the view of an outlined worksheet.

10. You can quickly rearrange the data sequence when you use Excel's _____ feature.

True/False

Circle T if the statement is true or F if the statement is false.

T F 1. You can sort a data range using conditional formatting.

T F 2. When numbers are sorted in ascending order, the largest number is on top.

T F 3. You can create a custom AutoFilter that will isolate data that falls between a high and low number.

T F 4. You can filter data to display all cells with a specific background color and cells that contain specific text.

T F 5. In a case-sensitive sort, lowercase letters will be sorted before uppercase letters.

T F 6. To temporarily isolate a specific list of rows in a worksheet containing data, use the Sort feature.

T F 7. The Data Validation command enables you to locate and remove duplicate values in a worksheet.

T F 8. To outline data, the data must have a blank line that includes a formula that references all the cells in the detail rows for that group.

T F 9. When a table is inserted in a worksheet, the Design tab is added to the Ribbon and Table tools are available.

T F 10. Data validation enables you to allow only specific values to be entered in cells.

Competency Assessment

Project 7-1: Analyze Semiannual Sales Data

Litware, Inc., has divided its sales representatives into two teams that are in competition for sales rewards. The sales report worksheet has been color coded to identify team members. In this exercise, you will sort the team data.

GET READY. LAUNCH Excel if it is not already running.

@ The *Semi Annual Sales* file for this lesson is available on the book companion website or in WileyPLUS.

1. **OPEN** the *Semi Annual Sales* data file for Lesson 7.

2. Click the Data tab to make it active.

3. Select A4:H12. The data range should include the column headings but not the monthly totals.

4. Click Sort in the Sort & Filter group. My Data Has Headers should be selected by default. If not, select it.

5. In the Sort dialog box, select Total (or Column H) in the Sort by field. In the Sort On field, select Values. Select Largest to Smallest (descending) in the Order field. Click OK. The sales representative with the highest total sales is listed first. The rest are listed in descending order.

6. With the data still selected, click Sort. Sort by Sales Representative. Sort on Font Color. In the Order fields, select Red and On Top. Click OK. The red team is listed first. Within the red team, representatives are listed in descending order in terms of sales.

7. **SAVE** the workbook as *Semi Annual Sales 7-1*. **CLOSE** the file.

LEAVE Excel open for the next project.

Project 7-2: Ensuring Data Integrity

Create a workbook that you will use to collect survey responses from a random sample of students at your college. Your survey will consist of ten questions, and you will survey ten students.

GET READY. LAUNCH Excel if it is not already running.

1. Click the File tab and open a new blank workbook.

2. Select A2, key Survey Questions, and press Tab.

3. Key Student 1 and press Tab. Key Student 2 and press Tab.

4. Select B2:C2. Use the fill handle to complete the series to Student 10 (cell K2).

5. Select A3 and key In what year did you begin college? Press Enter.

6. Key Have you met with an advisor this year? Press Enter.

7. Key How many hours per week do you study? Press Enter.

8. Select B3:K3. On the Data tab, click Data Validation.

9. On the Settings tab, in the Allow box, select Whole number. In the Data box, select less than or equal to. In the Maximum field, enter the current year in 20XX format.

10. Click the Input Message tab. In the Input message box, key Enter year in 20XX format. Click OK. The input message should be displayed when you close the dialog box.

11. Select B4:K4. Click Data Validation.

12. Click the Settings tab if necessary. In the Allow box, select List. In the Source box, key Yes, No. Click OK. A drop-down arrow should be displayed next to the active cell.

13. Resize the columns if necessary.

14. **SAVE** the workbook as *Survey 7-2* and then **CLOSE** the file.

LEAVE Excel open for the next project.

Proficiency Assessment

Project 7-3: Filter Data on Multiple Criteria

The Litware sales manager needs to filter the sales report data in a variety of ways so that he can use it in team meetings to acknowledge those who have achieved sales objectives and to motivate the teams. Create the filters for the sales manager.

GET READY. LAUNCH Excel if it is not already running.

@ The *Sales Teams* file for this lesson is available on the book companion website or in WileyPLUS.

1. **OPEN** *Sales Teams* from the data files for this lesson.

2. Select A4:H12. Click Filter. Click the arrow in the Total column.

3. Click Number Filters and then click Greater Than. Key 100,000 in the dialog box. Click OK. Four sales representatives are displayed.

4. Click Filter to display all data. Select any cell that contains data and create a filter to display the Red Team's statistics. (Hint: Because entire rows are color coded, you do not have to select the data. Data does not have to be sorted when you filter for color.)

5. **SAVE** the workbook as *Red Team*.

6. Click Filter to display all data. Click Filter again to display the filter arrows.

7. Click a filter arrow and display the Blue Team's statistics.

8. **SAVE** the workbook as *Blue Team*. **CLOSE** the workbook.

LEAVE Excel open for the next project.

Project 7-4: Sort and Filter Using Conditional Formatting

Each year *Fortune Magazine* surveys employees and publishes a list of the ten best employers based on employee ranking. The Top Ten worksheet contains additional information about the top ten companies in terms of their size (number of employees), percentage of minorities, and percentage of women. In this exercise, you will sort using conditional formatting to determine how many women in the workforce are employed by Top Ten companies.

GET READY. LAUNCH Excel if it is not already running.

@ The *Top Ten* file for this lesson is available on the book companion website or in WileyPLUS.

1. **OPEN** the *Top Ten* data file for this lesson.

2. Select the data range, including the column headings. Click Sort on the Data tab.

3. Sort the data by % Minorities. Click Cell Icon in the Sort On field.

4. Under Order, place the green flagged data (highest) on top. Click **OK**. Because you sorted by one criterion, the highest is on top, but the red and yellow are intermixed.

5. Click **Sort** to add a second criterion to sort on yellow flags, which represent the middle range.

6. With the data range selected, click **Filter**. Arrows are added to the column headings.

7. Click the filter arrow in the % Women column. Choose to filter by color.

8. Select the green arrow. Women comprise more than 60 percent of the workforce in two of the top ten companies.

9. **SAVE** the workbook as *Top Ten 7-4*. **CLOSE** the workbook.

LEAVE Excel open for the next project.

Mastery Assessment

Project 7-5: Subtotal Data

As a motivational tool, Litware's sales manager wants to group the teams and enter a subtotal as well as the grand total. In this exercise, you will complete this task.

GET READY. LAUNCH Excel if it is not already running.

@ The *Semi Annual Sales* file for this lesson is available on the book companion website or in WileyPLUS.

1. **OPEN** the *Semi Annual Sales* data file for this lesson.

2. Select the data range only and sort by font color with the Blue Team on top.

3. Clear contents and formatting from the Totals row.

4. Select the Blue Team and group the rows. Group the Red Team.

5. Insert a column to the left of column A. Merge and center the title and subtitle to include the new column.

6. Key Team in A4. Select B4:B14.

7. Click the Format Painter and format column A. In column A, key Red or Blue to identify the salesperson's team.

8. Create team subtotals in the Total column.

9. Collapse the outline to Level 2 so that only the team totals and grand total are displayed.

10. **SAVE** the workbook as *Teams 7-5*, and then **CLOSE** the file.

LEAVE Excel open for the next project.

Project 7-6: Create a Table in a Worksheet

The Records Management Director at Contoso has asked you to create a table within the Salary workbook.

GET READY. LAUNCH Excel if it is not already running.

@ The *Salary* file for this lesson is available on the book companion website or in WileyPLUS.

1. **OPEN** the *Salary* data file for this lesson.

2. Sort the data by Job Category and then by Job Title.

3. Click Format as Table on the Home tab. Select Table Style Light 10 on the Quick Styles list.

4. In the Format As Table dialog box, select the records management personnel data as the data for the table.

5. Add a Total Row to the table.

6. Rename the table column labels to match those in the worksheet (Last Name, First Name, Job Category, Job Title, Hours, and Salary).

7. **SAVE** the workbook as *Records Management Table*. **CLOSE** the workbook.

LEAVE Excel open for the next project.

In this lesson, you worked with salary data for a medical facility. The salary figures were based on average earnings for employees in medical care facilities in the Midwest. Go online and research salary data for your chosen profession. Identify three positions in which you might like to work. Conduct research into the average salary in those professions in three different cities in different parts of the country. For example, you might find earnings information for accountants in New York City, New York; St. Louis, Missouri; and Seattle, Washington. Create a worksheet to report your research findings. Format all data appropriately. Save your worksheet as *Salary Research* and exit Excel.

Workplace *Ready*

MANAGING LISTS IN EXCEL

Microsoft Excel provides numerous templates that can be downloaded and used to start new worksheets. Templates are time-saving tools that eliminate the need for you to spend time setting up the structure of a worksheet and applying complex formatting and formulas.

All you need to do is enter the raw data, because the template has built-in formatting and formulas.

When you click the File tab and click New in Backstage view's navigation bar, the New Workbook window opens, as shown in the Figure 7-31. There are buttons to Recent templates and Sample templates in the top section to the right of the Blank workbook button. The Office.com Available Templates are organized into categories of templates that can be downloaded from Microsoft Office Online. Although some are personal-use templates, the majority are business templates. You can browse templates by category and select and download a template of your choice. You can then use it as the basis for a new workbook.

Figure 7-31

Available templates

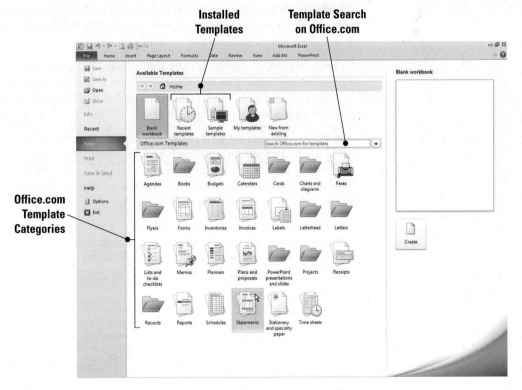

The Expense Budget template (Figure 7-32) can be downloaded from Microsoft Office Online.

Figure 7-32

Expense budget template

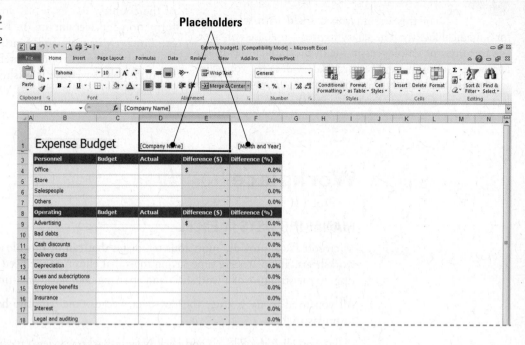

Download the **Expense Budget spreadsheet** file and explore this template that can be used in a business setting. This template should be located in the Budgets category and in the Business Budgets folder. The templates are organized alphabetically. You can use this template to create a basic expense budget and take advantage of the built-in formulas and structure. Templates are a great tool if you do not have the time to design a formatted workbook from the ground up. You can simply input your data, make a few minor adjustments as needed, and save and use the workbook as your own.

Placeholders are important text directives specified by the author of the template that direct the user where to add specific data in specific cells within the template. They are always surrounded by square brackets and have specific text directives.

In this template, placeholders mark cells in which to enter your company's name and the date. Categories of expenses are identified in column B. You can insert cells and rows if necessary. The existing cells and rows can be deleted or moved and the labels can be edited to reflect the line items in your company's budget.

You can key the data for your company's budget amounts and actual expenditures in columns C and D. The data cells in columns E and F contain formulas to calculate the difference between budget and actual expenditures as values and percentages. When you enter data, both calculations are completed automatically. When you scroll to the bottom of the worksheet, you see that formulas have been created to total each column.

You can easily see that using this template to create a company expense budget would take far less time than creating the worksheet from scratch. With a template you just enter the data—Excel provides the formulas and performs all the calculations.

LESSON SKILL MATRIX

Skill	Exam Objective	Objective Number
Building Basic Formulas	Use basic operators.	5.1.1
	Revise formulas.	5.1.2
	Precedence: Order of evaluation.	5.2.1
	Precedence using parentheses.	5.2.2
	Precedence of operators for percent versus exponentiation.	5.2.3
Using Cell References in Formulas	Create formulas that use relative and absolute cell references.	5.3.1
Using Cell Ranges in Formulas	Define a cell range.	5.6.2
	Edit ranges in formulas.	5.5.2
	Rename a named range.	5.5.3
	Define ranges in formulas.	5.5.1
Summarizing Data with Functions		
Using Formulas to Create Subtotals	Enter a cell range definition in the formula bar.	5.6.1
Controlling the Appearance of Formulas		

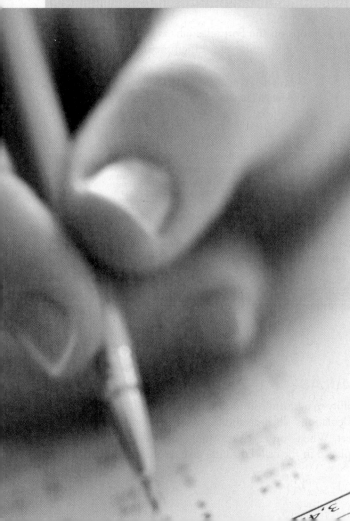

KEY TERMS

- absolute cell reference
- arguments
- constant
- external reference
- formula
- function
- mathematical operator
- mixed reference
- name
- operand
- reference
- relative cell reference
- scope

Most people agree that it is vitally important for a business to have a realistic budget. It is equally important for an individual to have a personal budget—a plan for managing income and expenses.

Katie Jordan has been managing, or more accurately, spending her money without a formal budget. In fact, the only budget she prepared was one she scribbled on the back of her résumé immediately after being offered what she considered to be her dream job. Since that time, Katie has changed jobs several times. Now, she wants to purchase a condominium, and she realizes that she needs to create a comprehensive personal budget that will enable her to realize her goal of home ownership.

Katie uses Excel in her job as a marketing analyst at Tailspin Toys. She plans to use Excel to track her expenditures and to develop a realistic budget. She has conducted online research and developed a preliminary budget. This is her first step toward financial independence. Formulas make Excel a powerful tool. In this lesson, you will learn to write simple formulas and use many of Excel's functions with built-in formulas that enable you to perform many types of calculations.

SOFTWARE ORIENTATION

Formulas Tab

In this Lesson, you'll use command groups on the Formulas tab, as shown in Figure 8-1. These commands are your tools for building formulas and using functions in Excel.

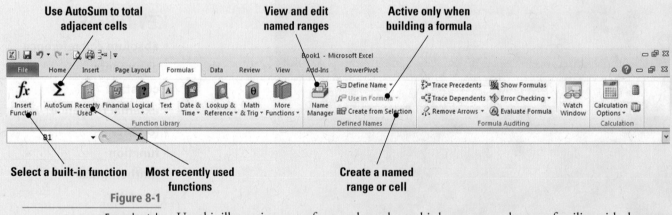

Use AutoSum to total adjacent cells

View and edit named ranges

Active only when building a formula

Select a built-in function   **Most recently used functions**

Create a named range or cell

Figure 8-1

Formulas tab

Use this illustration as a reference throughout this lesson as you become familiar with the command groups on the Formulas tab and use them to create formulas.

BUILDING BASIC FORMULAS

The real strength of Excel is its ability to perform common and complex calculations. A **formula** is an equation that performs calculations, such as addition, subtraction, multiplication, and division, on values in a worksheet. When you enter a formula in a cell, the formula is stored internally and the results are displayed in the cell. Formulas give results and solutions that help you assess and analyze data.

The Bottom Line

Creating a Formula that Performs Addition

A formula consists of two elements: operands and mathematical operators. **Operands** identify the values to be used in the calculation. An operand can be a constant value, a cell reference, a range of cells, or another formula. A **constant** is a number or text value that is entered directly into a formula. **Mathematical operators** specify the calculations to be performed. To allow Excel to distinguish formulas from data, all formulas begin with an equal sign (=).

In this exercise, you will learn how to create basic formulas that perform mathematical computations and apply the formulas using various methods.

Take Note

You can begin a formula with a + or − as the beginning mathematical operator, but Excel changes it to = when you press Enter.

When you build a formula, it appears in the formula bar and in the cell itself. When you complete the formula and press Enter, the value displays in the cell and the formula displays in the formula bar. You can edit a formula in the cell or in the formula bar the same way you can edit any data entry.

STEP BY STEP | **Create a Formula that Performs Addition**

GET READY. Before you begin these steps, **LAUNCH** Microsoft Excel and **OPEN** a blank workbook.

1. Select **A1** and key =25+15. Press Tab. Excel calculates the value in A1, and displays the sum of *40* in the cell.
2. In B1, key +18+35. Press Tab. The sum of the two numbers, *53*, appears in the cell.

Take Note

Formulas should be keyed without spaces, but if you key spaces, Excel eliminates them when you press Enter.

3. Select **B1** to display the formula for that cell in the formula bar. As illustrated in Figure 8-2, although you entered + to begin the formula, when you pressed Enter, Excel replaced the + with = as the beginning mathematical operator. This is the Excel formula auto correct feature.

Figure 8-2

Formula begins with equal sign

Cell containing formula

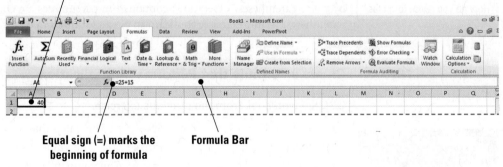

Equal sign (=) marks the beginning of formula   **Formula Bar**

4. Select **A3**. Click the formula bar and key =94+89+35. Press Enter. The sum of the three numbers, *218*, appears in the cell.
5. Select **A3** and click the formula bar. Select 89 and key 98. Press Enter. Notice that your sum changes to *227*.

PAUSE. LEAVE the workbook open to use in the next exercise.

CERTIFICATION
READY | **5.1.1**

How do you create a formula that performs addition?

Creating a Formula that Performs Subtraction

The same methods you used to create a formula to perform addition can be used to create a formula to perform subtraction. When you create a subtraction formula, enter = followed by the positive number and then enter a minus sign to indicate subtraction. When you create a subtraction formula, the minus sign *must* precede the number to be subtracted. In this exercise, you practice creating a formula that performs subtraction.

STEP BY STEP   **Create a Formula that Performs Subtraction**

USE the workbook from the previous exercise.

1. Select A5. Key =456−98. Press Enter. The value in A5, *358*, appears in the cell.
2. Select A6 and key =545−13−8. Press Enter. The value in A6 should be *524*.
3. In A8, create a formula to subtract 125 from 189. The value in A8 should be *64*.

Troubleshooting   If your formula returned a negative value (i.e., –64), you reversed the order in which the numbers should have been entered.

PAUSE. LEAVE the workbook open to use in the next exercise.

CERTIFICATION READY   5.1.1

How do you create a formula that performs subtraction?

When you entered a formula to subtract 125 from 189, you could have entered =189−125 or = −125+189. Either formula would yield a positive 64. If the positive number is entered first, it is not necessary to enter a plus sign.

If you find that you've made a mistake in your formula (such as returning the negative number mentioned earlier), you can select the cell with the erroneous function, press F2 to take you to the formula bar, and edit your function. Once you've made your corrections, press Enter to revise.

Take Note   When you have a cell selected, pressing F2 will always activate the formula bar for that cell.

Creating a Formula that Performs Multiplication

CERTIFICATION READY   5.1.2

How do you revise formulas?

The formula to multiply 33 by 6 is =33*6. If a formula contains two or more operators, operations are not necessarily performed in the order in which you read the formula. The order is determined by the rules of mathematics, but you can override standard operator priorities by using parentheses. Operations contained in parentheses are completed before those outside parentheses. In this exercise, you learn to create formulas that perform multiplication.

STEP BY STEP   **Create a Formula that Performs Multiplication**

USE the workbook from the previous exercise.

1. Select D1. Key =125*4 and press Enter. The value that appears in D1 is *500*.
2. Select D3 and key =2*7.50*2. Press Enter. The value in D3 is *30*.
3. Select D5 and key =5*3. Press Enter. The value in D5 is *15*.
4. Select D7 and key =5+2*8. The value in D7 is *21*.
5. Select D9 and key =(5+2)*8. The value in D9 is *56*.

CERTIFICATION READY   5.1.1

How do you create a formula that performs multiplication?

PAUSE. LEAVE the workbook open to use in the next exercise.

When you added parentheses to the last formula you entered in this exercise, you changed the order of the calculations. When you entered the formula without parentheses, Excel multiplied 2 by 8 and added 5 for a value of 21. When you entered (5+2)*8, Excel performed the addition first and returned a value of 56. The order of calculations will be further illustrated in the next exercise.

Creating a Formula that Performs Division

The forward slash is the mathematical operator for division. When a calculation includes multiple values, you must use parentheses to indicate the part of the calculation that should be performed first.

STEP BY STEP   **Create a Formula that Performs Division**

USE the workbook from the previous exercise.

1. Select **D7** and create the formula =**795/45**. Press **Enter**. Excel returns a value of *17.66667* in D7.

Take Note   The results of the formula calculation rounded the value 17.66667 after the seventh digit (eighth character) because the standard column width is 8.43. In other words, the value was rounded at that number of places only because of the column width.

2. Select **D7**. Excel applied the number format to this cell when it returned the value in step 1. Click the **Accounting Number Format ($)** button, on the Home tab in the Numbers group, to apply the accounting format to cell D7. The number is rounded to *$17.67* because two decimal places is the default setting for the accounting format.

3. Select **D9** and create the formula =**65−29*8+97/5**. Press **Enter**. The value in D9 is *−147.6*.

CERTIFICATION READY   **5.1.1**

How do you create a formula that performs division?

4. Select **D9**. Click in the formula bar and place parentheses around 65–29. Press **Enter**. The value in D9 is *307.4*.

5. **CLOSE** but do not save the workbook.

PAUSE. LEAVE Excel open to use in the next exercise.

Excel does not necessarily perform the operations in the same order that you enter or read them in a formula, which is left to right. Excel uses the rules of mathematics to determine which operations to perform first when a formula contains multiple operators. This is also known as the order of evaluation in Excel.

The order is:

CERTIFICATION READY   **5.2.1**

How do you determine the order of evaluation for mathematical operators in an Excel formula?

- negative number (−)
- percent (%)
- exponentiation (^)
- multiplication (*) and division (/)
- addition (+) and subtraction (−)

For example, consider the following equation:

$$5 + 6 * 15 / 3 - 1 = 34$$

Following mathematical operator priorities, the first operation would be 6 multiplied by 15 and that result would be divided by 3. Then 5 would be added and finally, 1 would be subtracted, giving you 34. Figure 8-3 illustrates the formula entered into Excel.

Figure 8-3

Structure of a formula

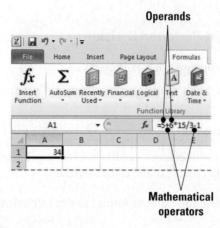

CERTIFICATION READY   5.2.2

How do you use parentheses in a formula to change the order of calculation?

When you use parentheses in a formula, you indicate which calculation to perform first, which overrides the standard operator priorities. Therefore, the result of the following equation would be significantly different from the previous one. Figure 8-4 illustrates the Excel formula. Here is the mathematical formula:

$$(5 + 6) * 15 / (3 - 1) = 82.5$$

Figure 8-4

Parentheses control the order of operations

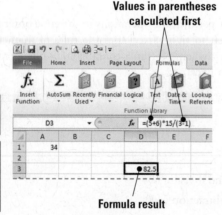

CERTIFICATION READY   5.2.3

How do you know whether exponents or percentages are calculated first in an Excel formula?

USING CELL REFERENCES IN FORMULAS

The Bottom Line

A cell **reference** in a formula identifies a cell or a range of cells on a worksheet and tells Excel where to look for the values you want it to calculate in the formula. Using cell references (cell names; A1, B1, and so on) enables you to re-use the formulas you write, by updating the data in the formulas, rather than rewriting the formulas themselves. With references, you can use values contained in different parts of a worksheet in one formula or use the value from one cell in several formulas. You can also refer to cells on another worksheet in the same workbook, as well as to other workbooks. Excel recognizes two types of cell references—relative and absolute.

Using Relative Cell References in a Formula

A cell reference identifies a cell's location in the worksheet, based on its row number and column letter. When you include a **relative cell reference** in a formula and copy that formula, Excel changes the reference to match the column or row to which the formula is copied. A relative cell reference is, therefore, one whose references change "relative" to the location where it is copied or moved. You use relative cell references when you want the reference to automatically adjust when you copy or fill the formula across rows or down columns in ranges of cells. By default, new formulas use relative references. In this exercise, you practice creating and using relative cell references in formulas.

You are about to learn two methods for creating formulas using relative references:
- By keying in an equal sign to mark the entry as a formula and then keying the formula directly into the cell; and
- By keying an equal sign and then clicking a cell or cell range included in the formula (rather than keying cell references).

The second method is usually quicker and eliminates the possibility of typing an incorrect cell or range reference. When you complete the formula and press Enter, the value displays in the cell and the formula displays in the formula bar.

| STEP BY STEP | Use Relative Cell References in a Formula |

GET READY. LAUNCH Microsoft Excel if it is not already open.

The *Personal Budget* file for this lesson is available on the book companion website or in WileyPLUS.

WILEY PLUS **EXTRA**

WileyPLUS Extra! features an online tutorial of this task.

1. **OPEN** the *Personal Budget* data file for this lesson.
2. Select **B7** and key **=sum(B4:** (colon). As shown in Figure 8-5, cell B4 is outlined in blue, and the reference to B4 in the formula is also blue. The ScreenTip below the formula identifies B4 as the first number in the formula. The reference to B4 is based on its relative position to B7, the cell that contains the formula.

Figure 8-5

Color-coordinated cell references

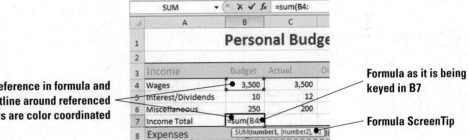

Cell reference in formula and outline around referenced cells are color coordinated

Formula as it is being keyed in B7

Formula ScreenTip

3. Key **B6** and press **Enter**. The total of the cells, *3,760*, appears in B7.
4. Select **B15**. Key **=sum(** and click **B10**. As shown in Figure 8-6, B10 appears in the formula bar and a flashing marquee appears around B10. Excel now knows that you are selecting this cell to be used in the formula.

Figure 8-6

Including a cell in a formula

Select first cell to include formula

8	Expenses	Budget	Actual	Difference
9	Home			
10	Mortgage/Rent	950	950	
11	Utilities	236	230	
12	Telephone	56	67	
13	Home Repairs	100	75	
14	Home Security	35	35	
15	Home Total	=sum(b10:		
16	Daily Living	SUM(number1, [number2], ...)		

5. Click and drag the flashing marquee to B14. As shown in Figure 8-7, the formula bar reveals that values within the B10:B14 range will be summed (added). Note, this step allows you to input a range of cells in the formula by highlighting instead of typing the formula in the cell.

Take Note You can use either uppercase or lowercase when you key a cell reference in a formula. For example, it would not matter whether you keyed B4 or b4 in the formula you entered.

Figure 8-7

Extend the cell range for a formula

SUM		✕ ✓ f_x	=SUM(B10:B14)	
	A	B	C	D
1		**Personal Budget**		
2				
3	Income	Budget	Actual	Difference
4	Wages	3,500	3,500	
5	Interest/Dividends	10	12	
6	Miscellaneous	250	200	
7	Income Total	3,760		
8	Expenses	Budget	Actual	Difference
9	Home			
10	Mortgage/Rent	950	950	
11	Utilities	236	230	
12	Telephone	56	67	
13	Home Repairs	100	75	
14	Home Security	35	35	
15	Home Total	=SUM(B10:B14)		
16	Daily Living			

6. Press Enter to accept the formula. Select B15. As illustrated in Figure 8-8, the value is displayed in B15 and when you click on the cell the formula is displayed in the formula bar. Take note that each cell reference is the cell's unique name. No matter what numeric value is assigned in the cell, the cell reference (B1, C10, etc.) never changes.

Figure 8-8

A formula displayed in the formula bar

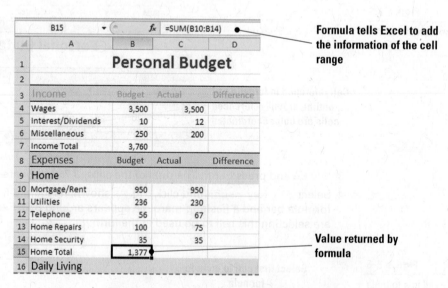

Formula tells Excel to add the information of the cell range

Value returned by formula

7. Once again, the goal of this step is to create a simple formula. Select D4 and key =. Click B4 and key −. Click C4 and press Enter. By default, when a subtraction formula yields no difference (a zero answer), Excel enters a hyphen.

Take Note   Open the Format Cells dialog box to change the way Excel displays "no difference" results. On the Numbers tab, you can choose to display 0, for example.

8. Select **D4** again. Click and drag the fill handle to D7 to select this range of cells. You are now copying the formula from the previous step into a new range of cells.

9. Use the fill handle to copy the formula in B7 to C7. Notice that the amount in D7 changes when the formula is copied. When you copied the formula to C7, the position of the cell containing the formula changed, so the reference in the formula changed to C7 instead of B7.

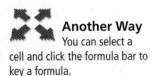

CERTIFICATION
READY   **5.3.1**

How do you create formulas that use relative cell references?

10. Select **D7** and click **Copy**. Select **D10:D15** and click **Paste**. Your formula has now been copied to the range of cells and Excel has automatically adjusted the cell references accordingly. Note that D7 is still highlighted by the flashing marquee.

11. Select **D17:D21** and click **Paste**. Your formula from D7 is now copied to the second range of cells and the references are adjusted. Note that the flashing marquee is still surrounding D7. You have the ability to copy one formula into multiple locations without having to recopy it.

Another Way
You can select a cell and click the formula bar to key a formula.

12. Create a Lesson 8 folder and **SAVE** your worksheet as *Budget*.

PAUSE. LEAVE the workbook open to use in the next exercise.

Using Absolute Cell References in a Formula

Sometimes you do not want a cell reference to change when you move or copy it. For example, when you review your personal budget, you might want to know what percentage of your income is budgeted for each category of expenses. Each formula you create to calculate those percentages will refer to the cell that contains the total income amount. The reference to the total income cell is an **absolute cell reference**—a reference that does not change when the formula is copied or moved.

Absolute cell references include two dollar signs in the formula. The absolute cell reference $B$7 in this exercise, for example, will always refer to cell B7 because dollar signs precede both the column (B) and row (7). When you copy or fill the formula across rows or down columns, the absolute reference will not adjust to the destination cells. By default, new formulas use relative references, and you must edit them if you want them to be absolute references.

STEP BY STEP   **Use Absolute Cell References in a Formula**

USE the workbook from the previous exercise.

1. Select **B15**. Use the fill handle to the right to copy the formula to C15. You have just extended the formula to cell C7 to calculate the information in the range of cells above C7.

2. Select **B21**. Key **=sum(** and select **B17:B20**. Press **Enter**. You have just created a formula to calculate the range of cells selected as illustrated in Figure 8-9. Note that the formula you copied and applied to D21 was automatically calculated when you pressed **Enter**.

Figure 8-9

Formulas copied and entered are applied to cell ranges

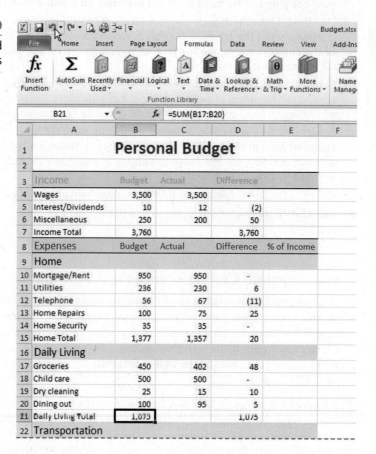

Take Note It is not necessary to key the closing parenthesis when you complete the selection for a formula. Excel supplies it when you press Enter.

3. Select **B21** and drag the fill handle to C21. You have copied the formula to the adjacent cell.

4. Select **E10**. Key = and click **B10**. Key / and click **B7**. Press **Enter**. You now have a decimal value of *.253* as your formula result.

5. Select **E10** again. On the formula bar, click in front of B7 to edit the formula; change B7 (relative cell reference) to **$B$7** (absolute cell reference). The edited formula should read =B10/$B$7 as illustrated in Figure 8-10. Press **Enter**. An absolute reference should be understood to be a value that you never want to change in your formula. By default, Excel will copy a formula into selected ranges as a relative cell reference unless you instruct it to do otherwise. Once you apply the absolute reference, Excel recognizes it and the program will not try to modify it to a relative reference again.

Figure 8-10

Adding an absolute reference
to a formula

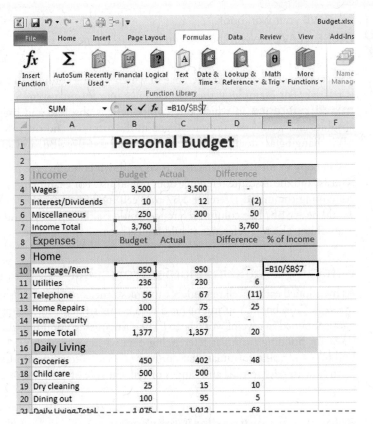

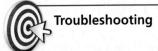 **Troubleshooting** When you enter a formula that will yield a result less than a whole number, be sure the cell is formatted for decimals. If the cell is formatted for whole numbers, the cell will display 0 or 1 rather than the expected value.

6. Select **E10** and drag the fill handle to E15. You have now applied the formula with the absolute reference $B$7 to each of the cells in the range.

7. With E10:E15 still selected, click the **Percent Style** button (%) in the Number group on the Home tab. Click **Increase Decimal**. The values should display with one decimal place and a % as illustrated in Figure 8-11.

Figure 8-11

Applying percent format to the
formula results

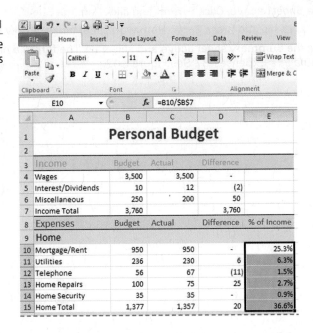

8. SAVE your workbook.

PAUSE. LEAVE the workbook open to use in the next exercise.

You can also create a mixed reference in which either a column, or a row, is absolute or the other is relative. For example, if the cell reference in a formula were $B7 or B$7, you would have a **mixed reference** in which one component is absolute and one is relative. The column is absolute and would remain unchanged in the formula, and the row is relative if the reference is $B7, changing as the mixed reference is copied to $B7, $B8, and so on.

If you copy or fill a formula across rows or down columns, the relative reference automatically adjusts, and the absolute reference does not adjust. For example, if you copied or filled a formula containing the mixed reference $B7 to a cell in column C, the formula in the destination cell would be =$B8. The column reference would be the same because that portion of the formula is absolute. The row reference would adjust because it is relative.

Referring to Data in Another Worksheet

As mentioned earlier, cell references can link to the contents of cells in another worksheet within the same workbook. You might need to use this strategy, for example, to create a summary of data contained in several worksheets. The principles for building these formulas are the same as those for building formulas referencing data within a worksheet. In this exercise, you practice building and using formulas that contain references to data in other worksheets. You will also learn how to refer to cells and ranges of cells outside of your active worksheet.

STEP BY STEP   **Refer to Data in Another Worksheet**

USE the workbook you saved in the previous exercise.

1. Click Sheet2 to make it the active sheet.
2. Select B4. Key = to indicate the beginning of a formula. Click Sheet1 and select B7. Press Enter. The value of cell B7 on Sheet1 is displayed in cell B4 of Sheet2. The formula bar displays =Sheet1!B7.
3. With Sheet2 still the active sheet, select B4 and drag the fill handle to D4. The values from Sheet1 row 4 are copied to Sheet2 row 4.
4. On the Home tab, click Format and click Rename Sheet. As you recall, you renamed worksheet tabs in previous exercises.
5. Key Summary and press Enter.
6. Make Sheet1 active. Click Format and click Rename Sheet.
7. Key Expenses and press Enter. Both worksheet tabs are now renamed.
8. Make the Summary sheet active and select B4. The formula bar now shows the formula as =Expenses!B7. See Figure 8-12.

Figure 8-12

Referred cell reference in another worksheet

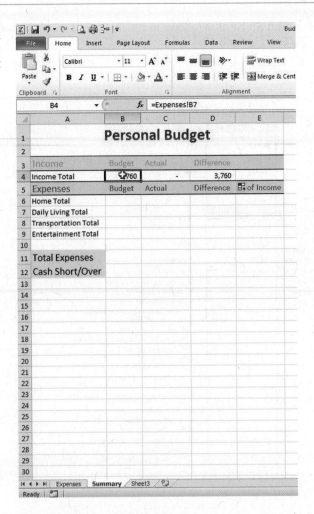

9. **SAVE** your workbook.

PAUSE. LEAVE the workbook open to use in the next exercise.

In this exercise, you referenced data in another worksheet within the Budget workbook. In the next exercise, you will reference data in another workbook. By renaming the worksheets within this workbook, you have prepared it for the next exercise.

Referencing Data in Another Workbook

An **external reference** refers to a cell or range on a worksheet in another Excel workbook, or to a defined name in another workbook. Although external references are similar to cell references, there are important differences. You normally use external references when working with large amounts of data and complex formulas that encompass several workbooks. In this exercise, you will learn how to refer to data in another workbook.

USE the workbook you saved in the previous exercise.

1. Click the File tab and click Options.
2. On the Options window, click Advanced.

3. Scroll to find *Show all windows in the Taskbar*, if it isn't already selected, select it and click **OK**. See Figure 8-13.

Figure 8-13

Advanced options in Excel options

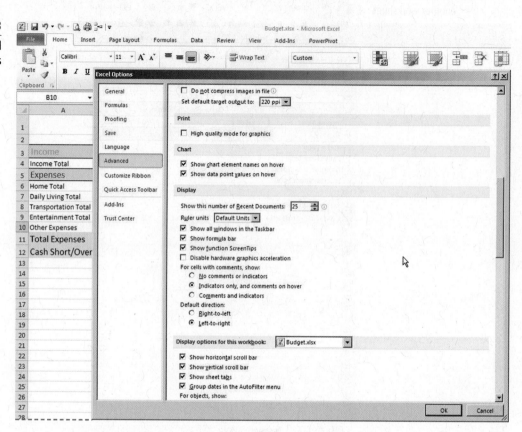

Troubleshooting If your system administrator has disabled the *Show all windows in the Taskbar* option, you will need to use the Switch Windows command in the Windows group on the View tab to move between the two workbooks.

The *Financial Obligations* file for this lesson is available on the book companion website or in WileyPLUS.

4. You are still in the Summary worksheet. In A10, key **Other Expenses** and press **Tab**.

5. **OPEN** the *Financial Obligations* data file for this lesson. This is the source workbook. The Budget workbook is the destination workbook.

6. Switch to the Budget workbook, and with B10 still active, key = to indicate the beginning of a formula. Change to the Financial Obligations workbook and select **B8**. A flashing marquee will identify this cell reference.

7. Press **Enter** to complete the external reference formula. Select **B10**. Your external reference has now been copied to this cell as illustrated in Figure 8-14. The formula bar displays square brackets around the name of the source workbook, indicating that the workbook is open. When the source is open, the external reference encloses the workbook name in square brackets, followed by the worksheet name, an exclamation point (!), and the cell range on which the formula depends.

Figure 8-14

External reference copied

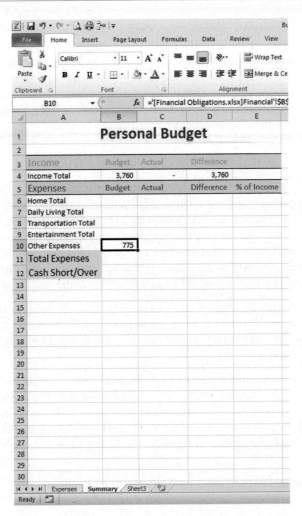

8. **CLOSE** the Financial Obligations workbook. When the source workbook is closed, the brackets are removed and the entire file path is shown in the formula. The formula bar in the Budget worksheet now displays the entire path for the source workbook as illustrated in Figure 8-15 because the source file is now closed.

Figure 8-15

File path to external reference

Entire file path to closed file

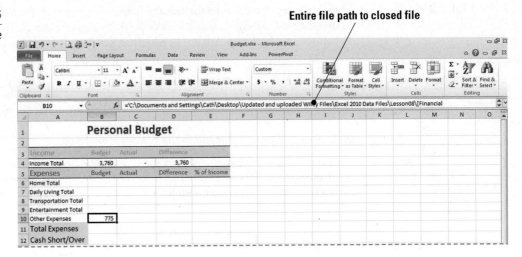

9. **SAVE** the destination workbook.

PAUSE. LEAVE the workbook open to use in the next exercise.

USING CELL RANGES IN FORMULAS

You can simplify formula building by naming ranges of data and using that name in selections and formulas rather than keying or selecting the cell range each time. In the business environment, you will often use a worksheet that contains data in hundreds of rows and columns. After you name a range, you can select it from the Name box and then perform a variety of functions, such as cutting and pasting it to a different workbook as well as using it in a formula. By default, a named range becomes an absolute reference in a formula.

Naming a Range

A **name** is a meaningful and logical identifier that you apply in Excel to make it easier to reference the purpose of a cell reference, cell range, constant, formula, or table. Naming a range clarifies the purpose of the data within the range of cells. Naming ranges or an individual cell according to the data they contain is a time-saving technique, even though it may not seem so when you work with limited data files in practice exercises. A good example could be to name a range such as B7:B17 as *Total Items* so that in future formula construction and reference, you only need to key Total Items and Excel will recognize the range to which you are referring.

You must select the range of cells you want to name before you use the Name box to create a named range. When you create a name using the Define Name command, you have the opportunity to select the range after you enter the name. This option is not available when you use the Name box.

All names have a scope, either to a specific worksheet or to the entire workbook. The **scope** of a name is the location within which Excel recognizes the name without qualification. For example, in step 1 in the next exercise, when you create the name Income_Total for cell B7, the New Name box, shown in Figure 8-16, identifies the scope as part of the workbook. This means the named cell can be used in formulas on the Expenses and the Summary worksheets in this workbook.

In this exercise, you will use three methods to name cells and ranges of cells. You will create the names by:

- Clicking Define Name on the Formulas tab and selecting the cell or range to be included in the name.
- Selecting a cell or range and entering a name in the Name box next to the formula bar.
- Selecting a cell or range that includes a label and clicking the Create from Selection button on the Formulas tab.

Take Note   There are several syntax rules for creating names. For example, the first character must be a letter, an underscore character (_), or a backslash (\). You cannot use a C, c, R, or r as a defined name, and you must use the underscore or period as word separators rather than spaces.

Name a Range

USE the workbook you saved in the previous exercise.

1. Select B7 on the Expenses worksheet and click Define Name in the Name Manager group on the Formulas tab. The New Name dialog box shown in Figure 8-16 opens with Excel's suggested name for the range.

Figure 8-16

New name dialog box

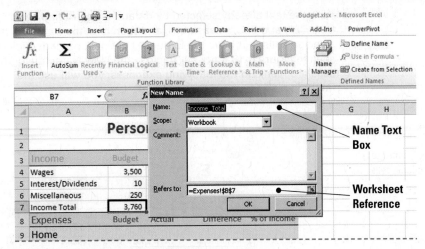

Name Text Box

Worksheet Reference

2. Click **OK** to accept Income_Total as the name for B7. Note that the Income_Total name now appears in the name box instead of the default cell reference of B7. See Figure 8-17.

Figure 8-17

Applying a defined name

Defined name applied

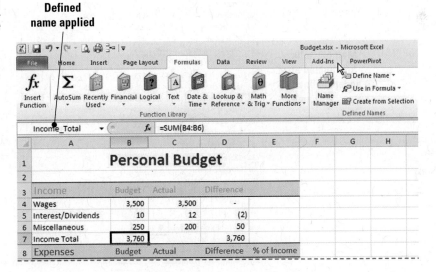

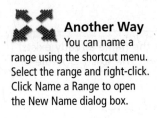

Another Way

You can name a range using the shortcut menu. Select the range and right-click. Click Name a Range to open the New Name dialog box.

3. Select **B36**. Click **Define Name**. In the New Name dialog box, with the Name box highlighted for entry, key **Total Expenses**. Accept the default in the *Scope* box.

4. Click the **Collapse Dialog** button and proceed to select the range that makes up total expenses.

5. With the text already selected by default in the *Refers to* box, press **Ctrl** and click **B15**, **B21**, **B28**, and **B33**, release Ctrl, and then click the **Expand Dialog** button. You have just selected cells that have the Expenses defined, named, copied, and applied to them as seen in Figure 8-18. Click **OK** to close the New Name dialog box. Some of the selected cells are blank. In the following exercises, you will use the names you just created to fill them.

Figure 8-18

Applying defined names to multiple cells

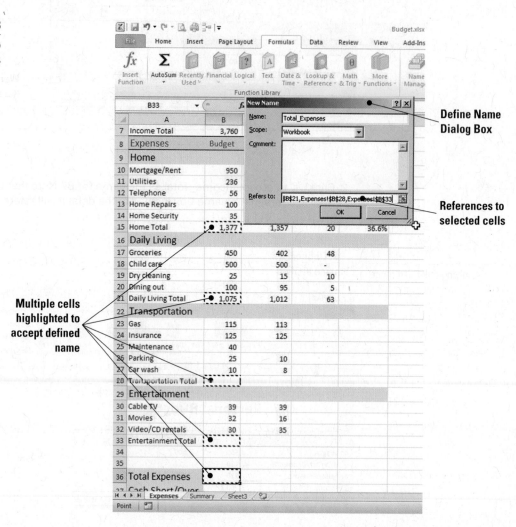

Troubleshooting If, in the process of naming a range, you receive a message that the name already exists, display the Name Manager (discussed later in this lesson) and edit the existing name or delete it and begin again.

6. Select **B23:B27** and click in the Name box to the left of the formula bar. Key **Transportation** and press **Enter**.

7. Select **B30:B32** and click **Define Name**. Key **Entertainment** in the Name box on the dialog box. Click **OK**.

8. Select **A15:B15**. Click **Create from Selection**. The left column will be selected as in Figure 8-19. Click **OK**. The dialog box closes. While naming this range doesn't change the current worksheet, you will use the range you just named in a later exercise.

Figure 8-19

Create names from selection

PAUSE. LEAVE the workbook open to use in the next exercise.

Changing the Size of a Range

If you need to change the parameters of a named range, you can easily redefine the range by using the Name Manager on the Formulas tab. The Name Manager contains all the information about named ranges. It allows you to view summaries of the names you have applied in the worksheet. In the following exercise, you will edit the range for Home_Total.

STEP BY STEP   **Change the Size of a Range**

USE the workbook from the previous exercise.

1. Click **Name Manager** on the Formulas tab. From the Name Manager window (see Figure 8-20), click to select **Home_Total** and click **Edit**. The Edit Name dialog box opens. You are going to change the scope (size) of the range rather than the name.

Figure 8-20

Name manager dialog box

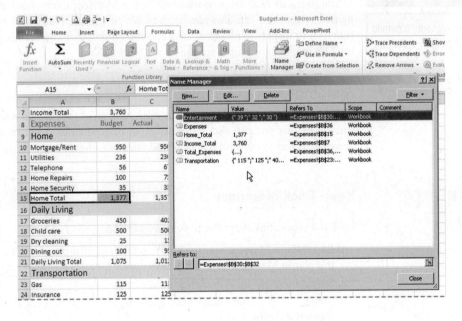

Take Note   Home_Total is the range you named in the Name a Range exercise earlier in this lesson, using the Create from Selection command.

2. The Home_Total range is identified in the Refers To box at the bottom of the Edit Name dialog box. Click the **Collapse Dialog** button and select **B10:B14**.

3. Click Expand Dialog to view the dialog box as shown in Figure 8-21. Click OK to accept your changes and close the dialog box.

Figure 8-21

Editing a previously named range

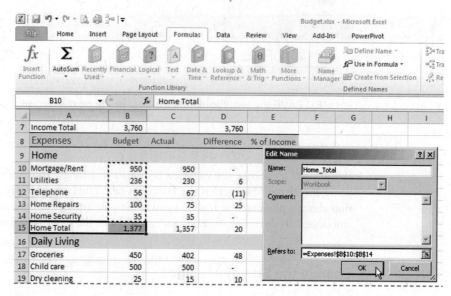

Figure 8-21

Editing a previously named range

4. Click Close to close the Name Manager dialog box. **SAVE** the workbook.

PAUSE. LEAVE the workbook open to use in the next exercise.

In the previous exercise, you used the Name Manager dialog box to extend the reference for a named range. You can also rename a range, or use the Names in combination with the Filter function to display names that meet specific criteria that you are filtering, such as names scoped to the worksheet or names scoped to the workbook.

Keeping Track of Ranges

Use the Name Manager dialog box to work with all of the defined names in the workbook. From this dialog box you can also add, change, or delete names. You can use the Name Manager as a convenient way to confirm the value and reference of a named reference or to determine its scope.

STEP BY STEP   **Keep Track of Ranges**

USE the workbook from the previous exercise.

1. Click Name Manager on the Defined Names group on the Formulas tab. You will use the Name Manager to modify previously created names and create new ones.

2. Select Income_Total and click Edit.

3. Select _Total in the Name field and press Delete. Click OK to accept your changes and close the dialog box.

4. Click New. Key Short\Over in the Name box. Be sure to use the backslash. You are specifying the name of a new range you will create in the next step. If you accidently key a forward slash, you will get an error dialog box. Click OK and return to the name and fix the error.

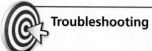 **Troubleshooting** You will receive an error message if you use the forward slash in a name. Although the forward slash is used in the Short/Over label on the worksheets, you can use only the underscore or the backslash as a word divider in a named range.

5. In the *Refers To* box, key =Income−Expenses. Click OK. You have now used names to create a formula.

6. Click Close to close the Name Manager dialog box. **SAVE** the workbook.
PAUSE. LEAVE the workbook open to use in the next exercise.

If you defined a named reference after you entered a cell reference in a formula, you may want to update the existing cell reference to the defined name. Select an empty cell, click the arrow next to Define Name, and click Apply Names. On the Apply Names dialog box, click one or more names, and click OK.

You can create a list of defined names in a workbook to make it simpler to keep track of your data. It is easier to remember names than to memorize cells and cell ranges. Just select an area of a worksheet with two empty columns, one for the name and one for a description. Select the upper-left cell of the list. Click Use in Formula and click Paste Names. Click Paste List.

Creating a Formula that Operates on a Named Range

You have created several named ranges in the previous exercises, which you will use in the next exercise to fill cells on the worksheets in your Budget workbook.

STEP BY STEP   **Create a Formula that Operates on a Named Range**

USE the workbook from the previous exercise.

1. On the Expenses worksheet, select B28. Key =sum(. Click Use in Formula in the Defined Names group on the Formulas tab. The Use in Formula drop-down list appears. It contains all the Defined names that you created as seen in Figure 8-22.

Figure 8-22

Use in Formula drop-down list

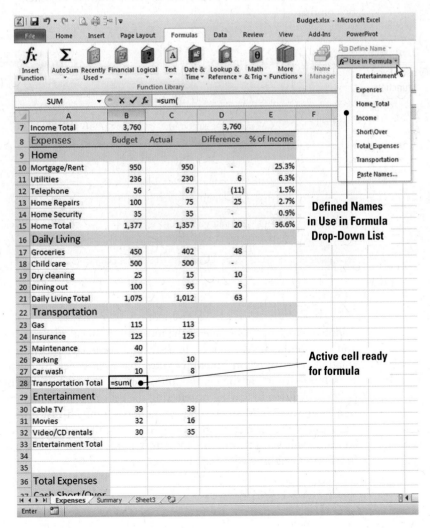

CERTIFICATION READY 5.5.1

How do you manage named ranges?

2. Click Transportation on the drop-down list. Key the closing parenthesis in the formula and press Enter. You have now defined the Transportation name for use in formulas for the selected range.

3. Select B33. Click the formula bar and key the following formula =sum(Entertainment), and press Enter.

4. On the Summary worksheet, select B11. Key the formula =sum(and click Use in Formula. Select Total Expenses from the list of named cells and ranges. Press Enter. SAVE the workbook.

PAUSE. LEAVE the workbook open to use in the next exercise.

SUMMARIZING DATA WITH FUNCTIONS

The Bottom Line

A **function** is a predefined formula that performs a calculation. Excel's built-in functions are designed to perform all sorts of calculations—from simple to complex. When you apply a function to specific data, you eliminate the time involved in manually constructing a formula. Using functions ensures the accuracy of the formula's results.

A function consists of a function name and function arguments and specified syntax. See Table 8-1 for a list of the most commonly used Excel functions. The arguments are enclosed in parentheses in the formula. This lets Excel know where the formula begins and where it ends. The arguments are in logical format from the left of the formula to the right in the parenthesis; (argument1, argument2, …) and are performed in that order, from left to right. Depending on the function, an **argument** can be a constant value, a single-cell reference, a range of cells, or even another function. If a function contains multiple arguments, the arguments are separated by commas.

Table 8-1

Most commonly used Excel functions

Function	Description	Formula Syntax
SUM	Takes all of the values in each of the specified cells and totals their values.	=SUM(first value, second value,...)
AVERAGE	Calculates the arithmetic mean, or average, for the values in a range of cells.	=AVERAGE(first value, second value,...)
MIN	Determines the smallest value of a given list of numbers or arguments.	=MIN(first value, second value,...)
MAX	Analyzes an argument list to determine the highest value (the opposite of the MIN function).	=MAX(first value, second value,...)

Using SUM

Adding a range of cells is one of the most common calculations performed on worksheet data. You can use the SUM function to easily and accurately select the cells to be included in a calculation. The AutoSum function makes that even easier, by calculating (by default) the total from the active cell to the first nonnumeric cell. In previous exercises, you created a formula to perform addition by keying or selecting the cells to include and connected them with the plus sign. Using the SUM or AutoSum function is a much easier way to achieve the same result. AutoSum is a built-in feature of Excel that recognizes adjacent cells in rows and columns as the logical selection to perform the AutoSum. In this exercise, you will use the most commonly used functions, beginning with the SUM function.

STEP BY STEP   ## Use SUM

USE the workbook from the previous exercise.

1. On the Expenses worksheet, select C28. Click Insert Function in the Function Library group on the Formulas tab. The Insert Function dialog box shown in Figure 8-23 opens.

Figure 8-23

Accept default name or create a name

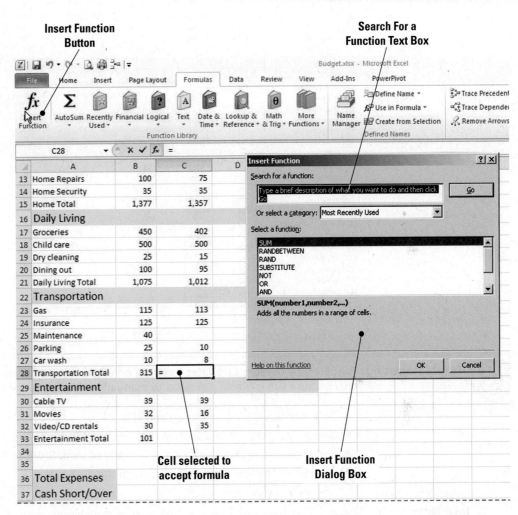

2. SUM is selected by default. Click OK. The Functions Arguments box for SUM opens.

3. In the Function Arguments box, the default range shown is C26:C27. Click the Collapse Dialog button in the Number1 field and select the cell range C23:C27. This has now applied the SUM function and its arguments to the selected cell range as illustrated in Figure 8-24.

Take Note

The Insert Function dialog box will select the most recently used function by default; in this case that is SUM. If you have used another function more recently, that function will be selected.

Figure 8-24

Change default range of cells

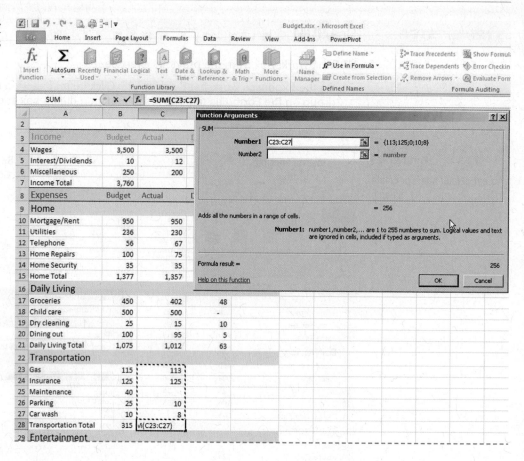

Troubleshooting AutoSum, by default, calculates the total only from the active cell to the first nonnumeric cell. Because C25 is blank, you need to manually select the range to be calculated.

4. Click the Expand Dialog button and click OK.

5. Select C33 and click AutoSum in the Function Library group.

6. Press Enter to accept C30:C32 as the range to sum. **SAVE** the workbook.

PAUSE. LEAVE the workbook open to use in the next exercise.

Take Note   Because it is used so frequently, AutoSum is available on the Formulas tab in the Function Library group and on the Home tab in the Editing group.

Using COUNT

Statistical functions, such as SUM and COUNT, are used to compile and classify data to present significant information. Use the COUNT function to count the number of numeric entries in a range. For example, in a worksheet used to calculate wages, you can apply the COUNT function to determine how many of the employees have worked over 40 hours in a work week. You will apply the COUNT function in the following exercise.

STEP BY STEP   **Use COUNT**

USE the workbook from the previous exercise.

1. On the Expenses worksheet, select A39 and key Expense Categories. Press Tab.
2. Click Insert Function in the Function Library group on the Formulas tab. The Insert Function dialog box opens.
3. On the Insert Function dialog box, key COUNT in the *Search for a Function* text box and click Go. The function will appear at the top of the function list and be selected by default in the Select a function window. Click on COUNT and click OK. You want to count only the expenses in each category and not include the category totals.
4. Click the Collapse Dialog button for Value1.
5. Select B10:B14 and press Enter. You have selected the range of cells for Value1 and Home_Total is now entered in the Value1 text box instead of the cell range.
6. Click the Collapse Dialog button for Value2 and select B17:20. Press Enter. B17:B20 now appears in the Value2 text box. You have selected the range of cells for Value2.

Take Note   As you add arguments, the Value fields on the Function Arguments dialog box expand to allow you to enter multiple arguments.

7. Collapse the dialog box for Value3. Select B23:B27 and press Enter. The identified range is one you named in a previous exercise. That name (Transportation) appears in the Value3 box rather than the cell range, and the values of the cells in the Transportation and Entertainment named ranges appear to the right of the value boxes.
8. In the Value4 box, key Entertainment. You have now manually applied the name Entertainment for Value4. Your entries in the Function Arguments dialog box should look similar to those shown in Figure 8-25.

Figure 8-25

Assign named ranges in function

Function Arguments Dialog Box   **Define Names assigned in Function Arguments**

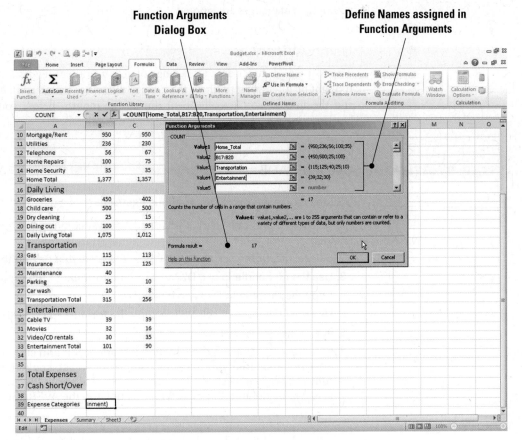

9. Click OK to accept the function arguments. Excel returns a value of 17 in B39. **SAVE** the workbook.

PAUSE. LEAVE the workbook open to use in the next exercise.

Take Note   Text or blank cells are ignored in a COUNT formula. If a cell contains a value of 0 (zero), the COUNT function will recognize it and count it as a cell with a number.

Using COUNTA

Use the COUNTA function to count the number of cells in a range that are not empty. COUNTA counts both text and values in a selected data range. You can use this formula to count the number of entries in a particular worksheet or range of cells. You will use this formula in the next exercise.

STEP BY STEP   **Use COUNTA**

USE the workbook from the previous exercise.

1. On the Expenses worksheet, select A40 and key Cells Containing Data. Press Tab.
2. Click Insert Function in the Function Library group on the Formulas tab. The Insert Function dialog box opens.

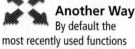 **Another Way**
By default the most recently used functions are displayed when the Insert Function dialog box opens. You can click the arrow in the category field and select All to

3. On the Insert Function dialog box, select COUNTA. If COUNTA does not appear in your list, key COUNTA in the *Search for a function* box and click Go. The function will appear at the top of the function list and be selected by default. Click OK.
4. Select B4:B33 in the Value1 box. Click OK. The formula is applied and Excel returns a value of 26.

PAUSE. LEAVE the worksheet open to use in the next exercise.

COUNTA returns a value that indicates the number of cells that contain data. Empty cells within the data ranges are ignored.

Using AVERAGE

The AVERAGE function adds a range of cells and then divides by the number of cell entries. It might be interesting to know the average difference between what you budgeted for expenses and the amount you actually spent during the month. Before you can calculate the average, however, you will need to finish calculating the differences.

STEP BY STEP   **Use AVERAGE**

USE the worksheet from the previous exercise.

1. Select D21 and right-click. Click Copy. You are copying the formula in D21 for the next step.
2. Select D23, right-click and click Paste. You have just pasted the formula into cell D23.
3. Use the fill handle in cell D23 to copy the formula to the range D24:D28.
4. Copy the formula in D28 and paste it to D30.
5. Use the fill handle in cell D30 to copy the formula to D31:D33.
6. In A41, key Average Difference and press Tab.
7. Click Recently Used in the Function Library group and click AVERAGE. If AVERAGE does not appear in your recently used function list, key AVERAGE in the *Search for a function* box and click Go. The function will appear at the top of the function list and be selected by default. Click OK. You are applying the AVERAGE formula to cell A42.

8. Click the Collapse Dialog button in Value1. Press Ctrl and select the category totals (D15, D21, D28, and D33). Notice that the arguments are separated by a comma.

9. Click Expand Dialog. Click OK. Your screen should resemble the screenshot in Figure 8-26. There is a $38 average difference between the amount budgeted and the amount you spent in each category.

Figure 8-26

AVERAGE formula applied to worksheet

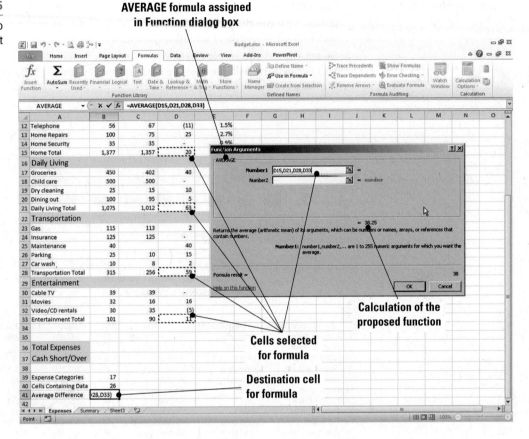

Take Note   The exact value returned for the AVERAGE formula was 38.25. Because column B is formatted for zero decimals, the value returned by the formula is 38.

10. **SAVE** and **CLOSE** the *Budget* workbook.

PAUSE. LEAVE Excel open to use in the next exercise.

Although you entered the numbers (cell references) as one number, if you open the Function Arguments dialog box after the formula has been entered, each cell reference is in a separate Number box.

Using MIN

The MIN formula returns the smallest number in a set of values. For example, a professor would use the MIN function to determine the lowest test score; a sales organization would determine which sales representative earned the lowest commission or which employee earns the lowest salary. Maximum values are usually calculated for the same set of data. You will learn to apply the MIN function in the next exercise.

STEP BY STEP   Use MIN

@ The *Personnel* file for this lesson is available on the book companion website or in WileyPLUS.

GET READY. OPEN the *Personnel* data file for Lesson 8.

1. Select A22 and key Minimum Salary. Press Tab.
2. Click the Recently Used button in the Function Library group on the Formulas tab. The MIN function is not listed. Key =min in cell B22 and double-click on MIN when it appears on the drop-down list below cell B22. Excel inputs the MIN command and an opening parenthesis is added to your formula.
3. Select E6:E19 and press Enter. You have now finished creating the formula arguments and applied the MIN function. Excel returns a value of $25,000 as the minimum salary for the personnel. See Figure 8-27.

Another Way
You can display the Insert Function dialog box by clicking the Insert Function

Figure 8-27

MIN function applied to worksheet

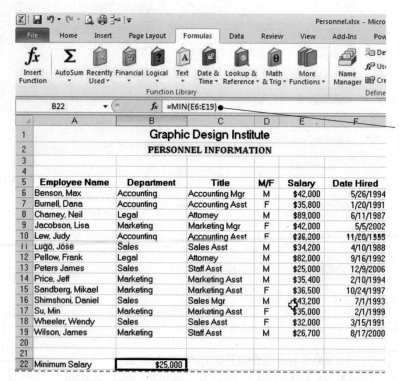

MIN formula applied to cell B22

4. **SAVE** the workbook as *Analysis*.

PAUSE. LEAVE the workbook open to use in the next exercise.

Using MAX

The MAX function returns the largest value in a set of values. Minimum values are usually calculated for the same set of data.

STEP BY STEP   Use MAX

USE the worksheet from the previous exercise.

1. In A23, key Maximum Salary and press Tab.
2. Click Insert Function in the Function Library group and key MAX in the *Search for a function* box and click Go. When the MAX function appears, it will be selected by default, click OK.
3. Click the Collapse Dialog button in Number1 text box and select E6:E19.

4. Click the Expand Dialog button and click OK. Excel applies and calculates the function on the range and returns the maximum salary value of $89,000 in cell A24.

5. **SAVE** and **CLOSE** the workbook.

PAUSE. LEAVE Excel open to use in the next exercise.

USING FORMULAS TO CREATE SUBTOTALS

The Bottom Line

You can calculate subtotals using the SUBTOTAL function, but it is generally easier to create a list by using the Subtotal command in the Outline group on the Data tab. After the subtotal list has been created, you can edit it using the SUBTOTAL function.

Selecting Ranges for Subtotaling

Groups are created for subtotaling by sorting the data. Data must be sorted by groups to insert a SUBTOTAL function. Subtotals are calculated with a summary function, and you can use the SUBTOTAL function to display more than one type of summary function for each column.

STEP BY STEP   **Select Ranges for Subtotaling**

1. **OPEN** the *Personnel* data file for this lesson.
2. Select A5:F19 (the data range and the column labels). Click Sort in the Sort & Filter group on the Data tab.

Troubleshooting If you do not include the labels in the data selection, Excel will prompt you to include the labels so that you can sort by label rather than the column heading.

The *Personnel* file for this lesson is available on the book companion website or in WileyPLUS.

WILEY PLUS EXTRA

WileyPLUS Extra! features an online tutorial of this task.

3. On the Sort dialog box, select Department as the sort by criterion. Select the My data has headers check box if it is not selected. Click OK. The list is sorted by department.
4. With the data range still selected, click Subtotal in the Outline group on the Data tab. The Subtotal dialog box opens.
5. Select Department in the *At each change in* box. Sum is the default in the *Use function* box.
6. Select Salary in the *Add subtotal to* box. Deselect any other column labels. Select Summary below data if it is not selected. Click OK. Subtotals are inserted below each department with a grand total at the bottom.
7. With the data selected, click Subtotal. On the dialog box, click Average in the *Use function* box.
8. Click Replace current subtotals to deselect it. Click OK.
9. **SAVE** the workbook as *Dept Subtotals*.

PAUSE. LEAVE Excel open to use in the next exercise.

Take Note   Subtotals are calculated with a summary function, such as SUM, COUNT, or AVERAGE. You can display more than one type of summary function for each column. Grand totals, on the other hand, are derived from the detail data, not from the values in the subtotals. Therefore, when you used the AVERAGE summary function, the grand total row displayed an average of all detail rows in the list, not an average of the values in the subtotal rows.

Modifying a Range in a Subtotal

You can change the way data is grouped and subtotaled by modifying the subtotal range using the SUBTOTAL function. This option is not available when you create subtotals from the Data tab commands.

STEP BY STEP **Modify a Range in a Subtotal**

USE the worksheet you saved in the previous exercise.

1. Insert a row above the Grand Total row.
2. Key Sales/Marketing Total in B29.
3. Copy the subtotal formula from E27 to E29.
4. In the Formula bar, change the function 9 (which includes hidden values) to 109 (which ignores hidden values) to exclude the sum and average subtotals for the individual departments within the data range. Otherwise, the formula result will include the average salary and the total salaries as well as the actual salaries for individual employees.
5. Replace the range in the Formula bar with E15:E25 and press Enter. The salaries for the sales and marketing departments combined are $310,000, which are now entered into the cell.
6. **SAVE** the workbook as *Dept Subtotals Revised*. **CLOSE** the workbook.

PAUSE. LEAVE Excel open to use in the next exercise.

CERTIFICATION READY   5.6.1

How do you enter a cell range definition in the formula bar?

Building Formulas to Subtotal and Total

In the previous exercise, you copied and modified a formula to create a subtotal for a combined group. You can accomplish the same result by using the SUBTOTAL function to build a formula and add subtotals to data that you cannot or do not want to sort into one category in order to use the built-in function in the Data tab's subtotal function.

STEP BY STEP **Build Formulas to Subtotal and Total**

@ The *Personnel* file for this lesson is available on the book companion website or in WileyPLUS.

1. **OPEN** the *Personnel* data file for this lesson.
2. Insert a row above row 11.
3. Select E11 and click Recently Used in the Formula Library group on the Formulas tab. The Recently Used formula drop-down list appears. Note that the SUBTOTAL function is not there. Click on the Insert Function option. Key SUBTOTAL in the *Search for a function* box and click Go. When the SUBTOTAL function appears, it will be selected by default, click OK.
4. Key 9 in the *Function_num* box on the Function Arguments dialog box.
5. Click the Collapse Dialog button in Ref1 and select E6:E10. You are inputting your first reference.
6. Click Expand Dialog and click OK to accept your changes and close the dialog box.
7. Select B11 and key Support Staff Total.
8. Select B21 and key Sales and Marketing Total.
9. Select E21 and click Recently Used. Click SUBTOTAL. Use the same procedure in step 4 to create a subtotal for the values in E12:E20. You are creating another subtotal formula. Format the subtotal for currency and expand the column to accommodate the data.

10. Press **Ctrl** and select row **11** and row **21**. Click **Bold** on the Home tab to emphasize the subtotals. Compare your worksheet to Figure 8-28.

Figure 8-28

SUBTOTAL applied in worksheet

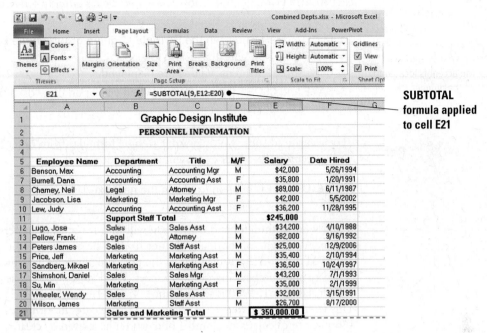

SUBTOTAL formula applied to cell E21

11. SAVE the workbook as *Combined Depts*.

PAUSE. LEAVE the workbook open to use in the next exercise.

When you use the Subtotal command on the Data tab, subtotal entries have a predefined format, and you can create multiple subtotals, as you did in a previous exercise. When you use the SUBTOTAL function, you must build the formula and label and format the subtotal entries manually.

Take Note   If the workbook is set to automatically calculate formulas, the Subtotal command recalculates subtotal and grand total values automatically when you edit the detail data.

CONTROLLING THE APPEARANCE OF FORMULAS

The Bottom Line   When you work with extremely large worksheets that contain numerous formulas, you sometimes need to see all formulas to audit the calculations in the worksheet. You can display and print the worksheet with all formulas visible.

Displaying Formulas on the Screen

When you create a formula, the result of the calculation is displayed in the cell and the formula is displayed in the Formula bar. You may need to see all formulas on the screen in order to audit them. As you learn in this lesson, you can click the Show Formulas command to display the formula in each cell instead of the resulting value.

STEP BY STEP   Display Formulas on the Screen

Another Way
You can also press Ctrl+` (grave accent) to switch between formulas and their values. The accent is located to the left of the number 1 key on most keyboards.

GET READY. With the workbook *Combined Depts* already open, perform the following steps:

1. Click Show Formulas in the Formula Auditing group on the Formulas tab. All worksheet formulas are displayed.
2. Click Show Formulas. Values are displayed.
3. **SAVE** and **CLOSE** the workbook. When you open the workbook again, it will open with values displayed.

X Ref

For security reasons, you may want to hide formulas from other workbook users. This and other security issues will be presented in Lesson 11.

PAUSE. LEAVE Excel open to use in the next exercise.

If you work with dates and times, you will find it useful to understand Excel's date and time system. Although you normally do not have to be concerned with serial numbers, when you displayed the worksheet formulas in the preceding exercise, you probably wondered what happened to the numbers in your worksheet. Excel stores dates as sequential serial numbers. By default, January 1, 1900 is serial number 1, and January 2, 1900 is serial number 2, and so on. This serial number date system allows you to use dates in formulas. For example, you can enter a formula to calculate the number of days you have lived by creating a formula to subtract your birth date from today's date.

Printing Formulas

When you audit the formulas in a large worksheet, you may find it useful to print the worksheet with the formulas displayed. To gain maximum benefit from the printed copy, print gridlines and row and column headers. In this exercise, you will display formulas for printing and adjust the print settings.

STEP BY STEP   Print Formulas

1. **OPEN** *Budget* from your Lesson 8 folder. This is the exercise you saved earlier.
2. Click Show Formulas in the Formula Auditing group on the Formulas tab. The formulas appear in the spreadsheet.
3. Click the Page Layout tab and click Print in Gridlines and Print in Headings in the Sheet Options group.
4. Click Orientation in the Page Setup group and click Landscape.
5. Click the File tab. Click on Print and view the Print Preview.
6. Click the Page Setup link at the bottom of the print settings to open the Page Setup dialog box.
7. On the Page tab of the dialog box, click Fit to: and leave the defaults as 1 page wide by 1 tall.
8. Click the Header/Footer tab. Click Custom Header and key your name in the left section. Refer to Figure 8-29. Click OK to accept your changes and close the Page Setup dialog box.

Figure 8-29

Custom print settings applied

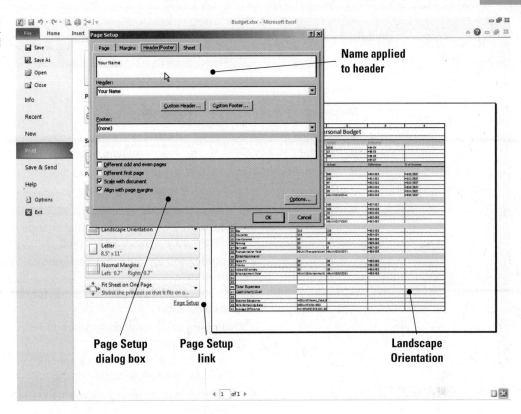

Page Setup dialog box   **Page Setup link**   **Landscape Orientation**

9. Click the Print button at the top-left corner of the Backstage view window. When prompted, click OK to print the document.

10. **SAVE** the workbook with the same name. **CLOSE** the workbook. **CLOSE** Excel.

SKILL SUMMARY

In This Lesson You Learned How To:	Exam Objective	Objective Number
Building Basic Formulas	Use basic operators.	5.1.1
	Revise formulas.	5.1.2
	Precedence: Order of evaluation.	5.2.1
	Precedence using parentheses.	5.2.2
	Precedence of operators for percent versus exponentiation.	5.2.3
Using Cell References in Formulas	Create formulas that use relative and absolute cell references.	5.3.1
Using Cell Ranges in Formulas	Define a cell range.	5.6.2
	Edit ranges in formulas.	5.5.2
	Rename a named range.	5.5.3
	Define ranges in formulas.	5.5.1
Summarizing Data with Functions		
Using Formulas to Create Subtotals	Enter a cell range definition in the formula bar.	5.6.1
Controlling the Appearance of Formulas		

Knowledge Assessment

Matching

Match each vocabulary term with its definition.

a. absolute cell reference   f. operand

b. constant   g. mathematical operator

c. external reference   h. relative cell reference

d. formula   i. mixed reference

e. function   j. scope

_____ 1. In formulas, cell references that change in relation to the location where they are moved or copied.

_____ 2. A predefined formula that performs calculations on values in a worksheet.

_____ 3. The components of a formula that identify the values to be used in the calculation.

_____ 4. Numbers or text values entered directly into a formula. These values are not calculated.

_____ 5. In a formula, a reference to a specific cell that does not change when the formula is copied or moved.

_____ 6. A reference to a cell or range on a worksheet in another Excel workbook.

_____ 7. An equation that performs calculations on values in a worksheet.

_____ 8. The formula component that specifies what calculations are to be performed.

_____ 9. A cell reference in which the column is absolute and the row is relative or vice versa.

_____ 10. The location within which a name is recognized without qualification.

Multiple Choice

Select the best response for the following statements.

1. Which of the following is not a mathematical operator?

    a. ×

    b. +

    c. −

    d. *

2. Which function automatically totals cells directly above or to the left of the cell containing the formula?

    a. COUNT

    b. AutoFill

    c. AutoSum

    d. SUM

3. Which of the following shows a formula for an external reference?

    a. =Sum(Expenses)

    b. =Sum(B6:b10)

    c. =Expenses!B7

    d. ='[Financial Obligations.xlsx]Sheet1'!$B$2

4. Which of the following shows a formula for a reference to another worksheet in the same workbook?
   a. =Sum(Expenses)
   b. =Sum(B6:b10)
   c. =Expenses!B7
   d. ='[Financial Obligations.xlsx]Sheet1'!$B$2

5. Which of the following shows a formula that references a named range?
   a. =Sum(Expenses)
   b. =Sum(B6:b10)
   c. =Expenses!B7
   d. ='[Financial Obligations.xlsx]Sheet1'!$B$2

6. Which character designates a cell reference as absolute?
   a. ^
   b. @
   c. $
   d. #

7. The COUNTA function
   a. counts the number of cells in a range that contain values.
   b. counts all cells in the range.
   c. counts the number of cells that are not empty.
   d. counts the text entries in the range.

8. The COUNT function is an example of a _____ function.
   a. logical
   b. financial
   c. statistical
   d. text

9. Which of the following is an acceptable name for a named range?
   a. C
   b. C_Contracts
   c. C/Contracts
   d. C Contracts

10. Which of the following statements accurately describes the default selection for AutoSum?
   a. By default, AutoSum totals all entries above the cell in which the formula is located.
   b. By default, AutoSum calculates the total from the active cell to the first nonnumeric cell.
   c. AutoSum does not have a default selection.
   d. You must make the selection before clicking AutoSum.

Competency Assessment

Project 8-1: Create Formulas to Calculate Income and Expenses

An employee at Tailspin Toys has entered second quarter income and expense data into a worksheet. You will enter formulas to calculate monthly and quarterly totals.

GET READY. LAUNCH Excel if it is not already running.

The *Tailspin Toys* file for this lesson is available on the book companion website or in WileyPLUS.

1. **OPEN** *Tailspin Toys* from the data files for this lesson.

2. Select E4 and key =B4+C4+D4 and press Enter.

3. Select B6. On the Formulas tab, in the Function Library group, click Insert Function.

4. In the Insert Function dialog box, select SUM and click OK.

5. In the Function Arguments dialog box, click the Collapse Dialog button and click B4. Key - and click B5.

6. Click the Expand Dialog button and click OK to close the dialog box.

7. Select B6 and use the fill handle to copy the formula to C6:D6.

8. Click B11 and click AutoSum in the Function Library group. Press Enter to accept B8:B10 as the cells to total.

9. Select B11 and use the fill handle to copy the formula to C11:D11.

10. Select B13 and click Insert Function in the Function Library group. On the Insert Function dialog box, SUM will be the default. Click OK.

11. Click the Collapse Dialog button for Number1 and click B6. Key - and click B11. Press Enter and click OK to close the dialog box.

12. Select B13 and use the fill handle to copy the formula to C13:D13.

13. Select E4. Click AutoSum in the Function Library group. Press Enter to accept the range as B4:D4. Copy the formula to E5:E14. Then delete the data in cells E7 and E12.

14. Select B15, key =B13-B14, and press Enter. Copy the formula to C15:E15.

15. **SAVE** the workbook as *Tailspin Toys 8-1* and then **CLOSE** the file.

LEAVE Excel open to use in the next project.

Project 8-2: Use AutoSum to Total Sales; Calculate Percentage of Increase

Blue Yonder Airlines has created a workbook to analyze sales for its first four years of operation. Enter formulas to determine the total sales for each division and the percentage increase/decrease each year.

GET READY. LAUNCH Excel if it is not already running.

@ The *Blue Yonder* file for this lesson is available on the book companion website or in WileyPLUS.

1. **OPEN** the *Blue Yonder* data file for this lesson.

2. Select F4 and click AutoSum in the Function Library group on the Formulas tab.

3. Press Enter to accept B4:E4 as the range to add.

4. Use the fill handle to copy the formula in F4 to F5:F8.

5. Select B12 and key =(C4-B4)/C4. Press Enter. This formula calculates the percentage increase in sales from 2005 to 2006. The numbers in parentheses yield the amount of the increase. The increase is then divided by the 2006 sales.

6. Select B12. Use the fill handle to copy the formula to B13:B15.

7. With the cell range B12:B15 still selected, use the fill handle to copy the formulas in the selected range to C12:D15.

8. Select F12. Key =(E4-B4)/E4 and press Enter. This enters a formula to calculate the percentage increase from the first year (2005) to the most recent (2008).

9. Copy the formula in F12 to F13:F15.

10. **SAVE** the workbook as *Blue Yonder 8-2* and then **CLOSE** the file.

LEAVE Excel open for the next project.

Proficiency Assessment

Project 8-3: Calculate Totals and Percentages

In the previous project, you calculated total sales for Blue Yonder's first four years of operation. You also calculated the percentage of increase or decrease in sales for each year. In this project, you will calculate expense totals and percentage increase or decrease.

GET READY. LAUNCH Excel if it is not already running.

@ The *Blue Yonder Expenses* file for this lesson is available on the book companion website or in WileyPLUS.

1. **OPEN** the *Blue Yonder Expenses* data file for this lesson. Expense History worksheet should be the active worksheet.

2. Select B8 and click AutoSum to total the 2005 expenses.

3. Copy the formula in B8 to C8:F8.

4. Select F4 and click AutoSum to total Corporate Contracts expenses for the four-year period.

5. Copy the formula in F4 to F5:F7.

6. In B12, create a formula to calculate the percentage increase in Corporate Contracts expenses from 2005 to 2006. Begin with 2006 expenses minus 2005 expenses, divided by 2006. Use parentheses to instruct Excel which function to perform first.

7. Copy the formula from B12 to B13:B15 and to C12:D15.

8. In F12, create a formula to calculate the percentage increase in expenses from 2005 to 2008. Remember to construct the formula to subtract and then divide.

9. Click Percentage Style (%) in the Number group. If necessary, click Increase Decimal to display one position after the decimal point.

10. Copy the formula in F12 to F13:F15.

11. **SAVE** the workbook as *Blue Yonder Expenses 8-3* and then **CLOSE** the file.

LEAVE Excel open for the next project.

Project 8-4: Create Formulas in a Template Worksheet

Tailspin Toys wants to project income and expenses for the third quarter based on its performance in the second quarter. A template has been created for the projections. In this project, you will create formulas for the calculations that affect only this worksheet. In the next exercise, you will create formulas that refer to data in another worksheet in this workbook. You are creating a template, so the values returned by your formulas will be $0 until you use the template in the next exercise.

GET READY. LAUNCH Excel if it is not already running.

@ The *Tailspin Projections* file for this lesson is available on the book companion website or in WileyPLUS.

1. **OPEN** the *Tailspin Projections* data file for this lesson.

2. In the Third Qtr worksheet, key 0 (zero) as a placeholder in B4 and in B5.

3. Select B6 and enter a formula to subtract the cost of goods sold from sales. The value returned will be $0.

4. Key 0 as a placeholder in B8:B10.

5. Select B11 and click AutoSum to calculate total expenses.

6. Select B13 and enter a formula to subtract total expenses from the gross margin.

7. Federal taxes are estimated to be 34% net income. Select B14 and enter a formula to multiply net income before taxes by 34%.

8. In B15, enter a formula to calculate net income after taxes.

9. **SAVE** the workbook as *Tailspin Projections 8-4*.

LEAVE the workbook open for the next project.

Mastery Assessment

Project 8-5: Refer to Data in Another Worksheet

Tailspin Toys wants to set goals for the third quarter based on its performance in the second quarter. Its goal is to increase sales by 10% while keeping costs and expenses to 5%. You will create formulas to calculate the projections.

USE the workbook you saved in Project 8-4.

1. Make Third Qtr the active sheet and display the Formulas. The formula to establish the sales goal for third quarter will be second quarter total sales + (second quarter total sales *10%).

2. Select B4, click Recently Used in the Function Library group, and click SUM in the *Select a function* box. Select Second Qtr E4 as the Number1 function argument.

3. In the *Number2 argument* box, key +(and click **Second Qtr**. Select **E4**.

4. Continuing in the *Number2 argument* box, key *10%) and press **Enter**. Your completed formula should read =SUM('SecondQtr'!E4,+('Second Qtr'!E4*10%)).

5. On the Third Quarter worksheet, select **B5**. Click **Recently Used** in the Function Library group and click **SUM**. Select **Second Qtr E5** as the Number1 function argument.

6. In the *Number2 argument* box, key +(and click **Second Qtr**. Select **E5**.

7. Continuing in the Number2 argument box, key *5%) and press **Enter**.

8. Copy the formula in B5 to B8:B10.

9. **SAVE** the workbook as *Tailspin Projections 8-5* and then **CLOSE** the file.

LEAVE Excel open for the next project.

Project 8-6: Name a Range and Use the Range in a Formula

Blue Yonder Airlines wants to analyze the sales and expense data from its four-year history.

GET READY. LAUNCH Excel if it is not already running.

@ The *Income Analysis* file for this lesson is available on the book companion website or in WileyPLUS.

1. **OPEN** the *Income Analysis* data file for this lesson.

2. Select **B4:E4** and click **Define Name** on the Formulas tab. Accept the defaults in the dialog box and click **OK**.

3. Repeat Step 2 and name the other three income sources.

4. On the Analysis worksheet, select **B5** and create a formula to calculate the four-year average for corporate contract sales. Use the Corporate Contracts named range in the formula.

5. Create a formula using the appropriately named range in B6, B7, and B8.

6. In column C, create a formula to calculate the maximum sales for each division.

7. Show the formulas on the screen. Adjust column width, if necessary, to display the entire formulas.

8. Print the Analysis worksheet in landscape orientation with gridlines and column headings included.

9. **SAVE** the workbook as *Income Analysis 8-6* and then **CLOSE** the file.

LEAVE Excel open for the next project.

INTERNET READY

As mentioned at the beginning of this lesson, a personal budget helps you make sound financial decisions and enables you to reach financial goals. Various governmental organizations and private financial counselors recommend percentages of your income to allocate for housing, transportation, etc. Use web search tools to find recommended guidelines for the percentage of income you should allocate in various spending categories. Be sure to use "personal budget guidelines" to avoid business and government budget sites.

From your research, create a worksheet that lists the categories and percentages that you think are reasonable for your personal or family budget. Save the workbook as *My Budget*. close Excel.

Cross-Cultural Solutions, a nonprofit organization, offers three short-term international volunteer programs. Volunteers can choose from ten countries, with year-round start dates and programs that are one- to twelve-weeks long.

As international volunteers with Cross-Cultural Solutions, individuals work side-by-side with local people on locally designed and locally driven projects, allowing them to see and learn about a country through the eyes of its people. The organization sends more than 1,000 volunteers abroad each year. Excel is a valuable tool for organizing data related to volunteers, the programs they choose, and the start date and duration of their volunteer activity.

Project 1: Sorting and Filtering Data

In this project, you will sort and filter the list of individuals who are scheduled to begin their volunteer experience in July and August.

GET READY. LAUNCH Excel if it is not already running.

@ The *Volunteers* data file for this lesson is available on the book companion website or in WileyPLUS.

1. **OPEN** the *Volunteers* data file.
2. With the Data tab active, select any cell in column D. Click Sort in the Sort & Filter group.
3. The Sort dialog box opens. In the Sort by field, select Program.
4. Click Add Level. In the Then by box, select Location.
5. Click Add Level. In the Then by box, select Start Date. Click OK.
6. **SAVE** the document as *Volunteers Project 1*.
7. Click Filter in the Sort & Filter group.
8. Click the arrow in the Duration column. On the drop-down list that appears, click the (Select All) check box to deselect all filters. Click the 6 Weeks check box, and click OK.
9. Click the arrow in the Start Date column, and deselect August. Click OK.
10. Click Quick Print to print the list of volunteers who will depart in July and remain on location for six weeks.
11. Select any cell in the data range. Click Remove Duplicates in the Data Tools group.
12. In the Remove Duplicates dialog box, click Select All, then click OK. A dialog box indicates that one duplicate entry was removed.
13. Click Filter to display all data.
14. **SAVE** the workbook.

LEAVE the workbook open for the next project.

Project 2: Managing Worksheets in a Workbook

In this exercise, you will increase the ease of accessing data by creating a worksheet for each program.

GET READY. USE the workbook from the previous project.

1. Select A1:F19, then click Copy in the Clipboard group on the Home tab.
2. Select Sheet2, click A1, and click Paste in the Clipboard group.
3. Click the Paste Options button, then click Keep Source Column Widths.
4. With Sheet2 active, click Format on the Home tab, then click Move or Copy Sheet. On the Move or Copy dialog box, in the Before Sheet list, select Sheet3. Click Create a Copy and click OK.
5. Click the Insert Worksheet icon. This creates Sheet5.

6. With Sheet1 active, click Format, then click Rename Sheet. Key Summary and press Enter. Click the Sheet2 tab and rename it Insight Abroad.

7. Click the Sheet2(2) tab, and rename the worksheet Intern Abroad. Click the Sheet3 tab, and rename the worksheet Volunteer Abroad.

8. On the Summary worksheet, select A20:F45 (Intern Abroad volunteers), and click Copy. Click the Intern Abroad tab, then select A5. Click Paste. This replaces data on the worksheet.

9. On the Summary worksheet, select A1:F4, and click Copy. Click the Volunteer Abroad tab, select A1, and click Paste.

10. Click the Paste Options button, and click Keep Source Column Widths.

11. Select A46:F87 on the Summary worksheet, and click Copy. Select A5 on the Volunteer Abroad worksheet, and click Paste.

12. With the Summary worksheet active, press Ctrl and click the Sheet5 tab to group the two worksheets.

13. In the Cells group, click Format, point to Hide & Unhide, and click Hide Sheet. Three worksheets remain visible.

14. Click the File tab, then click Print. In the Print Settings area, click the arrow in the Print Active Sheets area, then click Print Entire Workbook.

15. In the Cells group on the Home tab, click Format. Point to Hide & Unhide, then click Unhide Sheet. Select Summary, and click OK. Select Format, and unhide Sheet5.

16. With Sheet5 active, right-click the Sheet tab and select Delete Sheet.

17. Click the Summary tab, then click Format. Click Move or Copy Sheet. In the Move or Copy dialog box, click (move to end). Click OK.

18. **SAVE** the workbook as *Volunteers Project 2* and **CLOSE** the file.

LEAVE Excel open for the next project.

Project 3: Sorting and Subtotaling Data

Cross-Cultural Solutions is supported in part by individual and corporate tax-deductible contributions. Contributors are asked to select a fund to which their contribution will apply.

GET READY. LAUNCH Excel if it is not already running.

@ The *Contributions* file for this lesson is available on the book companion website or in WileyPLUS.

1. **OPEN** the *Contributions* data file.

2. Click the Data tab.

3. Select any data cell. Click Sort in the Sort & Filter group on the Data tab.

4. In the Sort dialog box, select Fund and click OK.

5. Click Subtotal in the Outline group on the Data tab. The Subtotal dialog box opens.

6. In the *At each change in* box, select Fund. Select or accept Sum in the *Use function* box and Amount in the *Add subtotal to* box. Click OK.

7. Adjust column widths if necessary to display all data.

8. **SAVE** the workbook as *Contributions Project 3*, and **CLOSE** the file.

LEAVE Excel open for the next project.

Project 4: Sorting and Subtotaling Data

In Project 3, you determined the amount contributed to each fund. Now you will use formulas and functions to perform additional analyses in preparation for Cross-Cultural Solutions' annual fund-raising drive.

GET READY. LAUNCH Excel if it is not already running.

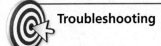

The *Contributions* file for this lesson is available on the book companion website or in WileyPLUS.

1. **OPEN** *Contributions* from the data files.
2. Click the Formulas tab. Select cell A36. Key Total Contributions.
3. Select C36 and click AutoSum in the Function Library group. C5:C35 should be selected by default. Press Enter.
4. Select A36:C36. Click Cell Styles on the Home tab. Click Total under Titles and Headings.
5. Select A38 and key Count. Press Tab.
6. On the Formulas tab, click Insert Function. Select Count and click OK.
7. Select C5:C35 in the Value1 box. Click OK.
8. In A39, key Contributions <$1,000, and press Tab.
9. Click Insert Function and select SUMIF. Click OK. Select C5:C35 in the Range box.

Troubleshooting If the function you want to use is not visible in the *Select a function* box on the Insert Function dialog box, key the function in the *Search for a function* box and click Go.

10. In the Criteria box, key <1000. Click OK.
11. Select A40 and key Average Individual. Press Tab.
12. Click Insert Function, and click AVERAGE. Click OK. Select C25:C35 in the Number1 box. Click OK. A triangle appears in the upper-left corner of B40 and an error message button is displayed. Click the arrow, then click Ignore Error.
13. Select A41, key Contributions >=5000, and press Tab.
14. Click Recently Used in the Function Library group, then click SUMIF.
15. In the Range box, select C5:C35 and press Tab.
16. In the Criteria box, key >=5000. Click OK.
17. Select B39:B41, and click Accounting Number Format in the Number group on the Home tab.
18. Click Decrease Decimal twice.
19. **SAVE** the workbook as *Contributions Project 4* and **CLOSE** the file.

CLOSE Excel.

9 Using Advanced Formulas and Securing Workbooks

LESSON SKILL MATRIX

Skill	Exam Objective	Objective Number
Using Formulas to Conditionally Summarize Data	Use a series of conditional logic values in a formula.	5.4.3
	Edit defined conditions in a formula.	5.4.2
	Create a formula with values that match conditions.	5.4.1
Using Formulas to Look Up Data in a Workbook		
Adding Conditional Logic Functions to Formulas	Use the IF function to apply conditional formatting.	8.3.3
Using Formulas to Format Text		
Using Formulas to Modify Text		
Securing Your Workbook Before Sharing It with Others		
Distributing a Workbook by Email	Send a worksheet via email or SkyDrive.	7.1.1
Tracking Changes to a Workbook		
Adding Comments to a Workbook	Insert comments.	7.2.1
	View comments.	7.2.2
	Edit comments.	7.2.3
	Delete comments.	7.2.4

KEY TERMS

- **arguments**
- **array**
- **authentication**
- **certificate authority (CA)**
- **change history**
- **conditional formula**
- **digital certificate**
- **digital signature**
- **lookup functions**
- **password**
- **shared workbook**
- **strong password**
- **table**
- **track changes**

248

Fabrikam, Inc., uses several of Excel's analytical tools to review sales data during strategic planning activities. Fabrikam's owners have created a standard bonus program as a part of the company's employee-retention efforts, as well as a performance bonus program to recognize sales agents who have been instrumental in achieving the company's strategic goals. The standard bonus is based on years of service to Fabrikam, and the performance bonus is awarded when an agent reaches his or her sales goal for the year. To determine which agents will receive the performance bonus, Fabrikam's accountants must create formulas to analyze the company's sales data. Excel's built-in formulas are the perfect solution to compute and display all the calculations the accountants need. You will learn to apply these formulas in the exercises in this lesson.

SOFTWARE ORIENTATION

The Formulas Tab

In this lesson, you will use commands on the Formulas tab to create formulas to conditionally summarize data, look up data, apply conditional logic, and format and modify text. The Formulas tab is shown in Figure 9-1.

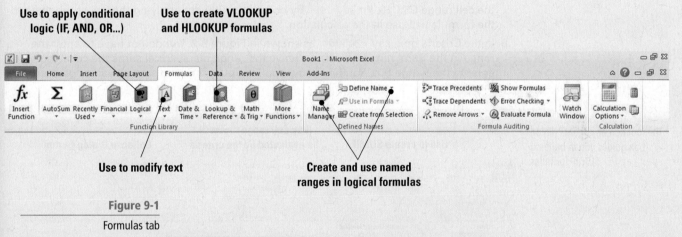

Use to apply conditional logic (IF, AND, OR...)

Use to create VLOOKUP and HLOOKUP formulas

Use to modify text

Create and use named ranges in logical formulas

Figure 9-1

Formulas tab

The formulas tab contains the command groups you will use to create and apply advanced formulas in Excel. Use this illustration as a reference throughout the lesson.

USING FORMULAS TO CONDITIONALLY SUMMARIZE DATA

The Bottom Line

As you learned in Lesson 8, a formula is an equation that performs calculations, such as addition, subtraction, multiplication, and division, on values in a worksheet. When you enter a formula in a cell, the formula is stored internally and the results are displayed in the cell. Formulas give results and solutions that help you assess and analyze data. As you also learned, you can use a conditional format, which changes the appearance of a cell range based on a criterion, to help you analyze data, detect critical issues, identify patterns, and visually explore trends.

Conditional formulas add yet another dimension to data analysis by summarizing data that meets one or more criteria. A **conditional formula** is one in which the result is determined by the presence or absence of a particular condition. Conditional formulas used in Excel include the functions SUMIF, COUNTIF, and AVERAGEIF.

Using SUMIF

The SUMIF function calculates the total of only those cells that meet a given criterion or condition. The syntax for the SUMIF function is SUMIF(range, criteria, sum_range). The values that a function uses to perform operations or calculations in a formula are called **arguments**. Thus, the arguments of the SUMIF function are range, criteria, and sum range, which, when used together, create a conditional formula in which only those cells that meet a stated criterion are added. Cells within the range that do not meet the criterion are not included in the total.

STEP BY STEP	**Use SUMIF**

@ The *Fabrikam Sales* file for this lesson is available on the book companion website or in WileyPLUS.

GET READY. Before you begin these steps, **LAUNCH** Microsoft Excel. Then, do the following:

1. **OPEN** the *Fabrikam Sales* file for this lesson.

2. Select cell A20 and key Sum of sales over $200,000. Press Enter. If necessary, select A20 and click Wrap Text in the Alignment group on the Home tab. You have now formatted the cell to wrap the text that will be keyed.

3. Select C20. Click the Formulas tab and in the Function Library group, click Insert Function. The Insert Function dialog box opens. Within the dialog box, key SUMIF in the *Search for function* text box and click Go. The SUMIF function will appear at the top of the function list and will be selected by default in the *Select a Function* window.

4. Click OK to close the Insert Function dialog box; the Function Arguments dialog box now opens automatically because you selected a formula. This dialog box allows you to edit the formula you selected.

5. In the Function Arguments dialog box, click the Collapse Dialog 🔳 button and select the cell range C5:C16. Press Enter. By doing this, you are applying the cell range that the formula will use in the calculation.

6. In the Criteria box, key >200000, as shown in Figure 9-2. You do not have to enter the range in the Sum_range box. If you leave the range blank, Excel sums the cells you enter in the Range box. You have now applied your criteria to sum all values greater than $200,000.

Figure 9-2

The function arguments dialog box guides you in building SUMIF formulas

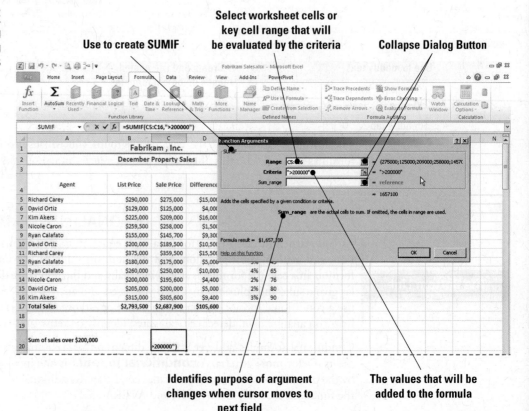

Use to create SUMIF

Select worksheet cells or key cell range that will be evaluated by the criteria

Collapse Dialog Button

Identifies purpose of argument changes when cursor moves to next field

The values that will be added to the formula

Troubleshooting It is not necessary to key dollar signs or commas when entering dollar amounts in the Function Arguments dialog box. If you key them, Excel removes them from the formula and returns an accurate value.

7. Click **OK** to accept the changes and close the dialog box. You see that $1,657,100 of Fabrikam's December revenue came from properties valued in excess of $200,000. (See Figure 9-3.)

Figure 9-3

Function arguments being applied

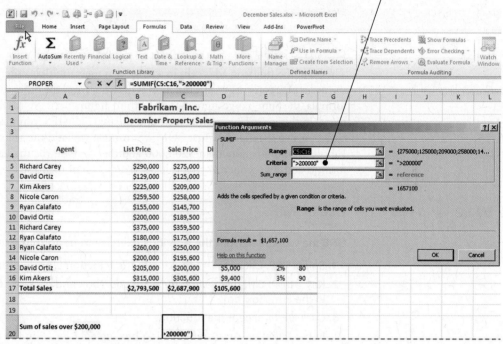

Take Note The result of the SUMIF formula in C20 does *not* include the property value in C15 because the formula specified values greater than $200,000. To include this value, the criterion would have to be >= (greater than or equal to).

8. Select cell **C21**, click **Recently Used** in the Function Library group, and click **SUMIF** to once again open the Function Arguments dialog box. The insertion point should be in the Range box.

Take Note When you click Recently Used, the last function that you used appears at the top of the list. Similarly, when you click Insert Function, the Insert Function dialog box opens with the last-used function highlighted.

9. Select **E5:E16** in the Range field. The selected range is automatically entered into the text box. Press **Tab**.

10. Key **<3%** in the Criteria box and press **Tab**. You are entering the criteria to calculate all values less than 3%.

CERTIFICATION READY   5.4.3

How do you use a SUMIF formula to conditionally summarize data?

11. Select **C5:C16** in the Sum_range field. Click **OK** to accept your changes and close the dialog box. Excel returns a value of $1,134,200.

12. Click the **File** tab and select **Save As**. Create a Lesson 9 folder.

13. **SAVE** the workbook as *December Sales* in the Lesson 9 folder.

PAUSE. LEAVE the workbook open for use in the next exercise.

Table 9-1 explains the meaning of each argument in the SUMIF syntax. Note that if you omit Sum_range from the formula, as you did in the first calculation in the preceding exercise, Excel evaluates and adds the cells in the range if they match the criterion.

Table 9-1

Arguments in the SUMIF syntax

Argument	Explanation
Range	The range of cells that you want the function to evaluate. Blank and text values are ignored.
Criteria	The condition or criterion in the form of a number, expression, or text entry that defines which cells will be added.
Sum_range	The actual cells to add if the corresponding cells in the range match the criteria.

Using SUMIFS

The SUMIFS function adds cells in a range that meet multiple criteria. It is important to note that the order of arguments in this function is different from the order used with SUMIF. In a SUMIF formula, the Sum_range argument is the third argument; in SUMIFS, however, it is the first argument. In this exercise, you will create and use two SUMIFS formulas, each of which analyzes data based on two criteria. The first SUMIFS formula will add the selling price of the properties that Fabrikam sold for more than $200,000 and that were on the market 60 days or less. The second formula adds the properties that sold at 98% (<3%) of their listed price within 60 days.

STEP BY STEP   **Use SUMIFS**

USE the workbook from the previous exercise to perform the following actions:

1. Select C22. Click Insert Function in the Function Library group on the Formulas tab.
2. Key SUMIFS in the *Search for a Function* box and click Go. SUMIFS will be highlighted in the Function box.
3. Click OK to accept the function.
4. In the Function Arguments dialog box, select C5:C16 in the Sum_range box. This adds your cell range to the argument of the formula.
5. In the Criteria_range1 box, select F5:F16. In the Criteria1 box, key <=60. This specifies that you want to calculate only those values that are less than or equal to 60. When you move to the next text box, notice that Excel places quotation marks around your criteria. It applies these marks to let itself know that this is a criterion and not a calculated value.
6. In the Criteria_range2 box, select C5:C16. You are now choosing your second cell range.
7. In the Criteria2 box, key >200000. Click OK. You have now applied a second criterion that will calculate values greater than 200,000. Excel calculates your formula, returning a value of $742,000.
8. Select C23 and click Recently Used in the Function Library group.
9. Select SUMIFS. In the Sum_range box, select C5:C16.
10. In the Criteria_range1 box, select F5:F16. Key <60 in the Criteria1 box.
11. In the Criteria_range2 box, select E5:E16. Key <3% in the Criteria2 box. Your Function Arguments dialog box should look like Figure 9-4. Click OK. After applying this formula, Excel returns a value of $433,000. (See Figure 9-4.)

CERTIFICATION
READY   **5.4.2**

How do you create a formula that sums only those values that meet multiple criteria?

Figure 9-4

SUMIFS formula applies two or more criteria

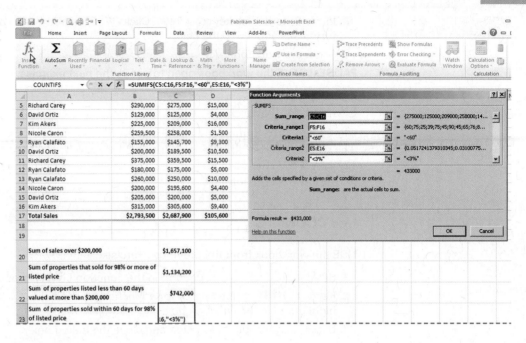

12. **SAVE** the workbook.

PAUSE. LEAVE the workbook open to use in the next exercise.

The formulas you used in this exercise analyzed the data on two criteria. You can continue to add up to 127 criteria on which data can be evaluated.

Because the order of arguments is different in SUMIF and SUMIFS, if you want to copy and edit these similar functions, be sure to put the arguments in the correct order (first, second, third, and so on).

Using COUNTIF

When used in a conditional formula, the COUNTIF function counts the number of cells in a given range that meet a specific condition. The syntax for the COUNTIF function is COUNTIF(range, criteria); the range is the range of cells to be counted by the formula, and the criteria are the conditions that must be met in order for the cells to be counted. The condition can be a number, expression, or text entry. In this exercise, you practice using the COUNTIF function to calculate values >=200,000. The range you will specify in this COUNTIF formula is the selling price of homes sold during the specified period. The criterion selects only those homes that sold for $200,000 or more.

STEP BY STEP   **Use COUNTIF**

USE the workbook from the previous exercise.

1. Select **C24**. Click **Insert Function** in the Function Library group.
2. Key **COUNTIF** in the *Search for a Function* box and click **Go**. COUNTIF will be highlighted in the Function dialog box.
3. Click **OK** to accept the function and close the dialog box. This opens the Function Arguments dialog box.

CERTIFICATION READY   **5.4.1**

How do you create a formula that counts the number of cells in a range that meet a specified condition?

4. In the Function Arguments dialog box, select **B5:B16** in the Range box. You have now selected your range for calculation.
5. In the Criteria box, key **>=200000**. Click **OK**. You have set your criteria of values greater than or equal to $200,000. Excel returns a value of 9.
6. Select **C25** and click **Recently Used** in the Function Library group.
7. Select **COUNTIF**. In the Functions Arguments box, in the Range box, select **C5:C16**.

8. In the Criteria box, key >=200000. Click OK. Excel returns a value of 7 when the formula is applied to the cell.

9. SAVE the workbook.

PAUSE. LEAVE the workbook open to use in the next exercise.

Using COUNTIFS

The COUNTIFS formula counts the number of cells within a range that meet multiple criteria. The syntax is COUNTIFS(range1, criteria1, range2, criteria2, and so on). You can create up to 127 ranges and criteria. In this exercise, you will perform calculations based on multiple criteria for the COUNTIFS formula.

STEP BY STEP | **Use COUNTIFS**

USE the workbook from the previous exercise.

1. Select C26. Click Insert Function in the Function Library group.

2. Key COUNTIFS in the *Search for a function* box and click Go. COUNTIFS will be highlighted in the Function box.

3. Click OK to accept the function and close the dialog box.

4. In the Function Arguments dialog box, select F5:F16 in the Criteria_range1 box. You have selected your first range for calculation.

5. In the Criteria1 box, key >=60. The descriptions and tips for each argument box in the Function Arguments dialog box are replaced with the value when you navigate to the next argument box, as illustrated in Figure 9-5. The formula result is also displayed, enabling you to review and make corrections if an error message occurs or an unexpected result is returned. You have now set your first criterion. Excel shows the calculation up to this step as a value of 8.

Figure 9-5

Arguments and results for COUNTIFS formula

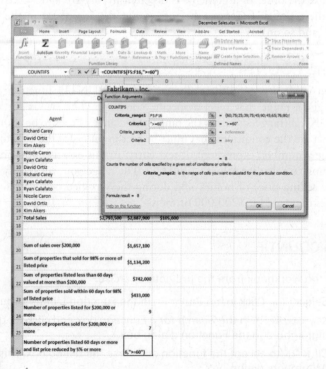

6. In the Criteria_range2 box, select E5:E16. You have selected your second range to be calculated.

7. In the Criteria2 box, key >=5%. Click OK. You have set your second criterion. When you click OK, Excel returns a value of 2.

8. SAVE the workbook.

PAUSE. LEAVE the workbook open to use in the next exercise.

A cell in the range you identify in the Function Arguments box is counted only if *all* of the corresponding criteria you specified are true for that cell. If a criterion refers to an empty cell, COUNTIFS treats it as a 0 value.

Take Note

When you create formulas, you can use the wildcard characters question mark (?) and asterisk (*) in your criteria. A question mark matches any single character; an asterisk matches any sequence of characters. If you want to find an actual question mark or asterisk, type a grave accent (`) preceding the character. You will apply this technique later in the lesson.

Using AVERAGEIF

The AVERAGEIF formula returns the arithmetic mean of all the cells in a range that meet a given criteria. The syntax is AVERAGEIF(range, criteria, average_range). In the AVERAGEIF syntax, *range* is the set of cells you want to average. For example, in this exercise, you use the AVERAGEIF function to calculate the average number of days properties valued at $200,000 or more were on the market before they were sold. The range in this formula is B5:B16 (cells that contain the listed value of the homes that were sold). The criterion is the condition against which you want the cells to be evaluated, that is, >=200000. Average_range is the actual set of cells to average—the number of days each home was on the market before it was sold.

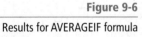

Use AVERAGEIF

USE the workbook from the previous exercise.

1. Select **C27** and click **Recently Used** in the Function Library group.
2. Click **AVERAGE**. Key **B5:B16** in the Number1 box and click **OK**. A mathematical average for this range is returned.
3. Select **C28** and click **Insert Function** in the Function Library group.
4. Select **AVERAGEIF** from the function list or use the function search box to locate and accept the AVERAGEIF function; the Function Arguments dialog box now opens.
5. In the Function Arguments dialog box, select **B5:B16** in the Range box.
6. In the Criteria box, key **>=200000**.
7. In the Average_range box, select **F5:F16**. Click **OK** to close the dialog box. Excel returns a value of 63.33, as illustrated in Figure 9-6.

Figure 9-6

Results for AVERAGEIF formula

8. **SAVE** the workbook.

PAUSE. LEAVE the workbook open to use in the next exercise.

Using AVERAGEIFS

An AVERAGEIFS formula returns the average (arithmetic mean) of all cells that meet multiple criteria. The syntax is AVERAGEIFS(average_range, criteria_range1, criteria1, criteria_range2, criteria2, and so on). You will learn to apply the AVERAGEIFS formula in the following exercise.

STEP BY STEP   **Use AVERAGEIFS**

USE the workbook from the previous exercise.

1. Select C29. Click Insert Function in the Function Library group.
2. Key AVERAGEIFS in the *Search for a function* box and click Go. AVERAGEIFS will be highlighted in the Function box.
3. Click OK to accept the function and close the dialog box.
4. In the Function Arguments dialog box, select F5:F16 in the Average_range box. Press Tab.
5. In the Criteria_range1 box, select B5:B16 and press Tab. You have selected your first criteria range.
6. In the Criteria1 box, key <200000. You have set your first criteria.
7. In the Criteria_range2 box, select E5:E16 and press Tab. You have now selected your second criteria range.
8. In the Criteria2 box, key <=5%. Click OK. Excel returns a value of 60.
9. **SAVE** and **CLOSE** the workbook.

PAUSE. LEAVE Excel open to use in the next exercise.

You entered only two criteria for the SUMIFS, COUNTIFS, and AVERAGEIFS formulas you created in the previous exercises. However, in very large worksheets, you often need to use multiple criteria in order for the formula to return a value that is meaningful for your analysis. You can enter up to 127 conditions that data must match in order for a cell to be included in the conditional summary that results from a SUMIFS, COUNTIFS, or AVERAGEIFS formula.

The following statements summarize how values are treated when you enter an AVERAGEIF or AVERAGEIFS formula:

- If Average_range is omitted from the function arguments, the range is used.
- If a cell in Average_range is an empty cell, AVERAGEIF ignores it.
- If a range is blank or contains a text value, AVERAGEIF returns the #DIV0! error value.
- If a cell in a criterion is empty, AVERAGEIF treats it as a 0 value.
- If no cells in the range meet the criteria, AVERAGEIF returns the #DIV/0! error value.

Take Note   You can reference another worksheet in the same workbook in a conditional formula, but you cannot use references to another workbook.

USING FORMULAS TO LOOK UP DATA IN A WORKBOOK

The Bottom Line

When worksheets contain long and sometimes cumbersome lists of data, you need a way to quickly find specific information within these lists. This is where Excel's **lookup functions** come in handy. Lookup functions are an efficient way to search for and insert a value in a cell when the desired value is stored elsewhere in the worksheet or even in a different workbook. VLOOKUP and HLOOKUP are the two lookup formulas that you will be using in this section. These functions can return cell references identifying where certain information is found, or they can return the actual contents of the found cell. As you work through the following exercises, note that the term **table** refers to a range of cells in a worksheet that can be used by a lookup function.

Using VLOOKUP

The V in VLOOKUP stands for *vertical*. This formula is used when the comparison values are located in a column to the left of the data that you want to find. The VLOOKUP function syntax is LOOKUP(lookup_value, table_array, col_index_num).

An **array** is used to build single formulas that produce multiple results or that operate on a group of arguments. You create and use array constants whenever you need to add sets of values that don't change (such as month names or pi) to your array formulas. Constants in your formulas process faster because they reside in memory and not in the workbook. The data in a table array must be arranged in rows and columns. It can be a constant or a formula. The VLOOKUP function searches for a value in the first column of a table array on the worksheet and then returns a value from a specific column, in the same row as the value it found, into a different location in the worksheet. In the next exercise, you will apply this formula to calculate employee bonuses.

When working with VLOOKUP and HLOOKUP functions and arguments, there are several key points to keep in mind:

- If lookup_value is smaller than the smallest value in the first column of table_array, VLOOKUP returns the #N/A error value.
- Table_array values can be text, numbers, or logical values. Uppercase and lowercase text is equivalent.
- The values in the first column of the table_array selection must be placed in ascending sort order, otherwise VLOOKUP may not give the correct value. The lookup table you use in this exercise lists years of service in ascending order.
- If the Range_lookup argument is True or omitted, an exact or approximate match is returned. If VLOOKUP cannot find an exact match, it returns the next largest value that is less than the value you have specified in lookup_value.
- If Range_lookup is False, VLOOKUP will find only an exact match. If an exact match is not found, the error value #N/A is returned.

STEP BY STEP	Use VLOOKUP

 The *Fabrikam Bonus* file for this lesson is available on the book companion website or in WileyPLUS.

GET READY. LAUNCH Microsoft Excel if it is not already open.

1. **OPEN** the *Fabrikam Bonus* data file for this lesson.
2. With the Bonus sheet active, select C15:F24 in the worksheet. Click the Formulas tab, and then click Define Name in the Defined Names group. The New Name dialog box opens.
3. Key Bonus in the Name box on the New Name dialog box. Click OK to close the dialog box. You have defined the range name.

Take Note

Arguments used in VLOOKUP or HLOOKUP are not case sensitive, so you can key them in uppercase, lowercase, or any combination of uppercase and lowercase characters. Also, the VLOOKUP and HLOOKUP function names are not case sensitive.

WileyPLUS Extra! features an online tutorial of this task.

4. Select E5 and click Insert Function.
5. In the *Search for a Function* box, key VLOOKUP and click OK. The Function Arguments dialog box opens with the cursor in the Lookup_value box.
6. Key D5 and press Tab. The insertion point moves to the Table_array box.
7. In the Table_array box, click the Collapse Dialog box button. In the Defined Names group, click Use in Formula and select Bonus. Press Tab. The insertion point moves to the next text box.
8. In the Col_index_num box, key 2, which is the column containing the standard bonus amounts. Press Tab.

9. In the Range_lookup box, key **True**; the same bonus is paid for a range of years, so you enter True in the Range_lookup box so that a value will be returned for all agents who have been with the company more than one year. Your Function Arguments dialog box should look similar to the one shown in Figure 9-7. Click **OK**. Excel returns a value of $750.

Figure 9-7

VLOOKUP in function arguments dialog box

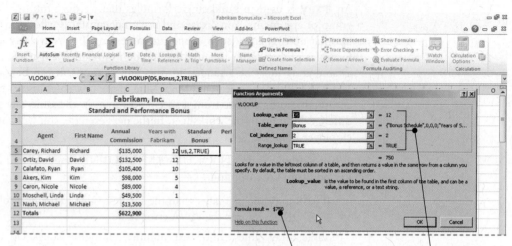

Value to be returned   All conditions entered

10. Using the fill handle in E5, copy the formula to the range E6:E11. This will calculate bonuses for the other sales agents. The N/A error message appears in E11 because a value is not available for agents who have been employed for less than one year. (Agents become eligible for a bonus only after a full year of service.) You will change this error message in another exercise.

11. **SAVE** the workbook as *Employee Bonus*.

PAUSE. LEAVE the workbook open to use in the next exercise.

Take Note

True in the Range_lookup box will return the closest value. False returns only an exact value. If you leave the Range_lookup box empty, Excel will enter True when you click OK.

Table 9-2 shows the argument components used in the VLOOKUP and HLOOKUP formulas. Refer also to Figure 9-8 and Figure 9-9.

Table 9-2

Function syntax for VLOOKUP

Key Combination	Formatting Applied
Lookup_value	The value to be found in the column or row; this can be a constant value, a text value enclosed in quotation marks, or the address or name of a cell that contains a numeric or text constant.
Table_array	Two or more columns of data. Use a reference to a range or a range name. The values in the first column of Table_array are the values searched by Lookup_value.
Row_index_num	The numeric position of the row that is to be searched for by HLOOKUP.
Col_index_num	The numeric position of the column that is to be searched for by VLOOKUP. The column number in Table_array from which the matching value must be returned. A Col_index_num of 1 returns the value in the first column in Table_array; a Col_index_num of 2 returns the value in the second column in Table_array, and so on.
Range_lookup	A logical value that specifies whether you want VLOOKUP to find an exact match or an approximate match. If the function is to return the nearest value, even when there is no match, this value should be set to True; if an exact match is required, this value should be set to False; if this argument is not included, the function assumes the value to be True.

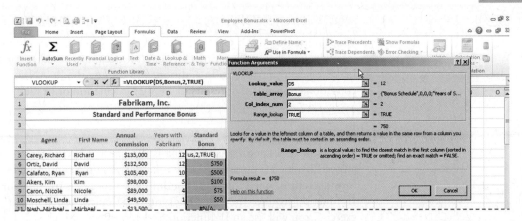

Figure 9-8

VLOOKUP in the function
arguments dialog box

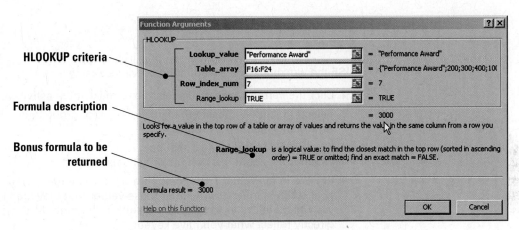

Figure 9-9

HLOOKUP in the function
arguments dialog box

Using HLOOKUP

HLOOKUP searches for a value in the top row of a table or an array and then returns a value in the same column from a row you specify in the table or array. Use HLOOKUP when the comparison values are located in a row across the top of a table of data and you want to look down a specified number of rows. In the following exercise, you will use an HLOOKUP formula to determine who is eligible for the performance bonus.

STEP BY STEP   **Use HLOOKUP**

USE the workbook from the previous exercise.

1. Select F5 and click Insert Function in the Function Library group.

2. In the *Search for a Function* box, key HLOOKUP and click OK. The *Function Arguments* dialog box opens with the cursor in the Lookup_value box.

3. Enter the HLOOKUP formula =HLOOKUP("performance award",F16:F24,7,true) in the argument boxes, as shown in Figure 9-9. Click OK. The performance bonus of 3000 is entered into the cell.

4. SAVE the workbook.

PAUSE. LEAVE the workbook open to use in the next exercise.

It may be difficult to remember the syntax for an HLOOKUP or VLOOKUP function. Remember, you can always use the Function Arguments dialog box to help you remember the order of the arguments for any and all formulas. When you click in each field, review the tips that appear on the right side of each box, as well as the explanation below the argument boxes that tells the purpose of each argument in the formula.

ADDING CONDITIONAL LOGIC FUNCTIONS TO FORMULAS

The Bottom Line

You can use the AND, OR, and NOT functions to create conditional formulas that result in a logical value, that is, True or False. Such formulas test whether conditions are true or false and make logical comparisons. In addition, you can use the IF, AND, and OR functions to create a conditional formula that results in another calculation or in values other than True or False.

Using IF

The result of a conditional formula is determined by the state of a specific condition or the answer to a logical question. An IF function sets up a conditional statement to test data. An IF formula returns one value if the condition you specify is true and another value if it is false. The IF function requires the following syntax: IF(logical_test, value_if_true, value if false). In this exercise, you will use an IF function to determine who is eligible for the performance bonus.

STEP BY STEP **Use IF**

USE the workbook you saved in the previous exercise.

1. Click the Performance worksheet tab to make it the active worksheet.

2. Select **D5**. Click **Logical** in the Function Library group and click **IF**. The Function Arguments dialog box opens.

3. Key **C5>=B5** in the Logical_test box. This component of the formula determines whether the agent has met his or her sales goal.

4. Key **Yes** in the Value_if_true box. This is the value returned if the agent met his or her goal. Keep in mind as you enter these values that they aren't case sensitive. Keying **yes** will therefore yield the same results in the formula. The output text in the cell will directly reflect what you have keyed.

5. Key **No** in the Value_if_false box and click **OK**.

6. With D5 still selected, use the fill handle to copy the formula to D6:D11. Excel returns the result that four agents have earned the performance award by displaying Yes In the cells. (See Figure 9-10.)

Figure 9-10

Using the IF function

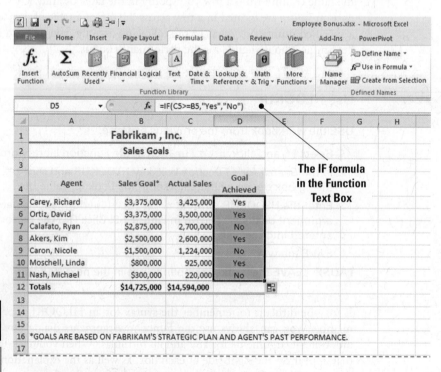

The IF formula in the Function Text Box

CERTIFICATION
READY 8.3.3

How do you use the IF function to apply conditional formatting?

7. **SAVE** the workbook.

PAUSE. LEAVE the workbook open to use in the next exercise.

Using AND

The AND function returns True if all its arguments are true and False if one or more arguments are false. The Syntax is AND(logical1, logical2, and so on). In this exercise, you will use the AND function to determine whether Fabrikam's total annual sales met the strategic goal *and* whether the sales goal exceeded the previous year's sales by 5 percent.

STEP BY STEP   **Use AND**

USE the workbook from the previous exercise.

1. Click the Annual Sales sheet tab.
2. Select B5. Click Logical in the Function Library group and click the AND option. The *Function Arguments* dialog box opens with the cursor in the Logical1 box.
3. Select B3, key <=, select B16, and press Enter. This argument represents the first condition: Did actual sales exceed the sales goal? Because this is the first year, only one logical test will be entered.
4. Select C5, click Recently Used, and click AND. In the Logical1 box, key C3<=C16.
5. In the Logical2 box, key C16>=B16*1.05. Click OK. The formula returns True, which means that both conditions in the formula have been met. The AND function arguments are illustrated in Figure 9-11.

Figure 9-11

AND function arguments

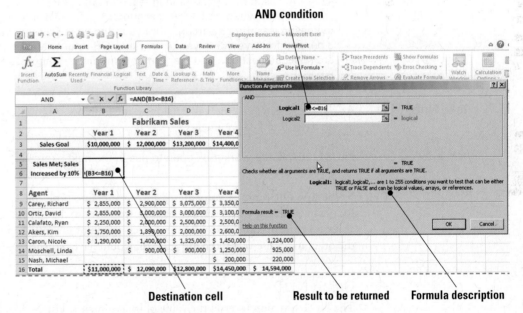

6. Select C5 and copy the formula to D5:F5.
7. SAVE the workbook.

PAUSE. LEAVE the workbook open to use in the next exercise.

Again, the AND function returns a True result only when both conditions in the formula have been met. For example, consider the results you achieved in the preceding exercise. Sales in the second year exceeded sales for the previous year; therefore, the first condition is met. Year 2 sales also exceeded Year 1 sales by 5 percent. Because both conditions are met, the formula returns a True result.

Now consider the arguments for the logical tests for year 3 (the formula in D5). Sales did not exceed the sales goal; therefore, the first argument returns a False value. However, sales did exceed the previous year's sales by 5 percent. When only one condition has been met, the formula returns False.

Using OR

The syntax for an OR formula is similar to that for an AND formula; however, OR returns True if *any* argument is True, and returns False only when *all* arguments are False. With this formula, the arguments must evaluate to logical values such as True or False or to arrays or references that contain logical values. In this exercise, you will create a formula that evaluates whether sales increased each year during two different data periods. The OR formula will return True if any of the periods increased.

STEP BY STEP   **Use OR**

USE the workbook from the previous exercise.

1. With the Annual Sales worksheet active, select A18 and click Logical in the Function Library group.
2. Click OR. The Function Arguments dialog box opens. You will create a formula that answers the following question: Did Carey's sales increase by 3% in year 3 or year 4?
3. In the Logical1 box, key D9>=C9*1.03 and press Tab. This argument will answer the first half of the question: Did Carey's sales increase by 3% in the first time period?
4. In the Logical2 box, key E9>=D9*1.03. This argument will answer the second half of the question: Did Carey's sales increase in the second time period?
5. Click OK to close the dialog box. The formula returns True, indicating that Carey's sales increased by 3 percent in at least one of the identified years. A False finding is returned only when both logical arguments are false. In this case, Mr. Carey's sales increased less than 3 percent from year 2 to year 3 but increased by more than 3 percent from year 3 to year 4. Because OR returns a False result only if all conditions are false, at least one of the arguments in this case equates to true.
6. **SAVE** the workbook.

Take Note   As you add arguments, the Value fields on the Function Arguments dialog box expand to allow you to enter multiple arguments.

PAUSE. LEAVE the workbook open to use in the next exercise.

In the first OR formula you entered in this exercise, both logical tests returned a True value. Mr. Carey's sales in year 3 were at least 3 percent more than in year 2. His year 4 sales were also at least 3 percent more than his year 3 sales. If one of the tests had resulted in a True value and the other in a False value, the formula still would have returned a True value in A18.

Using NOT

The NOT function reverses the value of its arguments. Use NOT when you want to make sure a value is not equal to one particular value. If the logical value is false, NOT returns True. In the following exercise, you will use the NOT function to answer the following question: Did Calafato's year 5 sales exceed his year 4 sales by 3 percent?

STEP BY STEP   **Use NOT**

USE the workbook from the previous exercise.

1. On the Annual Sales worksheet, select A19 and click Logical in the Function Library group.
2. Select NOT from the list of logical formulas.
3. In the Function Arguments dialog box, key F11>=E11*3% and click OK. False is returned by the formula. Thus, Calafato's year 5 sales were at least 3 percent greater than his year 4 sales. Notice that the NOT formula returns the opposite response of what would be returned by an IF formula. For example, if an IF formula returned the value of "top," then NOT would return the value of "bottom."

4. SAVE the workbook.

PAUSE. LEAVE the workbook open to use in the next exercise.

In this exercise, you want to be sure that in year 5, Calafato's sales increased by at least 3 percent over the previous year. The NOT conditional formula results in a logical value (True or False) and can be used for this logical test—returning the opposite value of what would be returned by an IF formula.

Using IFERROR

An error message is returned when a formula does not contain sufficient arguments to return a value. Use the IFERROR function to trap and handle errors in a formula. This function returns a value you specify if a formula evaluates to an error; otherwise, it returns the result of the formula. The syntax is IFERROR(value, value_if_error). In the IFERROR syntax, *value* is the argument that is checked for an error. In the next exercise, you will use this formula to determine eligible bonuses.

STEP BY STEP   **Use IFERROR**

USE the workbook you saved in the previous exercise.

1. Click the Bonus worksheet tab. Select **E11** and click to place the insertion point after the = in the formula bar to edit the formula. You are going to add the IFERROR formula to correct the formula error that gave the N/A result in a previous exercise.

2. Key **IFERROR(** before VLOOKUP. Leave the existing formula intact. Press **End**. This will take you to the end of the formula.

Take Note   You will notice that we write formulas such as IFERROR and VLOOKUP in all uppercase. These terms are not case sensitive, but Microsoft always writes them in uppercase in the formula lists and Help system because doing so makes reading formulas much easier. Thus, it is best to get in the habit of using formulas in uppercase.

3. At the end of the original formula, key, **"Not Eligible")**. As shown in Figure 9-12, the complete formula is =IFERROR(VLOOKUP(D11,Bonus,2,True),"Not Eligible"). Be sure to include the closing parenthesis and the preceding comma or Excel will return an error that the formula is incorrect.

Figure 9-12

Editing a formula to specify a message when an error occurs

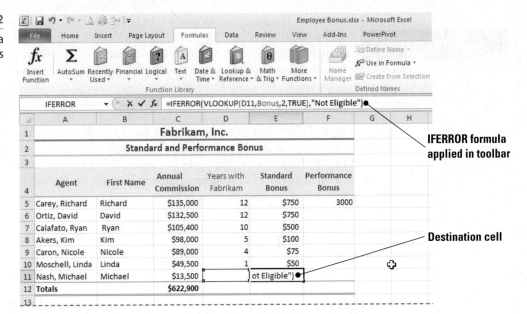

4. Press **Enter**. The #N/A error message is replaced with the message that the agent is not eligible for the bonus. If you select E11 and click the Insert Function button next to the formula bar, you will see that the original VLOOKUP formula appears in the Value box (first argument) in the IFERROR formula. As illustrated in Figure 9-13, that argument returned a #N/A error. The Value_if_error box contains the text to replace the error message.

Figure 9-13

IFERROR function arguments

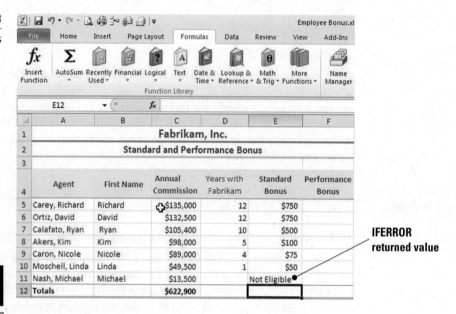

IFERROR
returned value

CERTIFICATION
READY   8.3.3

How do you use the IFERROR function to apply conditional formatting?

5. **SAVE** the workbook.

PAUSE. LEAVE the workbook open to use in the next exercise.

IFERROR will recognize and evaluate the following errors: #N/A, #VALUE!, #REF!, #DIV/0!, #NUM!, #NAME?, or #NULL!. In this exercise, you replaced the N/A error message with the "Not Eligible" response of why one of the sales agents did not receive a bonus when the VLOOKUP formula was applied.

USING FORMULAS TO FORMAT TEXT

The Bottom Line

You may be familiar with Microsoft Word's Convert Text command that enables you to change the capitalization of text. Similarly, in Excel, you can use PROPER, UPPER, and LOWER formulas to capitalize the first letter in a text string or to convert uppercase to lowercase or vice versa.

Using PROPER

The PROPER function capitalizes the first letter in a text string and any other letters in text that follow any character other than a letter. All other letters are converted to lowercase. In the PROPER(text) syntax, *text* can be text enclosed in quotation marks, a formula that returns text, or a reference to a cell containing the text you want to capitalize. In this exercise, you will use PROPER to change uppercase or lowercase text to title case text.

STEP BY STEP	Use PROPER

USE the workbook from the previous exercise.

1. Click the Performance worksheet tab. Select A17 and click Text in the Function Library group on the Formulas tab.

2. Scroll down the list and click PROPER. The Function Arguments dialog box opens.

3. Select A16 and click OK. The uppercase text in A16 is entered in A17 in title case. Note that all the text in the cell changes to proper case except for the S at the end of the word Fabrikam'S. Do not panic—you will address this in another step. (See Figure 9-14.)

Figure 9-14

Copying cell content

4. With A17 still selected, click Copy in the Clipboard group on the Home tab.

Take Note   Notice that the s letters following the apostrophe in Fabrikam's and Agent's are capitalized. Text that follows any character other than a letter is capitalized when you use the PROPER formula. Thus, you will need to proofread carefully when you convert capitalization.

5. Select A14 and click the arrow under Paste in the Clipboard group.

6. Click Paste Values, then click Values. 123 The text appears in A14. Click A14 and change the letters following the apostrophes to lowercase text.

7. Select A16:A17 and press Delete. The duplicate lines of text are removed.

8. **SAVE** the workbook.

PAUSE. LEAVE the workbook open to use in the next exercise.

The PROPER function capitalizes the first letter in each word in a text string. All other letters are converted to lowercase. That is why you edited the text after it was converted in the previous exercise. Because Excel recognized the apostrophe as a break, it capitalized the next letter. In the PROPER(text) syntax, text can be enclosed in quotation marks or cell references can be selected as you selected them in the previous exercise.

When you created the formula to convert the uppercase text to title case, you had two lines of text. If you deleted the original text in A16, the converted text in A17 would have been deleted as well. When you used the Paste Values option, the contents of A17 were pasted to A14 rather than the formula, which would be dependent on the text remaining in A16. After you pasted the results rather than the formula, you were able to remove the duplicate lines of text.

Using UPPER

The UPPER function allows you to convert text to uppercase (all capital letters). The syntax is UPPER(text), with text referring to the text you want converted to uppercase. Text can be a reference or a text string. Converting capitalization in text is a two-step process. You cannot enter the formula in the text's present location, so after the text has been converted, you must cut and paste the text to the desired location. The Paste Values command pastes the contents without the formula so that you can remove the duplicate data.

STEP BY STEP   **Use UPPER**

USE the workbook you saved in the previous exercise.

1. With the Performance worksheet still active from the previous exercise, select **A13** and click **Text** in the Function Library group.
2. Scroll down the list of functions, if necessary, and select **UPPER**. The Function Arguments dialog box opens.
3. Select **A14** as the text to convert and click **OK**. The text from A14 is entered in A13 in uppercase letters.
4. Click the **Home** tab. Select **A13** and click **Copy** in the Clipboard group.
5. With A13 still selected, click the arrow under Paste. Click **Paste Values** and click **Values**. With this action, you replaced the UPPER function in A13 with the actual result (value) of the function.
6. Select A14 and press Delete. **SAVE** the workbook.

PAUSE. LEAVE the workbook open to use in the next exercise.

Using LOWER

The LOWER function converts all uppercase letters in a text string to lowercase. LOWER does not change characters in text that are not letters. You will use the LOWER formula in the following exercise to apply lowercase text.

STEP BY STEP   **Use LOWER**

USE the workbook from the previous exercise.

1. Click the Annual Sales worksheet tab. Select **B20** and click **Text** in the Function Library group.
2. Scroll down the list of functions to select the **LOWER** formula.

3. Select **B19** as the text to convert and click **OK**. The text from B19 is converted to lowercase, and it is displayed in B20 below the original uppercase text in B19. Your workbook should resemble Figure 9-15.

Figure 9-15

Applying the LOWER formula

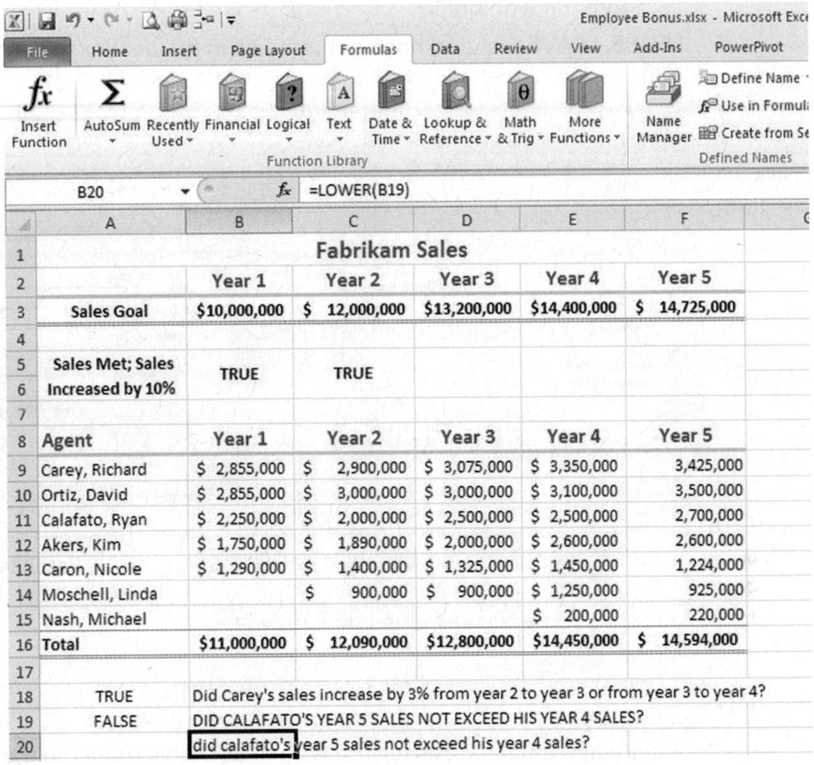

	A	B	C	D	E	F	G
1			Fabrikam Sales				
2		Year 1	Year 2	Year 3	Year 4	Year 5	
3	Sales Goal	$10,000,000	$ 12,000,000	$13,200,000	$14,400,000	$ 14,725,000	
4							
5	Sales Met; Sales	TRUE	TRUE				
6	Increased by 10%						
7							
8	Agent	Year 1	Year 2	Year 3	Year 4	Year 5	
9	Carey, Richard	$ 2,855,000	$ 2,900,000	$ 3,075,000	$ 3,350,000	3,425,000	
10	Ortiz, David	$ 2,855,000	$ 3,000,000	$ 3,000,000	$ 3,100,000	3,500,000	
11	Calafato, Ryan	$ 2,250,000	$ 2,000,000	$ 2,500,000	$ 2,500,000	2,700,000	
12	Akers, Kim	$ 1,750,000	$ 1,890,000	$ 2,000,000	$ 2,600,000	2,600,000	
13	Caron, Nicole	$ 1,290,000	$ 1,400,000	$ 1,325,000	$ 1,450,000	1,224,000	
14	Moschell, Linda		$ 900,000	$ 900,000	$ 1,250,000	925,000	
15	Nash, Michael				$ 200,000	220,000	
16	Total	$11,000,000	$ 12,090,000	$12,800,000	$14,450,000	$ 14,594,000	
17							
18	TRUE	Did Carey's sales increase by 3% from year 2 to year 3 or from year 3 to year 4?					
19	FALSE	DID CALAFATO'S YEAR 5 SALES NOT EXCEED HIS YEAR 4 SALES?					
20		did calafato's year 5 sales not exceed his year 4 sales?					

4. **SAVE** the workbook.

PAUSE. LEAVE the workbook open to use in the next exercise.

It is important that you always review text after you have changed its case. For example, the agent's name in B20 should be capitalized, as well as the first word in the sentence. If you replace the text in B19 with the lowercase text in B20, you will need to edit the text.

USING FORMULAS TO MODIFY TEXT

The Bottom Line

The SUBSTITUTE function allows you to edit data and substitute new text for existing text. Formulas can also be used to convert text to columns.

Using SUBSTITUTE

Excel's SUBSTITUTE function is especially useful when you need to edit data and you want to substitute new text for existing text in a text string. Use SUBSTITUTE when you want to replace specific text in a text string; use REPLACE when you want to replace any text that occurs in a specific location in a text string, such as when a name change occurs.

STEP BY STEP **Use SUBSTITUTE**

USE the workbook from the previous exercise.

1. Click the Annual Sales worksheet tab if necessary. Select **B22**, click **Text** in the Function Library, and click **SUBSTITUTE**; the Functions Arguments dialog box opens.
2. Select **B18** in the Text box.

3. Key 3 in the Old_text box. This is the text you want to replace.

4. Key 5 in the New_text box.

5. Key 1 in the Instance_num box (the Function Arguments settings are explained in Figure 9-16). Click OK.

6. **SAVE** the workbook.

PAUSE. LEAVE the workbook open to use in the next exercise.

Figure 9-16

SUBSTITUTE function arguments

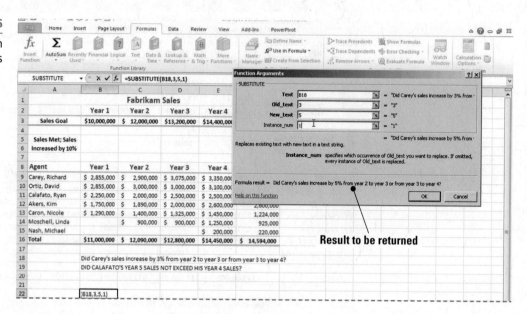

When you want to use existing text with small changes, you can use the SUBSTITUTE function. In the Function Arguments dialog box, Text can be the actual text you want to substitute, or it can be a cell reference. Here, you wanted to use the text in B18 with one change. Figure 9-16 illustrates the function arguments that result in changing 3% to 5% in the new text. The number 3 occurs three times in the original text. The last function argument indicates which occurrence should be replaced.

Converting Text to Columns

You can use the Convert Text to Columns Wizard to separate simple cell content, such as first names and last names, into different columns. Depending on how your data is organized, you can split the cell contents based on a delimiter (divider or separator), such as a space or a comma, or based on a specific column break location within your data. In the following exercise, you will convert the data in column A to two columns.

STEP BY STEP **Convert Text to Columns**

USE the workbook from the previous exercise.

1. Click the Performance worksheet tab. Select any cell in column B. Right-click to open the shortcut menu. Click Insert and click Entire Column. Click OK.

2. Select A5:A11. Click the Data tab and click Text to Columns in the Data Tools group.

3. The Text Wizard opens with Delimited selected as the default because Excel recognized that the data in the selected range is separated by a comma. Click Next to move to the next step in the wizard.

4. Select Comma as the delimiter. If other delimiters are checked, deselect them and click Next.

5. Select **Text** as the Column data format and click **Finish**. A warning window opens to confirm you want to replace the contents of the destination cells. Click **OK**. The first names of the agents are moved to column B. (See Figure 9-17.)

Figure 9-17

Converting text to columns

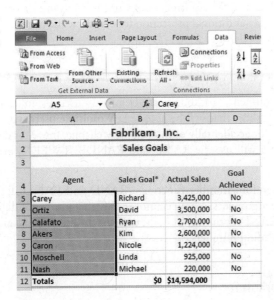

Another Way
You can also use text functions such as LEFT, MID, and RIGHT to convert text data from one column to multiple columns.

6. Select **A4**, key **Last Name**, and press **Tab**.

7. With B4 selected, key **First Name** and press **Tab**.

8. **SAVE** the workbook with the same name. **CLOSE** the workbook.

CLOSE Excel.

SOFTWARE ORIENTATION

The Review Tab

Microsoft Excel provides several layers of security and protection that allow you to control who can access and change your Excel data. Commands on the Review tab (Figure 9-18) enable you to protect an entire workbook file so that only authorized users can view or modify your data (the highest level of protection). You can also protect certain worksheet or workbook elements to prevent users from accidentally or deliberately changing, moving, or deleting important data. Data protection is especially important when files are shared and edited by multiple users.

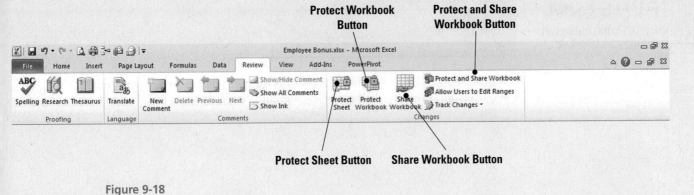

Figure 9-18

Review tab

Use this illustration as a reference throughout this lesson as you learn to share and edit files using Excel's security and protection options.

SECURING YOUR WORK BEFORE SHARING IT WITH OTHERS

A **password** is text that must be keyed before a user can access a workbook, worksheet, or worksheet elements. You can secure an entire workbook by restricting who can open and/or use the workbook data and by requiring a password to view and/or save changes to the workbook. You can also provide additional protection for certain worksheets or workbook elements with or without applying a password.

Protecting a Worksheet

In a work environment, workbooks are frequently used by more than one employee. When you create a worksheet that will be accessed by multiple users, you often need to protect it so that a user does not accidentally or intentionally change, move, or delete important data. In the next exercise, you will use the RAND and RANDBETWEEN formulas to create unique ID numbers.

Excel has two random number functions: RAND and RANDBETWEEN. RAND does not require function arguments, so you cannot specify the number of digits you want in the number returned by a RAND formula. In contrast, RANDBETWEEN allows you to determine the beginning and ending numbers.

STEP BY STEP | **Protect a Worksheet**

GET READY. Before you begin these steps, **LAUNCH** Microsoft Excel.

1. **OPEN** *Employee Data* from the data files for this lesson.

2. Select **G4** on the SSN worksheet. On the Formulas tab, click Insert Function. The Insert Function dialog box is displayed.

3. Key Rand in the *Search for a function* box and click Go. As shown in Figure 9-19, two random number functions are displayed in the *Select a function* box.

The *Employee Data* file for this lesson is available on the book companion website or in WileyPLUS.

Figure 9-19

Formulas to generate random numbers

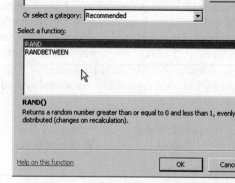

WileyPLUS Extra! features an online tutorial of this task.

4. Select RANDBETWEEN and click OK. This formula will create a random number for each employee that can be used for identification purposes.

5. In the Function Arguments dialog box, key 10000 in the Bottom box and 99999 in the Top box, as shown in Figure 9-20. Click OK. As one of the first steps in information security, employees are usually assigned an Employee ID number that can replace Social Security numbers on all documents. Your formulas returned a five-digit number for each employee.

Figure 9-20

Generating a five-digit random number

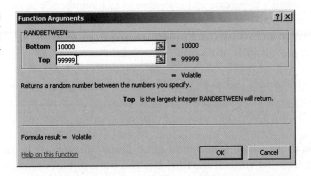

6. Copy the formula in G4 to G5:G33. Each employee is now assigned a random five-digit ID number.

7. With the range G4:G33 already selected, on the Home tab, click Copy. Click the Paste arrow, click Paste Values, and then click Values.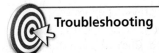

Troubleshooting The RANDBETWEEN formula generates a new random number each time a workbook is opened. To retain the Employee ID numbers created by the formula, you must replace the formula with the values.

8. With G4:G33 selected, click Format and then select Format Cells; the Format Cells dialog box opens.

9. On the Protection tab of the dialog box, make sure that Locked is selected and click OK. This prevents employee ID numbers from being changed when the worksheet has been protected.

10. On the Review tab, in the Changes group, click Protect Sheet.

11. Key L11!e01 in the *Password to unprotect sheet* box. The password is not displayed in the Password to unprotect sheet box. Instead, round dots (•) are displayed. Click OK.

12. You are asked to confirm the password. Key L11!e01 and click OK. You have just created and confirmed the password that will lock the worksheet. Passwords are meant to be secure. This means that all passwords are case sensitive. Thus, you must key exactly what has been assigned as the password—uppercase and lowercase letters, numbers, and symbols.

13. **SAVE** the workbook as *Payroll Data*. **CLOSE** the workbook.

PAUSE. LEAVE Excel open to use in the next exercise.

Take Note   Workbook and worksheet element protection should not be confused with workbook-level password security. Element protection cannot protect a workbook from users who have malicious intent.

Protecting a Workbook

Assigning a password is an effective way to prevent any user who does not know the password from opening a workbook. To protect an entire workbook, you can require a password to open and view the workbook. You can also require one password to open and view the workbook and a second password to modify workbook data. Passwords that apply to an entire workbook provide optimal security for your data.

Currently, the Payroll Data workbook you saved in the previous exercise can be viewed by anyone who has access to the computer system. You restricted the modification of the file, but you did not restrict access to the data. In this exercise, you will limit access to the workbook by requiring a password to open the document.

Excel passwords can contain up to 255 letters, numbers, spaces, and symbols. Passwords are case sensitive, so you must type uppercase and lowercase letters correctly. If possible, select a strong password that you can remember so that you do not have to write it down. A **strong password** is one that combines uppercase and lowercase letters, numbers, and symbols—consider the example password of L11!e01 that you used in the previous exercise. A password that uses 14 or more characters, however, is considered to be more secure. Passwords that use birthdates, house numbers, pet names, etc. provide little protection.

Take Note   It is vitally important that you remember passwords assigned to workbooks or worksheets. If you forget your password, Microsoft cannot retrieve it. If necessary, write down passwords and store them in a secure place away from the information you want to protect.

When you protect a worksheet, you can hide any formulas that you do not want to be visible. Select the cells that contain the formulas you want to hide. Then, on the Protection tab of the Format Cells dialog box, select the Hidden check box.

STEP BY STEP   **Protect a Workbook**

GET READY. LAUNCH Excel if it is not already running.

1. **OPEN** the *Payroll Data* file that you saved and closed in the previous exercise.
2. Click D11 and try to key a new value in the cell. A dialog box informs you that you are unable to modify the cell because the worksheet is protected. Click OK to continue.
3. Click the Performance worksheet tab and select D6.
4. On the Home tab, in the Cells group, click the Delete arrow, and click Delete Sheet Rows. Dr. Bourne's data is removed from the worksheet because this worksheet was left unprotected.
5. Click the SSN worksheet tab. Click Unprotect Sheet in the Changes group on the Review tab.
6. Key L11!e01 (the password you created in the previous exercise) and click OK.
7. D11 is still selected. Key 25, press Tab, and key 17000. Press Tab.
8. On the Review tab, in the Changes group, click Protect Workbook. The *Protect Structure and Windows* dialog box shown in Figure 9-21 opens. Click the Protect workbook f*or* Structure and Windows options in the dialog box.

Figure 9-21

Protecting the structure of a workbook

9. Key L11&E02 in the password box and click OK. Confirm the password as shown in Figure 9-22 and click OK.

Figure 9-22

Confirming the password to open a workbook

Take Note   The workbook password is optional, but if you do not supply a password, any user can unprotect the workbook and change the protected elements.

10. Click the File tab and select Save As.
11. In the Save As dialog box, click Tools and General Options in the Tools drop-down menu, as shown in Figure 9-23; the General Options dialog box opens.

Figure 9-23

Use the tools options in save as to restrict access to the workbook

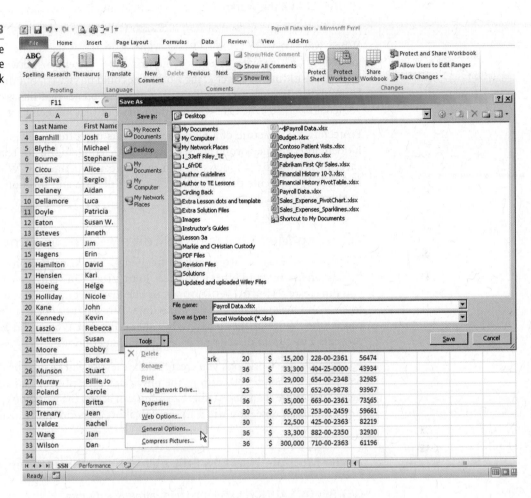

12. In the General Options dialog box shown in Figure 9-24, in the *Password to open* box, key L11&E02 and click OK.

Figure 9-24

Create a strong password to restrict access to the workbook

13. Reenter the password on the *Confirm Password* dialog box and click OK. The passwords must match exactly.
14. Click Save. Select Yes to replace the existing file. As the document is now saved, anyone who has the password can open the workbook and modify data contained in the Performance worksheet because that worksheet is not protected. However, to modify the SSN worksheet, the user must also know the password you used to protect that worksheet in the first exercise.

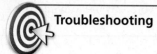 **Troubleshooting** When you confirm the password to prevent unauthorized viewing of a document, you are reminded that passwords are case sensitive. If the password you enter on the Confirm Password dialog box is not identical to the one you entered in the previous dialog box, you will receive an error message. Click OK to close the error message and reenter the password in the Confirm Password dialog box.

PAUSE. LEAVE the workbook open to use in the next exercise.

When you saved the Payroll Data workbook in the first exercise in this section, it could be viewed by anyone with access to your computer system or network. As you saw when you opened the file in this exercise, the workbook could be viewed, but the SSN worksheet could not be modified. If you saved the file with a different name, that file also would be protected, and you could not alter the data without the password that protects that worksheet.

Protecting the structure of a workbook prevents users from viewing worksheets that you have hidden; inserting new worksheets; or moving, deleting, hiding, or changing the names of worksheets. Selecting the Windows box on the Protect Structure and Windows dialog box (refer to Figure 9-21) prevents the user from changing the size and position of the windows when the workbook is opened.

Allowing Multiple Users to Edit a Workbook Simultaneously

Creating and updating workbooks is frequently a collaborative process. A worksheet or workbook is often routed to other employees so that they can verify data or make changes. In Excel, you can create a **shared workbook**, or one that is set up to allow multiple users on a network to view and make changes at the same time. When a user opens a shared workbook, he or she can see the changes made and saved by other users. The Protect and Share Workbook command prevents a user from disabling the change-tracking option.

For example, the workbook you create in this exercise will be used by the medical assistants, who will record all sample medications the physicians prescribe for patients. Sharing this workbook means that more than one medical assistant can access the workbook and enter data at the same time. In this exercise, you will learn how to allow users to simultaneously edit workbooks.

STEP BY STEP   **Allow Multiple Users to Edit a Workbook Simultaneously**

GET READY. LAUNCH Excel if it is not already running.

1. **CREATE** a new blank workbook.
2. Select A1:D1 and click Merge & Center in the Alignment group on the Home tab.
3. Key Sample Drugs Dispensed in the newly merged cell and press Enter.
4. Select A1, click Cell Styles, and then click Heading 1 in the Cell Style gallery that appears.
5. Begin in cell A3 and enter the following data:

Medical Assistant	Drug	Patient
Delamore, Luca	Cipro	Chor, Anthony
Hamilton, David	Ketek	Brundage, Michael
Hoeing, Helge	Lipitor	Charles, Matthew
Hamilton, David	Altace	Bishop, Scott
Esteves, Janeth	Zetia	Anderson, Nancy
Esteves, Janeth	Cipro	Coleman, Pat
Hagens, Erin	Avelox	Nayberg, Alex
Hagens, Erin	Norvasc	Kleinerman, Christian

6. Click on cell D3 and key Date. In the Date column, apply today's date to all the above records.

7. Select A3:D3 and apply the Heading 3 style.

8. Save the workbook as *Sample Medications*.

9. Click the Review tab, then click Share Workbook in the Changes group.

10. In the Share Workbook dialog box, click Allow changes by more than one user at the same time. This also allows workbook merging. Your identification will appear in the *Who has this workbook open now* box, as shown in Figure 9-25. Click OK.

Figure 9-25

Sharing a workbook

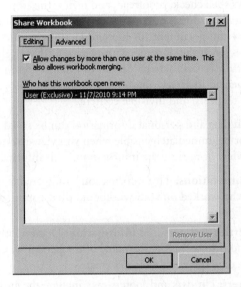

11. Click OK when the dialog box shown in Figure 9-26 opens.

Figure 9-26

Saving and closing a shared workbook

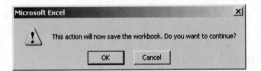

12. Click Protect Shared Workbook in the Changes group. Select the Sharing with track changes check box in the *Protect* Shared Workbook dialog box. Click OK.

13. Notice that [*Shared*] appears in the title bar.

SAVE and **CLOSE** the workbook.

PAUSE. LEAVE Excel open to use in the next exercise.

In a shared workbook, information is maintained about changes made in past editing sessions. The **change history** includes the name of the person who made each change, when the change was made, and what data was changed.

A shared workbook does not support all Excel features. For example, you can include merged cells, conditional formats, data validation, charts, and so on before a workbook is shared, but these features cannot be added by those who edit a shared workbook.

When you protected your shared workbook, you prevented those who use the workbook from removing the change history. By default, changes made in the workbook will be retained for 30 days. You can increase that time frame on the Advanced tab of the Share Workbook dialog box (refer to Figure 9-25).

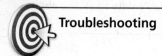

Troubleshooting If you want to assign a password to a shared workbook, you must assign it before the workbook is shared. You can also unshare a workbook and add the password. However, when you unshare a shared workbook, the change history is lost.

Using the Document Inspector

Before you share an important document with colleagues or individuals outside your organization, you should always spell check, proofread, and review the contents to ensure that everything is correct and the document does not contain anything you do not want to share with others. You should also review the document for hidden data or personal information that might be stored in the workbook or in the document properties. In Excel, the Document Inspector displays several different Inspectors that enable you to find and remove hidden data and personal information that is specific to Excel workbooks. Document Inspector will also locate custom XML data, hidden worksheets, and invisible content.

Several types of hidden data and personal information can be saved in an Excel workbook. This information might not be immediately visible when you view the document, but it still may be possible for others to view or retrieve the information. This information includes the following:

- **Comments and annotations:** This information would enable other people to see the names of people who worked on your workbook, their comments, and changes that were made to the workbook.

- **Document properties and personal information:** Document properties include the author, subject, and title, as well as the name of the person who most recently saved the workbook and the date the workbook was created.

- **Headers and footers:** Headers and footers may include the author's name, the date the file was created, etc.

- **Hidden rows, columns, and worksheets:** Columns D and E were hidden in the SSN worksheet to protect salary data. Before removing hidden rows or columns, be sure that their removal will not change calculations in your worksheet.

STEP BY STEP   **Use the Document Inspector**

OPEN *Employee ID* from the data files for this lesson. Then, perform these steps:

1. Click the File tab, click Save As, and key Employee ID Copy in the File name box to save a copy of the workbook. Click the Save button.

Troubleshooting It is a good idea to perform an inspection on a copy of your worksheet because you might not be able to restore hidden content that you remove in the inspection process. If you attempt to inspect a document that has unsaved changes, you will be prompted to save the document before completing the inspection.

WileyPLUS Extra! features an online tutorial of this task.

2. In the copy of your original workbook, click the File tab. Then, with Info clicked, click the Check for Issues button in the middle pane of the Backstage view window. Next, click Inspect Document. The Document Inspector dialog box opens, as shown in Figure 9-27.

Figure 9-27

Document Inspector dialog box

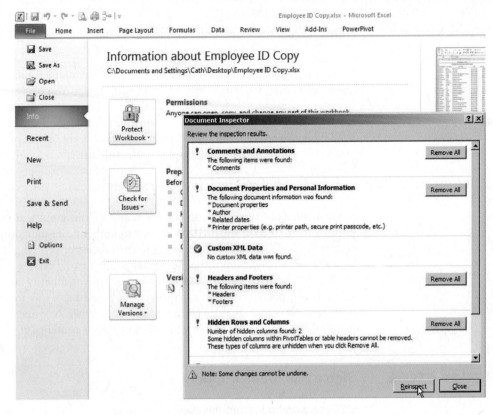

3. Click Inspect. The Document Inspector results shown in Figure 9-27 are returned.
4. Click Remove All for Comments and Annotations.

Take Note   You must remove each type of hidden data individually. You can re-inspect the document after you remove items.

5. Click Remove All for Document Properties and Personal Information.
6. Click Remove All for Hidden Rows and Columns. Headers and Footers should be the only hidden item remaining (Figure 9-28). Click the Close button to close the Document Inspector results dialog box.

Figure 9-28

Remove All command for hidden rows

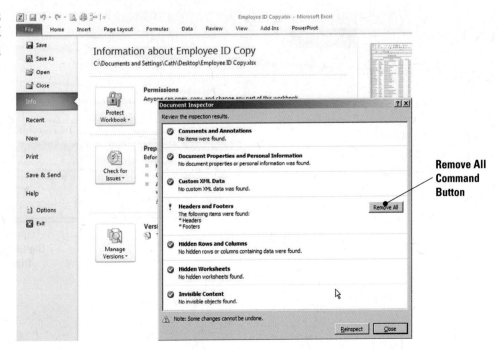

Remove All Command Button

7. SAVE the workbook.

PAUSE. LEAVE the workbook open to use in the next exercise.

When you opened the data file in this exercise, it contained hidden columns as well as other information that you didn't want to share with others. You first created a copy of your original worksheet because it is not always possible to restore data that the Document Inspector removes. For that reason, you removed sensitive information from the copy; the complete data is retained in the original workbook. If the original workbook was protected, the copy will also be protected, and Read-Only will display in the title bar.

Signing a Workbook Digitally

You can digitally sign a document for many of the same reasons you would sign a paper document. A **digital signature** is used to authenticate digital information using computer cryptography. **Authentication** refers to the process of verifying that people and products are who and what they claim to be. To digitally sign a workbook, you must have a current digital certificate. A **digital certificate** is a means of proving identity and authenticity. Digital certificates make it possible for digital signatures to be used as a way to authenticate digital information. You can get a digital ID from a Microsoft partner, or you can create your own digital ID. A digital signature is not visible within a document's contents.

STEP BY STEP | **Sign a Workbook Digitally**

USE the workbook from the previous exercise.

1. Click the **File** tab, click **Info**, then click **Protect Workbook**; when the *Protect Workbook* drop-down menu appears, click **Add a Digital Signature**. A dialog box opens that explains digital signatures. Read the message and click **OK**. If you or your organization does not have a valid digital certificate, the *Get a Digital ID* dialog box shown in Figure 9-29 opens.

Figure 9-29

Get a digital ID

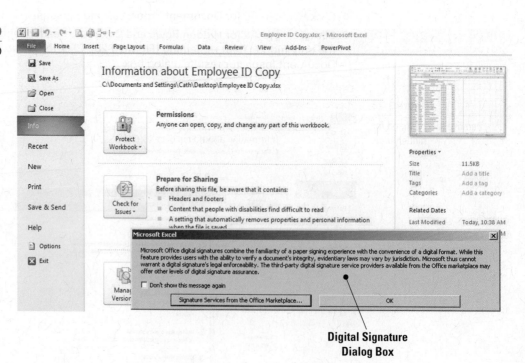

Digital Signature Dialog Box

Take Note The Get a Digital ID dialog box opens only if you select Add a Digital Signature and you do not have a digital certificate. If the document contains unsaved changes, the file is automatically saved when you click Add a Digital Signature.

If one or more digital certificates are available on your computer or network, a Sign dialog box opens so that you can sign the document.

2. Click OK. In the Get a Digital ID dialog box, click Create your own Digital ID and click OK.

3. Enter the information shown in Figure 9-30 and click Create.

Figure 9-30

Creating your own digital ID

4. In the *Purpose for signing this document* box that appears, key Transmission to CPA for tax purposes. Click Sign. A message is displayed indicating that your signature has been successfully saved with the document. If the document is changed, the signature will become invalid. Click OK. Backstage view now displays two new orange highlighted buttons in the middle of the Info screen. They are *View Signatures* with a title of Signed Workbook and *Protect Workbook* with a title of Permissions. See Figure 9-31.

Figure 9-31

Digital Signature created

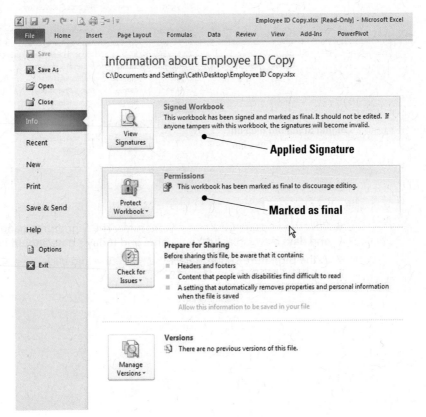

5. Click the Home tab. On the Status bar, in the bottom left corner of the Excel window, point to the Signature icon. A ScreenTip stating *This document contains signatures* is displayed. Note at the top of the worksheet that a notice indicates that *An author has marked this workbook as final to discourage editing*, as illustrated in Figure 9-32.

Marked as Final Notice in Worksheet

Digital Signature icon on status bar

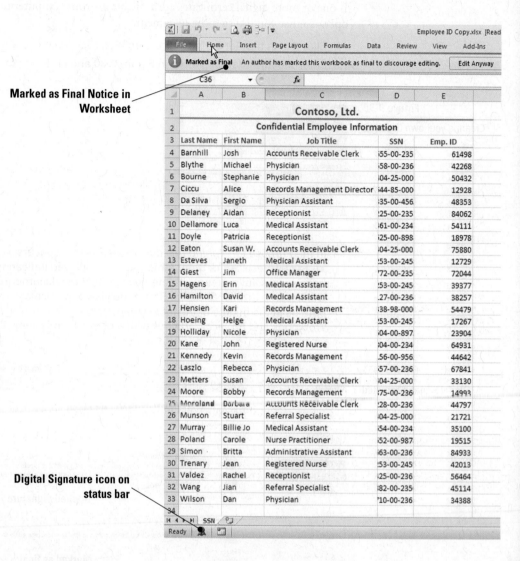

6. Click the File tab. Click View Signatures. The Signatures pane opens and the signature and date are displayed. Your name and today's date should be visible in the pane.

7. In the Signatures pane, select the signature and click the arrow to display the drop-down menu. Refer to Figure 9-33.

Signatures Pane

Figure 9-33

Digital signature drop-down
menu

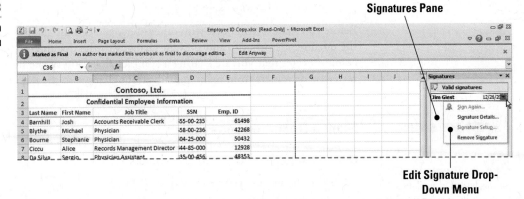

Signatures Pane

**Edit Signature Drop-
Down Menu**

Another Way
You can also click
the Signatures icon on the
Status bar to display the Signatures task pane.

8. Click Signature Details. The Signature Details dialog box indicates that the signature and the signed content have not been modified since the signature was applied. The worksheet is now protected so that the signature can be authenticated. Click the Close button to close the dialog box.

9. **SAVE** the workbook. (Remember, you named this file in the beginning of this section.)

CLOSE the workbook. **PAUSE. LEAVE** Excel open to use in the next exercise.

Take Note   The workbook was saved when you created the signature. There is no need to save again. If you use the Save As command after a signature has been added to a document, the signature will become invalid.

If you plan to exchange digitally signed documents, you should obtain a digital certificate from a reputable certificate authority. A **certificate authority (CA)** is a third-party entity that issues digital certificates to be used by others, keeps track of who is assigned to a certificate, signs certificates to verify their validity, and tracks which certificates are revoked or expired. Many organizations issue their own certificates, as you did in the exercise on behalf of Contoso, Ltd.

If you select the Get a digital ID from a Microsoft Partner option when you want to add a digital signature, you will be redirected to the Microsoft Office Marketplace where you can purchase a certificate.

If you do not want to purchase a digital certificate from a CA, you can create your own digital certificate as you did in this exercise. However, other people cannot verify the authenticity of your digital signature. It can be authenticated only on the computer on which you created the certificate.

When you review a signed document, you should look at the signature details and the certificate used to create that signature to find out if there are potential problems. When a workbook contains a signature, a Signature icon displays in the Status bar.

Marking a Document as Final

Before you share a workbook with other users, you can use the Mark as Final command to make the document read-only and prevent changes to the document. Marking a document as final communicates that you are sharing a completed version of the document, and it helps prevent reviewers or readers from making inadvertent changes to the document.

STEP BY STEP　　　**Mark a Document as Final**

@ The *Employee ID* file for this lesson is available on the book companion website or in WileyPLUS.

OPEN the *Employee ID* file for this lesson.

1. **SAVE** the workbook as *Employee ID Final*.
2. Click the File tab, click the Protect Workbook button in the left pane of the Backstage view window, and click Mark as Final, as shown in Figure 9-34.

Figure 9-34

Mark as Final

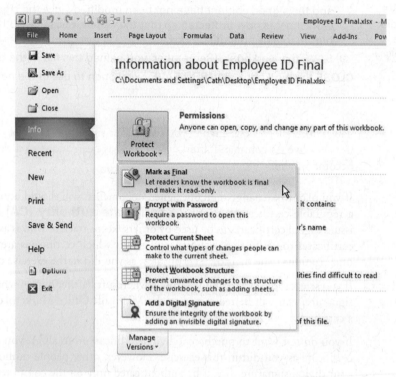

3. The Excel message dialog box opens indicating that the workbook will be marked as final and saved. This also means that the file has become read-only, meaning you can't edit it. Click OK.

4. An Excel message explains that the document has been marked as final. Click OK. If another dialog box is displayed indicating that this is the final version of the document, click OK. Click on the Home tab and notice a Marked as Final icon appears in the Status bar (Figure 9-35).

Figure 9-35

Marked as Final icon on the status bar

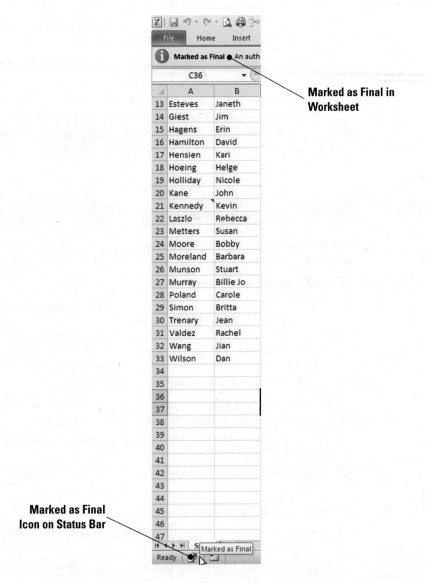

PAUSE. LEAVE the workbook open to use in the next exercise.

The Mark as Final command is not a security feature. Anyone who opens a workbook that has been marked as final can edit the document by removing the Mark as Final status from the document. Documents marked as final in an Excel 2007 workbook will not be read-only because Mark as Final was not an option in previous Excel versions.

To enable editing for a document that is marked as final, click the File tab, click on Protect Workbook, and click Mark as Final to deselect that option. The Read-Only designation will be removed from the workbook.

DISTRIBUTING A WORKBOOK BY EMAIL

The Bottom Line

The most common ways to share Excel data are by sending workbooks through email, by faxing workbooks, and by printing and distributing hard copies. Email allows you to share a workbook by routing it to one user who can make changes or add comments and then route the workbook to the next user. Changes can then be incorporated into a final document. You can email a workbook as an attachment from Excel or from your email program. You can also send a worksheet as an email message rather than as an attachment.

Distributing a Workbook by Email

The option to send a worksheet as an email message is available only from the Send to Mail Recipient command on the Quick Access Toolbar. When you add this command to the toolbar, you can use this option as a shortcut to send a workbook as an attachment. In the next set of exercises, you will learn how to send a workbook from Excel, send a worksheet as an email, and send a workbook as an attached file.

STEP BY STEP

Distribute a Workbook by Email

USE the workbook you saved in the previous exercise. Note that you must have an email program and Internet connection to complete the following exercises.

To send a workbook from Excel:

1. Click the File tab and click Save & Send in the navigation bar. Click Send Using E-mail in the Save & Send window. Click the Send as Attachment button. When you have Office 2010 installed, this feature will open Outlook by default. If you have changed your environment, your own personal email program will open. Notice that Excel automatically attaches the workbook to your email message.
2. Key your instructor's email address in the To field.
3. In the subject line, key Employee Final Attached as per request.
4. In the email message body, key The Employee ID Final workbook is attached.
5. Click Send. Your email with the workbook attached to it will now be sent to your instructor.

CLOSE the workbook. **LEAVE** Excel open for the next exercise.

To send a worksheet as an email message:

@ The *Employee ID* file for this lesson is available on the book companion website or in WileyPLUS.

1. **OPEN** the *Employee ID* file from the student data files for this lesson. **SAVE** the file as *Employee ID Recipient*.
2. Click the File tab, Click on Protect Workbook, and click Mark as Final.
3. Click the File tab and click Options in the Navigation bar. The *Excel Options* Window opens.
4. Click Customize Quick Access Toolbar. In the *Choose Commands From* field, click on E-mail to highlight. In the center bar between the left and right fields click Add. This step adds the email button to the Quick Access Toolbar.
5. In the Choose Commands drop-down box, click All Commands. Scroll and find Send to Mail Recipient and click to highlight it. In the center bar between the left and right fields, click Add. This step will add this command to the Toolbar.
6. Click OK to save both commands to the Toolbar.
7. On the Quick Access Toolbar, click Send to Mail Recipient.
8. The E-mail dialog box opens, as described in the first exercise in this group. Since the document is marked as final, *Send to Mail Recipients* is disabled. To disable Final, return to the Home tab and click the Edit Anyway button that appears at the top of the screen.

9. Click the Send the current sheet as the message body option, as shown in Figure 9-36, then click OK. The email window is now embedded in your Excel screen with the current worksheet visible as the body of the email.

Figure 9-36

E-mail dialog box

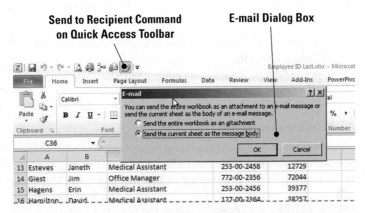

10. Key your instructor's email address in the To field.

11. Key Worksheet ready to e-mail in the subject line.

12. Click the Send this Selection button on the email message toolbar above the email information, as illustrated in Figure 9-37. Click OK.

Figure 9-37

Send to recipient

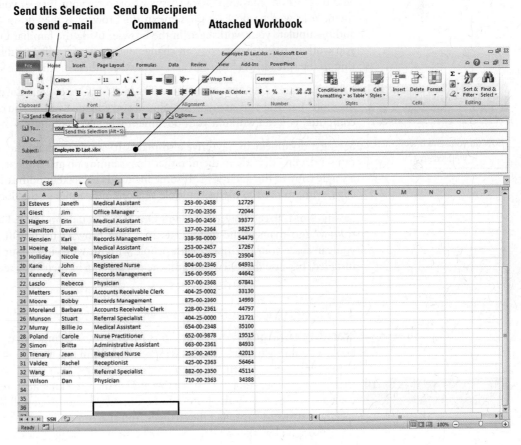

13. **SAVE** the workbook.

CLOSE the workbook. **LEAVE** Excel open for the next exercise.

To send a workbook from your email program:

1. **LAUNCH** your email program. Create a new email message.
2. Key your instructor's email address in the To field.
3. Key Employee ID Final ready to send in the subject line.
4. Click Attach File.
5. Navigate to the Lesson 9 folder where you saved *Employee ID Final*. Click the filename, then click Open.
6. In the message area, key The Employee ID Copy workbook is attached in the email message.
7. Click Send.
8. **CLOSE** the workbook.

 Troubleshooting Some email programs will not send a document as an attachment if the document is open on your computer. If you receive such a message, close the document, and click Send again.

PAUSE. LEAVE Excel open to use in the next exercise.

With the addition of Excel Web App to Office 2010, all you need to access your workbooks is a browser. Your colleagues can work with you, regardless of which version of Excel they have. When you click on an Excel workbook that is stored in a SharePoint site on a network or in Sky-Drive, the workbook opens directly in your browser. Windows Live SkyDrive is a virtual online storage area where users are able to store, access, and share thousands of documents, photos, and Microsoft Office files. SkyDrive password-protects your files so you control who has access to them. Your workbooks look the same in the browser as they do in Excel. You can also manage and manipulate your worksheets in the browser using the familiar look and feel of Excel. When you work in the browser, you can change data, enter or edit formulas, and apply basic formatting to the spreadsheet. You can also work with others on the same workbook at the same time.

When you save a document in Windows Live SkyDrive, your document is stored in a central location that you can access from almost anywhere. Even if you're away from your primary computer, you can work on your document whenever you have a connection to the web.

Saving a document in SkyDrive also makes it simple to share the document with others. You can send a link directly to them, rather than sending an attachment. This way, you preserve just a single copy of the document. If someone needs to make modifications, they do so in the same copy, with no need to merge multiple versions and copies of the document.

Saving Word, Excel, PowerPoint, and OneNote documents in SkyDrive enables you and others to view and manage the documents in a web browser using Office Web Apps. This means you can share your document with people without worrying about what application they have installed, because they view and edit the documents in their browser.

TRACKING CHANGES TO A WORKBOOK

The Bottom Line

Tracking changes is the ability to mark and track changes that have been made to a workbook. The ability to track changes is especially helpful in a workbook that is shared and modified by multiple users. When you turn on Track Changes, the workbook automatically becomes a shared workbook. You can customize the change-tracking feature to track specific types of changes, you can allow the feature to be turned on and off at will by various users, or you can specify a password to protect the changes. You also can decide whether to accept or reject changes to your original workbook data. When you turn off change tracking, the workbook is no longer a shared workbook.

Turning Track Changes On and Off

You can turn on change tracking using the Track Changes command, the Share Workbook command, or the Protect and Share Workbook command (all located on the Review tab). The Protect and Share Workbook command provides the highest level of security. When workbooks are shared, it is often important to know what changes were made by each user. The owner (creator) of the workbook can use change-tracking functions to manage the data in a shared workbook. The owner can use the change history record to manage the shared workbook by adding or removing users and resolving conflicting changes. In the next exercise, you will learn to track changes.

STEP BY STEP	**Turn Track Changes On and Off**

The *Sample Medications* file for this lesson is available on the book companion website or in WileyPLUS.

GET READY. LAUNCH Excel if it is not already running.

1. **OPEN** the *Sample Medications* data file for this lesson.
2. **SAVE** the workbook as *Samples* in the Lesson 9 folder.
3. On the Review tab, in the Changes group, click the Protect and Share Workbook button. The *Protect Shared Workbook* dialog box opens.
4. In the dialog box, click Sharing with track changes. When you choose this option, the Create Password text box becomes active. You can assign a password at this time, but it is not necessary. Click OK.
5. Click OK when asked if you want to continue and save the workbook. You have now marked the workbook to save tracked changes.

PAUSE. LEAVE the workbook open to use in the next exercise.

You can turn change tracking on and off in several ways. When you click the Share Workbook command on the Review tab, change tracking is automatically turned on. Using the Protect and Share Workbook command provides the highest level of security. Before the workbook is shared, the creator can enter a password that must be used to turn off change tracking. This protects the change history. Here, no one has the ability to delete any worksheet changes except the author.

Ⓧ Ref

The Track Changes command allows you to manage how changes are displayed on your screen. You will use this option in a following exercise .

Take Note

Turning off Track Changes removes the change history and removes the shared status of the workbook, but changes already shown in the document will remain until you accept or reject them.

Setting Track Change Options

The Advanced tab of the Share Workbook dialog box allows you to customize the shared use of the workbook. These options are normally set by the workbook author before the workbook is shared. In this exercise, you will modify these options.

STEP BY STEP   Set Track Change Options

USE the workbook from the previous exercise.

1. On the Review tab, in the Changes group, click Share Workbook; the Share Workbook dialog box opens.

2. Click the Advanced tab. See Figure 9-38.

Figure 9-38

Track changes options

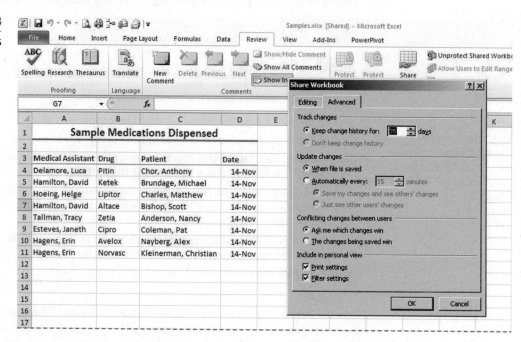

3. In the *Keep Change History For* box, click the scroll arrow to display 35.

4. Click OK to accept the default settings in the remainder of the options.

PAUSE. LEAVE the workbook open to use in the next exercise.

The Advanced tab contains four options. *Track changes* determines whether a change history is kept and the length of time it is kept. In a shared workbook, the change history documents changes made in past editing sessions. The information includes the name of the person who made each change, when the changes were made, and what data was changed. The default setting is 30 days. Contoso maintains a monthly record of the distribution of samples. Setting the change history to 35 days ensures that the office manger has sufficient time to review the workbook and resolve any conflicting changes before the change history is deleted.

Update changes controls when changes made to the shared workbook are incorporated into the workbook. *Conflicting changes between users* determines whose edits become part of the file if two or more people are attempting to edit at the same time. The workbook owner's changes usually take precedence. *Include in personal view* enables each user who edits the workbook to see a personal view of the workbook.

Inserting Tracked Changes

When you open a shared workbook, change tracking is automatically turned on. In most cases, the workbook owner will have entered a password to prevent a user from turning off change tracking. Thus, any text you key in the workbook will be tracked.

STEP BY STEP   **Insert Tracked Changes**

USE the workbook from the previous exercise.

1. On the Review tab, in the Changes group, click Track Changes; in the drop-down list that appears, click Highlight Changes. The Highlight Changes dialog box appears.

2. The *Track changes while editing* box is inactive because change tracking was activated when you shared the workbook. As shown in Figure 9-39, in *When*, click the down arrow and then select All. In *Who*, select Everyone. If the Highlight changes on screen option is not already selected, then select it. Click OK. A warning box appears; click OK to accept the warning as there are no current changes and you will make changes in the steps to follow.

Figure 9-39

Inserting tracked changes

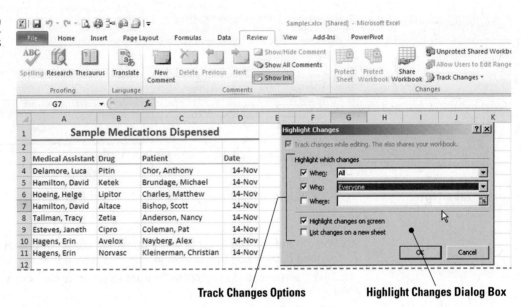

Track Changes Options   **Highlight Changes Dialog Box**

3. Click the File tab and click Options in the navigation bar. The Excel Options window opens.

4. In the General category, under *Personalize your copy of Microsoft Office*, in the User name box, key Luca Delamore. Click OK. You have changed the document user name that will be listed in the track changes.

5. Select A12 and enter the following information in A12, A13, and A14:

Delamore, Luca	Avelox	LaMee, Brian	14-Nov
Delamore, Luca	Ketek	Miller, Ben	14-Nov
Delamore, Luca	Cipro	Kearney, Bonnie	14-Nov

As you enter these changes, a colored triangle and comment box appear for each entry made. This makes it easy to view the changes later.

6. Click Save on the Quick Access Toolbar to save the changes you made under the user name Luca Delamore.

7. Click the File tab and select Options.

8. In the User name box, key Billie Jo Murray. Click OK. You are once again changing the user name and applying it to the document.

9. Key the following data in A15, A16, and A17. Note your changes to the worksheet, as illustrated in Figure 9-40:

Murray, Billie Jo	Zetia	Peters, James	15-Nov
Murray, Billie Jo	Cipro	Smith, Samantha	15-Nov
Murray, Billie Jo	Ketek	Ruth, Andy	15-Nov

Figure 9-40

Tracked changes in
a worksheet

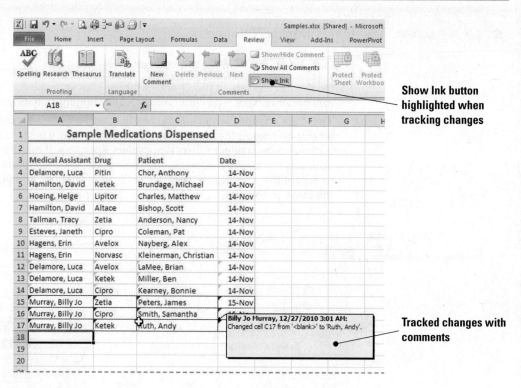

Take Note   Make a note of the name that you remove. You will restore the original user name at the end of this lesson.

10. Point to the colored triangle in the upper-left corner of one of the cells in which you entered data. A box opens with information about the changes made to that cell.

11. Click **Save** on the Quick Access Toolbar to save the changes you made under the user name Billie Jo Murray.

PAUSE. LEAVE the workbook open to use in the next exercise.

On a network, you do not see changes made by other users until both they and you save your changes. To save your changes to a shared workbook and to see the changes that other users have saved since your last save, click Save on the Quick Access Toolbar. Note that when you are working in a network environment, you can click Share Workbook in the Changes group and see a list of other users who have the workbook open.

Sometimes conflicts occur when two users are editing a shared workbook and try to save changes that affect the same cell. When the second user tries to save the workbook, Excel displays the Resolve Conflicts dialog box. Depending on the options established when the workbook was created and shared, you can either keep your change or accept the change made by the other user.

You can also display a list that shows how past conflicts have been resolved. These can be viewed on a separate worksheet that displays the name of the person who made the change, when and where it was made, what data was deleted or replaced, and how conflicts were resolved.

Deleting Your Changes

As noted previously, the changes you make in a shared workbook are not visible to other users until you save your work. Changes thus become a part of the change history only when you save. If you change your mind before saving, you can edit or delete any change. Changes must be saved before you can accept or reject them. If you do not save, Excel displays a message that the workbook must be saved before you can accept or reject changes. When you have saved your workbook and you want to delete a change, you can either enter new data or reject the change you made before saving.

Delete Your Changes

USE the workbook from the previous exercise.

1. Click the File tab and click Options.

2. In the General category, under *Personalize your copy of Microsoft Office*, in the User name box, key Erin Hagens. Click OK. You have again changed the user of the workbook for change tracking purposes.

3. Select A17 and enter the following data in A17, A18, and A19. You will replace data in row 17.

Hagens, Erin	Cipro	Berry, Jo	15-Nov
Hagens, Erin	Norvasc	Corets, Eva	15-Nov
Hagens, Erin	Altace	Beebe, Ann	15-Nov

SAVE the changes.

Take Note   Undo is inactive in a shared workbook. If you accidentally replace your data or another user's, you will need to reject the change to restore the data you replaced.

4. Click Track Changes and click Accept/Reject Changes from the drop-down menu that appears. Excel displays a message box confirming that you want to save the workbook; click OK. The Select Changes to Accept or Reject Dialog box opens.

5. On the Select Changes to Accept or Reject dialog box, click the Who drop-down arrow and select Erin Hagens, then click OK. You have just asked Excel to return only the tracked changes made by Erin Hagens. (See Figure 9-41.)

Figure 9-41

Select changes to accept or reject dialog box

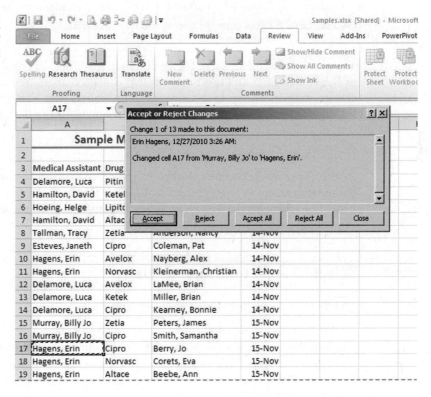

6. A17 is selected on the worksheet and the change you made to A17 is displayed. Click Reject. A17 displays the text you replaced and the cell selector moves to B17.

7. Reject the changes to B17, C17, and D17. Click Close.

8. Key the following information, beginning in A20:

| Hagens, Erin | Cipro | Berry, Jo | 15-Nov |

9. **SAVE** the workbook.

PAUSE. LEAVE the workbook open to use in the next exercise.

If you replace another user's data and you want to restore the original data, you should reject your change. If you instead delete text you entered as a replacement for other text, you will leave the cell or range blank. Rejecting your change restores the entry that you replaced.

Accepting Changes from Another User

After a shared workbook has been edited, you can easily identify which cells have been changed and determine whether you want to keep or reject the changes. You can choose to accept or reject all changes at one time without reviewing each change, or you can accept or reject them individually. In the following exercise you will learn how to accept changes from other users.

STEP BY STEP   **Accept Changes from Another User**

USE the workbook from the previous exercise.

1. Click the File tab and click Options.
2. In the General category, under *Personalize your copy of Microsoft Office*, in the User name box, key Jim Giest. Click OK.
3. Click Track Changes and select Accept/Reject Changes from the drop-down list.
4. *Not yet reviewed* will be selected by default. In the Who box, select Luca Delamore. Click OK. The Accept or Reject Changes dialog box is displayed.
5. Click Accept as each change is tracked and displayed. The Accept or Reject Changes dialog box closes when you have accepted all changes made by Luca Delamore.

PAUSE. LEAVE Excel open to use in the next exercise.

You can also click the Collapse Dialog button in the Where box on the Select Changes to Accept or Reject dialog box and select the cells that contain changes. You can then accept or reject the changes in their entirety. In this exercise, some changes were highlighted by cell and others were highlighted by row, and you could accept or reject changes to the selected cell or range.

Rejecting Changes from Another User

As the owner of the Samples workbook, the office manager in the following exercise has the authority to accept or reject changes by all users. Rejecting changes, however, does not prohibit a user from changing the data again. When all users have made the necessary changes, the owner can remove users and unshare the workbook.

STEP BY STEP   **Reject Changes from Another User**

USE the workbook from the previous exercise.

1. Click Track Changes and click Accept/Reject Changes.
2. Click the Collapse Dialog button 📷 on the right side of the Where box.
3. Select the data in row 16 and click the Expand Dialog button. Click OK to close the Select Changes to Accept or Reject dialog box. The Accept or Reject Changes dialog box is displayed.
4. Click Reject for each cell containing data in the row. The data is removed and row 16 is now blank.
5. SAVE the workbook as *Samples Edited*.

PAUSE. LEAVE the workbook open to use in the next exercise.

When you have the opportunity to work with a shared workbook that is saved on a network, you will likely encounter conflicts when you attempt to save a change that affects the same cell as another user's changes. In the Resolve Conflicts dialog box, you can read the information about each change and the conflicting changes made by another user. The options set on the Advanced tab of the Share Workbook dialog box determine how conflicts are resolved.

Removing Shared Status from a Workbook

Before you stop sharing a workbook, make sure that all other users have completed their work and that you have accepted or rejected all changes. Any unsaved changes will be lost when you stop sharing and the history worksheet will be deleted. Thus, before you remove the shared status from a workbook, you should print the history worksheet and/or copy it to another workbook. In this exercise, you will remove shared status from a workbook.

STEP BY STEP   **Remove Shared Status from a Workbook**

USE the workbook from the previous exercise.

1. On the Review tab, in the Changes group, click Track Changes, and then click Highlight Changes.

2. In the *When* box, All is selected by default. This tells Excel to search through all tracked changes made to the worksheet.

3. Clear the Who and Where check boxes if they are selected.

4. Click the List Changes On a New Sheet check box. Click OK. A History sheet is added to the workbook.

5. On the History worksheet, click the Select All button in the corner of the worksheet adjacent to the first column and first row. Click the Home tab, and then click the Copy button in the Clipboard group.

6. Press Ctrl+N to open a new workbook.

7. In the new workbook, in the Clipboard group on the Home tab, click Paste.

8. **SAVE** the new workbook as *Medications History*. **CLOSE** the workbook.

Take Note   It is a good idea to print the current version of a shared workbook as well as the change history, because cell locations in the copied history may no longer be valid if additional changes are made.

9. In the shared workbook, on the Review tab, click Unprotect Shared Workbook.

10. Click Share Workbook. The *Share Workbook* dialog box is displayed. On the Editing tab, make sure that you (Jim Giest) are the only user listed in the *Who Has This Workbook Open Now* list.

11. Clear the *Allow Changes By More Than One User At The Same Time* option. This also allows the workbook merging check box to become active. Click OK to close the dialog box.

12. A dialog box opens to prompt you about removing the workbook from shared use. Click Yes to turn off the workbook's shared status. The word Shared is removed from the title bar.

13. **SAVE** and **CLOSE** the workbook.

PAUSE. LEAVE Excel open to use in the next exercise.

When shared status has been removed from a workbook, changes can be made like they are made in any workbook. You can, of course, turn change tracking on again, which will automatically share the workbook.

ADDING COMMENTS TO A WORKBOOK

The Bottom Line

In Excel, you can add a note to a cell by inserting a comment. You can also edit the text in comments and delete any comments that you no longer need. Comments are marked by a red triangle in the upper-right corner of the cell. When you point to this triangle, the comment appears in a box next to the cell, along with the name of the user logged on to the computer at the time the comment was created.

Inserting a Comment

Comments are a useful technique for calling attention to important or significant data and providing insights from the user that explain more about the data. For example, say that Contoso's employees are evaluated on three performance measures. The manager uses comments to note incidents related to these measures. In this exercise, you will learn how to insert comments.

STEP BY STEP   **Insert a Comment**

@ The *Personnel Evaluations* file for this lesson is available on the book companion website or in WileyPLUS.

GET READY. LAUNCH Excel if it is not already running.

1. **OPEN** the *Personnel Evaluations* data file for this lesson.
2. Select cell F11. On the Review tab in the Comments group, click New Comment. The comment text box opens for editing.
3. Key Frequently to work late. Then, click outside the comment box. (See Figure 9-42.)

Figure 9-42

New comment text box

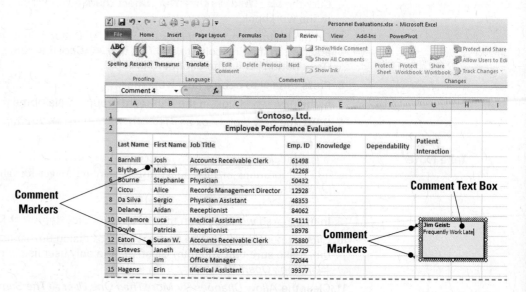

4. Select E8. Click New Comment and key Currently completing Masters degree program for additional certification. Click outside the comment box. The box disappears and a red triangle remains in the upper-right corner of the cell the comment was placed in.
5. Select F20. Click New Comment and key Adjusted hours for family emergency. Click outside the comment box.
6. Select G4. Click New Comment and key Consider salary increase. Click outside the comment box.
7. **SAVE** the workbook as *Performance Evaluations*.

PAUSE. LEAVE the workbook open to use in the next exercise.

CERTIFICATION READY   7.2.1

How do you insert comments?

As previously mentioned, Contoso, Ltd., conducts an annual employee performance review. In this workbook, the manager uses comments to note events or actions that he wants to recall when he conducts employees' annual reviews. Excel automatically displays the name that appears in the Name box under Global Office Settings on the Excel Options dialog box. If you don't want to use a name, you can select it in the comment and press Delete.

Viewing a Comment

When you rest your pointer over the red triangle that indicates that a cell has a comment attached to it, the comment is displayed. You can keep selected comments visible as you work, or you can display all comments using commands in the Comments group on the Review tab. The Show/Hide Comment and Show All Comments commands allow you to display or hide comments as needed. The Previous and Next commands allow you to move from one comment to another without selecting the cells.

STEP BY STEP   **View a Comment**

USE the workbook you saved in the previous exercise.

1. Select E8 and click Show/Hide Comment in the Comments group on the Review tab. Note that the comment remains visible when you click outside the cell.
2. Select G4 and click Show/Hide Comment. Again, the comment remains visible when you click outside the cell.
3. Select E8 and click Show/Hide Comment. The comment is hidden.
4. In the Comments group, click Next twice to navigate to the next available comment. The comment in cell F11 is displayed.
5. In the Comments group, click Show All Comments. Both your comments and those entered by others are displayed.
6. In the Comments group, click Show All Comments again to hide all comments and make sure they are no longer displayed. **SAVE** the workbook.

PAUSE. **LEAVE** the workbook open to use in the next exercise.

CERTIFICATION READY   7.2.2

How do you view comments?

Editing a Comment

Comments can be edited and formatted as needed. You can format a comment using most of the formatting options on the Home tab in the Font group. However, the Fill Color and Font Color options are not available for comment text. To edit a comment, select the cell containing the comment and click Edit Comment.

STEP BY STEP   **Edit a Comment**

USE the workbook from the previous exercise.

1. Select cell F11 and click the Edit Comment button on the Review tab. (See Figure 9-43.)

Figure 9-43

Editing a comment

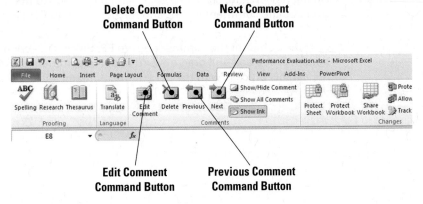

Delete Comment Command Button

Next Comment Command Button

Edit Comment Command Button

Previous Comment Command Button

2. Following the existing comment text, key Placed on probation. Then click any cell between F11 and E8.

3. Click Previous. The comment in E8 is displayed.

4. Select the comment text in E8 and key MA completed; can now prescribe medications.

5. Select G4 and click Edit Comment.

6. Select the text in the comment attached to G4. On the Home tab, click Bold.

7. Select F14, click the Review tab, and click Edit Comment.

8. Select the name and the comment text. Right-click and select Format Comment.

9. In the Format Comment dialog box, click the arrow in the Color box and click Red. Click OK to apply the format and close the dialog box.

10. SAVE the workbook.

PAUSE. LEAVE the workbook open to use in the next exercise.

CERTIFICATION READY   7.2.3

How do you edit comments?

Deleting a Comment

Of course, you can delete comments from a workbook when they are no longer needed. Unless the workbook is protected, any user can delete comments—so you should consider protecting a workbook that contains sensitive or confidential information. In this exercise, you will learn to delete a comment.

STEP BY STEP   **Delete a Comment**

Another Way
To delete a comment, you can click Show/Hide on the Review tab to display the comment and then double-click the comment text box and press Delete. You can also right-click on the comment and choose Delete from the drop-down menu that appears.

USE the workbook from the previous exercise.

1. Select F20. The comment for this cell is displayed.

2. On the Review tab, click Delete in the Comments group.

3. SAVE the workbook with the same name.

PAUSE. LEAVE the workbook open to use in the next exercise.

CERTIFICATION READY   7.2.4

How do you delete a comment?

Printing Comments in a Workbook

Anyone with access to a workbook can view the comments made by all users. As you learned in a previous exercise, comments can be removed from a workbook before the workbook is shared or copies are distributed. Comments can also be printed as they appear in the worksheet or on a separate page following the workbook. You will learn how to print comments in this exercise.

STEP BY STEP   **Print Comments in a Workbook**

USE the workbook from the previous exercise.

1. On the Review tab, click Show All Comments. Notice that the comment in E8 slightly overlaps the comment in F11, and the comment in F11 slightly overlaps the comment in F14.

2. Click the border of the comment box in E8. Select the center sizing handle at the bottom of the box and drag upward until the comment in F11 is completely visible. Repeat this process with the F11 comment. (See Figure 9-44.)

Figure 9-44

Setting up a workbook to print with comments

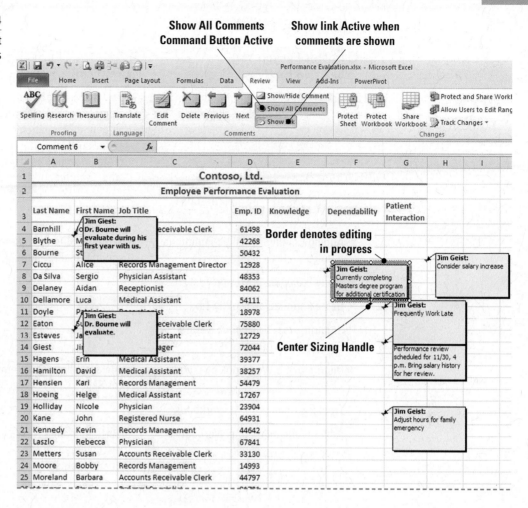

3. On the Page Layout tab in the Page Setup group, click *Orientation*. Confirm that Landscape is the orientation.

4. In the Page Setup group, click the *Page Setup* dialog box launcher.

5. On the Sheet tab in the Comments box, by default *As displayed on sheet* is selected. Click *Print Preview*. The Print Options window in Backstage opens. In the *Print Options* screen, click the *Next* arrow at the bottom of the window to view Page 2, and notice that it contains one line.

6. In the Print Settings, for Scaling, choose *Fit Sheet on One Page*.

7. Click *Print*.

8. **SAVE** and **CLOSE** the workbook.

CLOSE Excel.

When you print comments as they appear on the worksheet, the data in some cells may be covered. To print comments on a separate page, select *At end of sheets* in the Comments box on the Sheet tab of the Page Setup dialog box.

SKILL SUMMARY

In This Lesson You Learned How To:	Exam Objective	Objective Number
Using Formulas to Conditionally Summarize Data	Use a series of conditional logic values in a formula.	5.4.3
	Edit defined conditions in a formula.	5.4.2
	Create a formula with values that match conditions.	5.4.1
Using Formulas to Look Up Data in a Workbook		
Adding Conditional Logic Functions to Formulas	Use the IF function to apply conditional formatting.	8.3.3
Using Formulas to Format Text		
Using Formulas to Modify Text		
Securing Your Workbook Before Sharing It with Others		
Distributing a Workbook by Email	Send a worksheet via email or SkyDrive.	7.1.1
Tracking Changes to a Workbook		
Adding Comments to a Workbook	Insert comments.	7.2.1
	View comments.	7.2.2
	Edit comments.	7.2.3
	Delete comments.	7.2.4

Knowledge Assessment

Matching

Match each vocabulary term with its definition.

a. AND function
b. arguments
c. array
d. conditional formula
e. HLOOKUP

f. OR function
g. SUMIF
h. SUMIFS
i. Table
j. VLOOKUP

_____ 1. A function used to look up information stored in the first column of an Excel table in the worksheet.

_____ 2. A function in which a True result is returned if data meets any condition specified in the formula.

_____ 3. The values that a function uses to perform operations or calculations.

_____ 4. A function in which a True result is returned if data meets all conditions specified in the formula.

_____ 5. In a worksheet, a range of cells that can be used by a lookup formula.

_____ 6. A formula component used to build single formulas that produce multiple results.

_____ 7. A function in which the result is determined by the state of multiple criteria.

_____ 8. A function that references the first row of an Excel table in the worksheet in order to look up information stored in the same column.

_____ 9. A function that returns the total number of cells that meet one condition.

_____ 10. A function in which the result is determined by the state of a particular condition.

Multiple Choice

Select the best response for the following statements.

1. Which of the following functions would you use to convert text from uppercase to title case?
   a. UPPER
   b. PROPER
   c. LOWER
   d. SUBSTITUTE

2. Which function automatically counts cells that meet multiple conditions?
   a. COUNTIF
   b. COUNT
   c. COUNTIFS
   d. SUMIFS

3. Which function automatically counts cells that meet a specific condition?
   a. COUNTIF
   b. COUNT
   c. COUNTIFS
   d. SUMIFS

4. In the formula =SUMIFS(C5:C16,F5:F16,"<=60,"B5:B16,">200000"), the range of cells to be added is:
   a. =C5:C16.
   b. =F5:F16.
   c. =B5:B16.
   d. =C5:F16.

5. In the formula =SUMIFS(C5:C16,F5:F16,"<=60,"B5:B16,">200000"), <=60 means:
   a. if the value in C5:C16 is greater than or equal to 60, the value in C5:16 will be included in the total.
   b. if the value in F5:F16 is greater than or equal to 60, the value in C5:16 will be included in the total.
   c. if the value in B5:BF16 is less than or equal to 60, the value in C5:16 will be included in the total.
   d. if the value in F5:F16 is less than or equal to 60, the value in C5:16 will be included in the total.

6. *Criteria range* in a formula refers to:
   a. the worksheet data to be included in the formula's results.
   b. the range containing a condition that must be met in order for data to be included in the result.
   c. the type of formula being used for the calculation.
   d. the type of data contained in the cells to be included in the formula.

7. Which function returns one value if a condition is true and a different value when the condition is *not* true?

   a. AND

   b. OR

   c. IF

   d. IFERROR

8. Which function returns a value if all conditions are met?

   a. AND

   b. OR

   c. IF

   d. IFERROR

9. Which function specifies the result that will be returned if no values meet the specified condition(s)?

   a. AND

   b. OR

   c. NOT

   d. IFERROR

10. Which function reverses the value of the function arguments?

    a. AND

    b. NOT

    c. IF

    d. IFERROR

Competency Assessment

Project 9-1: Creating SUMIF and SUMIFS Formulas to Conditionally Summarize Data

Salary information for Contoso, Ltd., has been entered in a workbook so the office manager can analyze and summarize the data. In the following exercise, you will calculate sums with conditions.

GET READY. LAUNCH Excel.

@ The *Salaries* file for this lesson is available on the book companion website or in WileyPLUS.

1. **OPEN** the *Salaries* data file for this lesson.

2. Select F4 and click Insert Function in the Function Library group.

3. If the SUMIF function is not visible, key SUMIF in the *Search for a function* box and click Go. Select SUMIF from the *Select a function* list. Click OK.

4. In the Function Arguments dialog box, select C4:C33 in the Range field.

5. In the Criteria box, key >100000.

6. Click OK. Because the range and sum range are the same, it is not necessary to enter a sum range.

7. Select F5 and click Insert Function. Select SUMIFS and click OK.

8. In the Function Arguments dialog box, select C4:C33 as the sum range.

9. Select D4:D33 as the first criteria range.

10. Key >=10 as the first criterion.

11. Select C4:C33 as the second criteria range.

12. Key >60000 as the second criterion. Click OK to finish the formula.

13. **SAVE** the workbook as *Salaries 9-1*. **CLOSE** the file.

LEAVE Excel open to use in the next project.

Project 9-2: Creating COUNTIF and AVERAGEIF Formulas

In this exercise, you will enter COUNTIF and AVERAGEIF formulas to analyze and summarize grades for a course at the School of Fine Arts.

GET READY. LAUNCH Excel if it is not already running.

@ The *SFA Grades* file for this lesson is available on the book companion website or in WileyPLUS.

1. **OPEN** the *SFA Grades* data file for this lesson.
2. Select N4 and click Insert Function in the Function Library group on the Formulas tab.
3. If the COUNT function is not visible, key COUNT in the *Search for a function* box and click Go. Select COUNT from the *Select a function* list. Click OK.
4. Select L4:L41 in the Value1 field. Click OK.
5. Select N5 and click Insert Function.
6. Select COUNTIF and click OK.
7. In the Range field, key $M$4:$M$41. This is an absolute reference.
8. Key A in the Criteria field and click OK.
9. Copy the formula in N5 to N6:N8.
10. Select N6. In the formula bar, select A (the criterion) and key B. Press Enter.
11. Select N7. In the formula bar, select A (the criterion) and key C. Press Enter.
12. Select N8. In the formula bar, select A (the criterion) and key D. Press Enter.
13. Select N10, click Insert Function, and select AVERAGEIF.
14. Select M4:M41 as the range to evaluate.
15. Key A as the criterion. Select L4:L41 in the Average_range field. Click OK.
16. **SAVE** the workbook as *SFA Grades 9-2* and then **CLOSE** the file.

LEAVE Excel open for the next project.

Proficiency Assessment

Project 9-3: Creating LOOKUP Formulas

In this project, you will use a lookup table to determine an employee's end-of-year bonus.

GET READY. LAUNCH Excel if it is not already running.

@ The *Contoso Bonus* file for this lesson is available on the book companion website or in WileyPLUS.

1. **OPEN** the *Contoso Bonus* data file for this lesson.
2. Select B36:C44 and on the Formulas tab, click Define Name.
3. Key Bonus in the Name box and click OK.
4. Select E4 and click Lookup & Reference in the Function Library group. Click VLOOKUP.
5. Select D4 in the Lookup_value field. Press Tab.
6. Key Bonus in the Table_array field. Press Tab.
7. Key 2 in the Col_index_num field. Press Tab.
8. Key True in the Range_lookup field. Click OK.
9. Use the fill handle to copy the formula from E4 to E5:E33.
10. **SAVE** the workbook as *Contoso Bonus 9-3*, and then **CLOSE** the file.

LEAVE Excel open for the next project.

Project 9-4: Separating Text into Columns

In this project, you will separate student names into two columns rather than one.

GET READY. LAUNCH Excel if it is not already running.

1. **OPEN** the *SFA Grades 9-2* file that you saved in Project 9-2.
2. Select any cell in column B. On the Home tab, click the Insert Cells button and click Insert Sheet Columns. A new column B has been created.
3. Select A4:A41. Click the Data tab and click Text to Columns in the Data Tools group.
4. The *Convert Text to Columns Wizard* opens with Delimited checked as the default because Excel recognized that the data in the selected range is separated. Click Next.
5. Select Comma as the delimiter. If other delimiters are checked (such as Tab), deselect them and click Next.
6. Select Text as the Column data format and click Finish.
7. Select A3, key Last Name, and press Tab.
8. Select B4, key First Name, and press Tab.
9. **SAVE** the workbook as *SFA Grades 9-4*. **CLOSE** the workbook.

LEAVE Excel open for the next project.

Mastery Assessment

Project 9-5: Creating Conditional Logic Formulas

Professor Garrett Young has asked you to create formulas to identify the highest and lowest achieving students in one of his classes.

GET READY. LAUNCH Excel if it is not already running.

@ The *Grades* file for this lesson is available on the book companion website or in WileyPLUS.

1. **OPEN** the *Grades* file for this lesson.
2. Select M4 and click Logical in the Function Library group.
3. Select IF on the function list.
4. Key L4>=90%.
5. In the Value_if_true box, key High.
6. In the Value_if_false box, press Spacebar. (Pressing the spacebar will insert a space so that the cells that do not meet the criterion will be blank.) Click OK.
7. Using the fill handle, copy the formula in M4 to M5:M27.
8. Select N4, click Logical, and click IF.
9. Key L4<70%.
10. In the Value_if_true box, key Low.
11. In the Value_if_false box, press Spacebar. Click OK.
12. Copy the formula in N4 to N5:N27.
13. **SAVE** the workbook as *Grades 9-5* and then **CLOSE** the file.

LEAVE Excel open for the next project.

Project 9-6: Using Formulas to Format Text

Utilize formulas to format text on financial paperwork on short-term investments for Fabrikam, Inc.

GET READY. LAUNCH Excel if it is not already running.

@ The *Financing* file for this lesson is available on the book companion website or in WileyPLUS.

1. **OPEN** the *Financing* data file for this lesson.
2. On the Investments worksheet, select A12 and click Text on the Formulas tab. Enter a formula to convert the text in A4 to title case (i.e., PROPER(A4)).
3. Select A12 and drag the fill handle to A18.

4. With A12:18 selected, click **Copy** in the Clipboard group on the Home tab.

5. Select **A4** and click the arrow under Paste in the Clipboard group.

6. Click **Paste Values** and click **Values**. The data from A12:A18 is copied to A4:A10.

7. Select **A12:A18** and press **Delete**. The duplicate lines of text are removed.

8. **SAVE** the workbook as *Financing 9-6* and then **CLOSE** the file.

LEAVE Excel open for the next project.

INTERNET READY

If you are employed, does your employer provide a seniority-based bonus similar to the one offered by Fabrikam in the practice exercises? If your employer offers a bonus program, create a lookup table similar to the ones you used in this chapter that could be used to assign bonus amounts to employees.

Go online and research a company where you would like to seek employment when you complete your coursework. What salary and benefits are provided? If you can locate data related to a bonus or profit-sharing program, create a lookup table with the information. Create only the lookup table that could be added to a salary worksheet. For example, Payscale .com, a private research group, reported that in 2006, the average annual bonus for an administrative assistant was $800. Such a bonus might be tied to years of service or to an employee's performance ranking.

Create a worksheet to report your research findings. Format all data appropriately. Save your worksheet as *Bonus and Incentives*. Close Excel.

Workplace *Ready*

As you learned in this lesson, assigning a strong password is an important security precaution.

Visit http://www.microsoft.com/athome/security/privacy/password.mspx to learn more about creating a strong password.

Based on your review of the suggestions for creating strong passwords, create a list of passwords that you need to change to secure your personal information and protect the integrity of data you create. Do not list your actual passwords; rather, identify the password usage. For example, you might indicate that you need to change the password that you use to access your college email account or your personal email account. Determine a safe storage vehicle for the new passwords you create (in case you forget them).

10 Creating Charts and PivotTables

LESSON SKILL MATRIX

Skill	Exam Objective	Objective Number
Building Charts	Create charts based on worksheet data.	6.1
Formatting a Chart with a Quick Style		
Formatting the Parts of a Chart Manually		
Modifying the Chart		
Creating PivotTables	Create charts based on worksheet data.	6.1
	Show or hide data markers.	6.4.7
	Create a sparkline chart.	6.4.4
	Use Line chart types.	6.4.1
	Use Column chart types.	6.4.2
	Use Win/Loss chart types.	6.4.3
	Customize a sparkline.	6.4.5
	Format a sparkline.	6.4.6

KEY TERMS

- axis
- chart
- chart area
- chart sheet
- data labels
- data marker
- data series
- embedded chart
- legend
- legend keys
- plot area
- PivotTable
- sparkline
- title

Fourth Coffee owns espresso cafes in 15 major markets. Its primary income is generated from the sale of trademarked, freshly brewed coffee and espresso drinks. The cafes also sell a variety of pastries, packaged coffees and teas, deli-style sandwiches, and coffee-related accessories and gift items. In preparation for an upcoming budget meeting, the corporate manager wants to create charts to show trends in each of the five revenue categories for a five-year period and to project those trends to future sales. Because Excel allows you to track and work with substantial amounts of data, it is sometimes difficult to see the big picture by looking at the details in a worksheet. With Excel's charting capabilities, you can summarize and highlight data, reveal trends, and make comparisons that might not be obvious when looking at the raw data. You will use charts, PivotTables and several other useful tools to filter and present the data for Fourth Coffee.

SOFTWARE ORIENTATION

The Insert Tab

The Insert tab contains the command groups you'll use to create charts in Excel (see Figure 10-1). To create a basic chart in Excel that you can modify and format later, start by entering the data for the chart on a worksheet. Then, you can select that data and choose a chart type to graphically display the data. Simply by choosing a chart type, a chart layout, and a chart style—all of which are within easy reach on the Insert tab's ribbon—you will have instant professional results every time you create a chart.

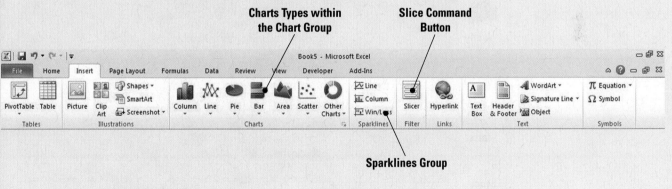

Figure 10-1

Insert tab

Use this illustration as a reference throughout this lesson as you become familiar with and use Excel's charting capabilities to create attention-getting illustrations that communicate an analysis of your data.

BUILDING CHARTS

A **chart** is a graphical representation of numeric data in a worksheet. Creating a chart is quick and easy in Excel, and the program provides a variety of chart types from which to choose. To build a chart in Excel, you must first select the data that will be included in the chart, then choose the type of chart in which you want to display the data.

When you want to create a chart or change an existing chart, you can choose from 11 chart types and numerous subtypes. Table 10-1 gives a brief description of each Excel chart type.

Table 10-1

Chart types

Icon	Chart Name	Function	Data Arrangement
Column	Column	Useful for showing data changes over a period of time or illustrating comparisons among data.	Columns or rows
Line	Line	Useful for showing trends in data at equal intervals. Displays continuous data over time set against a common scale. Values are represented as points along a line.	Columns or rows
Pie	Pie	Useful for showing the size of items in one data series, proportional to the sum of the items. Data points are displayed as a percentage of a circular pie.	One column or row
Bar	Bar	Useful for illustrating comparisons among individual items. Useful when axis labels are long or values are durations. Values are represented as horizontal rectangles.	Columns or rows
Area	Area	Useful for emphasizing magnitude of change over time; can be used to draw attention to the total value across a trend. Shows relationship of parts to the whole. Values represented as shaded areas.	Columns or rows
Scatter	Scatter	Useful for showing relationships among the numeric values in several data series or plotting two groups of numbers as one series of XY coordinates.	Columns or rows
Stock	Stock	Useful for illustrating the fluctuation of stock prices or scientific data.	Columns or rows in a specific order
Surface	Surface	Useful for finding optimum combinations between two sets of data. Use this chart when categories and data series are numeric values.	Columns or rows

Doughnut	Doughnut	Useful for displaying the relationship of parts to a whole; can contain more than one data series. Values are represented as sections of a circular band.	Columns or rows
Bubble	Bubble	Useful for comparing three sets of values. The third value determines the size of the bubble marker.	Columns with x values in first column and y values in adjacent columns
Radar	Radar	Useful for showing the trends of values relative to a center point; represents values as points that radiate from the center. Lines connect values in the series.	Columns or rows

Selecting Data to Include in a Chart

Excel's Ribbon interface makes it incredibly simple to create a chart. As you will see in the following exercise, you can create one of the common chart types by clicking its image on the Insert tab. More important than the chart type, however, is the selection of the data you want to display graphically. What aspects of the data do you want viewers to notice? The answer to that question is a major factor in selecting an appropriate chart type. In this exercise, you will learn to select data for use in an Excel chart that returns your calculations and data in a color-coded pie chart with sections identified by numbers, legends, titles, and other various data information.

STEP BY STEP | **Select Data to Include in a Chart**

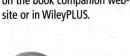
The *Financial History* file for this lesson is available on the book companion website or in WileyPLUS.

WileyPLUS Extra! features an online tutorial of this task.

GET READY. Before you begin these steps, **LAUNCH** Microsoft Excel.

1. **OPEN** the *Financial History* file for this lesson.
2. Select B4:B10 (the 2004 data) on the Sales History worksheet.
3. On the Insert tab, in the Charts group, click the Pie button. Click the first 2-D Pie chart. A color-coded pie chart with sections identified by number is displayed and the Chart Tools tabs (Design, Layout, and Format) become available, with the Design tab active. This chart, however, doesn't work: It includes the column label (2004) and total sales amount as its two largest portions, and these amounts should not be included in an analysis of sales for 2004.
4. Click in the chart's white space and press Delete. The chart is now deleted and the Chart Tools tab disappears.

5. Select B5:B9, click the Insert tab, click Pie in the Charts group, and click the first 2-D Pie chart. The correct data is displayed, but the chart is difficult to interpret with only numbers to identify the parts of the pie as illustrated in Figure 10-2.

Figure 10-2

Pie chart before formatting

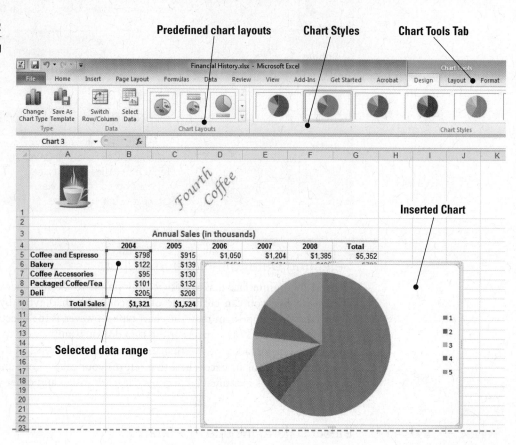

6. Click in the chart's white space and press Delete.

7. Select A4:B9, click the Insert tab, and click Pie in the Charts group. Click the first 2-D Pie chart. As illustrated in Figure 10-3, the data is clearly identified with a title and a label for each pie section.

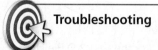

Troubleshooting When you insert a chart into your worksheet, the Chart Tools tabs (Design, Format, and Layout) become available in Excel's Ribbon with the Design tab active by default. You must select the Insert tab on the Ribbon each time you want to insert a chart.

Figure 10-3

Formatted pie chart

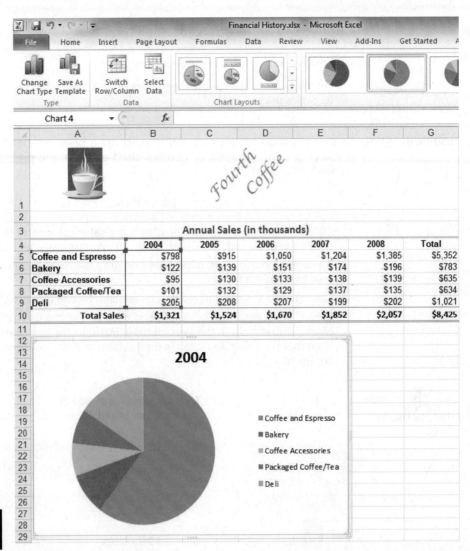

8. **CREATE** a Lesson 10 folder and **SAVE** the workbook as *Building Charts*.

PAUSE. LEAVE the workbook open to use in the next exercise.

This exercise illustrates that the chart's data selection must contain sufficient information to interpret the data at a glance. You will improve the display in subsequent exercises when you apply predefined layouts and styles. Excel did not distinguish between the column B label and its data when you selected only the data in column B. Although the label is formatted as text, because the column label was numeric, it was interpreted as data to be included in the graph. When you expanded the selection to include the row labels, 2004 was correctly recognized as a label and displayed as the title for the pie chart.

When you selected data and created a pie chart, the chart was placed on the worksheet. This is referred to as an **embedded chart**, meaning it is placed on the worksheet rather than on a separate **chart sheet**, a sheet that contains only a chart.

Choosing the Right Chart for Your Data

You can create most charts, such as column and bar charts, from data that you have arranged in rows or columns in a worksheet. Some charts, such as pie and bubble charts, require a specific data arrangement. The pie chart cannot be used for comparisons across periods of time or for analyzing trends. The column chart works well for comparisons. In a 2-D or 3-D column chart, each data marker is represented by a column. In a stacked column, data markers are stacked so that a column represents a data series. In this exercise, you learn how to create a column chart to illustrate the significant increase in coffee and espresso sales at Fourth Coffee during a five-year period.

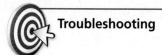

STEP BY STEP | **Choose the Right Chart for Your Data**

USE the workbook from the previous exercise.

1. On the Sales History worksheet, click on the pie chart's white space and press Delete to delete the pie chart.

Troubleshooting To delete a chart, click in the white space then press the Delete key on your keyboard. If you click on the graphic or another chart element and press Delete, only the selected element will be deleted.

2. Select A4:F9, click the Insert tab, and click Column in the Charts group on the Insert tab. Click 3-D Clustered Column on the drop-down list (first subtype under 3-D Column). The column chart illustrates the sales for each of the revenue categories for the five-year period. The Chart Tools tab appears with the Design tab active.

3. Anywhere on the chart, click, hold and drag the chart below the worksheet data and position it at the far left.

4. Click outside the column chart to deselect it. Notice that the Chart Tools tab disappears.

5. Select A4:F9, click the Insert tab, and click Line in the Charts group. Click 2-D Line with Markers (first chart in the second row). Position the line chart next to the column chart. Note that the Chart Tools tab is on the Ribbon with the Design tab active. Refer to Figure 10-4.

Figure 10-4

Bar chart and line chart

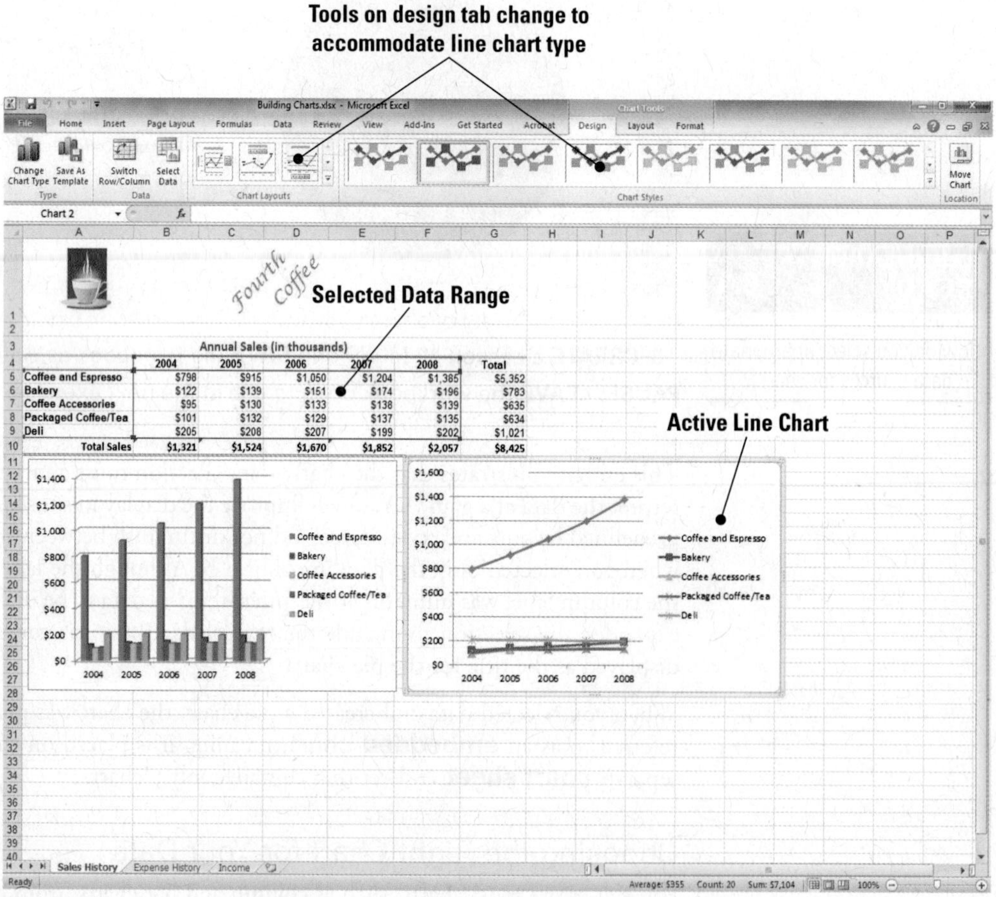

![Screenshot showing bar chart and line chart in Excel with annotations: "Tools on design tab change to accommodate line chart type", "Selected Data Range", and "Active Line Chart"]

6. **SAVE** the workbook with the same name, *Building Charts*.

PAUSE. LEAVE the workbook open to use in the next exercise.

The column and line charts provide two views of the same data, illustrating that the chart type you choose depends on the analysis you want the chart to portray. The pie chart, which shows values as part of the whole, accurately displayed the distribution of sales for one year. Column and line charts allow you to make comparisons over a period of time as well as comparisons among items.

The line chart you created in this exercise is shown in Figure 10-5. The chart includes data markers to indicate each year's sales. A **data marker** is a bar, area, dot, slice, or other symbol in a chart that represents a single data point or value that originates from a worksheet cell. Related data markers in a chart constitute a **data series**. The line chart is a good analysis tool. The chart you created illustrates not only the growth in coffee and espresso sales, but reveals a modest increase in bakery sales and static activity in the sale of packaged products.

Figure 10-5

Line chart with data markers

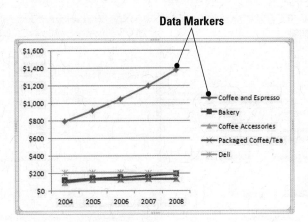

Creating a Bar Chart

Bar charts are similar to column charts and can be used to illustrate comparisons among individual items. Data that is arranged in columns or rows on a worksheet can be plotted in a bar chart. Clustered bar charts compare values across categories. Stacked bar charts show the relationship of individual items to the whole of that item. The side-by-side bar charts you create in this exercise illustrate two views of the same data. You can experiment with chart types and select the one that best portrays the message you want to convey to your target audience.

STEP BY STEP   **Create a Bar Chart**

USE the workbook from the previous exercise.

1. Click the Expense History workbook tab.
2. Select A4:F9. Click the Bar icon in the Charts Group on the Insert tab.

Take Note   A ScreenTip displays the chart type name when you rest the mouse pointer over a chart type or chart subtype.

3. Click the Clustered Bar in 3-D subtype. The data is displayed in a clustered bar chart and the Design tab is active on the Chart Tools tab.
4. Position the clustered bar chart on the left below the worksheet data.
5. Deselect the chart by clicking anywhere on the worksheet; select A4:F9. On the Insert tab, click the Bar icon in the Charts group.
6. Click Stacked Bar in 3-D.
7. Position the stacked bar graph next to the 3-D bar graph.
8. **SAVE** and **CLOSE** the workbook.

PAUSE. LEAVE Excel open to use in the next exercise.

The Charts group on the Insert tab contains six of the eleven chart types. To create one of these charts, select the worksheet data and click the icon. You can insert one of the other five chart types by clicking the Charts Dialog Box Launcher to open the Change Chart Type dialog box shown in Figure 10-6.

Figure 10-6

Change chart type dialog box

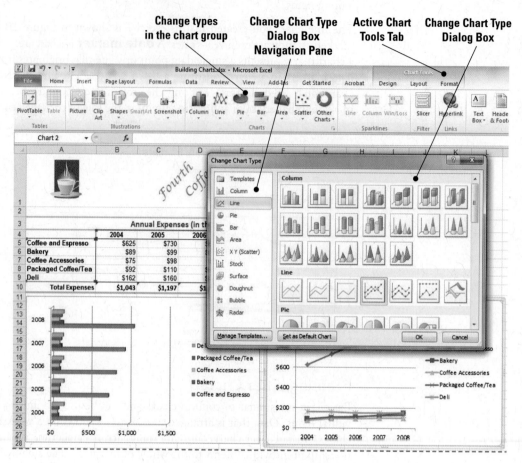

> **Another Way**
> You can open the Insert Chart dialog box by clicking Other Charts and then clicking All Chart Types at the bottom of the drop-down list.

When you click a chart type in the left pane of the dialog box, the first chart of that type is selected in the right pane. You can also scroll through the right pane and select any chart subtype.

When you apply a predefined chart style, the chart is formatted based on the document theme that you have applied. The Metro theme was applied to the Financial History workbook. The Metro theme colors were therefore applied to the charts you created in the preceding exercises.

FORMATTING A CHART WITH A QUICK STYLE

The Bottom Line

After you create a chart, you can instantly change its appearance by applying a predefined layout or style. Excel provides a variety of useful quick layouts and quick styles from which you can choose. As shown in Figure 10-7, when you create a chart, the chart tools become available and the Design, Layout, and Format tabs are added to the Ribbon.

Figure 10-7

Chart tools tab activates when a chart is inserted

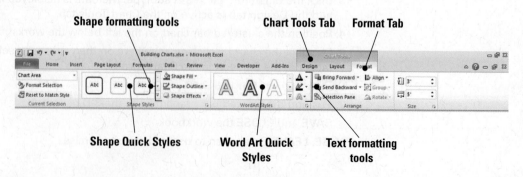

Formatting a Chart with a Quick Style

Predefined layouts and styles are timesaving features that you can use to enhance the appearance of your charts. Quick styles, as defined by Microsoft, are the Chart Styles available on the Chart Style group of the Design Tab in the Chart Tools tab. They are Quick Styles because you can click them in an instant instead of searching through the Chart Styles Gallery. In this exercise, you will apply a Quick Style to your chart.

STEP BY STEP   **Format a Chart with a Quick Style**

@ The *Financial History* file for this lesson is available on the book companion website or in WileyPLUS.

GET READY. LAUNCH Microsoft Excel if it is not already open.

1. **OPEN** the *Financial History* file for this lesson.
2. On the Expense History worksheet tab, select **A4:A9**. Press **Ctrl** and select **F4:F9**. You have selected two nonadjacent ranges to use for your chart.
3. On the **Insert** tab, click **Pie** in the Charts group and click **Pie** (the first option on the left) under 2-D. The 2008 data is displayed on the chart and the Design tab is active.

Figure 10-8

Quick Style applied to chart

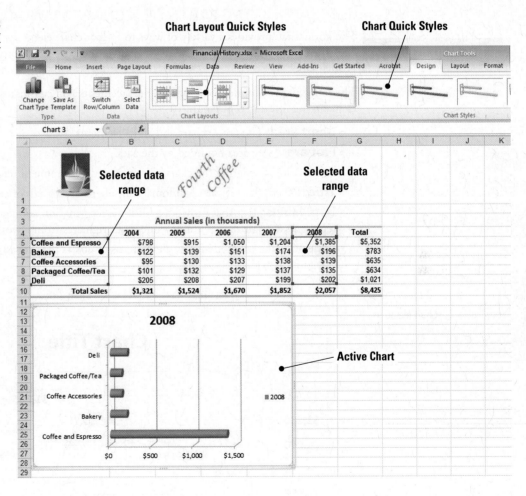

4. In the Chart Layouts group on the Design tab, click Layout 1. The pie chart now displays the percentage that each sales category contributes to total sales. When you apply Layout 1 and Style 4 to the expense chart, additional information is added to the chart and the appearance changes.

5. In the Chart Styles group, click Style 4. The chart's color scheme is changed. Position the chart below the data. You have just applied a Quick Style.

6. On the Sales History worksheet, select A4:A9. Press Ctrl and select F4:F9. You have again selected nonadjacent cell ranges to use in the next chart.

7. Click Bar in the Charts group and click Clustered Horizontal Cylinder (third row). The clustered bar chart appears on the worksheet.

8. Drag the chart below the worksheet data (see Figure 10-8).

9. Click Layout 2 in the Chart Layouts group on the Design tab. Click Style 4 in the Chart Styles group. You have applied your second Quick Style.

10. **SAVE** the workbook as *Chart Styles*.

PAUSE. LEAVE the workbook open to use in the next exercise.

Take Note To see all predefined styles, click the More arrow in the Chart Styles Group.

FORMATTING THE PARTS OF A CHART MANUALLY

The Format tab provides a variety of ways to format chart elements. To format a chart element, click the chart element that you want to change, then use the appropriate commands from the Format tab.

The following list defines some of the chart elements you can manually format in Excel. These elements are illustrated in Figure 10-9:

- **Chart area:** The entire chart and all its elements.
- **Plot area:** The area bounded by the axes.
- **Axis:** A line bordering the chart plot area used as a frame of reference for measurement.
- **Title:** Descriptive text that is automatically aligned to an axis or centered at the top of a chart.
- **Data labels:** Text that provides additional information about a data marker, which represents a single data point or value that originates from a worksheet cell.
- **Legend:** A box that identifies the patterns or colors that are assigned to the data series or categories in a chart.

Figure 10-9

Chart elements

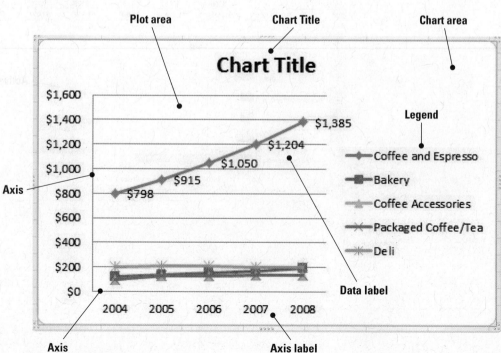

Changing a Chart's Fill Color or Pattern

Use commands on the Format tab to add or change fill colors or patterns applied to chart elements. Select the element to format and launch the Format dialog box or use the commands in the Shape Styles group on the Format tab to add fill color or a pattern to the selected chart element. When you select any chart element and click Format Selection, an element-specific dialog box opens. For example, if you click the data series, the Format Data Series dialog box opens. The Shape Fill color choices are those associated with the theme applied to the worksheet. You can use the Shape Fill command to fill any shape with color, gradient, or texture. In this exercise, you will customize the look of your chart by modifying the fill colors and patterns.

STEP BY STEP   **Change the Chart's Fill Color or Pattern**

USE the workbook from the previous exercise.

1. Click in the chart area of the Clustered Horizontal Cylinder chart on the Sales History worksheet to display the Chart Tools on the Ribbon.

2. Click the **Format** tab and click **Format Selection** in the Current Selection group. The Format Chart Area dialog box opens. See Figure 10-10.

Figure 10-10

Format chart area dialog box

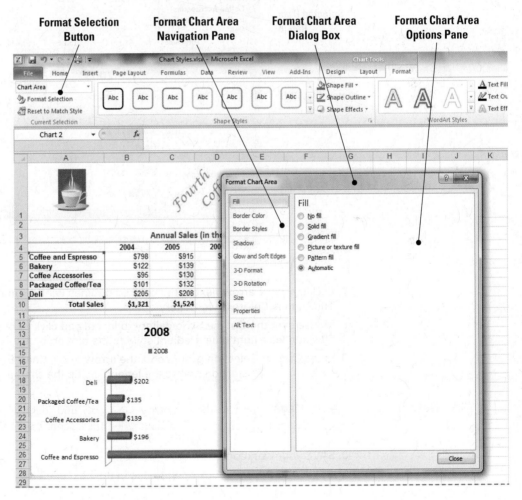

| **Format Selection Button** | **Format Chart Area Navigation Pane** | **Format Chart Area Dialog Box** | **Format Chart Area Options Pane** |

Take Note   To display the Chart Tools, you must select the chart. If a worksheet cell is active, the Design, Layout, and Format tabs are not available.

3. Select **Solid fill**. Click the **Color** arrow and click **Olive Green, Accent 3, Lighter 40%**. A light green fill has been added to the entire background chart area.

4. Select **Picture or texture fill**. Click the **Texture** arrow and click **Newsprint** (center of selection options). The textured format replaces the color fill as the background in the chart area.

5. Click Close to close the dialog box.

6. In the Current Selection group, click the arrow in the Chart Elements selection box and click Plot Area. The plot area in the chart becomes active as illustrated in Figure 10-11.

Figure 10-11

Chart elements area

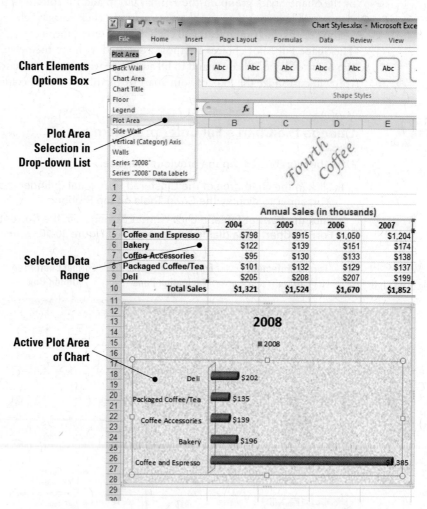

7. Click the More arrow next to the colored outlines window in the Shape Styles group. The Outline Colors Style Gallery opens.

8. Mouse over the Outline Style gallery to locate and click Subtle Effect – Blue, Accent 1. This applies a light blue gradient style to the plot area.

9. In the Current Selection group, click the arrow in the Chart Elements selection box and click Legend. This action makes the legend inside the chart active. Press Delete.

Take Note | **Legend Keys** appear to the left of legend entries and identify the color-coded data series. Because this chart contains only one data series, the legend is unnecessary.

10. **SAVE** your workbook.

PAUSE. LEAVE the workbook open to use in the next exercise.

When you use the mouse to point to an element in the chart, the element name appears in a ScreenTip. You can select the element you want to format by clicking the arrow next to the Chart Elements box in the Current Selection group on the Format tab. Figure 10-11 shows the list of chart elements in the bar chart on the Sales History worksheet. This list is chart specific. Legend will no longer be listed after you deleted that element from the chart. When you click the arrow, the list will include all elements that you have included in the displayed chart.

Changing the Chart's Border Line

You can outline any or all chart elements. Just select the element and apply one of the predefined outlines or click Shape Outline to format the shape of a selected chart element. You can apply a border around any chart element as well as around the entire chart. Select an element or the chart and use the colored outlines in the Shape Styles group on the Format tab, or click Shape Outlines and choose a Theme or Standard color for the border.

STEP BY STEP   **Change the Chart's Border Line**

USE the workbook you saved in the previous exercise.

1. In the Current Selection group, click the arrow in the Chart Elements selection box and click Chart Area. The chart area section on the chart becomes active.

2. Click the more arrow next to the colored outlines window in the Shape Styles group. The Outline Colors Style Gallery opens.

3. Scroll through the outline styles to locate and click Colored Outline – Blue, Accent 1. The chart is outlined with a light blue border.

4. In the Current Selection group, click the arrow in the Chart Elements selection box and click Plot Area.

5. Mouse over the Outline Style gallery to locate and click Colored Outline – Red, Accent 2. A red border is placed around the plot area.

6. In the Current Selection group, click the arrow in the Chart Elements selection box and click Walls. This activates the walls inside your chart. Mouse over the Outline Style gallery to locate and click Colored Outline – Black, Dark 1. Your chart will resemble Figure 10-12.

Figure 10-12

Formatted chart elements

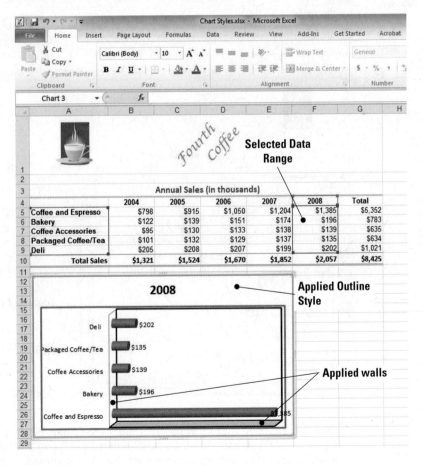

7. SAVE your workbook.

PAUSE. LEAVE the workbook open to use in the next exercise.

Formatting the Data Series

The chart is a communication tool, and you use formatting to call attention to significant data. When you clarified the chart title in the pie chart, you clarified the chart's contents. In this exercise, you make the bar chart's content easier to understand when you add a data series and format the series to call attention to the figures. You can apply fill color to the data series; outline the series with a border; change the shape; or add special effects to the columns, bars, and so on, that represent the data series.

STEP BY STEP   **Format the Data Series**

USE the workbook you saved in the previous exercise.

1. Select the chart on the Sales History worksheet. Click the arrow in the Chart Elements selection box and select Series "2008". This makes the cylinders in the chart active.

2. In the Shape Styles group, click Shape Fill. The color gallery opens.

3. Point to Texture. Click Denim. Your chart cylinders have now had the Denim texture applied.

4. Click the arrow in the Chart Elements selection box and click Series "2008" Data Labels. The data labels in your chart are now active.

5. Click Shape Outline in the Shape Styles group. This opens the color gallery.

6. Click Blue under Standard Colors.

7. Mouse over the data series for coffee and espresso on the bottom cylinder to activate the crosshair cursor. Click and hold the left mouse button to drag the data series above the bar so that the label is completely visible. See Figure 10-13.

Figure 10-13

Move a formatted data series

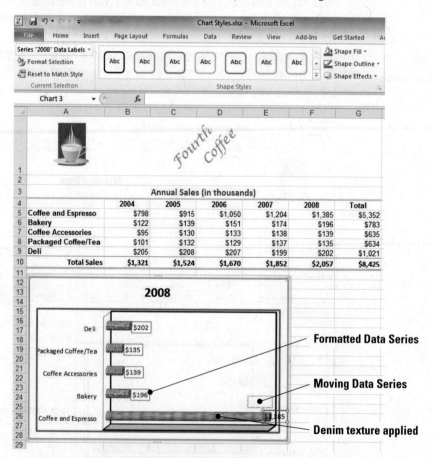

8. Click the Expense History worksheet tab. In the Chart Elements selection box click Chart Title. Place your insertion point behind the 8 and key Expenses at the end of the existing text. You have edited the chart title, and it should read 2008 Expenses.

9. SAVE the workbook. CLOSE the workbook.

PAUSE. LEAVE Excel open to use in the next exercise.

Take Note   The data series is the most important element of the chart. Use formatting tools to call attention to the graphic and the label.

Modifying a Chart's Legend

You can modify the content of the legend, expand or collapse the legend box, edit the text that is displayed, and change character attributes. A finished chart should stand alone—that is, the chart should contain sufficient data to convey the intended data analysis. In the chart you modify in this exercise, changing the font colors in the legend to match the blocks in the columns provides an additional visual aid that enables the viewer to quickly see the income contribution for each category. In the next exercise, you will learn to modify a chart's legend.

STEP BY STEP   **Modify a Chart's Legend**

The *Financial History* file for this lesson is available on the book companion website or in WileyPLUS.

OPEN the *Financial History* file for this lesson.

1. On the Sales History worksheet, select the cell range A4:F9.
2. Click Column in the Charts group on the Insert tab; the Column chart options menu appears.
3. Select Stacked Column in 3D from the Column chart menu; the chart is inserted and the *Chart Tools* tabs become available.
4. Click the more arrow at the bottom right of the Chart Layouts group When the Layout gallery opens, click Layout 4. The legend has moved and appears below the plot area.

Take Note

WILEY PLUS EXTRA

WileyPLUS Extra! features an online tutorial of this task.

When you applied Layout 4 to the column chart, the legend was placed at the bottom of the chart. You can click the legend border and move it to any location on the chart. All other elements of the quick layout will remain the same.

5. Click to select the chart's legend and in the Outline styles, click the Colored Outline – Blue, Accent 1 style. This will enclose the legend in a light blue border as illustrated in Figure 10-14.

Figure 10-14

Formatted legend

Format Selection Button

![Excel screenshot showing the Financial History.xlsx worksheet with a stacked column 3D chart. The Annual Sales (in thousands) data table shows Coffee and Espresso, Bakery, Coffee Accessories, Packaged Coffee/Tea, and Deli rows for years 2004-2008 with a Total column. The chart below has a formatted legend enclosed in a light blue border.]

Formatted Legend

6. With the legend still selected right-click to display the shortcut menu. Click **Font**; the Font dialog box appears.

7. In the Font dialog box, select **Small Caps** in the Effects option area and click **OK**. This applies the small capital letter format to the text in the legend.

8. Place your mouse cursor directly on the text for Coffee and Espresso in the legend; right-click to display the shortcut menu and click **Font**. The *Font* dialog box opens.

9. In the Font dialog box, click the **Font color** button, and then click **Green** from the drop-down color palette. Click **OK** to apply the color to the Coffee and Espresso legend text and close the dialog box.

10. Repeat step 9 for each legend item and apply the following font colors:

    Bakery: **Red**

    Coffee Accessories: **Orange**

    Packaged Coffee/Tea: **Light Blue**

    Deli: **Blue**

11. **SAVE** the file as *Chart 1*.

PAUSE. LEAVE the workbook open to use in the next exercise.

MODIFYING A CHART

The Bottom Line

You can modify a chart by adding or deleting elements or by moving or resizing the chart. You can also change the chart type without having to delete the existing chart and create a new one. Adding elements to a chart can provide additional information that was not available in the data you selected to create the chart. For example, the stacked column chart you worked with in the preceding exercise does not have a title and it does not indicate that the sales amounts are in thousands. That kind of information can be displayed in labels. Labels make it easy to understand chart data. You can display series names, category names, and percentages in data labels. To prevent data labels from overlapping, and to make them easier to read, you can adjust their positions on the chart. In this exercise, you learn to use the Layout tab commands to add chart labels.

STEP BY STEP   **Add Elements to a Chart**

USE the workbook from the previous exercise.

1. With the chart still active click the **Layout** tab.

2. Click **Axis Titles** in the Labels group, then point to the Primary Vertical Axis Title in the drop-down menu that appears; the Primary Vertical Axis Title options list is displayed.

3. Click **Vertical Title**. An Axis title text box appears in the chart. Select the Axis Title text, and key **(In Thousands)** in the title text box.

4. Click **Chart Title** in the Labels group. Click **Above Chart** in the drop-down menu that appears. A text box displaying Chart Title is inserted above the columns.

5. Select the text and replace it with **Sales History**.

6. Click **Data Labels** in the Labels group. Click **None**. The Labels are removed from each column in the chart. Click on **Data Labels** again to restore the labels showing the dollar amount of sales in each category.

Take Note   Because of the chart size, the data labels are difficult to read. You will correct this in a subsequent exercise.

7. Click **Gridlines** in the Axes group. Point to Primary Horizontal Gridlines and click **Major Gridlines**.

8. In the Labels group, click **Axis Titles** then and point to **Primary Horizontal Axis Title**. The drop-down menu appears.

9. Click **Title Below Axis**.

10. Key **Annual Sales** in the Axis Title text box as illustrated in Figure 10-15.

Figure 10-15

Editing an Axis title

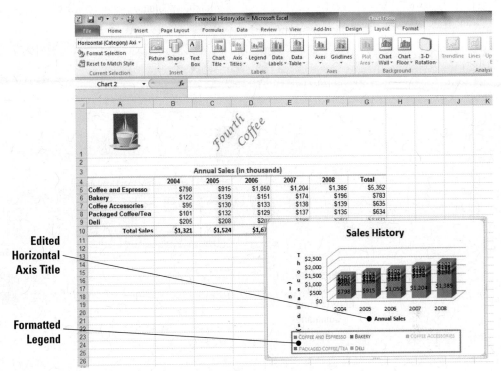

Edited
Horizontal
Axis Title

Formatted
Legend

Another Way
Rather than select and replace the text in the text boxes, you can key the new text in the formula bar. When you press Enter, the new text replaces the generic text in the title boxes.

11. **SAVE** the workbook with the same name.

PAUSE. LEAVE the workbook open to use in the next exercise.

Deleting Elements from a Chart

When a chart becomes too cluttered, you may need to delete nonessential elements. You can use the Layout tab commands to delete chart elements, or you can select an element on the chart and press the Delete key. You can also select an element in the Current Selection group and press Delete. You will use this next exercise to delete elements from the chart.

STEP BY STEP   **Delete Elements from a Chart**

USE the workbook from the previous exercise.

1. On the Layout tab in the Labels group, click **Axis Titles** and point to Primary Horizontal Axis Title. Click **None**. There is now no horizontal axis title in the chart.

2. Click **Gridlines** in the Axes group, point to Primary Horizontal Gridlines. Click **None**. There are now no gridlines in the chart.

3. Click the Design tab and click Switch Row/Column. The data display is changed to have all sales for one category stacked as illustrated in Figure 10-16.

Figure 10-16

Using switch row/column

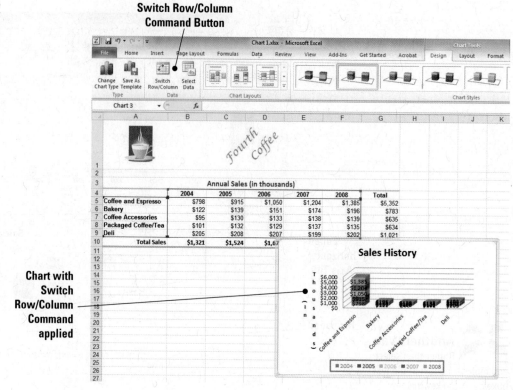

Switch Row/Column Command Button

Chart with Switch Row/Column Command applied

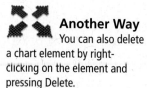

Another Way
You can also delete a chart element by right-clicking on the element and pressing Delete.

4. Click Switch Row/Column to Undo.

5. **SAVE** the workbook.

PAUSE. LEAVE the workbook open to use in the next exercise.

Take Note   It is important to remember that whether the chart is embedded in the worksheet or located on a chart sheet, the chart is linked to the worksheet data. Any changes in the worksheet data will be reflected in the chart. Likewise, if the worksheet data is deleted, the chart will be deleted as well.

Moving a Chart

When you insert a chart, by default, it is embedded in the worksheet. You can click a corner of a chart or the midpoint of any side to display move handles (four-sided arrow). You can use the move handles to drag the chart to any location on the worksheet. Sometimes you want a chart to be on a chart sheet so that it can be reviewed without the worksheet data. In this exercise, you will move charts in the workbook.

Move a Chart

USE the workbook from the previous exercise.

1. Click a blank area in the Sales History chart to deselect any previous actions.
2. Mouse over the chart to activate the move pointer (crosshairs). Click, hold and drag the chart so that it is centered in columns B to G.
3. The chart remains selected. Click the Design tab.
4. Click Move Chart in the Location group. The *Move Chart* dialog box shown in Figure 10-17 opens, with the default setting—New Sheet—selected. This setting places the chart as an object in a new worksheet.

Figure 10-17

Move chart dialog box

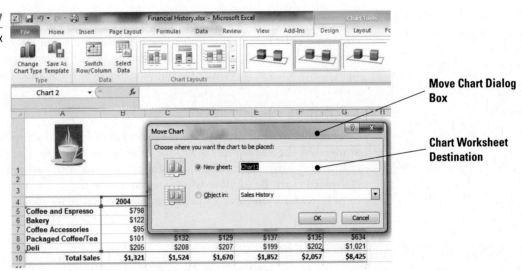

5. The New Sheet selection option is selected in the dialog box, key Sales History Chart in the text box. Click OK. A chart sheet is inserted before the Sales History sheet. The chart sheet becomes the active sheet, and the Chart Tools tabs are displayed as illustrated in Figure 10-18.

Figure 10-18

Chart sheet created

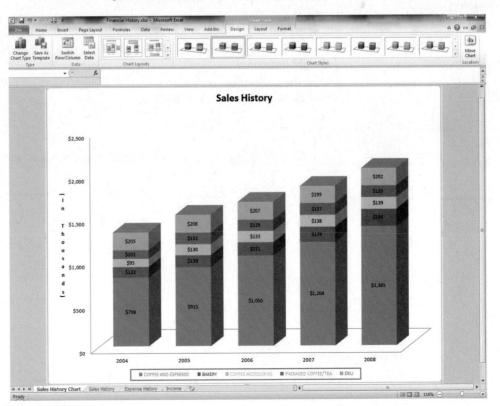

6. On the Layout tab, in the Labels group, click Legend. Click Show Legend at Right; the legend moves to the right side of the chart in the chart sheet, which makes the elements in the chart easier to read.

Take Note   The Chart Tools that you used on the Design, Layout, and Format tabs can be applied to the chart sheet. The data series amounts were difficult to read when you applied them to the embedded chart. They are easy to read and can be used for analysis when the chart is moved to a chart sheet.

7. **SAVE** and **CLOSE** the workbook.

PAUSE. LEAVE Excel open to use in the next exercise.

You can move chart elements or move the entire chart. In previous exercises, you moved an embedded chart by dragging it to a new location. When you move the chart to a new sheet, it becomes even more important for the chart to be self-explanatory. Moving the legend to the right makes it easier to identify the building blocks in the stacked columns.

Resizing a Chart

You can click a corner of a chart or the midpoint of any side to display sizing handles (two-sided arrow). Use the side handles to change chart height or width. Use the corner sizing handles to change both height and width. Increasing the size of a chart makes it easier to read, especially an embedded chart. Be cautious when you reduce the size of a chart, however. Titles and legends must be readable. In this exercise you will learn to resize the chart.

STEP BY STEP   **Resize a Chart**

GET READY. LAUNCH Microsoft Excel if it is not already open.

@ The *Financial History 2* file for this lesson is available on the book companion website or in WileyPLUS.

1. **OPEN** the *Financial History 2* file for this lesson.

2. Click a blank area in the chart on the Expense History worksheet to make the chart active and display the Chart Tools tabs.

3. Click the top-left sizing handle and drag the left edge of the chart to the bottom of row 9 at the left edge of the worksheet. You are using the sizing handles to resize the chart.

4. Click the top-right sizing handle and align the right edge of the chart with the column G right boundary.

5. Click the bottom-center sizing handle and drag the chart boundary to the bottom of row 35 as shown in Figure 10-19.

Figure 10-19

Resizing chart with sizing
handles

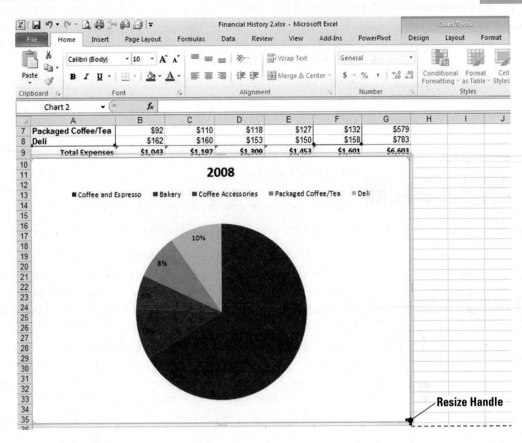

6. Click the Sales History worksheet tab to make the Sales History worksheet active. Click
   a blank area in the chart. Click the Format tab.

7. In the Size group, click the Shape Height up arrow until the height is 3.5.

8. In the Size group, click the Shape Width down arrow until the width is 4.0.

9. **SAVE** the workbook as *Chart 2*. **CLOSE** the workbook.

PAUSE. LEAVE Excel open to use in the next exercise.

Choosing a Different Chart Type

For most 2-D charts, you can change the chart type and give it a completely different look. If a
chart contains multiple data series, you can also select a different chart type for any single data
series, creating a combined chart. You cannot combine a 2-D and a 3-D chart, however.

STEP BY STEP   **Choose a Different Chart Type**

GET READY. LAUNCH Microsoft Excel if it is not already open.

@ The *Financial History*
file for this lesson is available
on the book companion website or in WileyPLUS.

1. **OPEN** the *Financial History* file for this lesson.

2. On the Expense History worksheet, select A4:F9.

3. On the Insert tab, click Bar and click Stacked Bar in 3-D. This inserts the stacked bar in
   a 3-D chart into your worksheet. The Design tab becomes active as soon as the chart is
   inserted into the worksheet.

4. Click Layout 2 in the Charts Layout group.

5. Select the chart title text box and key Expense History.

6. On the *Design* tab, click Change Chart Type.

7. Click Stacked Horizontal Cylinder in the Change Chart type dialog box. Click OK.

8. On the Sales History worksheet, select A4:B9. On the Insert tab, click Pie. Click Pie
   under Pie 2D.

9. Click Layout 1 on the Design tab.

10. Click Change Chart Type and click Exploded Pie in 3-D. Click OK.

11. SAVE the workbook as *Chart 3*. CLOSE the workbook.

CLOSE Excel.

CREATING PIVOTTABLES

A **PivotTable** report is a collaborative way to quickly condense large amounts of data. Use a PivotTable report to analyze and display the numerical data in detail and to answer unforeseen questions about your data. In this exercise, you will learn to create basic pivottables.

A PivotTable report is especially designed for:

- Querying large amounts of data in many different ways.
- Subtotaling and gathering numeric data, summarizing data by categories and subcategories, and creating custom calculations and formulas.
- Expanding and collapsing levels of data to filter your results, and drilling down finer points from the summary data for areas of importance.
- Moving rows to columns or columns to pivot rows to examine different summaries of the data.
- Filtering, sorting, grouping, and conditionally formatting the most useful and interesting subset of data to enable you to focus on the information that you want.
- Providing concise, eye-catching, and interpreted online or printed information.

Creating and Adding Data to a Basic PivotTable

You often use a PivotTable report when you want to examine and analyze related totals. Examples are when you have a long list of figures to calculate or you want to compare several facts about each piece of numerical data. In this exercise, you will create a basic PivotTable report.

STEP BY STEP   **Create and Add Data to a Basic PivotTable Report**

The *Financial History* file for this lesson is available on the book companion website or in WileyPLUS.

OPEN *Financial History* from the student data files.

1. On the Sales History worksheet, select cells A4:G9.

2. On the Insert tab, click the PivotTable icon to access the drop-down menu, and then click PivotTable. The Create PivotTable dialog box opens. Accept the defaults as shown in Figure 10-20.

Figure 10-20

Create PivotTable dialog box

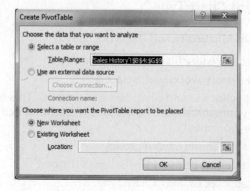

3. Click OK. The PivotTable Tools tab appears on the Ribbon. It contains an Options tab (default) and Design tab. Your screen should resemble Figure 10-21.

Figure 10-21

New PivotTable in worksheet

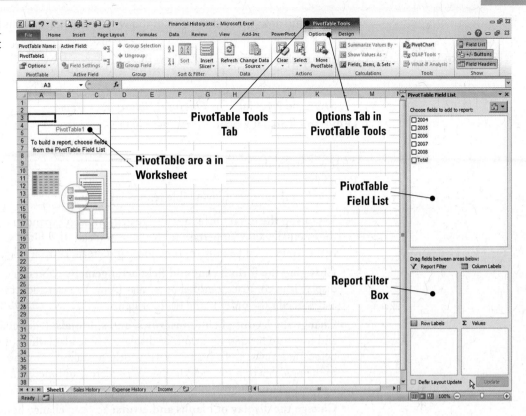

4. On the right side of the screen, in the *PivotTable Field list*, click to place check marks in each box for the years 2004–2008 and Total. You have now formatted your basic PivotTable report.

5. Click and hold on Total in the field list, then drag it to the Report Filter box as shown in Figure 10-22, then release. The Total filter now appears in cells A1:B1.

Figure 10-22

Dragging total to report filter

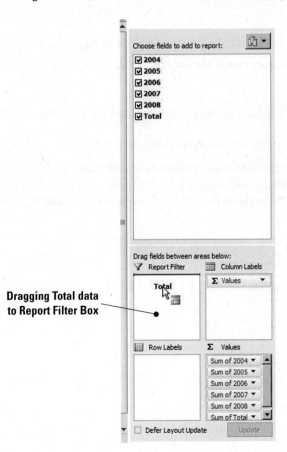

6. Move the new sheet to the end of the workbook. Rename the worksheet PivotTable.

Take Note   When you click on any empty cell on the PivotTable, the Field list will disappear. To make it reappear, you simply need to click on any active cell that is showing data.

7. SAVE the PivotTable as *Financial History PivotTable*.
LEAVE the workbook open for the next exercise.

After you create the initial PivotTable report by defining the data source, arranging fields in the PivotTable Field List, and choosing an initial layout, you can perform the additional tasks as you work with and improve a PivotTable report, including:

- **Exploring the data:** Once initially created, you can expand and collapse data, and show the essential facts that pertain to the data. You can sort, filter, and group fields and data items. You can edit summary functions, and create custom calculations and formulas.

- **Changing the form layout and field arrangements:** You can edit the PivotTable report to display it in compact, outline, or tabular form. You can add, rearrange, and remove fields and also edit the order of the fields or items.

- **Change the layout of columns, rows, and subtotals:** Excel enables you to turn column and row field headers on or off, or display or hide blank lines, display subtotals above or below their rows, and adjust column widths on refresh. You also can move a column field to the row area or a row field to the column area, and merge or unmerge cells for outer row and column items.

- **Change the display of blanks and errors:** You can change how errors and empty cells are displayed, change how items and labels without data are shown, and display or hide blank lines.

- **Changing the format of the PivotTable:** You can apply manual and conditional formatting to cells and ranges, and you can edit the overall look by applying a PivotTable format style.

Adding Data from Another Worksheet to the PivotTable

In this exercise, you will add data from another worksheet in your workbook PivotTable.

STEP BY STEP   **Add Data from Another Worksheet to the PivotTable**

USE the workbook from the previous exercise.

1. On the Expense History worksheet, select cells A4:G9.
2. On the Insert tab, click the PivotTable icon then Click PivotTable. The Create PivotTable dialog box opens. Click the Existing Worksheet radio button as shown in Figure 10-23.

Figure 10-23

Create PivotTable dialog box

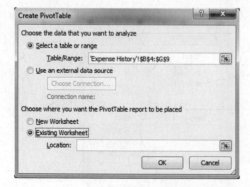

3. Click on the PivotTable worksheet and highlight cells A8:F9. These cells should now be visible in the Create PivotTable dialog box as seen in Figure 10-24. Click OK. A new PivotTable with the data from the Expense History worksheet has now been inserted into the PivotTable worksheet.

Figure 10-24

Settings in the Create PivotTable dialog box

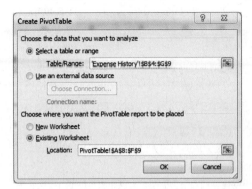

4. Your data from the Expense History sheet is now viewable in the PivotTable sheet.
5. Format the data to the worksheet by selecting the check boxes for the years 2004–2008 and Total in the *PivotTable Field List*. Click, hold and drag Total to the Report filter box.
6. **SAVE** the workbook as *Sales vs. Expenses PivotTable*.

LEAVE the workbook open for the next exercise.

Adding Charts to the PivotTable

A PivotTable chart is an essential tool to help organize and arrange specific data from workbooks or worksheets.

STEP BY STEP   **Add a Chart to the PivotTable**

USE the workbook from the previous exercise.

1. On the PivotTable worksheet, select cells A3:F4.
2. On the Insert tab, in the Charts group, click Column, 2D, Clustered Column. You have inserted the Clustered Column chart to reflect the data from the Expenses PivotTable.
3. Click, hold, and drag the chart to the left side, aligning the top with Row 12. You have moved the chart for better viewing.
4. Select cells A8:F9. Click on the Insert tab, in the Charts group, click Bar, 2D, Clustered Bar. You have inserted the Clustered Bar chart to reflect the data from the Expenses PivotTable. You will be able to differentiate the data easier by having unlike charts on the worksheet.
5. Click, hold, and drag the Bar chart to be adjacent below the first chart (Row 29).
6. Click on the Column chart to activate. In the Chart Layout group, click Layout 1. The new layout has changed the style of the chart.
7. In the Chart Styles group, choose and apply Style 4. Note that the style of the chart has changed.
8. Edit the Chart Title to read Sales History. You have retitled the chart.
9. Click on the Bar chart to activate. In the Chart Layout group, click Layout 2. Note that the style of the chart has changed.
10. In the Chart Styles group, choose and apply Style 5. The new layout can be seen applied in the workbook.

11. Edit the Chart Title to read **Expense History**. Your completed charts are visible in Figure 10-25.

Figure 10-25

PivotTable with charts

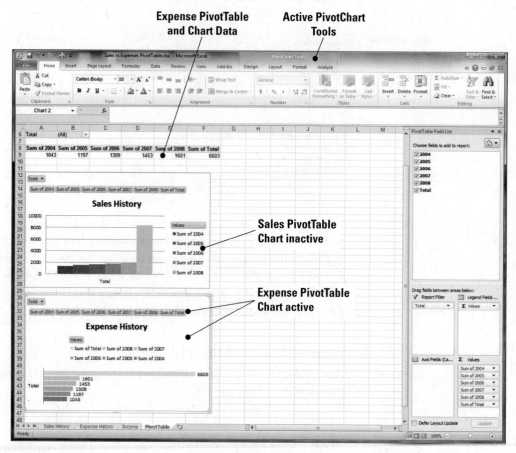

Expense PivotTable and Chart Data

Active PivotChart Tools

Sales PivotTable Chart inactive

Expense PivotTable Chart active

12. **SAVE** the workbook as *Sales_Expenses_Charts*.

LEAVE the workbook open for the next exercise.

Using the Slicer to Bring Data Forward

NEW to Office 2010

In previous versions of Microsoft Excel, you could use report filters to filter data in a PivotTable report, but it was not easy to view the current filtering state when you chose to filter on multiple data. New to Microsoft Excel 2010, you have the option to use slicers to filter the data. **Slicers** are easy-to-use filtering mechanisms that contain a set of buttons that allow you to quickly filter the data in a PivotTable report, without the need to open drop-down lists to find the items that you want to filter. In addition to quick filtering, slicers also indicate the current filtering state, which makes it easy to understand what exactly is shown in a filtered PivotTable report.

When you select an item, that item is included in the filter and the data for that item will be displayed in the report. In this exercise you create two simple slicers to filter your data.

STEP BY STEP | **Use the Slicer to Bring Data Forward**

USE the workbook from the previous exercise.

1. The PivotTable worksheet is still active. Click on cell **A4** to select it.

2. Click on the **Insert** tab and click on the **Slicer** icon. The Insert Slicers dialog box appears, as shown in Figure 10-26.

Figure 10-26

Insert Slicers dialog box

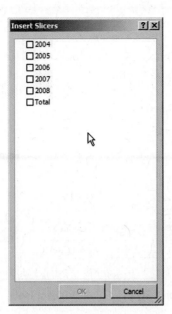

3. In the Insert Slicers dialog box is a check box list of the data from the PivotTable. Click to select the Total check box and click OK. The slicer is now inserted in the worksheet and the Slicer Tools tab on the Ribbon is now active.

4. To move the Slicer, click, hold, and drag it next to the Sales History chart in column G as shown in Figure 10-27.

Figure 10-27

Newly inserted slicer

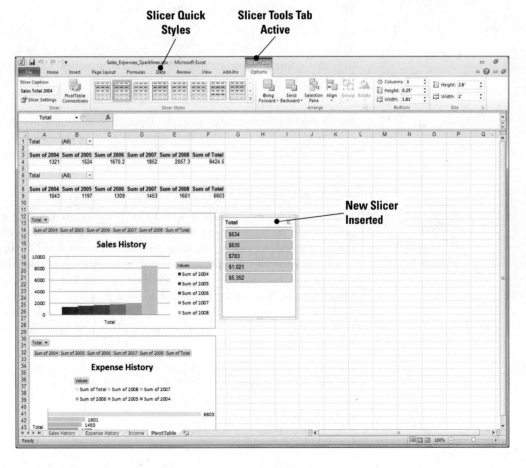

5. Right-click on the Slicer to access the short-cut menu. Click Slicer Settings. The Slicer Settings dialog box opens.

6. The insertion point appears in the Name text box. Key Sales Slicer. Press Tab twice.

7. The insertion point is now in the Caption text box. Key Sales Total 2004 and click OK.

8. On the Slicer Tools Options tab on the Ribbon, in Slicer Styles, choose Slicer Style Light 2. The toolbar should resemble Figure 10-28.

Figure 10-28

Slicer Tools tab

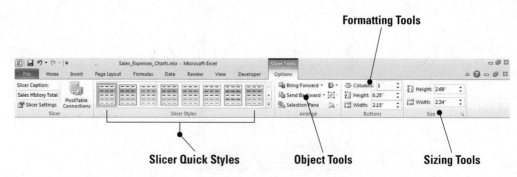

9. Click to activate cell A9.

10. Repeat steps 2 through 7, substituting Expenses Slicer and Expenses Total 2004, and move it next to the Expense History chart.

11. In Slicer Styles, choose and apply Slicer Style Light 3. The slicer's styles have been formatted to match their respective charts.

12. **SAVE** the workbook as *Sales_Expense_Slicers*.

LEAVE the workbook open for the next exercise.

CERTIFICATION READY 6.4.7

How do you use the Slicer to bring data forward?

When you use a regular PivotTable report filter to filter on multiple items, the filter indicates only that multiple items are filtered, and you have to open a drop-down list to find the filtering details. However, a slicer clearly labels the filter that is applied and provides details so that you can easily understand the data that is displayed in the filtered PivotTable report.

Slicers are usually associated with the PivotTable in which they are created. However, you can also create stand-alone slicers that are referenced from Online Analytical Processing (OLAP) Cube functions (database), or that can be associated with any PivotTable at a later time.

Adding Sparklines to a PivotTable

NEW to Office 2010

Sparklines make it easy to show a data trend. Data presented in a row or column is useful, but patterns can be hard to spot at a glance. The context for these numbers can be provided by inserting sparklines next to the data. New to Microsoft Excel 2010, a **sparkline** is a tiny chart in a worksheet cell that provides a visual representation of data. Taking up a small amount of room, a sparkline can display a trend based on adjacent data in a clear and compact graphical representation. You can use sparklines to show trends in a series of values, such as sales increases or decreases, economic cycles, or to highlight maximum and minimum values, without having to build a detailed chart in your worksheet. It is best to position a sparkline closest to its data for best results.

Unlike charts on an Excel worksheet, sparklines are not objects—a sparkline is actually a tiny chart in the background of a cell. Because a sparkline is a tiny chart embedded in a cell, you can enter text in a cell and use a sparkline as its background. In the next exercise, you will apply a sparkline to the worksheet.

STEP BY STEP   **Add Sparklines to a PivotTable**

USE the workbook from the previous exercise.

1. In the PivotTable worksheet, highlight cells A4:E4.
2. On the Insert tab, in the Sparklines group, click on the Line icon. The Create Sparklines dialog box appears. This will allow you to insert a Sparkline Line chart into the destination cell.

Take Note   There are three types of sparkline charts in Excel 2010—line, column, and win/loss.

3. Click cell J19 to add the cell to the Location Range as shown in Figure 10-29. Click OK. The newly created sparkline is inserted into the worksheet. Note that the Sparkline Tools Design tab is now active on the Ribbon.

Figure 10-29

Sparklines tools active on the ribbon

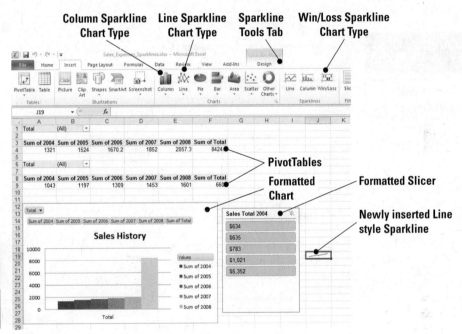

CERTIFICATION READY   6.4.4

How do you create a Sparkline?

4. Right-click on the column J header to format the width to a size of 35.
5. Right-click on the Row 19 header and format to the height of 45. Click on J19 to make it active. It was deselected when you formatted the column and row.
6. On the Sparklines Design tab, in the Show group, place checkmarks in all 6 options. These options are for data settings on the sparkline itself. They Show: high point, low point, negative point, first point, last point, and markers. If you do not select any of these show points, then you will just have a basic line in the cell. As you activate these options, you will see the sparkline change with each click as well as your sparkline itself.
7. In the Sparkline Style group, choose and apply Sparkline Style Accent 2, Darker 50%. The style of the sparkline has now been formatted.
8. In cell J19, key Sales History Trend. Press Enter.
9. Click on the Sparkline. From the Home tab, center the text and decrease the font to size 8. Sparklines allow text to be entered into the background as labels. You have just added a label, aligned it, and resized it.

10. Repeat steps 1 through 7 to create a second sparkline using the following criteria:

> Sparkline type: **Column**
>
> Data from cells: **A9:E9**
>
> Location cell: **J38**
>
> Row 38 height: **45**
>
> Show group: **all options**
>
> Sparkline style: **Sparkline Style Accent 3, Darker 50%**
>
> Cell text: **Expense History Trend, centered, size 8, top aligned**

Your completed sparklines should resemble the image in Figure 10-30.

Figure 10-30

Completed Sparklines in worksheet

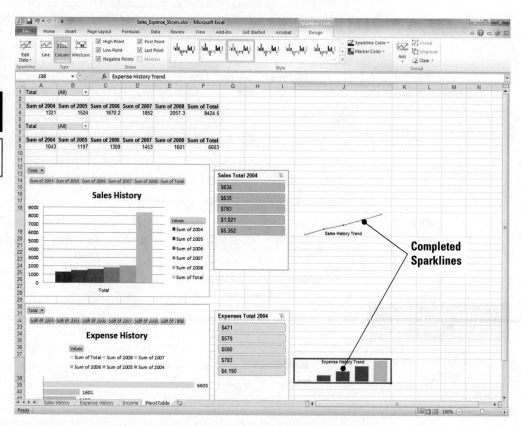

11. **SAVE** the workbook as *Sales_Expenses_Sparklines*. **CLOSE** the workbook.
LEAVE Excel open for the next exercise.

You can quickly see the relationship between a sparkline and its underlying data, and when your data changes, you can see the change in the sparkline immediately. In addition to creating a single sparkline for a row or column of data, you can create several sparklines at the same time by selecting multiple cells that correspond to underlying data, as shown in Figure 10-31.

Figure 10-31

Data ranges in sparklines

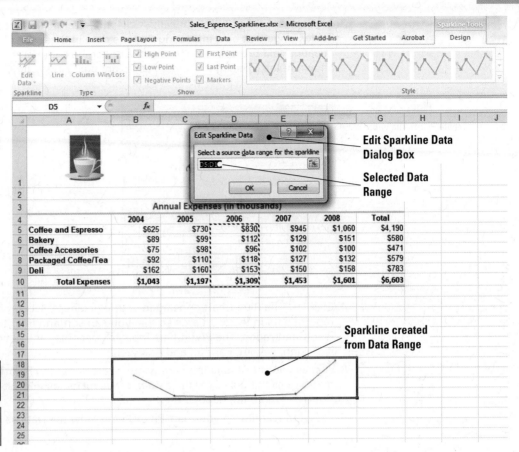

Edit Sparkline Data
Dialog Box

Selected Data
Range

Sparkline created
from Data Range

You can also create sparklines for rows of data that you add later by using the fill handle on an adjacent cell that contains a sparkline.

One advantage of using sparklines is that, unlike charts, sparklines are printed when you print a worksheet that contains them.

Creating a PivotChart Report

A PivotChart report provides a graphical representation of the data in a PivotTable report. A PivotChart report displays data series, categories, data markers, and axes just as typical charts do. You can change the chart type and other options such as the titles, the legend placement, the data labels, and the chart location. Like a PivotTable report, a PivotChart report is interactive. Modifications that you make to the field layout and data in the associated PivotTable report are instantly reflected in the PivotChart report.

STEP BY STEP   **Create a PivotChart Report**

OPEN the *Financial History PivotTable* you created earlier in this lesson.

1. Click on cell B20. This will be the cell where your PivotChart will be inserted.

2. On the Insert tab, click the PivotTable down arrow icon and then click Insert PivotChart in the drop-down menu that appears. The Create PivotTable with PivotChart dialog box opens with the Select a Table or Range option selected by default.

3. In your worksheet, highlight cells A3:F4; the reference to these cells appears in the Table/Range text box, indicating that the data in these cells is to be analyzed. In the Location text box at the bottom of the dialog box, a reference to cell B20 appears, as shown in the Existing Worksheet Location: box. Figure 10-32.

Figure 10-32

Create PivotTable with Pivotchart dialog box

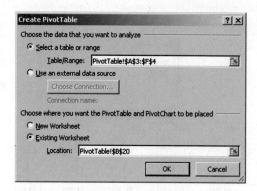

4. Click OK. The PivotChart appears in your worksheet, accompanied by PivotChart report filters in the chart area so that you can sort and filter the essential data of the PivotChart report. The PivotChart Tools tab becomes active with the following tabs in it: Design, Layout, Format, and Analyze.

5. Just as you chose data in the previous exercise for the PivotTable, you will place check marks in all the boxes for the data in the PivotTable Field list and click, hold, and drag Sum of Total to the Report Filter.

6. Click, hold, and drag your new PivotChart below the Data as shown in Figure 10-33.

Figure 10-33

New PivotChart report

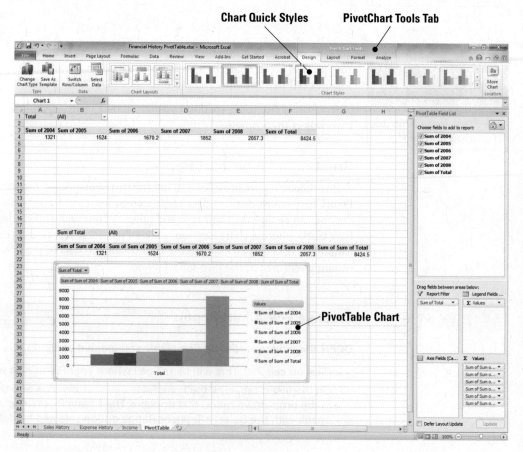

7. **SAVE** the PivotChart as *Sales_Expense_PivotChart*. **CLOSE** the workbook. **CLOSE** Excel.

SKILL SUMMARY

In This Lesson You Learned How To:	Exam Objective	Objective Number
Building Charts	Create charts based on worksheet data.	6.1
Formatting a Chart with a Quick Style		
Manually Formatting the Parts of a Chart		
Modifying a Chart		
Creating PivotTables	Create charts based on worksheet data.	6.1
	Show or hide data markers.	6.4.7
	Create a sparkline chart.	6.4.4
	Use Line chart types.	6.4.1
	Use Column chart types.	6.4.2
	Use Win/Loss chart types.	6.4.3
	Customize a sparkline.	6.4.5
	Format a sparkline.	6.4.6

Knowledge Assessment

Matching

Match each vocabulary term with its definition.

a. axis
b. chart
c. chart area
d. chart sheet
e. data labels
f. data marker
g. data series
h. embedded chart
i. legend
j. title

_____ 1. A box that identifies the patterns or colors that are assigned to a data series or categories in a chart.

_____ 2. A graphical representation of numeric data in a worksheet.

_____ 3. A bar, area, dot, slice, or other symbol in a chart that represents a single data point or value that originates from a worksheet cell.

_____ 4. A chart that is placed on a worksheet rather than on a separate sheet.

_____ 5. A sheet in a workbook that contains only a chart.

_____ 6. The entire chart and all its elements.

_____ 7. Related data points that are plotted in a chart.

_____ 8. A line bordering the chart plot area used as a frame of reference for measurement.

_____ 9. Descriptive text that is automatically aligned to an axis or centered at the top of a chart.

_____ 10. A label that provides additional information about a data marker, which represents a single data point or value that originates from a worksheet cell.

Multiple Choice

Select the best response for the following statements.

1. Which chart type shows values as parts of a whole?
   a. Column
   b. Bar
   c. Area
   d. Pie

2. What type of chart appears on a worksheet with other data?
   a. Chart sheet
   b. Embedded
   c. PivotChart
   d. Mixed

3. What part of a chart do you click when you want to select the entire chart?
   a. Chart area
   b. Plot area
   c. Chart title
   d. Legend

4. What happens to a chart if the source data is deleted?
   a. Nothing.
   b. The chart will move to the area where the data was located.
   c. The data in the chart is deleted.
   d. You will be asked if you want the chart deleted.

5. What is the first step that should be taken when creating a chart?
   a. Providing a name for the chart
   b. Selecting the chart type
   c. Selecting the range of cells that contain the data the chart will use
   d. Choosing the data labels that will be used in the chart

6. If you want to print only the chart in a worksheet, what should you do before printing?
   a. Click the chart to select it and then print.
   b. Select the *Print chart only* option in the Page Setup dialog box.
   c. Move the chart to a new sheet by itself and then print that sheet.
   d. You cannot print only the chart if it is part of a larger worksheet.

7. To change the location of a legend on a chart, use the Legend command on which Ribbon tab?
   a. Insert
   b. Format
   c. Layout
   d. Design

8. A column chart represents values as
   a. Horizontal bars
   b. Vertical bars
   c. Horizontal lines
   d. Vertical lines

9. To move a chart from a worksheet to a chart sheet
   a. Use the move handles and drag it to the new location.
   b. Use the Move Chart Location command on the Design tab.
   c. Cut the chart from the worksheet and paste it to a new workbook sheet.
   d. You cannot move the chart after it has been created.

10. Which of the following statements is **not** true?

    a. You can change both the height and width of a chart with commands on the Format tab.

    b. You can use the sizing handles to change the height and width of a chart.

    c. You must delete an existing chart in order to have the data displayed in a different chart type.

    d. When a chart sheet is created, it no longer appears on the worksheet containing the data series.

Competency Assessment

Project 10-1: Create a Pie Chart

Blue Yonder Airlines has created a workbook to analyze sales for its first four years of operation. The manager wants to create charts that reflect an analysis of the data.

GET READY. LAUNCH Excel.

The *BY Financials* file for this lesson is available on the book companion website or in WileyPLUS.

1. **OPEN** the *BY Financials* file for this lesson.
2. On the Income worksheet, select A3:A7. Press **Ctrl** and select E3:E7.
3. Click the Insert tab. Click Pie and click Pie in 3-D.
4. Click Layout 1 in the Chart Layouts group on the Design tab.
5. Click Move Chart Location.
6. Select New Sheet and click OK.
7. Right-click the Chart1 tab and click Rename.
8. Key 2008 Income Chart and press Enter.
9. **SAVE** the workbook as *BY Financials 10-1*.
10. **CLOSE** the workbook.

LEAVE Excel open for the next project.

Project 10-2: Create a Bar Chart

Create a bar chart to analyze trends in Fourth Coffee's income before taxes.

The *Financial History* file for this lesson is available on the book companion website or in WileyPLUS.

1. **OPEN** the *Financial History* file for this lesson.
2. Make the Income worksheet active. Select A4:F9 and click the Insert tab.
3. Click Bar in the Charts group, and click 100% Stacked Horizontal Cylinder.
4. Click in the Chart Area and click the Layout tab.
5. Click Legend and click Show Legend at Bottom.
6. Click the Chart Area to display the move handles. Move the chart so that the top-left corner is aligned with B12.
7. Click the bottom-right sizing handle and increase the size of the chart so that it fills B12:G29.
8. **SAVE** the workbook as *Financial History 10-2*.

LEAVE the workbook open to use in the next project.

Project 10-3: Modify a Bar Chart

In the previous project, you created a bar chart to analyze trends in Fourth Coffee's income before taxes. Modify the chart by adding additional chart elements.

USE the workbook from the previous project.

1. Select the chart area and click Chart Title in the Labels group on the Layout tab.
2. Click More Title Options and click Gradient fill.
3. In the Preset colors box, click Moss (first option in the third row) and click Close. The Chart Title text box is selected.
4. In the Chart Title text box, key Income Before Taxes and press Enter.
5. Click Axis Titles and click Primary Vertical Axis Title.
6. Click Rotated Title. The Axis Title text box is selected.
7. In the Axis Title text box, key in thousands and press Enter.
8. Right-click the Axis Title text box and click Font.
9. Click Font color and click Green. Click OK.
10. **SAVE** the workbook as *Financial History 10-3*.
11. **CLOSE** the file.

LEAVE Excel open for the next project.

Project 10-4: Create a Line Chart

In this exercise, you will build Line charts to view the results of the data calculations with data markers.

GET READY. LAUNCH Excel if it is not already running.

@ The *BY Financials* file for this lesson is available on the book companion website or in WileyPLUS.

1. **OPEN** the *BY Financials* file for this lesson.
2. On the Annual Sales worksheet, select A3:E7. Click Line on the Insert tab.
3. Click Stacked line with Markers.
4. Apply Layout 3.
5. Click Chart Title and key Blue Yonder Airlines in the formula bar.
6. Click Plot Area and click Format Selection.
7. Click Border Color and click Gradient line.
8. Click Preset Colors and click Daybreak (first row, fourth option from left).
9. Click Direction and click Linear Diagonal. Click Close.
10. Click Chart Area, click Format Selection, and click Solid fill.
11. In the Fill Color area, click Color and click Blue, Accent 1, Lighter 80%.
12. Click Close.
13. **SAVE** the workbook as *BY Financials 10-4*.

LEAVE the workbook open for the next project.

Project 10-5: Create a Doughnut Chart

In this exercise, you will apply data results in a doughnut chart.

GET READY. LAUNCH Excel if it is not already running.

1. **USE** the workbook from the previous project.
2. Click the Annual Expenses tab. Select A3:E7 and click Other Charts on the Insert tab.
3. Click Doughnut.
4. Click Layout 2.
5. On the Format tab, click the Size dialog box launcher. Set both height and width to 5 inches.
6. Key Annual Expenses as the chart title.
7. Print the chart only.
8. **SAVE** the workbook as *BY Financials 10-5*. **CLOSE** the workbook.

LEAVE Excel open for the next project.

Project 10-6: Fixing the Fitness Classes Worksheet

Fourth Coffee's corporate manager wants to change the chart type and some of the formatting in the chart prepared in a previous exercise.

GET READY. LAUNCH Excel if it is not already running.

@ The *Income Chart* file for this lesson is available on the book companion website or in WileyPLUS.

1. **OPEN** the *Income Chart* file for this lesson.
2. Select the chart. Click the Design tab.
3. Click Layout 3.
4. On the Layout tab, click Axis Titles, click Primary Horizontal Axis Title, choose Title Below Axis, and then key Percentage of Income below the axis.
5. Click Data Labels and add data labels to the bars.
6. Right-click the chart title and click Font. Click Font color and click Red – Accent 2 under Theme Colors.
7. Click Small Caps and click OK.
8. On the Layout tab, in the Current Selection group, click the down arrow next to Chart Title and choose Legend.
9. Click Colored Outline – Red Accent 2 on the Format tab.
10. On the Design tab, click Move Chart Location. Click New Sheet and click OK.
11. **SAVE** the workbook as *Income Chart 10-6* and then **CLOSE** the file.

LEAVE Excel open for the next project.

INTERNET READY

Customized chart styles cannot be saved and applied to other charts. However, you can save a customized chart as a template. Use Excel Help to learn how to save a chart as a template that can be used later. Open your *Income Chart 10-6* workbook and save it as a template file to the Lesson 10 folder. Save the workbook as *Chart Template*. Close Excel.

11 Adding Pictures and Shapes to a Worksheet

LESSON SKILL MATRIX

Skill	Exam Objective	Objective Number
Inserting Pictures	Insert illustrations.	6.2.1
	Modify clip art SmartArt.	6.2.5
Adding Shapes	Position illustrations.	6.2.2
	Modify shapes.	6.2.6
Copying or Moving a Graphic		
Formatting Graphics	Size illustrations.	6.2.3
	Rotate illustrations.	6.2.4
Adding Graphic Enhancements Using Picture Tools	Change artistic effects on an image.	6.3.3
	Use picture color tools.	6.3.2
	Make corrections to an image.	6.3.1
	Modify screenshots.	6.2.7

KEY TERMS

- clip
- clip art
- Clip Organizer
- connector
- flowchart
- organization chart
- Quick Styles
- SmartArt graphic
- Text pane

Adding a chart, picture, or other illustration to a worksheet captures attention and immediately portrays an idea of what the worksheet is all about. The manager of Margie's Travel often inserts pictures, clip art, shapes, and SmartArt graphics into the Excel worksheets she sends to clients. Providing potential travelers with actual photos or other representations of highlights in vacation areas is an effective communication tool for a travel agency.

SOFTWARE ORIENTATION

The Insert Tab

Microsoft Office includes a gallery of media images you can insert into worksheets such as pictures, clip art, shapes, and SmartArt graphics. You can also insert a text box that can be positioned anywhere on the worksheet or insert WordArt to call attention to a worksheet or chart's primary message. Use the Insert tab shown in Figure 11-1 to insert illustrations and special text.

Insert graphics illustrations   **Insert decorative text**

Figure 11-1

Insert tab

Use this figure as a reference throughout this lesson as you become skilled in inserting and formatting illustrations within a worksheet.

INSERTING PICTURES

The Bottom Line

While the old adage *a picture is worth a thousand words* is perhaps an exaggeration, a visual feature adds interest and calls attention to statistical data presented in worksheets. Unlike a worksheet background that is displayed but does not print, pictures, clip art, shapes, and SmartArt graphics are included in worksheet printouts. Graphic objects can be used with charts to focus attention on relevant data.

Inserting a Picture from a File

Pictures can be an integral part of creating a compelling worksheet. You can insert or copy pictures into a worksheet from image providers or files on your computer, such as your favorite digital photographs. A well-chosen picture can portray a powerful message, or it can be used to enhance a chart or other Excel graphic display. Using Excel's Insert Picture command, you can customize the presentation of worksheet data with selected photographs. In the next exercise, you will insert pictures from a file.

The manager of Margie's Travel is preparing a worksheet with detailed travel arrangements for a client's annual sales meeting to be held at a hotel in Yosemite National Park. The client wants to combine the business travel with a family vacation package. The manager will use your worksheet with photos of the area and add the financial data related to the proposal. The visuals can be formatted to enhance the data and call attention to the most important aspects of the workbook.

STEP BY STEP | Insert a Picture from a File

GET READY. Before you begin these steps, **LAUNCH** Microsoft Excel and create a new Blank workbook.

1. Click the Sheet1 tab. Click Format in the Cells group on the Home tab and click Rename Sheet from the drop-down menu that appears. Key Vernal Fall to replace the selected Sheet1 text, and press Enter. Use the same process to rename Sheet2 to El Capitan and to rename Sheet3 to Sequoias.

2. Select A1 on the Vernal Fall worksheet. On the Insert tab, click Picture. The Insert Picture dialog box opens.

3. In the dialog box directory, navigate to the data files for this lesson, and then click *Vernal Fall*. Click Insert. The picture is inserted and, as shown in Figure 11-2, the Format tab with Picture Tools is added to the Ribbon.

Figure 11-2

Picture Tools on the Format tab

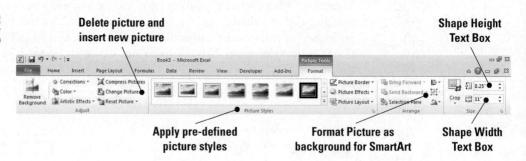

4. Select the number in the Shape Height text box, key 5, and press Enter. The image changes to a height of 5 inches, with its width automatically proportioned.

5. Select A1 on the El Capitan worksheet. Click the Insert tab and click Picture. In the Insert Picture dialog box, navigate to the data files for this lesson and click the El Capitan image, then click Insert. The picture is inserted and the Picture Tools become available.

6. Select the Shape Height value, key 5, and press Enter.

7. Select A1 on the Sequoias worksheet. Click the Insert tab and click Picture. In the dialog box, click Sequoias to select it from the data files for this lesson. Click Insert to insert the picture.

8. Select the Shape Height value, key 5, and press Enter.

9. Create a Lesson 11 folder and **SAVE** the workbook as *Yosemite*.

PAUSE. LEAVE the workbook open to use in the next exercise.

Take Note When you change the picture height, the width is automatically adjusted.

Inserting a Clip Art Picture

A **clip** refers to a single media file including art, sound, animation, or movies. A **clip art** image is a single piece of readymade art, often appearing as a bitmap or a combination of drawn shapes. You can insert a clip art image into a worksheet from Microsoft Office Online, other image providers, or files on your computer. When you search for clip art in Excel, your search results can include clip art, photographs, movies, and sound files. In this exercise, you will insert clip art into your worksheet.

Insert a Clip Art Picture

USE the workbook from the previous exercise.

1. Click on any blank cell in the Sequoia worksheet. On the Home tab, click Insert and click Insert Sheet. Click the rename option in the Cells group, and then click Insert Sheet from the drop-down menu that appears. Click to select the text in the new worksheet's tab, and then rename the sheet Clip Art.

2. On the *Insert* tab, click Clip Art. The Clip Art task pane opens on the right side of the Excel window.

Take Note   If you are connected to the Internet, the search results can return numerous clip art images from Microsoft Office Online as well as the images in your clip art files. If you are not connected to the Internet, the search results will be limited to images stored in your clip art collections.

3. Click the Results should be drop-down arrow and place a check mark in all media types. In the *Search for* field, key waterfall and click Go. Results are displayed similar to those shown in Figure 11-3.

Figure 11-3

Default settings for clip art search

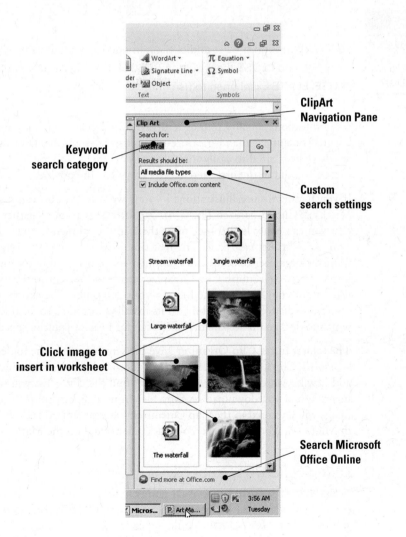

Keyword search category

ClipArt Navigation Pane

Custom search settings

Click image to insert in worksheet

Search Microsoft Office Online

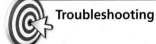

Troubleshooting If waterfall images are not returned by your search, connect to the Internet to include search results from Microsoft Office Online or insert one of the waterfall images from the data files for this lesson.

4. Your results will return more than just graphics. Be sure not to select any audio or video file. Click any image in the search results to insert a waterfall into the Clip Art worksheet.

5. In the Clip Art task pane, click the arrow in the *Results should be* field. Deselect all media types except Illustrations (as shown in Figure 11-4). Click **Go**. The results include only clip art images.

Figure 11-4

Restrict search to Illustrations only

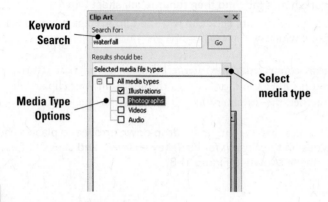

Keyword Search

Select media type

Media Type Options

CERTIFICATION READY   6.2.1

How do you insert a clip art image into a worksheet?

6. Scroll through the list and click an image to insert a waterfall clip art image.

7. **SAVE** and **CLOSE** the workbook. **CLOSE** the Clip Art task pane.

PAUSE. LEAVE Excel open to use in the next exercise.

The professional-quality photos returned by a clip art search are usually more appropriate in a business document than caricature-type artistic designs. Some of the photos in the clip art gallery have been sized to easily insert into a document, and you do not always need to adjust the size, as you did in the first exercise, to easily view the picture.

If you frequently use illustrations in your worksheets, you can organize your favorites in the Microsoft Clip Organizer. The **Clip Organizer** is a way to gather and store your own clips so that you can easily locate and insert them into documents. You can access the Clip Organizer from the Clip Art task pane. The first time you open the Clip Organizer, you are asked if you want the organizer to scan your computer for photos and other media files and organize them into separate collections. Clip Organizer creates a shortcut to the files in their original location; it does not copy or move the files on your computer. The shortcuts let you preview, open, or insert a media file without going to its installed location. You can let the Clip Organizer decide which folders and hardware drives to scan for files, or you can specify where to search.

The folders in the Clip Organizer have the same names as the folders in which the original files are stored. Clip Organizer automatically adds keywords to media files. You can modify, delete, or add new keywords to ensure that you will find the clip when you want to insert it into a document. When you download or copy files from a clip art source such as Microsoft Online, the image will be stored in the Clip Organizer. Clips organized and saved in Excel can then be used in Microsoft Word and PowerPoint documents and on the Margie's Travel website.

Using SmartArt Graphics

A **SmartArt graphic** is a visual representation of information and ideas. SmartArt graphics can be used with other images and decorative text. When you insert a SmartArt image into your worksheet, The **Text pane** should appear to the left of a SmartArt graphic, containing bullets that represent the shapes in the graphic. The Text pane works like an outline or a bulleted list that maps information directly to the graphic. You can use the pane to enter and edit the text that appears in the graphic.

SmartArt should not be confused with clip art. Clip art is an actual image. SmartArt is a graphical representation of something other than an image that you would want to add to a worksheet. An example would be a flowchart. The SmartArt library has many different styles and themes that can be applied to the worksheet. You can build the flowchart, add text to it, change its appearance, move the objects on the worksheet, and make it ready for presentation. In this next exercise, you will apply SmartArt graphics.

STEP BY STEP   **Use SmartArt Graphics**

@ The *Cruise Dates* file for this lesson is available on the book companion website or in WileyPLUS.

OPEN the *Cruise Dates* file for this lesson.

1. On the Mexico worksheet, select C24.

2. On the Insert tab, in the Illustrations group, click SmartArt. The *Choose a SmartArt Graphic* dialog box is displayed as shown in Figure 11-5.

Figure 11-5

Select layout for SmartArt graphic

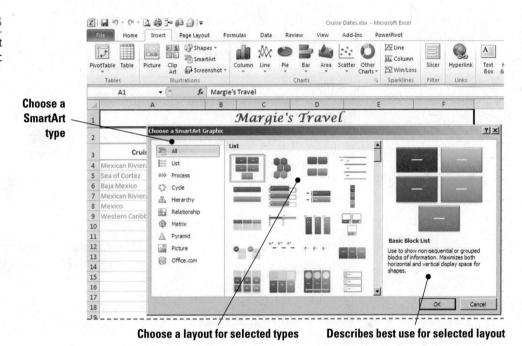

3. In the *Choose a SmartArt Graphic* dialog box, click Cycle in the type pane on the left side of the dialog box.

4. Click Block Cycle (top row, third from left) in the layout pane on the right side of the dialog box. Click OK. The Cycle graphic image is inserted and SmartArt Tools are available on the Design and Format tabs. When it is inserted, the graphic is joined by its Text pane. This pane allows the user to enter the information to be contained in the SmartArt graphic.

5. On the Design tab, shown in Figure 11-6, click the Text Pane button in the Create Graphic group if the Text pane is not displayed when the graphic is inserted. Point to the Block Cycle layout name at the bottom of the Text Pane to see a ScreenTip; holding a description of the best use for the selected SmartArt layout.

Figure 11-6

SmartArt Tools tab

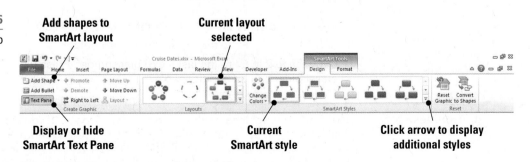

6. The Text pane and the SmartArt graphic have placeholder text that you can replace with your information. The first Text placeholder will be selected as shown in Figure 11-7. Key **May 20**. As you key text in the Text pane, it is displayed in the first block of the Cycle graphic.

Figure 11-7

SmartArt graphic with text pane

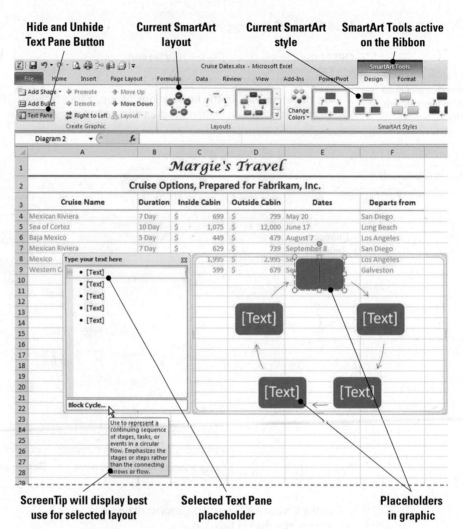

Hide and Unhide Text Pane Button

Current SmartArt layout

Current SmartArt style

SmartArt Tools active on the Ribbon

ScreenTip will display best use for selected layout

Selected Text Pane placeholder

Placeholders in graphic

7. Click, hold, and drag the SmartArt graphic to rest below the cells in the worksheet. Select **E5** in the data range and click **Copy**.

8. Click the graphic, select the second **[Text]** placeholder, and click **Paste**. The date of June 17 that you copied has now been pasted into the second graphic.

Take Note   If you press Enter when you key or copy text to a text placeholder, a new block is added to the SmartArt graphic image. You can delete an unwanted block by deleting the placeholder. When you click outside the SmartArt graphic, the Text pane closes. Click the graphic to display the pane to insert or paste additional text.

9. Copy **E6** and paste the date in the third [Text] placeholder.

10. Copy the text in **E7** to the fourth [Text] placeholder.

11. Copy the text in **E8** to the last [Text] placeholder. Press **Enter** to add an additional text placeholder and an additional block to the Cycle graphic.

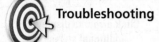

Troubleshooting   Each SmartArt graphic contains a fixed number of spaces. If you enter too much information, it will not be displayed. Content that is not displayed is identified with a red X in the Text pane. The content is still available if you switch to another SmartArt layout with more space, but if you close the workbook with the same layout, the hidden information is lost.

12. Copy the text in E9 to the last block.
13. Click outside the image to view the Cycle graphic image as it is displayed in your worksheet. Note that the text pane is now hidden from view and only the graphic with its formatting remains. The deselected graphic is shown in Figure 11-8. To view the graphic with its text pane refer to Figure 11-7.

Figure 11-8

SmartArt graphic with text pane hidden

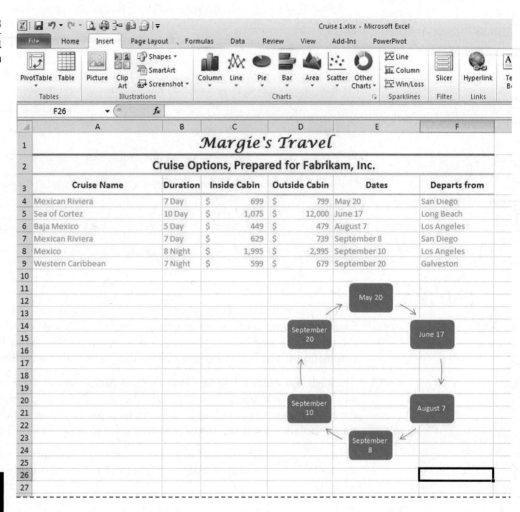

CERTIFICATION READY 6.2.5

How do you insert and modify SmartArt graphics?

14. **SAVE** the workbook as *Cruise 1*.

PAUSE. LEAVE the workbook open to use in the next exercise.

When choosing a layout for a SmartArt graphic, determine what you want to convey and how your information should appear, then try different layouts until you find the one that best illustrates your message. Your graphic should be clear and easy to follow. Single descriptive words and short descriptive phrases are recommended for your graphic. Table 11-1 lists the seven types of SmartArt graphics and a short description of the purpose of each type.

Table 11-1

SmartArt graphic types and purposes

Graphic Type	Purpose of Graphic
List	Show nonsequential information
Process	Show steps in a process or timeline
Cycle	Show a continual process
Hierarchy	Show a decision tree Create an organization chart
Relationship	Illustrate connections
Matrix	Show how parts relate to a whole
Pyramid	Show proportional relationships with the largest component on the top or bottom
Picture	Manipulate multiple graphics in a style and order
Office.com	Additional Styles available online

If you cannot find the exact layout that you want, you can add and remove shapes in your SmartArt graphic to adjust the structure of the layout. When you add or remove shapes and edit the text, the arrangement of the shapes and the amount of text within those shapes is updated automatically. The original design and border of the layout is maintained.

Although you cannot drag text into the Text pane, you can copy and paste to the pane. Also, you can copy from the Text pane to any Microsoft Office program. When you click away from the SmartArt graphic, the Text pane disappears. You can show or hide the Text pane by clicking the control on the left side of the SmartArt graphic or by clicking Text Pane on the Design tab.

In general, SmartArt graphics work best with small amounts of text. Larger amounts of text detract from the visual appeal of the graphic and make it more difficult to convey your message visually.

ADDING SHAPES

The Bottom Line

You can add a shape to a workbook or combine multiple shapes to create a drawing or a more complex shape. Available shapes include lines, basic geometric shapes, arrows, equation shapes, flowchart shapes, stars, banners, and callouts.

Inserting Basic Shapes

You can use a shape to call attention to an important aspect of worksheet data. Excel provides a variety of basic shapes that you can insert. You can add shapes to a chart or add shapes on top of a SmartArt graphic to customize the chart or SmartArt graphic. When you use more than one shape, it does not matter which shape you insert first. You can use the Bring to Front and Send to Back commands to place the shape containing text on top so that the text is visible. In this exercise, you insert and format basic shapes in Excel, and place one shape on top of another to achieve a desired result.

STEP BY STEP   **Insert Basic Shapes**

USE the workbook from the previous exercise.

1. On the Alaska worksheet, click A5. Click Shapes in the Illustrations group on the Insert tab. The Shapes gallery shown in Figure 11-9 opens.

Figure 11-9

Select a shape from the shapes gallery

Shapes Command Button

Shapes Styles Gallery

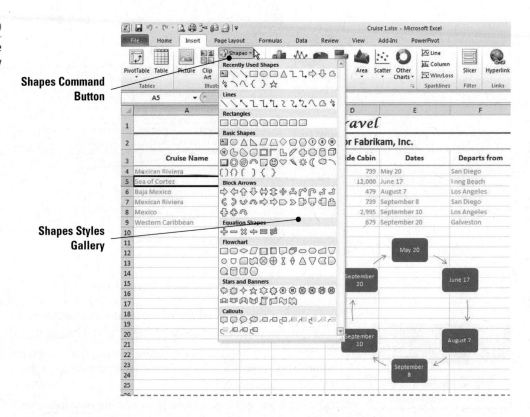

2. Click Rounded Rectangle in the Rectangles group in the Shapes gallery and click A5 to place the rectangle in that cell. Use the handles on the rectangle to resize the rectangle to hide the text in row 5 from A5 to the right boundary of F5 of the worksheet.

3. On the Format tab, in the Shape Styles group, click Colored Outline—Orange, Accent 6 (first outline style). This places the colored border around the graphic.

4. Click Shape Fill in the Shape Styles group and click No Fill. Click an empty cell to deselect the rectangle. The text in your cells is now visible since you chose the no fill option. The colored outline shape calls attention to the Southbound Glacier Discovery cruise that leaves Seattle on June 4.

5. Click WordArt in the Text group on the Insert tab. In the WordArt gallery, click Fill—Orange, Accent 6 Outline – Accent 6, Glow—Accent 6 (second row, second style). The WordArt sample text *Your Text Here* is placed on the worksheet.

6. Click the Home tab, place your insertion point in the number in the Font Size box and key 36. Press Enter.

7. The Your text here text is still selected; replace it by keying Lowest Price of the Summer in the WordArt text box.

8. Move the WordArt text box so that it is several rows directly below the last row of data and aligned with the data range.

9. On the Insert tab, click Shapes and click Double Arrow (third option from the left) in the Lines group. Click C5 to position the arrow from C5 to the WordArt below the data range. Refer to Figure 11-10.

Figure 11-10

SmartArt Shapes inserted

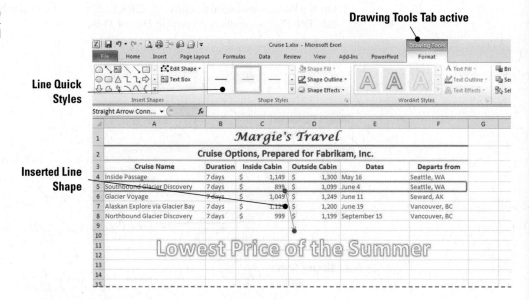

Line Quick Styles

Drawing Tools Tab active

Inserted Line Shape

10. Click the Insert tab. On the Mexico worksheet, click Shapes. In the Rectangles group, click Snip Same Side Corner Rectangle (fourth from left) in the Rectangles section of the gallery. Click in the center of the existing SmartArt to place the new shape.

11. Click Colored Outline—Orange, Accent 6 in the Shape Styles group.

12. Use the shape's handles to resize the rectangle and drag the rectangle to cover the SmartArt graphic. Click Send Backward in the Arrange group on the Format tab.

13. **SAVE** your workbook.

PAUSE. LEAVE the workbook open to use in the next exercise.

CERTIFICATION READY   **6.2.1**

How do you add a basic shape to a worksheet?

Drawing Lines

You may want to add a line to point to data in a specific location, create a signature line, or separate text. A **connector** is a line that has connection points at the ends of the line and stays connected to the shape to which you have connected it. Straight, elbow, and curved lines are available. In this exercise, you add two text boxes to your worksheet, and then insert connector lines to connect the text boxes.

STEP BY STEP   **Draw Lines**

USE the workbook from the previous exercise.

1. On the Advertising worksheet, on the Insert tab, in the Text group, click Text Box.

2. Select A2 and draw a text box that covers A2:A4. Your cursor will become an upside-down cross when you have chosen the text box option. You simply point to the place where you want to start the box, click, hold, and drag to the area of the worksheet where you want the text box to end and then release the mouse. It might take several tries before you get used to the process. See Figure 11-11 for a visual aid.

Figure 11-11

Creating a text box

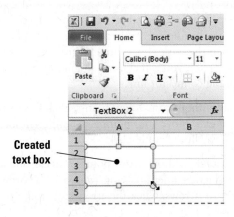

Created text box

3. Click **inside the box** and then key **Cruise** in the text box.

4. Click the **Insert** tab. Click **Text Box** and select **C5**. Using the same process you learned in step 2, draw a text box that covers C5:C7.

5. Key **Relax** in the text box.

6. Click the **Insert** tab. Click **Text Box** and select **E8**. Draw a text box that covers E8:E10.

7. Key **Enjoy** in the text box.

8. On the Insert tab, click **Shapes** in the Illustrations group. In the Lines section of the gallery, click **Elbow Double-Arrow Connector** (sixth from the left). Red circular dots (the connection points) appear on the text boxes as you move your pointer over them.

9. Click on the **Cruise** textbox to reveal the connection points. Black indicators show where you can attach a connector.

10. Click the **right connection point** on the Cruise text box and drag the connection arrow to the left connection point on the Relax text box.

11. Use the same procedure in step 8 to connect the Relax text box to the Enjoy text box. Your worksheet should look like Figure 11-12.

Figure 11-12

Use connector lines to connect shapes

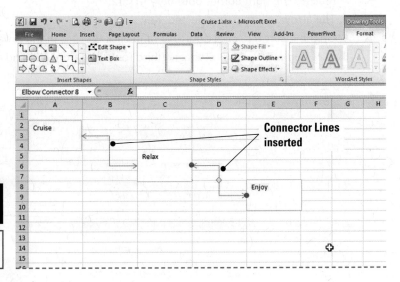

Connector Lines inserted

CERTIFICATION
READY   6.2.6

How do you draw lines to connect shapes?

12. Click the border of the Cruise text box to display the move arrow. Drag the box to A8. The connection line remains with the text box.

13. Move the Cruise text box to A2:A4.

Take Note   After you have connected the text boxes, you can move the connection line independently, but not the boxes that the connector links.

14. **SAVE** your workbook.

PAUSE. LEAVE the workbook open to use in the next exercise.

When you rearrange shapes that are joined by connectors, the connectors move with the shapes. You can move the end of a connector to detach it from the shape. You can then attach it to another connection site on the same shape, attach it to another shape, or delete the connector. When you select the connector, you can click the diamond shape in the center of the connector and change the angle of the connector line.

If you want to draw a line without connection points, click Freeform in the Shapes gallery. Click one position in the document, move your pointer to a different location, and click again. When you are finished drawing the line, double-click.

If you attach shapes with a line without arrow points, you can add an arrowhead to the line after it has been attached to a shape. Under Drawing Tools on the Format tab, click the arrow next to Shape Outline and point to Arrows. Click the arrow style you want.

Inserting a Block Arrow

Insert block arrows when you want to show steps in a process or show a timeline. You can insert a block arrow from the Shapes gallery, or you can insert a SmartArt graphic and select the Continuous Arrow Process. The SmartArt Continuous Arrow Process arrow is used to show a timeline or sequential steps in a task, process, or workflow. The standard block arrow can serve the same purpose or be used to call attention to data in the worksheet. In this exercise, you will insert block arrows into the worksheet.

STEP BY STEP	Insert a Block Arrow

USE the workbook from the previous exercise.

1. On the Hawaii worksheet, click the Insert tab if necessary and then click Shapes. Under Block Arrows, click Right Arrow.
2. Move the insertion crosshairs to A11 and drag the block so that the arrow point touches the right corner boundary of B12.
3. The arrow will remain selected. Key Explore the Islands!.
4. On the Insert tab, click SmartArt, and click Process in the SmartArt type pane.
5. Click Continuous Arrow Process (third row, third from left) and click OK. See Figure 11-13.

Figure 11-13

Selecting a SmartArt Process

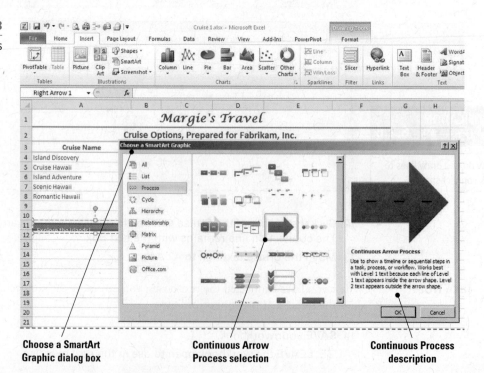

Choose a SmartArt
Graphic dialog box

Continuous Arrow
Process selection

Continuous Process
description

6. Click any edge of the SmartArt image to display the move pointer and click and drag the pointer to move the image below the block arrow shape.

7. The first placeholder is already active. Key Call Today!.

8. In the second placeholder, key Sail this Summer!.

9. Select the third [Text] placeholder and press Backspace to delete the third placeholder bullet.

10. **SAVE** and **CLOSE** the workbook.

PAUSE. LEAVE Excel open to use in the next exercise.

There is little difference between the two block arrows you inserted in this exercise. You can size either arrow to fit your needs. The major difference is that text entered in the SmartArt graphic is entered in a text box so messages can be separated, as illustrated in the exercise.

Creating a Flowchart

A **flowchart** is a schematic representation of a process—a working map for reaching your final product or decision. A flowchart shows the steps in a process, such as in the instructions for assembling a new computer, a diagram of a manufacturing plant's work flow, or the required steps for responding to a request for proposal (RFP). You can create a flowchart by inserting Flowchart shapes and connectors or use a Process SmartArt graphic. You can add more detail when you create a flowchart by using the flowchart shapes. The SmartArt graphic saves time but provides less detail. The flowchart's intended use and the amount of detail needed determine which style should be used. In the next exercise, you construct a flowchart.

Flowchart shapes provide an indication of what happens during the flow of work. In the Flowchart worksheet, for example, the chart begins with a Preparation shape. A diamond shape is used to indicate a decision. Connector arrows point one direction if the decision is no, and point the other direction if the decision is yes. See Figure 11-14.

Figure 11-14

Basic flowchart components

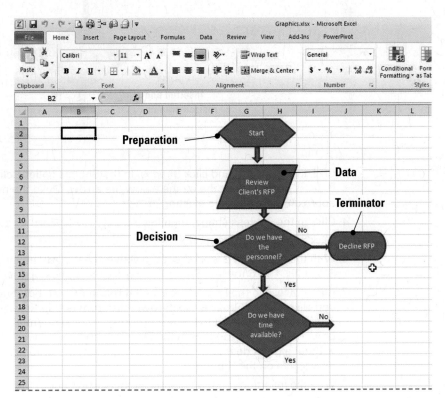

STEP BY STEP   Create a Flowchart

The *Graphics* workbook file for this lesson is available on the book companion website or in WileyPLUS.

OPEN the *Graphics* workbook file for this lesson.

1. On the Flowchart 1 worksheet, click the Insert tab, and then click Shapes to produce the Shapes gallery.

2. In the Block Arrows section of the gallery, click Down Arrow. The arrow is now inserted in the worksheet. Move the newly inserted arrow to the bottom point of the last diamond shape. Adjust the arrow's size to resemble the existing arrows. Move again to have the arrow reside directly below the point of the diamond as shown in Figure 11-15.

Figure 11-15

Block arrow placed and resized

WileyPLUS Extra! features an online tutorial of this task.

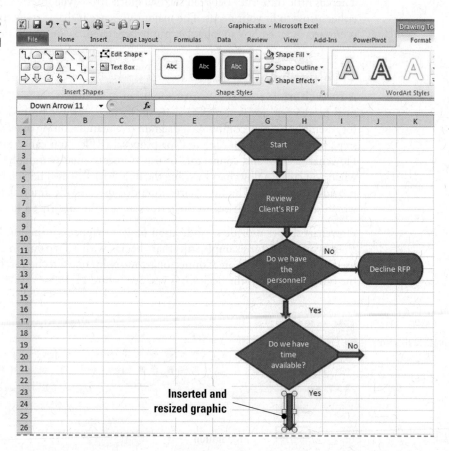

Inserted and resized graphic

3. Click the Insert tab and click Shapes. In the Shapes gallery, click the Flowchart: Process shape. Insert the image below the arrow. Make the newly inserted arrow the approximate size of the existing arrows.

4. Click in the Process shape, then key Prepare worksheet to calculate potential earnings.

5. Click Sheet2 and rename it Flowchart 2.

6. With the Flowchart 2 worksheet the active sheet, click the Insert tab, and click SmartArt. The *Choose a SmartArt Graphic* dialog box opens.

7. Click Process in the Type pane. Scroll through the list, pointing to the process to locate and click Vertical Process (sixth row, third from left) in the Layout pane. The Vertical Process layout is used to show a progression or sequential steps in a task, process, or work flow from top to bottom. This SmartArt layout works best with Level 1 text without a great deal of detail. Click OK to insert the graphic. The SmartArt Tools tab is now active on the Ribbon.

8. With the insertion point in the first [Text] placeholder in the Text pane, key Review RFP.

9. In the second placeholder, key Personnel?.

10. In the third placeholder text box, key Time?. Press Enter. You have now added another text box in the text pane.

CERTIFICATION
READY   6.2.5

How do you use shapes and
SmartArt graphics?

11. Key Prepare Worksheet. The size and shape of the rectangles in the diagram change as you enter a longer text string.

12. **SAVE** the workbook as *Graphics 1*.

PAUSE. LEAVE the workbook open to use in the next exercise.

Creating an Organization Chart

One of the most common uses for the Hierarchy layout is a company organization chart. An **organization chart** graphically illustrates the management structure of an organization. When you choose this layout, additional functionality, such as the assistant shape and hanging layouts, become available. In the next exercise, you will create and modify an organization chart.

STEP BY STEP   **Create an Organization Chart**

USE the workbook you saved in the previous exercise.

1. Click the Sheet3 tab. Right-click, click Format, click Rename Sheet; the Sheet3 text in the worksheet tab is selected.

2. Key Organization Chart and press Enter.

3. On the Insert tab, click SmartArt to open the *Choose a SmartArt Graphic* dialog box.

4. Click Hierarchy in the Shape Type pane. Click Organization Chart in the layout pane and click OK.

5. In the first [Text] placeholder, key Margie Shoop, CEO, and press Enter. You have added a new text placeholder.

6. Click Demote in the Create Graphic group on the Design tab to demote the box to Level 2. This moves the box one level below the CEO and to the left. Key John Y. Chen and press Enter. You have now added another Text placeholder.

7. Click Demote and key Jamie Reding. Press Enter. This new text placeholder is now one level below John Y. Chen.

8. Key Stephanie Conway and press Enter. You have now created another text placeholder.

9. Click Promote and key Ciam Sawyer. Press Enter. You have now created another text placeholder.

10. Click Demote and key Jeffrey Ford. This now moves the text placeholder one level below Ciam Sawyer.

11. Click inside the text of the first text placeholder (Margie Shoop, CEO) in the Text pane, then click the drop-down list arrow next to Add Shape in the Create Graphic group on SmartArt Tools Design tab. The Add Shape drop-down list appears.

Take Note   You can select a diagram shape and click Add Shape. You can then choose the position and shape type that should be added.

Another Way
When you key text in a Text pane placeholder, you can select the next placeholder by clicking it rather than pressing Enter. Press **Enter** when you need additional positions in the organization chart.

12. Click Add Assistant in the drop-down list that appears. Key Brenda Diaz, Assistant in the new text placeholder that appears in Text pane.

13. Select any blank placeholders in the Text pane and click Delete. If necessary, press Backspace to delete the last blank text placeholder. Move the graphic to the upper left corner of the worksheet.

14. Click outside the graphic. Your organization chart should look like Figure 11-16.

Figure 11-16

Organization chart created
with SmartArt Tools

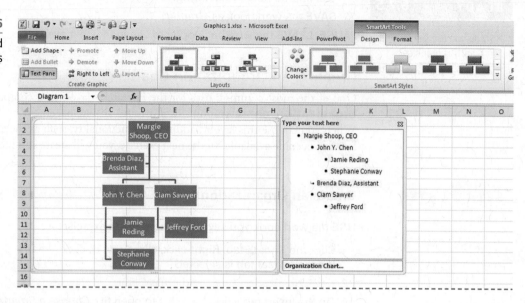

15. SAVE your workbook.

PAUSE. LEAVE the workbook open to use in the next exercise.

In this exercise, you created a standard organization chart for Margie's Travel. In a subsequent exercise, you will modify the SmartArt graphic by changing the reporting level of some positions. You can adjust levels in the organizational chart by selecting the shape or the bulleted item in the Text pane and then clicking Promote or Demote.

When two individuals share the top-level responsibilities, their positions should be connected by a broken line. The SmartArt Organization Chart layout does not provide this type of connection. You can insert a broken line and connect the two blocks.

Character formatting such as bold or italic can be applied in the Text pane. This formatting will be displayed in the graphic, but not in the Text pane.

COPYING OR MOVING A GRAPHIC

Pictures, clip art, shapes, and SmartArt graphics are not always inserted where you want them for an effective presentation. You can move a graphic manually, or specify its exact size by using options in the Size group on the Format tab. When you want to move a graphic incrementally, use the arrow keys, which provide precision. Click the graphic border and move the graphic for a significant change in location.

Copying or Moving a Graphic

You can copy a SmartArt graphic, or any other graphical display, and paste it to another location within the worksheet, paste it to another worksheet or workbook, or paste it to another Microsoft Office program. You can move a shape in a SmartArt graphic, or you can move the whole graphic. This flexibility allows you to customize the design of the graphical display. In this exercise, you will move and copy graphics.

Copy or Move a Graphic

 Another Way
In a previous exercise, you copied text from worksheet cells and pasted it in a bullet point in a SmartArt graphic. You can also copy and paste text within the Text pane.

 Another Way
When you have a SmartArt graphic that has multiple elements and you want to copy it, you can use Ctrl+A when the graphic is active to select all the elements of that graphic.

USE the workbook you saved in the previous exercise.

1. Click the Flowchart 2 tab to open the worksheet.
2. Click the SmartArt graphic to select it. Press the up, down, left, or right directional arrows on your keyboard to move the graphic so that it fills F4:H18.
3. Click anywhere in the Flowchart 2 graphic. Click Copy on the Home tab to copy the graphic.
4. Click the Flowchart 1 worksheet, select D32, and click Paste; the graphic appears in cell D32.
5. Click the right-center border of the graphic and drag the border to the right boundary of column M.
6. Click the first rectangle (Review RFP) in the organization chart and drag it to the left and down so that it is parallel to the second rectangle (Personnel?). Notice that the arrow now points to the right toward the other rectangle.
7. **SAVE** the workbook.

PAUSE. LEAVE the workbook open to use in the next exercise.

FORMATTING GRAPHICS

The Bottom Line

The formatting styles such as font, fill color, and effects that are applied when you insert a shape or SmartArt graphic are based on the underlying document theme of the worksheet. You can apply a Quick Style to an entire graphic or apply formatting components to various parts of a graphic.

Applying Styles to Shapes

Quick Styles are combinations of different formatting options. They are displayed in a thumbnail in various Quick Style galleries on the Format tab that is added to the Ribbon when a graphic is inserted in a worksheet. When you place your pointer over a style thumbnail on the Format tab, you can see how applying that style will affect your SmartArt graphic or shape. In this exercise, you change the appearance of a graphic by applying formatting to flowchart components to preview various formatting styles. After trying several effects, you can select a basic style to use throughout the flowchart rather than have such varying styles in one graphic. In the next exercise, you will be applying shape styles to the SmartArt.

Apply Styles to Shapes

USE the workbook from the previous exercise.

1. On the Flowchart 1 worksheet, at the top of the Organization chart, select the Start shape. The Drawing Tools tab is now active on the Ribbon.
2. Click the Format tab and click the more arrow next to the predefined Outline Styles in the Shape Styles group. This opens the Outline Colors gallery.
3. In row 4, click Subtle Effect – Red, Accent 2. You have now applied this style to the Start object.
4. Select the first diamond shape, press Shift, and select the second diamond. You have now selected both objects.
5. Click Shape Fill and click Red, Accent 2.
6. With the shapes still selected, click Shape Outline.
7. Click Dash Dot.
8. Click Shape Effects, point to Glow, and click the first option (Blue 5 pt. glow, Accent color 1) in the Glow gallery.

9. Click **Text Fill** in the WordArt Styles group and click **Dark Blue** in standard colors. You have changed the shape text as illustrated in Figure 11-17.

Figure 11-17

Organization chart with formatting applied

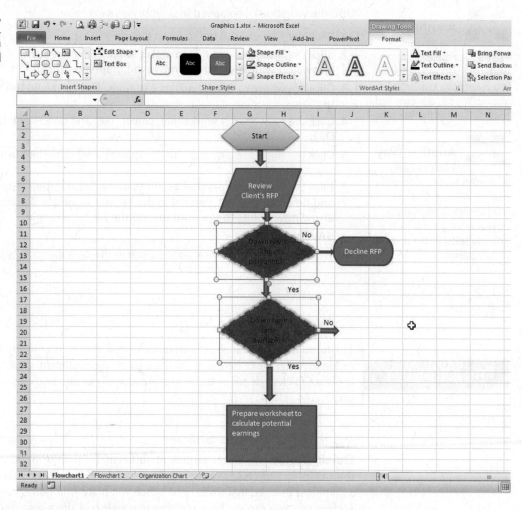

10. **SAVE** the workbook.

PAUSE. LEAVE the workbook open to use in the next exercise.

CERTIFICATION READY   6.2.5

How do you apply a style to SmartArt?

A word of caution is in order: To prevent the formatting of a graphic from overpowering the message, apply formatting sparingly. When a graphic is composed of individual shapes, you must select the shapes to which you want to apply formatting. As you will see in the next exercise, you can apply a predefined style to shapes or apply a style to the entire SmartArt graphic.

Applying Quick Styles to Graphics

SmartArt styles reflect the document theme that was chosen when the worksheet was created. You can apply a different style from those displayed on the Design tab, or you can modify elements within the graphic by changing the shape fill, outline, or effects. You can point to a style and see how that style will look in your display, rather than applying and undoing numerous styles in order to find the one you want to use. That way, you can see the effect without changing anything on your worksheet. In this exercise, you will format shapes by applying quick styles.

STEP BY STEP **Apply Quick Styles to Graphics**

USE the workbook from the previous exercise.

1. On the Flowchart 2 worksheet, select the SmartArt graphic. Click the Design tab. In the SmartArt Styles group, the style that is currently applied to the graphic, based on the Office theme, is selected. The style choices that are available in the SmartArt Styles group on the Design tab are based on the colors, fonts, and effects that comprise the Office theme.

2. Point to each style that is displayed to see the changes that applying the style would have on the SmartArt graphic. Click White Outline.

3. Click the more arrow in the bottom right corner of Smart Art styles and point to various styles in the *Best Match for Document* list to observe changes to the graphic.

4. Preview the styles in the 3-D group and click Metallic Scene (third row, first option on left). When you change the worksheet's theme, the options in the styles gallery change to reflect the new theme that you have applied to the worksheet.

5. Click Change Colors and click Colorful – Accent Colors. Notice that choices in the SmartArt Styles group have changed based on changing the graphics colors. When you insert a SmartArt graphic, a color diagram of the style you select is displayed on the *Choose a SmartArt Graphic* dialog box. The color combination displayed in that sample was applied to your graphic when you clicked Change Colors.

6. On the Organization Chart worksheet, click the SmartArt graphic. Click Subtle Effect in the SmartArt Quick styles window in the SmartArt Styles group.

7. SAVE the workbook as *Graphics 2*.

PAUSE. LEAVE the workbook open to use in the next exercise.

> **CERTIFICATION READY** 6.2.5
>
> How do you modify the style applied to a SmartArt graphic?

Resizing a Graphic

You can resize one or more shapes within a graphic or resize the complete SmartArt graphic. You can use the sizing handles on the side or corner of a graphic to increase or decrease its size, or you can specify a specific size for the height and width of a graphic or shape within the graphic. In this exercise, you will learn how to resize the graphic using the sizing tools on the Ribbon.

STEP BY STEP **Resize a Graphic**

USE the workbook from the previous exercise.

1. On the Organization Chart worksheet, click in the SmartArt graphic to select it.

2. Click the left-center sizing handle and drag it to the column G right boundary.

3. On the Format tab, click Size. In the Height box, key 5.5. In the Width box, key 6. You have now resized the shape.

4. Click the shape at the top of the diagram (Margie Shoop, CEO). Click the right sizing handle and drag to the right until the shape extends over the rest of the organization chart.

5. SAVE and CLOSE the workbook.

PAUSE. LEAVE Excel open to use in the next exercise.

> **CERTIFICATION READY** 6.2.3
>
> How do you resize a SmartArt graphic?

Rotating a Graphic

You can change a shape's position by rotating or reversing it. Reversing a shape is also referred to as creating a mirror image or flipping. When you rotate multiple shapes, they are not rotated as a group, but each shape is rotated around its own center. The predefined rotation options limit you to flipping the graphic. When you open the Size and Properties dialog box, you can rotate a graphic one degree at a time, which gives you a great deal of flexibility in placing the graphic at exactly the angle that calls attention to the most significant data in a worksheet. In the next exercise, you will learn to reposition by rotating the shape.

STEP BY STEP   Rotate a Graphic

@ The *Take a Summer Cruise* file for this lesson is available on the book companion website or in WileyPLUS.

OPEN the *Take a Summer Cruise* file for this lesson.

1. On the Hawaii worksheet, select the text in the standard block arrow (Explore the Islands!). Key Pick a Cruise!.

2. Click the Format tab. In the Arrange group, click Rotate and click Flip Horizontal. The arrow is reversed. The text will remain facing in the original direction.

3. Click Rotate and click Rotate Right 90°. The arrow is now pointing up.

4. Mouse over the graphic, displaying the move pointer, and move it so that the arrow tip is centered in the white space in A6.

5. Click the SmartArt graphic. On the Design tab, click Right to Left in the Create Graphics group. The graphic is reversed horizontally. The text also moved in correspondence with the movement of the arrow.

6. On the Format tab, click Arrange, and then click Selection Pane. On the *Selection and Visibility* pane, click Right Arrow 1.

7. On the Format tab, click Rotate and then click More Rotation Options. The Format Shape dialog box is displayed with the Size options showing.

8. On the *Size and rotate* area, click the down arrow in the Rotation field until the graphic rotation is 70°. Click Close.

9. Move the graphic so that all text is visible and the point is centered in the white space in A6 as illustrated in Figure 11-18.

Figure 11-18

Rotation applied to the Smart-Art shape

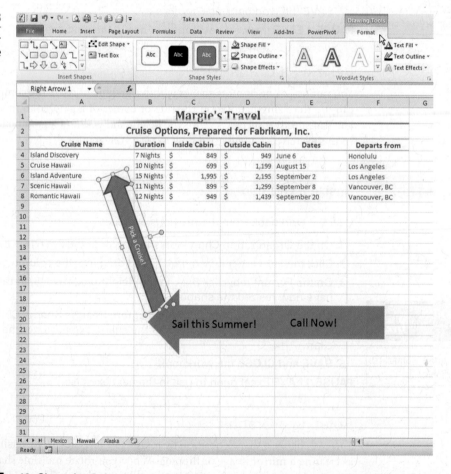

10. Close the Selection and Visibility pane. Also, on the Page Layout tab, in the Sheet Options group, deselect the worksheet Gridlines so they no longer display in the worksheet.

11. **SAVE** the workbook as *Cruise 2*.

PAUSE. LEAVE the workbook open to use in the next exercise.

CERTIFICATION READY   6.2.4

How do you rotate a SmartArt graphic?

If you have more than one graphic in a worksheet, display the Selection and Visibility pane so that you can easily select the graphic that you want to modify or format. Options on the Selection and Visibility pane allow you to hide graphics temporarily and to reorder the shapes on a worksheet. This feature is useful when you want to print a draft, but you do not need the graphics to display until you are ready to print the final document.

Resetting a Picture to Its Original State

Sometimes you make formatting changes and then want to restore a picture or graphic to its original formatting. The Reset Picture command on the Picture Tools Format tab will reset picture formatting to the formatting present when the file was last saved. In the next exercise, you will manipulate picture settings and then reset them back to their original state.

STEP BY STEP | **Reset a Picture to Its Original State**

USE the workbook from the previous exercise.

1. On the Mexico worksheet, select the picture. The Picture Tools tab is now active. Click the Format tab.

2. Click the Crop icon. On the drop-down list, click Crop to Shape and then in the Rectangles options, choose Snip Same Side Corner Rectangle. This crops the right and left top corners of the picture.

3. In the Picture Quick Styles window, in Picture Styles group, click Metal Frame (3rd style). The corners of the picture have now reappeared and there is a metal frame border in place.

4. Click the Corrections button in the Adjust group and the corrections drop-down list opens. In the Brightness and Contrast area, click Brightness: +20% Contrast: –40% (4th option in first row). You have now adjusted the brightness and contrast of the picture.

5. In the Adjust group, click the Color button. The Color drop-down list opens. On the list, in the Recolor section, click Dark Blue, Text color 2 Dark. You have now changed the image to reflect the applied colors as illustrated in Figure 11-19.

Figure 11-19

Reformatted picture

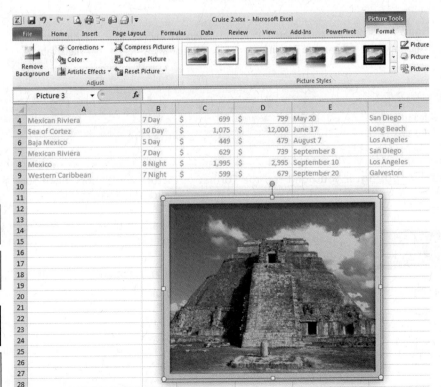

CERTIFICATION READY 6.3.1

How do you restore an image to its original form?

CERTIFICATION READY 6.3.1

How do you change the brightness and contrast in an image?

6. Click Reset Picture in the Adjust group.

7. **SAVE** the workbook with the same name. **CLOSE** the workbook.

LEAVE Excel open for the next exercise.

NEW to Office 2010

ADDING GRAPHIC ENHANCEMENTS USING PICTURE TOOLS

The Bottom Line

New to Office 2010 are enhanced photo editing capabilities. Along with the inclusion of Live Preview, this gives the application user the opportunity to create vibrant, stylistic, and professional picture edits without the need for a third-party program or add-in. Upon selection of your graphic, the picture tools are activated on the Ribbon. In this section, you will be applying artistic effects, color features, picture effects, corrections, borders, and managing picture properties.

Changing a Graphic with Artistic Effects

Located in the Adjust Group on the Ribbon, you will find the button for Artistic Effects. This new feature allows you to edit images to apply effects such as marker, crisscross etching, photocopy, pastels smooth, and glow edges, to list a few. The Artistic Effects feature allows for a more dynamic use of images in workbooks and worksheets. In this next exercise, you will choose and apply several artistic effects to images.

STEP BY STEP

Change a Graphic with Artistic Effects

GET READY. Before you begin these steps, **LAUNCH** Microsoft Excel and create a new Blank workbook.

The *Skyline* image file for this lesson is available on the book companion website or in WileyPLUS.

1. Click on the Insert tab. Choose the *Skyline* image from the Lesson 11 folder. The image is now inserted into the worksheet.

2. Move the image to align with cell B11.

3. Under Picture tools, on the Format tab, in the Adjust group, click the Artistic Effects button, shown in Figure 11-20.

Figure 11-20

Artistic Effects button

Artistic Effects Command Button   Picture Styles Quick Styles   Picture Tools Tab   Placeholders in graphic

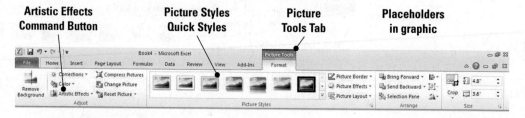

WileyPLUS Extra! features an online tutorial of this task.

Troubleshooting If you don't see the Format or Picture tools tabs, make sure that you have the picture selected and active and if needed click the Format tab.

4. Mouse over the effects' thumbnails in the gallery. Note that your Live Preview shows you what your changes will look like. Click on Cutout. You have now applied the artistic effect.

CERTIFICATION READY   **6.3.3**

How do you apply an artistic effect to a graphic?

5. **SAVE** the workbook as *Skyline 11* in the Lesson 11 folder. **CLOSE** the workbook.

LEAVE Excel open for the next exercise.

Take Note   If you compress a picture to reduce its size, the amount of detail retained in the image will change, making the image look different than before it was compressed. To avoid this, you should compress it before applying an artistic effect. You can recompress the file after you have saved your effects as long as you have not closed the program you are working in.

Using the Color Feature to Enhance Images

The Color tool is located in the Adjust group on the Ribbon. It allows you to apply changes and color to the image you are using. All these enhancements change the output and look of the picture, altering it from its original state. In this next exercise, you will use the Color tools to apply different colors to the picture and you will apply these photo enhancements—saturation, tone, contrast, and recolor.

STEP BY STEP

Use the Color Feature to Enhance Images

 The *Vintage Car* image file for this lesson is available on the book companion website or in WileyPLUS.

WILEY PLUS EXTRA

WileyPLUS Extra! features an online tutorial of this task.

GET READY. Before you begin these steps, **LAUNCH** Microsoft Excel and create a new Blank workbook.

1. Click on the Insert tab. Choose the *Vintage Car* image from the student data files for this lesson. Move the image to align with cell B11.

2. Under Picture tools, on the Format tab, within the Adjust group, click the Color button; the color gallery opens (see Figure 11-21).

3. In the Color Saturation section, mouse over the Saturation 33% thumbnail. You will see the picture change in the worksheet with Live Preview. Click on the thumbnail to apply the change. The picture has now changed on the worksheet.

4. Click the Color button in the Adjust group; the Color gallery opens. In the Color Tone section, mouse over the Temperature: 7200 K thumbnail. Click to apply. The image has now changed again to apply the new color style.

5. Click the Color button in the Adjust group; the Color gallery opens. In the Recolor section, mouse over several of the thumbnails and note the changes to your image in the workbook. Click on the Orange, Accent color 6 Light. Your image has now had the settings applied as illustrated in Figure 11-21.

Figure 11-21

Recolor application

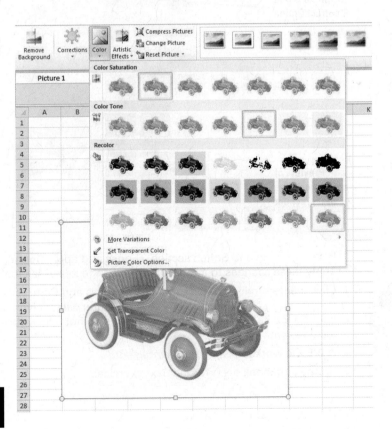

CERTIFICATION READY 6.3.2

How do you apply color enhancements to a graphic?

6. **SAVE** the workbook as *Antique Auto* in the Lesson 11 folder.

LEAVE the workbook open for the next exercise.

Take Note   You can use the color tool to enhance your image's original state. You can also use the tool to alter and modify any artistic effect or picture style you have applied. Remember, with Live Preview, you can view before applying any changes.

Making Corrections to a Graphic

The Corrections button is located in the Adjust group on the Ribbon. The Corrections tool allows you to adjust an image's brightness and contrast, and sharpness and softness. In the next exercise, you will use the Corrections tools to apply these corrections.

STEP BY STEP   **Make Corrections to a Graphic**

USE the workbook from the previous exercise.

1. With the image and the Format tab active, click on the Corrections button, in the Adjust group, to produce the Corrections option gallery, as seen in Figure 11-22.

Figure 11-22

Corrections group

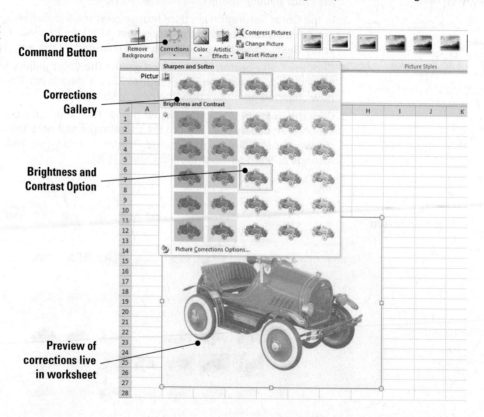

2. In the Sharpen and Soften section, choose and apply Soften: 50%. This setting will apply these changes to the picture and change its overall look.

3. Click the Corrections button. In the Brightness and Contrast section, choose and apply Brightness: +20% Contrast: –40%. This setting will apply these changes to the picture and change its overall look. These changes do not overwrite the previous step but are included with them.

4. **SAVE** the workbook as *Edited Vintage Auto*.

LEAVE the workbook open for the next exercise.

CERTIFICATION READY   6.3.1

How do you apply corrections to a graphic?

Applying a Picture Style

There are 28 built-in picture styles in Excel's Picture group. With the new Live Preview feature in Office 2010, you can simply mouse over the style of your choice and view the change on your screen *before* choosing and applying your style. In the next exercise, you will apply Picture styles to the graphic.

STEP BY STEP   **Apply a Picture Style**

USE the workbook from the previous exercise.

1. Click the drop-down arrow in the Picture Styles group to open the Picture Styles thumbnail galley, as shown in Figure 11-23.

Figure 11-23

Style options window

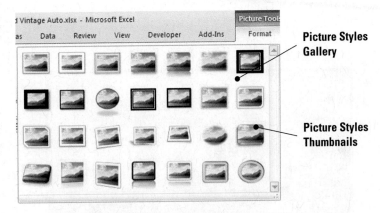

Picture Styles Gallery

Picture Styles Thumbnails

2. Mouse over several of the styles and note the changes with Live Preview.
3. Click to apply Snip Diagonal Corner, White.
4. **SAVE** the changes as *Vintage Auto Style*. **CLOSE** the workbook.

LEAVE Excel open for the next exercise.

Customizing Picture Borders

Once you have applied a picture style, you can modify and customize it. Besides the built-in presets, you can apply such enhancements as shadow, reflection, glow, soft edges, bevel, and 3-D rotation. Once again, the Live Preview feature allows you to view your choice onscreen before you choose and apply it to your image. You will enhance your pictures in this next exercise with picture borders.

STEP BY STEP   **Customize Picture Borders**

WileyPLUS Extra! features an online tutorial of this task.

OPEN the previously created *Skyline 11* file from the Lesson 11 folder to use with this exercise.

1. Click on the image to make it active. Click the Format tab.
2. Click the Picture Border command, in the *Theme Colors* gallery, choose and apply Red, Accent 2, Lighter 40%. The red border is now placed around the picture. Click on any empty cell to deselect the picture and view the border.
3. Click on the Picture Border command, point to Weight. From the Line Weight drop-down list, click Weight to open a menu of border weight (thickness) options (see Figure 11-24). Click on 4½ pt to place a border of that line weight around the image.

Figure 11-24

Picture border options

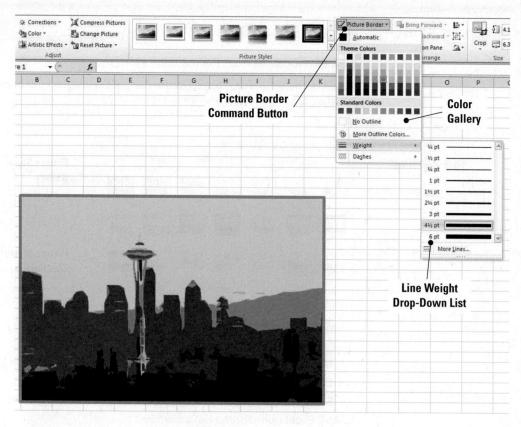

4. **SAVE** the workbook as *Skyline Style*.

LEAVE workbook open for the next exercise.

NEW to Office 2010

Applying a Picture Effect

Picture Effects are not to be confused with Artistic Effects. Picture Effects are located in the Picture Styles Group. Once you have applied a picture style, you can modify and customize it. Besides the built-in presets, you can apply such enhancements as shadow, reflection, glow, soft edges, bevel, and 3-D rotation. The Live Preview feature allows you to view your choice onscreen before you choose and apply it to your image. In the next exercise, you will apply a picture effect to the image.

STEP BY STEP   **Apply a Picture Effect**

USE the workbook from the previous exercise.

1. Click the image and the Format tab to make both active. Click on the Picture Effects command to open the Picture Effects menu. Take a few moments to browse through the choices.

CERTIFICATION READY   6.2.6

How do you apply Picture Effects to a graphic?

2. Point to the Soft Edges button, click on 2.5 Point. The 2.5 point soft edges style has been applied to the border of the picture.

3. **SAVE** your changes.

LEAVE Excel open for the next exercise.

Using Picture Properties

When you have your image selected, you can click on the drop-down arrow in the corner of the Size and Properties group. This brings up the Properties dialog box associated with that particular image. At this time, you can view the property options that Excel has available to you. In this exercise, you will familiarize yourself with several of the Picture Properties options.

STEP BY STEP   **Use Picture Properties**

USE the workbook from the previous exercise.

1. Click both the image and the Format tab to make them active. Right-click on the image, and click Format Picture to open the Format Picture dialog box with the Picture Corrections dialog box open as shown in Figure 11-25.

Figure 11-25

Format Picture dialog box

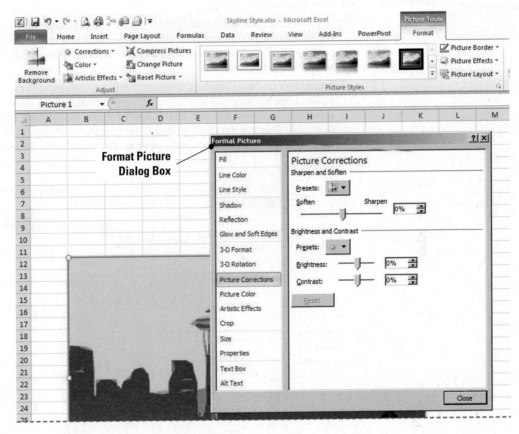

2. Click on Line Color in the Format Picture options pane. In Transparency, key 45, press Enter. This will apply a 45% transparency to the border around the image.

Take Note   You can undo any Picture property by clicking the undo option. This will not close the Property Options window.

CERTIFICATION READY   6.2.3

How do you apply size changes to a graphic?

3. Right-click on the picture, and click Format Picture. Click on Size in the Format Picture options pane. In the *Size and rotate* area, change Height to 2, and press Tab. The width will automatically format the picture to the proper scale of 3.07 inches. Click Close.

4. SAVE the workbook as *My Skyline*.

LEAVE Excel open for the next exercise.

You can use the Picture properties to modify the properties outside the presets. This will apply to your current project. When you start a new project, the properties will begin again with the default settings.

Using Screenshot to Capture and Crop Images

NEW to Office 2010

New to Office 2010, the Screenshot feature allows you to interact with your desktop and open applications to capture, crop, save, and modify your own custom images to enhance your spreadsheet, presentation, or document. When you click the Screenshot button, you can use the entire application window that you have chosen or use the Screen Clipping tool to crop it to the size you desire and need. In the next exercise, you will use screenshot to capture and crop images.

STEP BY STEP   **Use Screenshot to Capture and Crop Images**

USE the workbook from the previous exercise.

1. Minimize the workbook.

2. In Windows, click the Start button, point to programs, point to Microsoft Office and **OPEN** Word 2010. This action will open a blank Word document automatically. To proceed with this exercise, both Word and Excel should be the only two programs open on the toolbar.

3. From the Windows toolbar, click on the Excel worksheet to make it the active program again. Click on any cell in the worksheet to ensure you don't have your image selected. On the Insert tab, in the Illustrations group, click the Screenshot icon. The Available Windows gallery opens. This gives you thumbnails of all open available application windows to choose your screenshot from. Refer to Figure 11-26.

Figure 11-26

Available Windows gallery

Screenshot Command Button

Screen Clipping command

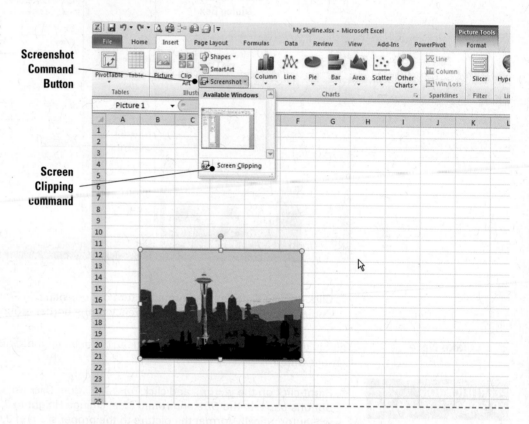

Take Note   Only your application windows that are not minimized to the taskbar will be available in the Available Windows box in Screenshot.

4. Mouse over the thumbnails in the Available Windows gallery. The ScreenTips will let you know what files and applications are open.

5. Take a few moments to close all the open applications except the blank Word document.

6. In the Taskbar, click the Screenshot button to open the Available Windows gallery. Place your mouse pointer on the open Word document and click on the thumbnail. Excel takes a screenshot of the entire Word document and Word window. Excel has also now inserted the entire Word screenshot into your worksheet.

7. Click on the screenshot image to activate it, click Delete to delete the image from the worksheet.

8. Click on the Insert tab. Click on Screenshot. In the Screenshot window, click on Screen Clipping. You will now notice that your screen has greyed out and you have a crosshair for a pointer. In any area of the Ribbon of the Word document, click, hold, and drag your crosshair anywhere in the gray area as illustrated in Figure 11-27. When you release your mouse button from cropping, your cropped image will insert into your worksheet.

Figure 11-27

Windows screen clipping window

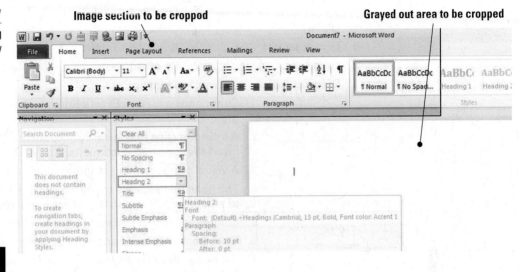

Image section to be cropped

Grayed out area to be cropped

CERTIFICATION READY   **6.2.7**

How do you use and modify screenshots?

9. Click, hold, and drag the image to align with the lower-right corner of cell A11.
10. **SAVE** the workbook as *Screenshot*. **CLOSE** the workbook.
CLOSE Excel.

SKILL SUMMARY

In This Lesson You Learned How To:	Exam Objective	Objective Number
Inserting Pictures	Insert illustrations.	6.2.1
	Modify clip art SmartArt.	6.2.5
Adding Shapes	Position illustrations.	6.2.2
	Modify shapes.	6.2.6
Copying or Moving a Graphic		
Formatting Graphics	Size illustrations.	6.2.3
	Rotate illustrations.	6.2.4
Adding Graphic Enhancements Using Picture Tools	Change artistic effects on an image.	6.3.3
	Use picture color tools.	6.3.2
	Make corrections to an image.	6.3.1
	Modify screenshots.	6.2.7

Knowledge Assessment

Matching

Match each vocabulary term with its definition.

a. clip
b. clip art
c. Clip Organizer
d. connector
e. Drawing Tools

f. flowchart
g. Quick Styles
h. SmartArt Graphic
i. SmartArt Tools
j. Text pane

_____ 1. Commands added to Excel's Ribbon when you insert a SmartArt graphic.

_____ 2. A listing of clips that is easily accessible so that you can locate and insert the clips into documents.

_____ 3. A visual representation of information and ideas.

_____ 4. The pane that appears to the left of a SmartArt graphic that you use to enter and edit text that appears in the graphic.

_____ 5. Commands added to Excel's Ribbon when you insert a shape.

_____ 6. A schematic representation of a process.

_____ 7. A line that has connection points at the end of the line and stays connected to the shapes to which you add it.

_____ 8. A single piece of readymade art, often appearing as a bitmap or combination of drawn shapes.

_____ 9. A single media file including art, sound, animation, or movie.

_____ 10. Collections of formatting options that make formatting documents and objects easier.

True/False

Circle T if the statement is true or F if the statement is false.

T F 1. When you insert a SmartArt graphic, the formatting is preset and cannot be changed.

T F 2. You can insert multiple images into one worksheet.

T F 3. The colors, fonts, and effects in a SmartArt graphic are based on the document theme that was applied to the worksheet.

T F 4. When you move a shape that has a connector line attached, you must select the connector to move it as well.

T F 5. You can hide a graphic on a worksheet without deleting it.

T F 6. You can rotate a SmartArt graphic, but you cannot rotate the individual parts of the graphic.

T F 7. When you create an organization chart, an assistant position is at the same level as the individual who is being assisted.

T F 8. You can rotate a graphic to any desired angle.

T F 9. You can restore a picture to its original formatting without reverting to a saved file.

T F 10. You can change a graphic without deleting the original.

Competency Assessment

Project 11-1: Insert Pictures and Clip Art

An employee at Blue Yonder Airlines wants to add graphics to a worksheet that summarizes annual sales.

GET READY. LAUNCH Excel.

The *Annual Sales* file for this lesson is available on the book companion website or in WileyPLUS.

1. **OPEN** the *Annual Sales* file for this lesson.
2. On the Insert tab, click Clip Art. The Clip Art task pane opens.
3. In the Results Should Be field, select Photographs. All other media types should be deselected. The ClipArt search feature will not work without an Internet connection.
4. Key Airplane in the *Search for* field and click Go.
5. Scroll through the search results and select an image of an airplane in an open sky. The image will be inserted and the Picture Tools tab will be activated.
6. In the Size group, click the value box in Shape Height, key 1, and press Enter.
7. Click the picture and move it to the blank space on the right side of A1.
8. Use the sizing handles to shrink the picture so that it fits into the blank space to the right of the title.
9. With the picture selected, use the keyboard arrow keys to align the picture against the right boundary of column B.
10. In the Picture Styles group, click Soft Edge Rectangle.
11. **SAVE** the workbook as *Annual Sales 11-1*. **CLOSE** the workbook and the Clip Art task pane.

LEAVE Excel open to use in the next project.

Project 11-2: Format and Resize SmartArt Graphics

The School of Fine Arts has created a SmartArt graphic to represent the steps a department must complete in order to add a new course to the department course offerings.

OPEN the *Curriculum* file for this lesson.

The *Curriculum* file for this lesson is available on the book companion website or in WileyPLUS.

1. Click to select the WordArt text box at the top of the worksheet.
2. On the Format tab, click More in the WordArt Styles group.
3. On the WordArt gallery, click Fill – Red, Accent2, Matte Bevel (last row).
4. Click to select the SmartArt graphic. Close the Text pane.
5. On the Design tab, click Change Colors and click Colored Outline - Accent 2.
6. Use the right-center sizing handle to decrease the graphic's width and align the graphic pane with the title.
7. Click Text Box on the Insert tab. Draw the text box in the center of the graphic.
8. Key New Course Cycle in the box. Widen the text box to accommodate the text you entered.
9. Click Shape Fill on the Format tab. Click Dark Red in standard colors.
10. Click in Shape Height value box and key 0.3. Press Enter.
11. Use the arrow keys to move the text box to the center of the SmartArt graphic.
12. **SAVE** the workbook as *Curriculum 11-2* and then **CLOSE** the file.

LEAVE Excel open for the next project.

Proficiency Assessment

Project 11-3: Insert Pictures and Shapes into SmartArt

1. **OPEN** *Curriculum* from the data files for this lesson.
2. On the Insert tab, click Picture.
3. Select the *Book* image from the student files for Lesson 11 and click Insert.
4. Resize the picture so it is the same size as the SmartArt graphic. Move the picture so that the graphic is hidden.
5. On the Format tab, click Brightness: +40% Contrast –40%.
6. Click Send Backward.
7. Click in the SmartArt graphic and press Ctrl+A to select all the shapes in the graphic.
8. In the Shape Styles group on the Format tab, click Colored Outline – Red, Accent 2. Click outside the SmartArt graphic.
9. **SAVE** the workbook as *Curriculum 11-3* and **CLOSE** the file.

LEAVE Excel open for the next project.

@ The *Book* image file for this lesson is available on the book companion website or in WileyPLUS.

Project 11-4: Format and Reset a Picture to Its Original State

GET READY. LAUNCH Excel if it is not already running.

1. **OPEN** the *Pictures* workbook file for this lesson.
2. Click the second picture in the first column. On the Format tab, click Selection Pane.
3. In the Selection and Visibility pane, click Picture 1.
4. In the Picture Styles group, click Reflected Rounded Rectangle.
5. Click Color and in the Recolor area click Sepia.
6. Click Picture 2 in the task pane. Click Picture Effects.
7. Point to Glow and click Red, 5 pt. glow, Accent color 2.
8. Select Picture 3 in the task pane and click Crop. Place the crop tool at the lower-right corner and drag up to the bottom of desktop in the picture. Click Crop again to complete the crop.
9. Select Picture 4 in the task pane. Click the Change Picture icon and select Book. Click Insert.
10. Click Picture 2 and click Reset Picture.
11. **SAVE** the workbook as *Pictures 11-4*. **CLOSE** the workbook.

LEAVE Excel open for the next project.

@ The *Pictures* workbook file for this lesson is available on the book companion website or in WileyPLUS.

Mastery Assessment

Project 11-5: Create an Organization Chart

Blue Yonder Airlines wants to create an organization chart. Use SmartArt graphics to create and format an organization chart.

GET READY. LAUNCH Excel if it is not already running.

1. **OPEN** a new blank workbook.
2. On the Insert tab, click SmartArt.
3. Click Hierarchy and click Organization Chart.

4. Enter the following information in the Text pane. When you have entered the names, the assistant shape should be connected to the line between the CEO and the two managers. Click Promote to move a shape to a higher level and click Demote to move a shape to a lower level as needed.

Name	Position	Reports to
Kim Ralls	Executive	
Mikael Sandberg	Corporate Sales/Charter Flights	CEO
John Evans	Flight School and Sky Diving	CEO
Frank Pellow	Sales Representative	Mikael Sandberg
Linda Russell	Sales Representative	Mikael Sandberg
Scott Seely	Sales Representative	John Evans
Tracy Tallman	Flight Instructor	John Evans
Katie Jordan	Sky Diving Instructor	John Evans
Elsa Leavitt	Assistant	

5. Move the SmartArt graphic to the upper-left edge of the worksheet.
6. Use a corner-sizing handle to expand the graphic so that it fits in A1:I20.
7. On the Design tab, click Subtle Effect.
8. **SAVE** the workbook as *Blue Yonder 11-5*. **CLOSE** the file.

LEAVE Excel open for the next project.

Project 11-6: Correct Shapes and Images

GET READY. LAUNCH Excel if it is not already running.

1. **OPEN** the *Advertising* file for this lesson.
2. Press Shift to select the shapes and change the height of the shape to 1 inch high by 1.35 inches wide.
3. Apply Colored Outline – Aqua, Accent 5 style to the shapes.
4. Rotate the shapes 20°.
5. Select the connectors and change the shape outline weight to 1½ pt and the shape outline to dark red.
6. Insert the *Ship* picture from the data files for this lesson.
7. Set shape height at 4.5 inches and accept the default width.
8. Change the picture brightness to +40%.
9. Send the picture behind the connected shapes.
10. **SAVE** the workbook as *Advertising 11-6*. **CLOSE** the workbook.

LEAVE Excel open for the next project.

@ The *Advertising* file for this lesson is available on the book companion website or in WileyPLUS.

@ The *Ship* file for this lesson is available on the book companion website or in WileyPLUS.

INTERNET READY

Use web search tools to find a travel agency that you could use to plan your next vacation.

View the pictures and vacation descriptions on the web page that represents the type of vacation you would like to take (i.e., the beach, the mountains, a cruise).

Open a new Excel workbook. Open the Clip Art task pane and click Clip Art on Office Online. Locate at least five pictures that represent your vacation. Download the selected images to your Clip Organizer in a Vacation folder. Insert the pictures into a worksheet for each picture. Title the worksheets to correspond to the vacation the picture represents. Add modifications to the graphics: outlines, styles, artistic effects, picture effects, and corrections. Add SmartArt graphics to go with each of the images to describe the type of vacation that the picture pertains to. Save the workbook as *Vacation Plan*. Close Excel.

Workplace *Ready*

FORMATTING PICTURES IN EXCEL

With the introduction of the new Picture tools in Office 2010, you now have the ability to insert, modify, and use more creative and professional-looking graphics in your workbooks.

With the ability to use these Picture tools across the Office 2010 suite, images you format in one application are portable and editable in another. For example, screenshots that are modified and used in a Word document can be copied and pasted to PowerPoint and Excel.

These improvements in picture editing will no doubt work well for anyone in the workplace from assistant and co-worker to CEO. The consistency in using only one application to insert and edit images can lead to lower software overhead, consistency of training and usage, and easier management of shared and frequently used documents.

Utilization of these editing tools can mean consistent and professional image branding in corporate or personal use.

Photos edited in Office 2010 can be inserted in email in Outlook, and copied to Word, Power-Point, and Excel for various uses. In a business venue, the tools can refine images for company logos, brochure photos, employee photo id pictures, and so on. On a personal note, an individual can edit family photos to create albums, calendars, cards, and many other items that had once needed an expensive software alternative to create.

Consider all the possibilities that these improved Picture editing features have to offer. Be creative and enjoy mastering the possibilities.

Cross-Cultural Solutions (CCS) is a nonprofit organization and a registered charity, which means that contributions made by companies and individuals are tax deductible. The organization is preparing for one of its annual fund-raising events—a formal dinner and charity auction.

As a CCS employee, you have already created a workbook to track corporate and individual contributions. The director now asks you to create charts to illustrate his presentation to potential contributors who will attend the fund-raising event.

Project 1: Creating a Summary Worksheet and Pie Chart

In this exercise, you will subtotal contributions by the budget category to which the contributions are to be applied, then you'll create formulas in a summary worksheet that references the subtotals. You will also use the summary worksheet to create a pie chart that illustrates the distribution of contributions among the organization's budget categories.

GET READY. LAUNCH Excel if it is not already running.

1. **OPEN** the *Contributions 1* workbook file.
2. Click the Data tab. Select any cell in the data. Click Sort in the Sort & Filter group.
3. The Sort dialog box opens. In the Sort by field, select Fund. Click OK.
4. **SAVE** the document as *Contributions Project 1*.
5. Click Subtotal on the Outline group. In the *At each change in field*, select Fund. Click OK.
6. Click the Summary tab and click B5. Key = and click the Year-to-Date Contributions tab. Click C12, and press Enter.
7. Select B6, and enter a formula that references the subtotal for general operating fund contributions.
8. Enter formulas in B7 and B8 that reference the appropriate subtotals.
9. Select B9, and click AutoSum on the Formulas tab to total the contributions.
10. Select B5:B8, then click Copy on the Home tab.
11. Click the arrow under Paste, click Paste Values, then click Values.
12. Click the Insert tab. Select A4:B8, and click Pie in the Chart group. Then click Pie in the 2-D Pie category.
13. Click the Design tab, then click Layout 1 in the Chart Layouts group.
14. Click the Layout tab, and select Chart Title in the Current Selection group.
15. Key Year-to-Date Contributions. Press Enter.
16. Select the chart title, and click the Format tab.
17. Click Shape Fill, then click Orange under Standard Colors.
18. Click the Design tab, and click Move Chart. Click New sheet, and click OK.
19. **SAVE** and **CLOSE** the workbook.

LEAVE Excel open for the next project.

@ The *Contributions 1* workbook file for this lesson is available on the book companion website or in WileyPLUS.

Project 2: Creating a Column Chart

Next you will create a chart that compares budgeted amounts with contributions received to date. This comparison will be used to establish the fund-raising goal.

GET READY. LAUNCH Excel if it is not already running.

1. **OPEN** the *Contributions 2* workbook file.
2. Click the Insert tab. On the Budget worksheet, select A4:C8, then click Column.
3. Click 3-D Clustered Column.
4. **SAVE** the document as *Contributions Project 2*.

@ The *Contributions 2* file for this lesson is available on the book companion website or in WileyPLUS.

5. Select Layout 2.

6. Select Chart Title in the Current Selection group on the Layout tab, and key Budgeted vs. Received. Press Enter.

7. Delete the legend.

8. Select Budgeted in the chart title, click Text Fill on the Format tab, and click Blue, Accent 1 under Theme Colors.

9. Select Received in the chart title, click Text Fill, and click Purple.

10. Select Series "Budgeted Amount" Data Labels in the Current Selection group on the Layout tab, and apply Blue, Accent 1 text fill.

11. Select Series "Received to Date" Data Labels, and apply Purple text fill.

12. Move the chart to a new sheet.

13. Name the chart sheet Budgeted vs. Received.

14. Select the Horizontal (Category) Axis, then select Text Fill. Click Purple.

15. If necessary, select and move the series amounts so that they are completely visible.

16. **SAVE** and **CLOSE** the workbook.

LEAVE Excel open for the next project.

Project 3: Adding Pictures to a Worksheet

Your next task is to enhance a worksheet's appearance by adding pictures and a background.

OPEN the *CCS Locations* workbook file.

@ The *Africa, Asia, Latin America,* and *Europe* images and *CCS Locations* file for this lesson are available on the book companion website or in WileyPLUS.

1. Click the Locations worksheet tab if necessary. Then click the Insert tab and select Picture.

2. Select the *Africa* image from the data files for this lesson. Click Insert.

3. Select the picture and move it to cell A5. Use the sizing handles to shrink the picture so that it fits within A5 without covering the text.

4. Click the Insert tab, then click Picture.

5. Select the *Asia* image from the data files for this lesson. Click Insert.

6. Click the Format tab. In the Size group, click Shape Height and key 1. The width of the picture should size proportionately.

7. Align the picture with the right boundary of A8.

8. Insert the *Latin America* image into cell A13. Size the picture so that it is centered below the text in the cell.

9. Insert the *Europe* image into cell A19. Set shape width to 1.2. The height of the picture should size proportionately. Align the picture with the top and right boundaries of cell A19.

10. Select the picture in A19, and click Picture Effects. Select Red Accent color 2, 5pt glow.

11. Click the Welcome worksheet tab, then select A1:O32. In the Alignment group on the Home tab, click Merge & Center.

12. Click Middle Align, then click Center Text. Key Welcome to Cross-Cultural Solutions' Annual Charity Auction.

13. Select the text and change the font to Lucida Calligraphy and the font size to 36. Click Wrap Text.

14. Click the Page Layout tab, and click Background. Select the *Sunset* image from the data files and click Insert.

15. Remove gridlines and headings from the view. Double-click a Ribbon tab to minimize the Ribbon. Increase or decrease the zoom so that the message background fills the screen.

16. **SAVE** the workbook as *CSS Locations Project 3* and **CLOSE** the file.

LEAVE Excel open for the next project.

Project 4: Tracking Changes in a Shared Workbook

As a result of the fund-raising event, several organizations and individuals have increased their contributions. Use change tracking to record the increases and to add comments related to the changes.

GET READY. LAUNCH Excel if it is not already running.

@ The *Contributions 1* file for this lesson is available on the book companion website or in WileyPLUS.

1. **OPEN** the *Contributions 1* file.
2. Click the File tab, then click Save As.
3. Click Tools, then click General Options.
4. Key Cont4! in the *Password to modify* box and click OK.
5. Reenter the password.
6. **SAVE** the workbook as *Contributions Project 4*.
7. Click the Review tab. Click Track Changes, then click Highlight Changes.
8. Click Track changes while editing. This also shares your workbook. Click Who, then click OK.
9. Click OK to save the workbook.
10. Click cell C7 and key 1500. Press Enter. In C7, click New Comment, and key Increased by Jim Hance.
11. Select A15 and click New Comment. Key Call Maria Hammond next week.
12. Select B27 and key Scholarship. Press Enter. In B27, insert a comment that reads Mark Hassal, General Manager, changed fund allocation.
13. **SAVE** and **CLOSE** the file.

CLOSE Excel.

Appendix A Microsoft Office Specialist (MOS) Skills for Excel 2010: Exam 77-882

Matrix Skill	Objective Number	Lesson Number
Managing the Worksheet Environment	1	
Navigate through a worksheet.	1.1	
Use hotkeys.	1.1.1	1
Use the Name box.	1.1.2	1
Print a worksheet or workbook.	1.2	
Print only selected worksheets.	1.2.1	2
Print an entire workbook.	1.2.2	2
Construct headers and footers.	1.2.3	5
Apply printing options.	1.2.4	2, 5
Personalize the environment by using Backstage.	1.3	
Manipulate the Quick Access Toolbar.	1.3.1	1, 2
Customize the Ribbon.	1.3.2	2
Manipulate Excel default settings (Excel Options).	1.3.3	2
Manipulate workbook properties (document panel).	1.3.4	2
Manipulate workbook files and folders.	1.3.5	2, 3
Creating Cell Data	2	
Construct cell data.	2.1	
Use Paste Special.	2.1.1	5
Cut cell data.	2.1.2	3, 4
Move cell data.	2.1.3	3, 4
Select cell data.	2.1.4	3, 4
Apply AutoFill.	2.2	
Copy cell data.	2.2.1	3
Fill a series.	2.2.2	3
Preserve cell format.	2.2.3	3
Apply and manipulate hyperlinks.	2.3	
Create a hyperlink in a cell.	2.3.1	4
Modify hyperlinks.	2.3.2	4

Matrix Skill	Objective Number	Lesson Number
Modify hyperlinked cell attributes.	2.3.3	4
Remove a hyperlink.	2.3.4	4
Formatting Cells and Worksheets	3	
Apply and modify cell formats.	3.1	
Align cell content.	3.1.1	4
Apply a number format.	3.1.2	4
Wrap text in a cell.	3.1.3	4
Use Format Painter.	3.1.4	4
Merge or split cells.	3.2	
Use Merge & Center.	3.2.1	4
Merge across.	3.2.2	4
Merge cells.	3.2.3	4
Unmerge cells.	3.2.4	4
Create row and column titles.	3.3	
Print row and column headings.	3.3.1	5
Print rows to repeat with titles.	3.3.2	5
Print columns to repeat with titles.	3.3.3	5
Configure titles to print only on odd or even pages.	3.3.4	5
Configure titles to skip the first worksheet page.	3.3.5	5
Hide or unhide rows and columns.	3.4	
Hide or unhide a column.	3.4.1	5
Hide or unhide a row.	3.4.2	5
Hide a series of columns.	3.4.3	5
Hide a series of rows.	3.4.4	5
Manipulate Page Setup options for worksheets.	3.5	
Configure page orientation.	3.5.1	5
Manage page scaling.	3.5.2	5
Configure page margins.	3.5.3	5
Change header and footer size.	3.5.4	5

Matrix Skill	Objective Number	Lesson Number
Create and apply cell styles.	**3.6**	
Apply cell styles.	**3.6.1**	**4**
Construct new cell styles.	**3.6.2**	**4**
Managing Worksheets and Workbooks	**4**	
Create and format worksheets.	**4.1**	
Insert worksheets.	**4.1.1**	**6**
Delete worksheets.	**4.1.2**	**6**
Reposition worksheets within a workbook.	**4.1.3**	**6**
Copy worksheets.	**4.1.4**	**6**
Move worksheets.	**4.1.5**	**6**
Rename worksheets.	**4.1.6**	**6**
Group worksheets.	**4.1.7**	**6**
Apply color to worksheet tabs.	**4.1.8**	**5**
Hide worksheet tabs.	**4.1.9**	**6**
Unhide worksheet tabs.	**4.1.10**	**6**
Manipulate window views.	**4.2**	
Split window views.	**4.2.1**	**1**
Arrange window views.	**4.2.2**	**1, 6**
Open a new window with contents from the current worksheet.	**4.2.3**	**1, 6**
Manipulate workbook views.	**4.3**	
Use Normal workbook view.	**4.3.1**	**1**
Use Page Layout workbook view.	**4.3.2**	**1**
Use Page Break workbook view.	**4.3.3**	**5**
Create custom views.	**4.3.4**	**5**
Applying Formulas and Functions	**5**	
Create formulas.	**5.1**	
Use basic operators.	**5.1.1**	**8**
Revise formulas.	**5.1.2**	**8**
Enforce precedence.	**5.2**	
Precedence order of evaluation.	**5.2.1**	**8**
Precedence using parentheses.	**5.2.2**	**8**

Matrix Skill	Objective Number	Lesson Number
Precedence of operators for percent vs. exponentiation.	5.2.3	8
Apply cell references in formulas.	5.3	
Relative and absolute references.	5.3.1	8
Apply conditional logic in a formula.	5.4	
Create a formula with values that match conditions.	5.4.1	9
Edit defined conditions in a formula.	5.4.2	9
Use a series of conditional logic values in a formula.	5.4.3	9
Apply named ranges in formulas.	5.5	
Define ranges in formulas.	5.5.1	8
Edit ranges in formulas.	5.5.2	8
Rename a named range.	5.5.3	8
Apply cell ranges in formulas.	5.6	
Enter a cell range definition in the formula bar.	5.6.1	8
Define a cell range.	5.6.2	8
Presenting Data Visually	6	
Create charts based on worksheet data.	6.1	10
Apply and manipulate illustrations.	6.2	
Insert illustrations.	6.2.1	11
Position illustrations.	6.2.2	11
Size illustrations.	6.2.3	11
Rotate illustrations.	6.2.4	11
Modify clip art SmartArt.	6.2.5	11
Modify shapes.	6.2.6	11
Modify screenshots.	6.2.7	11
Create and modify images by using the Image Editor.	6.3	
Make corrections to an image.	6.3.1	11
Use picture color tools.	6.3.2	11
Change artistic effects on an image.	6.3.3	11
Apply Sparklines.	6.4	
Use Line chart types.	6.4.1	10

Matrix Skill	Objective Number	Lesson Number
Use Column chart types.	6.4.2	10
Use Win/Loss chart types.	6.4.3	10
Create a Sparkline chart.	6.4.4	10
Customize a Sparkline.	6.4.5	10
Format a Sparkline.	6.4.6	10
Show or hide data markers.	6.4.7	10
Sharing Worksheet Data with other users	**7**	
Share spreadsheets by using Backstage.	7.1	
Send a worksheet via email or SkyDrive.	7.1.1	9
Change the file type to a different version of Excel.	7.1.2	3
Save as a PDF or XPS file.	7.1.3	3
Manage comments.	7.2	
Insert comments.	7.2.1	9
View comments.	7.2.2	9
Edit comments.	7.2.3	9
Delete comments.	7.2.4	9
Analyzing and Organizing Data	**8**	
Filter data.	8.1	
Define a filter.	8.1.1	7
Apply a filter.	8.1.2	7
Remove a filter.	8.1.3	7
Filter lists using AutoFilter.	8.1.4	7
Sort data.	8.2	
Use sort options.	8.2.1	7
Apply conditional formatting.	8.3	
Apply conditional formatting to cells.	8.3.1	4, 7
Use the Rule Manager to apply conditional formats.	8.3.2	4
Use the IF function to apply conditional formatting.	8.3.3	9
Clear rules.	8.3.4	4
Use icon sets.	8.3.5	4
Use data bars.	8.3.6	4

Appendix B Microsoft Office Professional 2010

Component	Requirement
Computer and processor	500 MHz or faster processor.
Memory	256 MB RAM; 512 MB recommended for graphics features, Outlook Instant Search, and certain advanced functionality.[1,2]
Hard disk	3.0 GB available disk space.
Display	1024×576 or higher resolution monitor.
Operating system	Windows XP (must have SP3) (32-bit), Windows 7, Windows Vista with Service Pack (SP) 1, Windows Server 2003 R2 with MSXML 6.0 (32-bit Office only), Windows Server 2008, or later 32- or 64-bit OS.
Graphics	Graphics hardware acceleration requires a DirectX 9.0c graphics card with 64 MB or more video memory.
Additional requirements	Certain Microsoft® OneNote® features require Windows® Desktop Search 3.0, Windows Media® Player 9.0, Microsoft® ActiveSync® 4.1, microphone, audio output device, video recording device, TWAIN-compatible digital camera, or scanner; sharing notebooks requires users to be on the same network.
	Certain advanced functionality requires connectivity to Microsoft Exchange Server 2003, Microsoft SharePoint Server 2010, and/or Microsoft SharePoint Foundation 2010.
	Certain features require Windows Search 4.0.
	Send to OneNote Print Driver and Integration with Business Connectivity Services require Microsoft .NET Framework 3.5 and/or Windows XPS features.
	Internet Explorer (IE) 6 or later, 32-bit browser only. IE7 or later required to receive broadcast presentations. Internet functionality requires an Internet connection.
	Multi-Touch features require Windows 7 and a touch-enabled device.
	Certain inking features require Windows XP Tablet PC Edition or later.
	Speech recognition functionality requires a close-talk microphone and audio output device.
	Internet Fax not available on Windows Vista Starter, Windows Vista Home Basic, or Windows Vista Home Premium.
	Information Rights Management features require access to a Windows 2003 Server with SP1 or later running Windows Rights Management Services.
	Certain online functionality requires a Windows LiveTM ID.
Other	Product functionality and graphics may vary based on your system configuration. Some features may require additional or advanced hardware or server connectivity; **www.office.com/products.**

[1] 512 MB RAM recommended for accessing Outlook data files larger than 1 GB.

[2] GHz processor or faster and 1 GB RAM or more recommended for OneNote Audio Search. Close-talking microphone required. Audio Search is not available in all languages.

Excel 2010 Glossary

A

absolute cell reference   A reference that does not change when a formula is copied or moved.

active cell   A cell that is highlighted or outlined by a bold black line.

argument   A component of a function that is enclosed in parentheses.

array   Used to build single formulas that produce multiple results or that operate on a group of arguments.

ascending order   An arrangement in which data appears alphabetically from A to Z.

attribute   A formatting characteristic.

authentication   The process of verifying that people and products are who and what they claim to be.

AutoComplete   An Excel feature that automatically enters the remaining characters of an entry if the first few typed characters match an existing entry in that column.

Auto fill   An option that automatically fills cells with data and/or formatting.

AutoFilter   A built-in set of filtering capabilities.

axis   A line bordering the chart plot area as a frame of reference for measurement.

B

Backstage   A view that enables you to easily navigate and customize different features that you frequently use in Excel.

boundary   The line between rows or columns.

C

cell   A box on the grid identified by the intersection of a column and a row.

certificate authority (CA)   A third-party entity that issues digital certificates to be used by others.

change history   Information maintained about changes made in past editing sessions, including the name of the person who made each change, when the change was made, and what data was changed.

character   A letter, number, punctuation mark, or symbol.

chart   A graphical representation of numeric data in a worksheet.

chart area   An entire chart and all its elements.

chart sheet   A sheet that contains only a chart.

clip   A single media file including art, sound, animation, or a movie.

clip art   A single piece of ready-made art, often appearing as a bitmap or a combination of drawn shapes.

Clip Organizer   A tool to gather and store your own clips so that you can easily locate them and insert them into documents.

column   Cells that run from top to bottom on the grid and are identified by letters.

column heading   The identifying letter of a column.

column width   The left-to-right width of a column.

command group   Task-specific groups divided among the command tabs appropriate to the work a user is currently performing.

command tab   Task-oriented tabs that are organized on the Ribbon.

comparison operator   A sign, such as greater than (>) or less than (<), that is used to compare two values.

conditional formatting   Automatic formatting based on established criteria.

conditional formula   A formula in which the result is determined by the presence or absence of a particular condition.

connector   A line that has connection points at its ends that stay connected to the shape to which you have connected it.

constant   A number or text value that is entered directly into a formula.

copy   To duplicate data from the worksheet that is available in the Clipboard.

copy pointer   A tool that allows users to drag a cell or range of cells to a new location.

criteria   Specifications that allot what data type users want to use in a cell or range of cells and how users want that data used, formatted, or displayed.

cut   To remove data from a worksheet that is still available in the Clipboard for use.

D

data labels   Text that provides additional information about a data marker, which represents a single data point or value that originates from a worksheet cell.

data marker   A bar, area, dot, slice, or other symbol in a chart that represents a single data point or value that originates from a worksheet cell.

data series   Related data markers in a chart.

default   A predefined setting. You can accept Excel's default option settings or you can change them.

default settings   Standard settings installed by an application as presets so that the application has the same settings each and every time it is accessed.

Definitive Command   A command that closes Backstage view and returns the user to a workbook.

descending order   An arrangement in which data appear alphabetically from Z to A.

Dialog Box Launcher   An arrow in the lower-right corner of some command group headers in the Ribbon tabs.

digital certificate   A means of proving identity and authenticity.

digital signature   A signature that is used to authenticate digital information using computer cryptography.

Document properties   Document information that identifies who created the document, when it was created, how large the file is, and other important information about the workbook.

document theme   A predefined set of colors, fonts, lines, and fill effects.

duplicate value   Occurs when all values in a row are an exact match for all the values in another row.

E

embedded chart   A chart that is placed on a worksheet rather than on a separate chart sheet.

external reference   A cell or range on a worksheet in another Excel workbook, or a defined name in another workbook.

F

Fast Command   A command that provides quick access to common functions and is located on the left navigation pane.

File tab   A tab that replaces the Office button in Microsoft Office 2010 and takes you to Backstage view.

fill handle   A small black square in the lower-right corner of a selected cell.

filter   A restriction that Excel uses to determine which worksheet rows to display.

flowchart   A schematic representation of a process, or a working map that helps users reach a final product or decision.

font   A set of text characteristics designed to appear a certain way.

footer   A line of text that appears at the bottom of each page in a document.

Format Painter   An Excel feature that allows users to copy formatting from a cell or range of cells to another cell or range of cells.

formula   An equation that performs calculations, such as addition, subtraction, multiplication, and division, on values in a worksheet.

formula bar   A bar located between the Ribbon and the worksheet in which users can edit the contents of a cell.

freeze   To keep certain rows or columns visible while the rest of a worksheet scrolls.

function   A predefined formula that performs a calculation.

G

gridlines   The lines that display around worksheet cells.

grouping   Organizing data so that it can be viewed as a collapsible and expandable outline.

group worksheets   A feature that allows users to enter and edit data on several worksheets at the same time or apply formatting to multiple worksheets.

H

header   A line of text that appears at the top of each page in a document.

Help system   A system in Excel 2010 that is rich in information, illustrations, and tips that can help users complete any task as they create a worksheet and workbook.

hide   To make a worksheet invisible.

hotkey   Another name for a Keytip.

hyperlink   An image or a sequence of characters that opens another file or a web page when users click it.

K

Keytips   Small "badges" revealed by pressing and releasing the Alt key, which displays keyboard shortcuts for specific tabs and commands on the Ribbon and Quick Access Toolbar.

keywords   Words assigned to document properties that make organizing and finding documents easier.

L

label   Text entered in a worksheet that is used to identify numeric data.

legend   A box that identifies the patterns or colors that are assigned to the data series or categories in a chart.

legend keys   A key that appears to the left of legend entries and identifies the color-coded data series.

lookup functions   Functions used to find information stored in a table in an Excel worksheet.

M

mathematical operator   An element that specifies a calculation to be performed.

merged cells   Cells created by combining two or more adjacent horizontal or vertical cells.

Mini toolbar   A toolbar displayed above the shortcut menu that users can use to apply selected formatting features.

mixed reference   A reference in which one component is absolute and one is relative.

move pointer   A tool that allows users to drag a cell or range of cells to a new location, replacing any existing data in the destination cells.

N

name   A meaningful and logical identifier that a user can apply to make it easier to understand the purpose of a cell reference, constant, formula, or table.

Name box   Located below the Ribbon at the left end of the formula bar. When the user keys a cell location in this box and presses Enter, the cursor moves to that cell.

natural series   A formatted series of text or numbers.

O

Office Clipboard   A location that collects and stores up to 24 copied or cut items, which are then available to be used in the active workbook and in other Microsoft Office programs.

operand   An element that identifies the value to be used in a calculation.

organization chart   A chart that graphically illustrates the management structure of an organization.

orientation   The way a workbook or worksheet appears on the printed page.

outline symbols   Symbols that are used to change the view of an outlined worksheet.

P

page break   A divider that breaks a worksheet into separate pages for printing.

Page Break Preview   A command on the View tab to control where page breaks occur.

password   Text that must be keyed before a user can access a workbook, worksheet, or worksheet element.

paste   To insert data from the Clipboard to a new location in a worksheet.

Paste Special   A function that performs irregular cell copying.

PivotTable   A report designed to quickly condense large amounts of data, which can be used to analyze and display the numerical data in detail and to answer unforeseen questions about data.

placeholders   Important text directives specified by the author of the template to direct the user where to add specific data in specific cells within the template.

plot area   The area bounded by the axes of a chart.

point   A unit used to measure the height of the characters in a cell.

Print options   Options to customize and manipulate a workbook for printing, such as margins, orientation, scale, and collation.

Print Preview   A window that displays a full-page view of a worksheet just as it will be printed.

Q

Quick Access Toolbar   A toolbar that permits fast and easy access to the tools a user employs most often in any given Excel session.

Quick Styles   Combinations of different formatting options.

R

reference   A component of a formula that identifies a cell or a range of cells on a worksheet.

relative cell reference   A reference that changes "relative" to the location where it is copied or moved.

Ribbon   A broad band that runs across the top of the window that organizes tools from the Menu toolbar into an easy-to-use interface.

row   Cells that run from left to right on the grid and are identified by numbers.

row heading   The identifying number of a row.

row height   The top-to-bottom height of a row.

S

scaling   Shrinking or stretching printed output to a percentage of its actual size.

scope   The location within which Excel recognizes an item without qualification.

ScreenTips   Small onscreen windows that display descriptive text when users rest the pointer on a command or control.

select   To click in an area to make it active.

selecting text   Highlighting text.

shared workbook   A workbook that is set up to allow multiple users on a network to view and make changes at the same time.

SmartArt graphic   A visual representation of information and ideas that can be used with other images and decorative text.

string   Any sequence of letters or numbers in a field.

strong password   A password that combines uppercase and lowercase letters, numbers, and symbols.

style   A set of formatting attributes that users can apply to a cell or range of cells more easily than by setting each attribute individually.

T

tab   Component of the navigation pane that a user can click to access groups of related functions and commands.

table   A range of cells in a worksheet that can be used by a lookup function.

template   Files designed with formatting and formulas, complete with designs, tools, and specific data types included.

Text pane   A pane that appears to the left of a SmartArt graphic that works like an outline or a bulleted list that maps information directly to the graphic.

title   Descriptive text that is automatically aligned to an axis or centered at the top of a chart.

track changes   The ability to mark and record the changes that have been made to a workbook.

U

unhide   To make a worksheet visible again.

W

workbook   A spreadsheet file.

worksheet   Sheets similar to pages in a document or a book in which you can enter information.

Z

zoom   A feature that allows users to make a worksheet appear bigger (zoom in) or smaller (zoom out).

Credits

Troubleshooting icon © Matthias Haas/iStockphoto

Another Way icon © Anatolii Tsekhmister/iStockphoto

Internet Ready Icon © Orlando Rosu/iStockphoto

Introduction

Page ix (XL jet airplane landing on runway): © Stephen Strathdee/iStockphoto

Page ix (Analyzing financial data): © Damir Cudic/iStockphoto

Page xxxi (Family at the doctor's office): © Kurt Paris/iStockphoto

Page xxxi (Doctors consult over an X-ray): © proxyminder/iStockphoto

Page xxxii (Townhome row): © Tony Casanova/iStockphoto

Page xxxiii (Doctor and patient): © iofoto/iStockphoto

Page xxxiv (XL jet airplane landing on runway): © Stephen Strathdee/iStockphoto

Page xxxv (Artist working on a painting): © StudioStella/iStockphoto

Page xxxvi (businessman in a meeting): © enis izgi/iStockphoto

Page xxxvi (Analyzing financial data): © Damir Cudic/iStockphoto

Page xxxvii (Businessman working at his desk): © Ben Blankenburg/iStockphoto

Page xxxix (Coffee shop series: Behind the counter): © Eliza Snow/iStockphoto

Page xl (Cruise ship): © Bjorn Heller/iStockphoto

Lesson 1

Chapter Opener (Family at the doctor's office): © Kurt Paris/iStockphoto

Lesson 2

Chapter Opener (Doctors consult over an X-ray): © proxyminder/iStockphoto

Lesson 3

Chapter Opener (Townhome row): © Tony Casanova/iStockphoto

Lesson 4

Chapter Opener (Doctor and patient): © iofoto/iStockphoto

Lesson 5

Chapter Opener (XL jet airplane landing on runway): © Stephen Strathdee/iStockphoto

Lesson 6

Chapter Opener (Artist working on a painting): © StudioStella/iStockphoto

Lesson 7

Chapter Opener (businessman in a meeting): © enis izgi/iStockphoto

Figure 7-6 (nurse holding medical chart): © Fuse/Getty Images, Inc.

Figure 7-7 (nurse holding medical chart): © Fuse/Getty Images, Inc.

Lesson 8

Chapter Opener (Analyzing financial data): © Damir Cudic/iStockphoto

Lesson 9

Chapter Opener (Businessman working at his desk): © Ben Blankenburg/iStockphoto

Lesson 10

Chapter Opener (Coffee shop series: Behind the counter): © Eliza Snow/iStockphoto

Lesson 11

Chapter Opener (Cruise ship): © Bjorn Heller/iStockphoto

Figure 11-21 (blue toy car): © Vasilis Nikolos/iStockphoto

Figure 11-22 (blue toy car): © Vasilis Nikolos/iStockphoto

Index